Sustainable Development and Green Innovation

EMERALD STUDIES IN FINANCE, INSURANCE, AND RISK MANAGEMENT

Series Editor: Simon Grima

Books in this series collect quantitative and qualitative studies in areas relating to finance, insurance, and risk management. Subjects of interest may include banking, accounting, auditing, compliance, sustainability, behaviour, management, and business economics.

In the disruption of political upheaval, new technologies, climate change, and new regulations, it is more important than ever to understand risk in the financial industry. Providing high-quality academic research, this book series provides a platform for authors to explore, analyse, and discuss current and new financial models and theories and engage with innovative research on an international scale.

Previously published:

Uncertainty and Challenges in Contemporary Economic Behaviour
Ercan Özen and Simon Grima

New Challenges for Future Sustainability and Wellbeing
Ercan Özen, Simon Grima and Rebecca Dalli Gonzi

Insurance and Risk Management for Disruptions in Social, Economic and Environmental Systems: Decision and Control Allocations Within New Domains of Risk
Simon Grima, Ercan Özen and Rebecca Emily Dalli Gonzi

Public Sector Leadership in Assessing and Addressing Risk
Peter C. Young, Simon Grima and Rebecca Dalli Gonzi

Big Data Analytics in the Insurance Market
Kiran Sood, Balamurugan Balusamy, Simon Grima and Pierpaolo Marano

Big Data: A Game Changer for Insurance Industry
Kiran Sood, Rajesh Kumar Dhanaraj, Balamurugan Balusamy, Simon Grima and R. Uma Maheshwari

The Adoption and Effect of Artificial Intelligence on Human Resources Management, Part A
Pallavi Tyagi, Naveen Chilamkurti, Simon Grima, Kiran Sood and Balamurugan Balusamy

The Adoption and Effect of Artificial Intelligence on Human Resources Management, Part B
Pallavi Tyagi, Naveen Chilamkurti, Simon Grima, Kiran Sood and Balamurugan Balusamy

Contemporary Studies of Risks in Emerging Technology, Part A
Simon Grima, Kiran Sood and Ercan Özen

Contemporary Studies of Risks in Emerging Technology, Part B
Simon Grima, Kiran Sood and Ercan Özen

The Framework for Resilient Industry: A Holistic Approach for Developing Economies
Narinder Kumar, Kiran Sood, Ercan Özen and Simon Grima

VUCA and Other Analytics in Business Resilience, Part A
Deepmala Singh, Kiran Sood, Sandeep Kautish and Simon Grima

VUCA and Other Analytics in Business Resilience, Part B
Deepmala Singh, Kiran Sood, Sandeep Kautish and Simon Grima

Finance Analytics in Business: Perspectives on Enhancing Efficiency and Accuracy
Sanjay Taneja, Pawan Kumar, Kiran Sood, Ercan Özen and Simon Grima

Enterprise Risk Management in Today's World: Enterprise-wide Risk Management and Strategy, Part A
Author: Jean-Paul Louisot; Editor: Simon Grima

Enterprise Risk Management in Today's World: A Current and Futuristic View of the Complexity, Resilience, Responsibility and Tools in ERM, Part B
Author: Jean-Paul Louisot; Editor: Simon Grima

Green Management: A New Paradigm in the World of Business
Swati Gupta, Sanjay Taneja, Ercan Özen, Kiran Sood and Simon Grima

Business Challenges and Opportunities in the Era of Industry 5.0
Simon Grima, Salih Serkan Kaleli, Mehmet Baygin and Engin Boztepe

Financial Landscape Transformation: Technological Disruptions
Manjit Kour, Sanjay Taneja, Ercan Özen, Kiran Sood and Simon Grima

Sustainable Development and Green Innovation: Managing Risk Through Interdisciplinary Approaches and Policy Strategies

EDITED BY

ADALAT MURADOV
Azerbaijan State University of Economics (UNEC), Azerbaijan

FARIZ AHMADOV
Karabakh University, Azerbaijan

NARGIZ HAJIYEVA
Azerbaijan State University of Economics (UNEC), Azerbaijan

KIRAN SOOD
Azerbaijan State University of Economics (UNEC), Azerbaijan

AND

SIMON GRIMA
University of Malta, Malta

emerald PUBLISHING

United Kingdom – North America – Japan – India – Malaysia – China

Emerald Publishing Limited
Emerald Publishing, Floor 5, Northspring, 21-23 Wellington Street, Leeds LS1 4DL.

First edition 2025

British Library Cataloguing in Publication Data
A catalogue record for this book is available from the British Library

ISBN: 978-1-83608-463-1 (Print)
ISBN: 978-1-83608-462-4 (Online)
ISBN: 978-1-83608-464-8 (Epub)

Printed and bound by CPI Group (UK) Ltd, Croydon, CR0 4YY

Contents

About the Editors

Adalat Muradov, born on 29 January 1962, is the Rector of Azerbaijan State University of Economics. He graduated with honours from Kiev State University in 1990 and earned his doctorate in 1998. A distinguished economist, he has held key roles in Azerbaijan's Ministry of Economy, serving in macroeconomic analysis and World Trade Organization (WTO) accession negotiations. He has authored multiple academic works and contributed to international economic programmes. Recognised for his contributions to education, he was awarded the Order of Glory in 2020. Fluent in English, Ukrainian, and Russian, he remains a leading figure in Azerbaijan's economic and academic landscape and author of books and articles in economics.

Fariz Ahmadov completed his bachelor's degree at Azerbaijan State University of Economics (UNEC) before earning his master's and doctoral degrees at Sakarya University in Türkiye. Since 2010, he has held various academic and administrative positions at UNEC. From 2023 to 2024, he served as UNEC's Vice-Rector for Science and Innovation. He has published over 10 articles in SCOPUS and Web of Science-indexed journals and more than 40 in other international journals. He has chaired six editions of the ISCEMR conference at UNEC. On 29 July 2024, he was appointed Vice-Rector for Science and Innovation at Karabakh University.

Nargiz Hajiyeva is the first female Political Scientist from Azerbaijan tenured as a Weiser Scholar (2024) at the University of Michigan, Ann arbour, and a Ludovika Scholar at Ludovika University of Public Service in Hungary. A recipient of the Swiss Federal Excellence Scholarship, she is proficient in seven languages. She serves as the Director of the Organization of Scientific Activities Unit and Chair of the Women Researchers Council at Azerbaijan State University of Economics, where she also lectures on Political Science and Leadership. Additionally, as the first Azerbaijani, she co-directs the 'Empirical Methods' Working Group at the Swiss Political Science Association in Switzerland. She has authored over 45 academic articles, 3 books, and 5 book chapters, contributing extensively to political science and international affairs.

Kiran Sood is a distinguished Professor at Chitkara Business School, Chitkara University, Punjab, India. She earned her doctorate with a focus on Product Portfolio Performance of General Insurance Companies and later completed her postdoctorate at Uşak University, specialising in environmental, social, and governance issues in the insurance industry. She is also an Affiliated Professor at the University of Malta and a Researcher at the Women Researchers Council at Azerbaijan State University of Economics. With over two decades of academic and industry experience, she has made significant contributions to research and education. Her extensive scholarly work includes numerous journal publications and conference presentations. An expert in insurance regulations, marketing, finance, and management, her research also explores economics and innovation in the insurance sector. As an accomplished Editor, she has overseen the publication of more than 20 books in collaboration with leading international publishers, including Emerald, CRC, Taylor & Francis, AAP, WILEY Scrivener, IET, River Publishers, and IEEE.

Simon Grima is the Deputy Dean of the Faculty of Economics, Management, and Accountancy, Associate Professor and the Head of the Department of Insurance and Risk Management. He is also a Professor at the University of Latvia, Faculty of Business, Management and Economics; a Visiting Professor at Università Cattolica del Sacro Cuore (commonly referred to as UNICATT or Catholic University of Milan) Milan; and an Affiliate Professor at Haxhi Zeka University, Kosovo. He served as the President of the Malta Association of Risk Management and was President of the Malta Association of Compliance Officers between 2013 and 2015 and between 2016 and 2018, respectively. He is again the current President of MARM since 2023. Moreover, he is the Co-Chair of the Scientific Education Committee of the Federation of European Risk Managers and is a member of the Strategic Risk Leaders Association, previously the Public Risk Management Association. His research focus is on governance, regulations, and internal controls and has over 30 years of experience varying between financial services, academia, and public entities. He has acted as co-chair and is a member of the scientific programme committee at some international conferences and is a chief editor, editor, and review editor of some journals and book series. He has been awarded outstanding reviewer for *Journal of Financial Regulation and Compliance* in 2017 and 2022 and the outstanding author contribution for the Book Series Contemporary Studies in Economic and Financial Analysis Emerald Literati Awards in 2024. Moreover, he acts as an independent director for financial services firms, sits on risk, compliance, procurement, investment, and audit committees and carries out duties as a compliance officer, internal auditor, and risk manager.

About the Contributors

George Abuselidze, Doctor of Economics (Dr. sc. oec.), is a Professor in Economics, Econometrics and Finance at Batumi Shota Rustaveli State University (Georgia) and a Researcher at the University of Georgia. He is a member of the editorial/advisory board of more than 50 journals and books, as well as the Director of the Sustainable Development Research Institute in Georgia. His research interests include economics, econometrics, and finance; business, management, and accounting; innovative economy; digital economy and finance; financial economics; public finance; money and interest rates; taxation, subsidies, and revenue; national budget, deficit, and debt; etc.

Kobla Sewornu Afadzinu is a Doctoral Student in the Faculty of Economics at the University of Szeged, Hungary, and is researching the topic 'Public Funds and their Audit: The Role of Ghana Audit Service'. He holds a master's degree in Accounting and Controlling from The Hague University in the Netherlands as well as a bachelor's degree in Accounting and Information Systems from Regent University of Science and Technology and a Higher National Diploma from Accra Polytechnic (now Accra Technical University). His research interest lies in public sector auditing, public financial management, financial innovations, and accounting in the public domain. His favourite pastimes include watching football, reading financial novels, and watching movies with his family.

Vusal Ahmadov holds a PhD in Economics from the University of Szeged. He currently delivers lectures on statistics, econometrics, microeconomics, macroeconomics, and labour economics in the Department of International Economics and Business at Azerbaijan State University of Economics and Advanced Microeconomics at Khazar University. He has published articles in international journals in the area of economic growth and remittances, and his research interest areas are development macroeconomics, international finance, and environmental economics.

Nazrin Akhundzada is a Lecturer in the Department of International Economics and Business and UNEC Business School, Azerbaijan State University of Economics. She holds an MA in Economics from Istanbul Technical University and an MS in Banking and International Finance from City University of London, Bayes Business School. Her research focusses on economic growth, development economics, business, and finance. An experienced educator, she has published on topics such as digital channels for Micro, Small and Medium Enterprises (MSMEs) and financial instability's impact on foreign direct investment.

Shubh Arora is working as an Associate Professor at Sharda University. She has over 15 years of rich academic and research experience. She holds a PhD in Marketing and an MBA in Marketing and Finance. She is committed to fostering dynamic learning environments and employs innovative teaching pedagogy and strategies to enhance student engagement and comprehension. Her expertise is evident in her extensive publication record, comprising over 10 papers in prestigious national and international journals indexed with SCOPUS, ABDC, UGC, and other databases.

Lukas Baschung is an Associate Professor at the Haute école de gestion Arc (HEG Arc) in Neuchâtel, which is part of the University of Applied Sciences and Arts Western Switzerland/HES-SO. He teaches public management and carries out research on various topics, such as quality management and resilience of public administrations, as well as on various public policies, for example, in the fields of higher education, research, innovation, and energy. He is the Head of the master's major programme 'Business in Eurasia' and the Dean of the Swiss Eurasian Institute of Management.

Zarina Burkadze is an Associate Professor of Political Science at Ilia State University, Tbilisi, Georgia. She is a founding member and Secretary General of the Georgian Association for Public Opinion Research, and author of *Great Power Competition and the Path to Democracy – The Case of Georgia, 1991–2020* (Rochester University Press, 2022). She received her PhD in Political Science from the University of Zurich and was a Fulbright Postdoctoral Scholar at the Institute for European, Russian, and Eurasian Studies (at the Elliott School of International Affairs, George Washington University) (2019–2020). She was also a Visiting Scholar at the Institute for Social Research at the University of Michigan. Her research interests revolve around the topics of democratisation, Europeanisation, democracy, and autocracy promotion. She enjoys teaching and delivers courses on research design, political violence, and democracy for bachelor-, master-, and doctoral-level students.

Aulonë Cenaj, PhD(c), has completed her bachelor's and master's studies at University 'Haxhi Zeka' in Kosovo. In 2022, she graduated in Business Management in Banking and Finance. She is currently studying for a PhD in Economics at South East European University. During her studies, she currently works as an Assistant at University 'Haxhi Zeka' in the following subjects: International Finance, Corporate Finance, Advanced Corporate Finance, and Corporate Governance. She has conducted several scientific research projects that provide scientific contributions to economic issues. During her studies, she has conducted research in the fields of public finance, green economy, banking sector, and other fields of particular economic importance.

Nino Chanadiri is a PhD student in Political Science at Ilia State University. Her main research interests include interethnic peace and conflict dynamics, international relations and security, as well as gender-related issues in conflict and post-conflict settings. As an author and analyst, she has been actively cooperating with think tanks and journals in Georgia and beyond, working on political topics and producing several articles and opinion papers on political and social developments in Eastern and Northern Europe. In addition to academic life, she has experience in local and international projects in the fields of peace, development, and education.

Hiranya Dissanayake is a Senior Lecturer in the Faculty of Business Studies & Finance at Wayamba University of Sri Lanka. With over a decade of teaching experience, she is known for her dedication to academic excellence and her commitment to student development. Her research interests include corporate governance, corporate sustainability, and bibliometric analysis, areas in which she has published extensively in reputable journals. She has also won multiple awards, including the CIMA Research Excellence Award and recognition for her contributions to corporate governance and sustainability. Beyond teaching, she has held leadership roles, including as a former Head of the Department of Accountancy, and has been actively involved in academic conferences and workshops and as a research supervisor for postgraduate students. She holds a BCom degree from the University of Colombo and an MSc degree in Applied Finance and is currently a PhD candidate in Management (Finance) at the University of Sri Jayewardenepura.

Kushtrim Gashi is an Assistant Professor at the Faculty of Economics, University 'Ukshin Hoti' Prizren. He holds a PhD from Swiss Management Center University in Switzerland and specialises in management. He teaches a variety of subjects, including quality management, negotiation and leadership skills, management economics, e-business, and digital business with artificial intelligence (AI). He is highly dedicated to student development, mentoring numerous bachelor's and master's theses, and helping students tackle complex research topics in business and management. In addition to his academic role, he actively contributes to university governance as a member of key committees such as the Central Quality Assurance Committee and the Faculty Council. His professional background includes positions in the financial sector as a credit analyst and in other organisations as a manager and director, demonstrating his diverse expertise in various sectors. His research interests focus on the intersection of management, technology, and data governance. He has published in international book chapters and journals, making significant contributions in areas such as AI, risk management, and sustainable business practices.

Anuradha Iddagoda is a Senior Lecturer of the Management Science Unit, Department of Mathematics, Faculty of Applied Sciences, University of Sri Jayewardenepura, Sri Lanka. She also served as a Guest Lecturer at the University of Rzeszów, Poland, in the years 2022, 2023, and 2024. She is a member of the Chartered Institute of Personnel Management Sri Lanka, Sri Lanka. Her research areas are human resource management, green human resource management, employee engagement, leadership, and work–life balance.

Szonja Jenei is an Economist working as an Assistant Professor at Széchenyi István University in Hungary, while also helping to manage their family business in the construction industry. She has a diverse background, having worked in healthcare, the cultural sector, and the business sector for nearly a decade, gaining strong experience in business administration and human resource management. Early in her career, she succeeded as a sales representative, boosting company revenues by promoting their products. She also holds certifications as a trainer and business coach, showing her dedication to ongoing professional growth.

Botond Géza Kálmán (1993) has earned his doctorate in Management at the Hungarian University of Agricultural and Life Sciences, with the topic of comparative financial literacy. In addition, he is a Master of Laws of England and Wales at Leeds Beckett University (UK). Also, he holds a juris doctor degree in Continental Law, two further MA degrees (Pedagogy and Public Service), and an MSc in Finance. His research topics are workplace stress, higher education and competitiveness. For 5 years, he was the director of an out-patient dental services LLC. He is an Associate Professor at Kodolányi János University and Budapest.

Duresa Kilaj, PhD(c), is a Teaching Assistant at the Faculty of Business, University 'Haxhi Zeka' in Peja, Kosovo, and an Import Manager at Afrimi AG Company. She specialises in banking, finance, and econometrics and is pursuing her PhD in Economics at South East European University, North Macedonia. With publications in Scopus and Web of Science journals and participation in international projects and conferences, she bridges academic knowledge with professional practice, aiming to advance sustainable development in economics, finance, and management.

Armand Brice Kouadio is an Associate Professor of Human Resource Management at the Haute école de gestion Arc (HEG Arc) in Neuchâtel, which is part of the University of Applied Sciences and Arts Western Switzerland/HES-SO. His teaching focusses on strategic human capital management, with an emphasis on equipping future leaders with the tools to navigate evolving organisational landscapes. His research delves into behavioural dynamics in organisational settings and the development of innovative personnel policies, highlighting the human challenges and opportunities presented by workplace modernisation, flexible working conditions, and the integration of technological advancements.

Svitlana Lavrynenko, PhD in Economics, is an Associate Professor of Management and Marketing at Polissia National University (Zhytomyr, Ukraine). Her research interests include approaches to shaping the innovative potential of enterprise management systems in the context of dynamic changes in the external environment. The research focusses on enterprise management in the era of digital transformation, contemporary trends, and innovative modernisation of enterprise management, business management, and business planning. Significant attention is paid to the intellectualisation and communicative integration of the management system as components of achieving its efficiency, effectiveness, and competitiveness.

Dhaval Maheta, a distinguished academician with a PhD in Management, is a Professor in the Department of Business and Industrial Management at Veer Narmad South Gujarat University, Surat. With 22+ years of academic and corporate experience, including roles at ICICI Bank and HDFC Ltd., he specialises in quantitative methods, financial management, research methodology, and financial derivatives. He has authored books, published 40+ research papers, and led a YouTube channel offering free tutorials on research software. A seasoned trainer, he has organised 150+ workshops and trained 10,000+ professionals in advanced data analysis and research methodologies.

Szilárd Malatyinszki is an Associate Professor. He is the Dean of the Faculty of Economics of János Kodolányi University, the Director of the KJE Orosház Education Center, and the Head of the Department of Economics and Management. He obtained a habilitation (postdoctoral) and doctoral certificate in the field of regional development. The topic of his PhD and habilitation is both the measurement of human resources at the settlement level in Békés County. The number of his scientific publications is over 120.

Fisnik Morina is an Associate Professor at the Faculty of Business, University 'Haxhi Zeka' in Peja, Kosovo, specialising in banking, finance, economics, and econometrics. He is the Vice Dean for Teaching, Student Affairs, and Scientific Research. He completed postdoctoral research in banking and finance at the University of Graz (2023) and in risk management at the University of Malta (2022). He has published extensively in Scopus and Web of Science, is internationally certified in modern teaching methods, and has led numerous international research projects in economics and finance.

Peter Novoszath is currently an Associate Professor at the University of Dunaújváros. He has published more than 140 scientific publications and several books, both in Hungary and abroad, which have been cited more than 215 times. He has also participated in the preparation and implementation of several research proposals. In addition, he currently teaches some of the international finance and economics courses at the University of Dunaújváros and closely cooperates with domestic and foreign scientific journals and associations (https://orcid.org/0000-0002-8755-685).

Tinatin Nozadze is a PhD candidate of Political Science at Ilia State University. Her main scientific interests are conflicts, political violence, and authoritarian regimes. Over the past years, she participated in different education and training courses, among which the most notable is the Winter School in Methods organised jointly by the Georgian Association for Public Opinion Research and Ilia State University. She has a deep theoretical and empirical knowledge regarding the topics related to international conflicts and politics. Her article 'Israeli-Palestinian Conflict and the Heterogeneous Interests of EU Member States' was published in the scientific works collection of Tbilisi Open University.

Cathérine Enorédia Odorige, PhD, is an Assistant Professor in the Department of Organisational Development and Communication Science, Social Science Institute, University of Dunaújváros, Hungary. She teaches and conducts research in the fields of business communication, development communication, culture and communication, emotional intelligence, and enterprise management. Other research and publication areas are sustainable development, European integration, migration, asylum, integration and inclusion of third-country nationals in the European Union, human trafficking, transnationalism, NGOs, intercultural communication, community-building, corruption, and transparency. She is an experienced project manager, specializing in the inclusion and integration of migrants in host countries. She is at the forefront of supporting migrant women and men in empowerment initiatives and in addressing sexual and gender-based violence (SGBV) (https://orcid.org/0000-0003-4477-5492).

Osakue Stevenson Omoera, PhD, is the Dean of the Faculty of Humanities and Chair Professor of Theatre and Film Studies in the Department of Theatre and Film Studies, Federal University Otuoke, Bayelsa State, Nigeria. He is an expert in applied media, film, and theatre studies. He is also an Adjunct Professor in the Department of Mass Communication, National Open University of Nigeria, Abuja. Widely published and extensively travelled, he brings close to 20 years of experience to bear in his teaching, research, and administrative responsibilities. Some of his latest publications are *Introducing Media Studies: A Holistic Approach to Understanding Communication* (2024) and *Audience Reception of Benin Cinema in Nigeria: Empirical Findings and Implications for Nollywood* (2024) (https://orcid.org/0000-0003-1086-7874).

Andriy Popovych is an Assistant Researcher at the Agricultural and Food Economics State Research Institute, Warsaw, Poland. His key areas of work and research focus are agricultural economics, environmental research, and food studies. Due to his former professional experience in financial management and analysis, the topics pertaining to financial markets are also among his current research interests.

Kirti Prashar, working as an Assistant Professor at Sharda University, specialises in commerce and marketing, possessing a wealth of knowledge backed by a master's degree in commerce, UGC National Eligibility Test certification, and the ongoing pursuit of a PhD in marketing. With more than 5 years of dedicated teaching and research experience, she has contributed significantly to academia through numerous publications. Her expertise extends beyond publication, serving as an editor and reviewer for reputable academic journals, with a good number of patents published under her name. She epitomises dedication, expertise, and passion in her pursuit of advancing knowledge and nurturing future generations of scholars and learners.

Niluka Rajakaruna is currently a Senior Lecturer in the Department of Accountancy at the Faculty of Business Studies & Finance, Wayamba University of Sri Lanka. She is reading for a PhD in Finance at the Management Science University of Malaysia. She holds an MSc in Applied Finance from the University of Sri Jayewardenepura (2021), a Master of Business Administration with a Merit Pass from

Wayamba University of Sri Lanka, and a Bachelor of Science Special Degree in Accountancy and Business Finance with a Second-Class Upper Division from the same university. She began her academic career as a Temporary Lecturer in 2012 and has since made significant contributions to teaching and research in her field.

Hem Shweta Rathore is currently working as an Assistant Professor at Amity School of Business, Amity University Uttar Pradesh (AUUP), Noida. She has 9 years of teaching and research. She has published 10 research papers in international and national journals, some of which are Scopus Indexed and UGC Care Listed Journals. One research scholar was awarded MPhil in the derivatives market under her supervision. At present, three scholars are pursuing their PhD in the Management and Commerce domain under her guidance. She is a reviewer with various journals indexed in Web of Science and Scopus. She is a lifetime member of the Indian Commerce Association.

Anna Slobodianyk, PhD in Economics, is an Associate Professor at the National Aviation University, Kyiv, Ukraine. Her research interests include economic competition, capital markets, exchange activity, institutional economics, information systems, and financial economics.

Liudmyla Tarasovych, PhD in Economics, is an Associate Professor and Head of the Department of Management and Marketing at Polissia National University (Zhytomyr, Ukraine). Her research interests include innovative approaches to marketing and management, focussing on adapting marketing strategies in a rapidly changing environment. She studies the role of marketing in managing socio-economic systems to effectively respond to global challenges and promote sustainable development. She pays special attention to social marketing as an effective tool for increasing competitiveness, stability of the rural economy, and community development through the integration of social responsibility and innovative approach.

Tetiana Usiuk, PhD in Economics, is an Associate Professor in the Department of International Economic Relations and European Integration at Polissia National University (Zhytomyr, Ukraine). Her research interests include regulatory competition in international agricultural business. She researches issues related to tariff and non-tariff regulation of international trade between countries and the development of trade wars in international agricultural markets. Certain aspects of her research relate to the problems of forming the institutional environment of Ukraine's foreign economic policy in the context of a full-scale war.

Rovena Vangjel (Troplini) has been the Head of the Department of Accounting and Finance at Universiteti "Aleksandër Moisiu" Durrës (UAMD) since September 2020 and holds the title of Associate Professor at University for Business and Technology (UBT), Kosovo as of February 2024. She has been a Lecturer at UAMD since 2009, contributing to financial development and economic growth. She has held administrative roles, including Head of the Finance Subject Group and Coordinator of the BSc Bank-Finance programme. She has published numerous scientific articles, served as a Project Leader and expert in various projects, and is a member of several international scientific committees and conferences.

Luan Vardari is a Vice-Rector for Teaching, Student Affairs and Scientific Research at the University 'Ukshin Hoti' Prizren, where he is also an Assistant Professor of Finance at the Faculty of Economics. He holds a PhD in Business Administration and an MA in Finance from Trakya University, where his research focusses on the stock markets of the Balkan countries. Previously, he was a Vice Dean and has built a strong academic presence, particularly in the areas of financial markets, portfolio optimization, and international finance. In addition to teaching at the university, he is the Founder and Editor-in-Chief of the *Prizren Social Science Journal*, for which he has authored numerous book chapters and academic articles. His leadership and contributions reflect his commitment to promoting financial education and supporting academic excellence at his institution.

Madhu Verma is an Assistant Professor at Sharda University, bringing a wealth of expertise in commerce and research to her role. With a master's degree in Commerce and qualification in the National Eligibility Test, she possesses a solid academic foundation and good teaching experience. Her dedication to research and data analysis is evident through her active engagement in related courses. Her effective verbal communication skills and critical thinking abilities enhance her teaching and research endeavours, making her a valuable asset to both her students and the academic community.

Maryna Yaremova, PhD in Economics, is an Associate Professor in the Department of Economics, Entrepreneurship and Tourism, Polissia National University (Zhytomyr, Ukraine). Her research interests include modelling strategies for the transition to a low-carbon economy, focussing on the environmental, economic, and social impact of sustainable natural resource management. She researches innovative technologies for recycling and reuse of materials and organic waste management to create closed production cycles. She pays special attention to using biomass to produce biofuels, biopolymers, and other environmentally friendly materials to solve global ecological problems.

Zsuzsanna Zugor, JD, L.L.M. (b. 1979, Székesfehérvár, Hungary), is a social politician and financial law specialist. A doctoral candidate at István Széchenyi Doctoral School, her research focusses on financial literacy's impact on labour market outcomes among disadvantaged groups. She serves as Chancellor and Associate Professor at János Kodolányi University, teaching Social Policy and Labour Market Training. Since 2014, she has been a curator for the Foundation Supporting the Poor. In 2023, she received the Hungarian Gold Cross of Merit for her contributions to social and economic development.

Foreword

One of the most significant transformative challenges of the new millennium is sustainable development and the green innovations leading to it. Pursuing sustainable development and green innovation has become a key agenda for policymakers, businesses, and researchers alike. Integrating interdisciplinary approaches and policy strategies has become increasingly prominent in the face of environmental challenges and the identification of effective solutions. In particular, the role of specific stakeholders, such as the state and municipalities, the role of corporate green strategies, and the contribution of funding institutions in the sustainability transition are all important.

This book, *Sustainable Development and Green Innovation: Managing Risk Through Interdisciplinary Approaches and Policy Strategies*, is part of the highly esteemed ESFIRM (Emerald Studies in Finance, Insurance, and Risk Management) series and aims to comprehensively explore the dynamic intersections of sustainability, finance, risk management, and policy making. This book explores the sustainability transition and related policy strategy from an interdisciplinary perspective. The book's guiding principle is that specific sectors can be drivers (or even barriers) to sustainable development, such as the financial sector, tourism, education, and energy, among others. The book's chapters provide a comprehensive overview of the background of technological, social, and policy innovations.

Good green governance is best understood through case studies. The book presents several sectoral and regional examples of policies that promote sustainability and can contribute to knowledge transfer on green issues.

From the strategic ambitions and constraints of Swiss energy companies to the complex role of stakeholder engagement in green innovation policy in Nigeria, the contributions reflect the global and multifaceted nature of sustainable development. The bibliometric review of green finance and banking literature also provides an in-depth synthesis of existing knowledge, helping to identify emerging trends and research gaps. Technology has an undeniable role to play in the transition to a green economy, and several chapters in the volume address the implications of artificial intelligence and machine learning for sustainable finance. These technological developments are shaping the future of financial markets and driving the emergence of innovative green solutions. In addition, case studies on sustainability practices in tourism and rural entrepreneurship highlight the need for targeted policy interventions that consider specific socio-economic and environmental contexts. This volume provides valuable insights into the effectiveness of different policy measures, such as those implemented in Georgia and the Visegrad region, to promote environmentally sustainable economic growth.

One of the book's conclusions is that the sustainability transition is decided in the minds and hearts of the people. Policy instruments and institutional solutions depend on people and their communities. Another important finding is that the multidimensional nature of sustainable development requires a holistic approach, considering economic and non-economic drivers. This book seeks to bridge the gap between theory and practice by presenting empirical studies and conceptual frameworks that can guide policymakers and practitioners in achieving sustainability goals. The authors make valuable recommendations emphasising the need for collaboration across sectors and disciplines to make meaningful progress. I am confident that this volume will inspire further research and help inform policy measures to facilitate the transition to a more sustainable and resilient future.

Tamás Pálvölgyi, PhD
Associate Professor
Head of Department of Water and Environmental Policies
Vice Dean for International Affairs and Strategy
Faculty of Water Sciences
University of Public Service
Hungary

Preface

In an era increasingly defined by climate change, technological upheaval, and socio-economic transformation, the pursuit of sustainable development has moved from the margins to the centre of global discourse. The world stands at an inflection point, where the convergence of environmental imperatives, financial innovation, and technological advancements demands new frameworks, strategies, and a new vision of growth. This volume, *Sustainable Development and Green Innovation: Managing Risk Through Interdisciplinary Approaches and Policy Strategies*, finds its purpose and relevance within this evolving context.

This volume combines an interdisciplinary collection of scholarly contributions examining the multifaceted green and sustainable development dimensions. From the empirical evaluation of green bond exchange-traded funds (ETFs) to the bibliometric mapping of green banking research, from the exploration of artificial intelligence and machine learning in sustainable finance to the role of social marketing in rural entrepreneurship, the chapters presented herein address the complex, interconnected challenges of promoting a green economy across diverse regional and sectoral landscapes.

Some contributions centre on the financial mechanisms catalysing green transformation. Green finance, encompassing green bonds, banking, and ESG (environmental, social, and governance)-focussed investment vehicles, is scrutinised through quantitative bibliometric reviews and empirical analysis. Studying green bond ETFs offers new empirical insights into the debated 'green premium', revealing the complexities of market dynamics, investor expectations, and certification processes. Concurrently, bibliometric analyses of green finance and banking literature reveal critical gaps, emerging trends, and global research collaborations, providing a structured roadmap for future academic inquiry.

Technology's transformative potential is a recurring theme throughout the volume. Chapters dedicated to the intersection of emerging technologies and sustainable finance illuminate the critical roles played by artificial intelligence, machine learning, and distributed ledger technologies (DLTs). These technologies offer powerful tools for enhancing transparency, improving risk assessment, optimising resource allocation, and embedding ESG principles into financial decision-making. Through systematic reviews and qualitative interviews, contributors explore how digital innovation can be harnessed to support the transition to a green economy while highlighting the ethical, regulatory, and implementation challenges accompanying technological adoption.

Policy frameworks and governance structures are another critical pillar of this volume. Regional analyses, particularly focussed on the Visegrad countries, demonstrate the nuanced and often uneven progress towards green growth within the European Union. By employing rigorous econometric techniques such as panel Fully Modified Ordinary Least Squares (FMOLS) and Dynamic Ordinary Least Squares (DOLS) models, the studies herein provide robust empirical evidence regarding the impact of policy stringency, carbon taxes, green finance, and technological innovation on greenhouse gas emissions, renewable energy adoption, and material productivity. These findings have significant implications for policymakers balancing economic growth, environmental sustainability, and social equity.

Socio-economic and educational dimensions of sustainability are also robustly addressed. The role of social marketing in promoting rural entrepreneurship is critically examined, emphasising the necessity of integrating social goals with business innovation to achieve inclusive and sustainable development. Stakeholder engagement strategies in education systems are analysed as vital for cultivating green innovation mindsets and fostering a new generation of sustainability champions. These chapters underscore that technological and financial innovation, while necessary, are insufficient without the active participation and empowerment of communities.

This volume is distinctive in its methodological diversity. Bibliometric analyses using Bibliophagy and VOSviewer provide quantitative mapping of research landscapes, thematic structures, and intellectual linkages across green finance and green banking domains. Qualitative methodologies, including case studies and interviews, enrich the analysis of technology adoption and social innovation. Econometric modelling enhances the empirical rigour of policy evaluations. The multi-method approach adopted by the contributors not only improves the validity and reliability of findings but also reflects the inherently interdisciplinary nature of sustainability science.

Several common threads weave through the diverse contributions. First, there is a need for systemic approaches that integrate financial innovation, technological advancement, social engagement, and policy reform. Second, recognising that regional, cultural, and institutional contexts profoundly shape the pathways and outcomes of green transitions. Third, there is an urgency to foster global collaboration, as no single nation or sector can address the magnitude of environmental challenges in isolation.

Importantly, the chapters in this volume do not shy away from identifying persistent barriers to sustainable development. Issues such as regulatory fragmentation, the 'greenwashing' of financial products, technological inequalities, limited access to green financing in developing economies, and the socio-political inertia resisting environmental reforms are critically examined. These challenges highlight the necessity for continued research, innovation, and dialogue.

This work also contributes significantly to filling gaps in the existing literature. The bibliometric reviews offer fresh insights into under-researched areas such as green credit policies, rural entrepreneurship in the context of social marketing, and the emerging intersections of AI and sustainable finance. Empirical analyses of green bond ETFs, an area previously underexplored relative to traditional green bonds, provide important evidence for investors and policymakers navigating the evolving landscape of sustainable finance.

By bringing together perspectives from Europe, South Asia, and Eastern Europe, including case studies from countries such as Kosovo, Georgia, Ukraine, India, and the Visegrad group, the volume offers a genuinely global view of sustainable development challenges and strategies. This international scope reinforces that while sustainability challenges are universal, solutions must be sensitive to local contexts.

The intended audience for this volume is broad. Academics and researchers will find rich empirical data, methodological innovations, and extensive literature mappings to support further inquiry. Policymakers and regulatory bodies will discover actionable insights into designing and implementing green finance mechanisms and technological regulations. Industry practitioners, particularly in the banking, finance, and technology sectors, will gain strategic perspectives on aligning business practices with sustainability imperatives. Students and educators will find the volume a valuable resource for understanding the complex interrelationships that define the field of sustainable development today.

Overall, this volume affirms that sustainable development is not a distant aspiration but an immediate necessity. Achieving it requires the collaborative efforts of diverse stakeholders operating across multiple scales and sectors. Financial markets must realign incentives towards long-term environmental stewardship. Technologies must be harnessed ethically and inclusively. Policies must be ambitious, coherent, and adaptive. Communities must be empowered to drive bottom-up change.

The editors and contributors hope that *Sustainable Development and Green Innovation: Managing Risk Through Interdisciplinary Approaches and Policy Strategies* will serve as both a scholarly reference and a catalyst for further research, dialogue, and action towards a greener, fairer and more resilient world.

Chapter 1, 'Swiss Energy Companies and Energy Transition: Between Strategic Ambitions and Internal and External Constraints', analyses the strategic management of Swiss energy companies facing the renewable transition, revealing how internal capabilities and external pressures shape energy strategies.

Chapter 2, 'Stakeholder Engagement as Policy Instrument for Green Innovation and Development: A Study of Nigeria's Government Engagement with Educators', examines how stakeholder engagement between government and educators in Nigeria acts as a catalyst for green innovation and sustainable entrepreneurship development.

Chapter 3, 'Green Finance and Sustainable Development: A Bibliometric Review', presents a bibliometric analysis of global green finance research trends, highlighting emerging themes, intellectual networks, and research gaps critical for sustainable development.

Chapter 4, 'The Role of Technology, AI, ML and DLT in Sustainable Finance and a Green Economy', explores how artificial intelligence, machine learning, and distributed ledger technologies drive transformation in sustainable finance and green economic systems.

Chapter 5, 'Greening the Future: A Comprehensive Approach to Sustainable Development', provides a holistic framework for addressing global environmental and socio-economic challenges through sustainable development policies, with an emphasis on innovation and risk management.

Chapter 6, 'Imperatives of Social Marketing in the Context of Rural Entrepreneurship', highlights how social marketing strategies can promote rural entrepreneurship, improve social welfare, and support sustainable economic development, particularly in transitional economies.

Chapter 7 'Sustainability of Tourism and Regional Airports Based on Good and Less Good Practices', investigates sustainability practices at regional airports, comparing successful and less effective initiatives to promote environmentally responsible tourism and aviation.

Chapter 8, 'Policy Strategies for Sustainable Development and Green Innovation', analyses policy mechanisms and strategies governments can employ to accelerate green innovation and ensure the successful transition towards sustainable economic models.

Chapter 9, 'Policy Instruments for Promoting Green Innovation in Economic Development: The Case of Georgia', focusses on the Georgian experience and assesses how specific policy instruments foster green innovation and contribute to environmentally sustainable economic development.

Chapter 10, 'Corruption Perception in the Light of Green Transition Indicators', examines the interplay between corruption perceptions and green transition efforts, emphasising how governance quality directly impacts environmental and sustainability outcomes.

Chapter 11, 'Financial Market Contribution to Sustainable Development: Two Approaches to Green Bonds ETF's Analysis', provides empirical analysis of green bond ETFs, testing the existence of a 'green premium' and evaluating their contribution to financing global sustainability initiatives.

Chapter 12, 'Green Growth Policy in Visegrad: Key Drivers from an Economic and Non-Economic Perspective', evaluates how policy instruments, economic factors, and EU environmental standards drive or constrain the green transition in the Visegrad Group countries.

Chapter 13, 'A Bibliometric Review on the Literature of Green Banking: Using Scopus Database (1997–2022)', conducts a bibliometric review of green banking literature, identifying major research areas, trends, influential authors, and outlining future directions for sustainable finance research.

Simon Grima
University of Malta, Malta
Kiran Sood
Azerbaijan State University of Economics (UNEC), Azerbaijan

Chapter 1

Swiss Energy Companies and Energy Transition: Between Strategic Ambitions and Internal and External Constraints

Lukas Baschung and Armand Brice Kouadio

HES-SO//Haute école de gestion Arc, Neuchâtel, Switzerland

Abstract

Purpose: If the Swiss political environment is generally rather favourable to the production of considerably more renewable energy (RE), the implementation of concrete projects by energy companies is influenced by various internal and external constraints. This chapter aims to describe, illustrate and analyse strategies and the nature of constraints, as well as their impact on the energy transition from energy enterprises' perspective.

Need for the study: The Swiss landscape of energy enterprises is highly diversified. Yet, it is unclear to what extent this diversity has an impact on the companies' strategies and constraints regarding the production of RE and, thereby, on green growth within Switzerland.

Methodology: This study is based on a mixed method consisting of qualitative interviews with CEOs from six Swiss energy enterprises and two experts as well as quantitative data generated on the basis of annual reports of most Swiss energy-producing enterprises (n = 105).

Findings: To varying extents, all company strategies seek to develop RE. The number of RE types produced or envisaged by public companies is generally higher than for private companies. Companies are influenced by external factors, such as legal opposition, regulations and customer and citizen behaviour, as well as internal factors, such as risk management capacities, human resources availability and innovation capacity.

Sustainable Development and Green Innovation: Managing Risk through Interdisciplinary Approaches and Policy Strategies, 1–18

Published under exclusive licence by Emerald Publishing Limited
doi:10.1108/978-1-83608-462-420251001

Practical implications: Each energy enterprise must choose its RE projects by considering its specific external and internal constraints in order to maximise its benefits and contribution to the national energy transition strategy.

Keywords: Energy companies; Switzerland; constraints; obstacles; energy transition; size; legal status

JEL codes: H12; L25; L33; P18; Q42

Introduction

Given the long tradition of hydropower in Swiss energy production (Tabi & Wüstenhagen, 2017), it can be considered that the topic of RE is not new in Switzerland. Nevertheless, attention to RE suddenly and greatly increased across all political parties with the Fukushima accident. In this context and due to growing awareness of the climate crisis, the Swiss federal government and parliament reformulated their energy strategy towards successive replacement of nuclear and fossil energy with RE (Díaz et al., 2017). Several federal laws were adapted in order to promote the production of RE. These legal changes were clearly confirmed by the votes of the Swiss population in 2017 and 2024. Simultaneously, Switzerland faces another major problem, namely, a high dependency from imports. In fact, 70% of Switzerland's energy supply depends on foreign fossil and nuclear fuels.[1] Since negotiations on an electricity agreement between Switzerland and the European Union (EU) were suspended in 2018, Switzerland has been increasingly isolated from the advancing EU market integration and mechanisms which are crucial for grid security (IEA, 2023). Consequently, Switzerland finds itself in a typical situation of the 'impossible energy trinity', which means to be a state 'which cannot simultaneously achieve energy security, sustainability, and sovereignty' (Thaler & Hofmann, 2022, p. 1). Given these circumstances of successive renouncement of nuclear energy and the uncertain relationship with the EU, the pressure to develop RE is high.

Despite the broad political support for the development of RE, the implementation of concrete projects often meets opposition, especially at the local level. Legal opposition, for instance, regarding the enlargement of hydropower plants or the installation of wind power plants, may block the implementation of projects for a long time, sometimes even several decades (IEA, 2023). Indeed, civil society organisations or individual citizens oppose RE projects, often with the argument that they want to preserve the landscape for functions such as nutrition, aesthetics, heritage or habitat (Kienast et al., 2017).

---

[1]Swiss Confederation – International energy policy (admin.ch); consulted in June 2024.

Swiss energy companies are situated at the centre of this field of tension between pressure for and opposition to the development of RE. In fact, they are the organisations which should plan and implement concrete RE development projects. Yet, there is a research gap concerning their strategies for the development of RE and the external and internal constraints they face. Such knowledge is a crucial source of information for public policies on RE. The case of Switzerland is particularly interesting because of its highly diversified energy companies. Indeed, they consist of approximately 600 firms, which vary greatly regarding variables such as size, energy production, legal status, and so on. This chapter examines to what extent the variables of size and legal status have an impact on the companies' strategies, which are based on the analysis of their annual activity reports, and the constraints they face, and these are based on semi-structured interviews with CEOs from six varying energy enterprises and two experts.

This introduction is followed by a literature review focussing on obstacles met for the development of RE in Switzerland and a description of the Swiss landscape of energy companies. The methodological section specifies the data used and the analysis performed, followed by a presentation and discussion of the results obtained.

Literature Review

Obstacles for the Development of Renewable Energies

The development of RE meets various kinds of obstacles. As reported by several studies, these obstacles concern the *human resources*, *social*, *technical*, *political*, *legal* and *economic* dimensions. A first study dedicated to the development of wind energy in China makes it clear that even if some conditions are met, such as the availability of a high production capacity, others, such as the shortage of professional talent in wind power technology, may slow down further development. Indeed, in the case of RE production, there needs to be a wide range of qualified labour in a wide range of professions: R&D professionals, senior management personnel, manufacturing professionals, senior technicians, as well as wind plant and turbine operations and maintenance personnel (Zhao et al., 2014). The nature of these obstacles impedes further development of RE and varies according to the type of RE. This becomes clear when comparing the results of the previous study with another Chinese study concerning hydrogen. Thus, a shortage of manufacturers, incomplete supporting facilities and hydrogen fuel safety issues are identified as being the main obstacles. In addition, the political and technical dimensions constitute another important hurdle (Wu et al., 2021). Paradoxically, the lack of stable legal regulations precisely constitutes another obstacle, as argued by a study on Polish biogas plants. Indeed, changing regulations have a negative impact on investment according to the employees of a biogas-producing firm (Bednarek et al., 2023).

RE sources do not only represent interesting opportunities for large energy enterprises, but also smaller, decentralised RE systems, which are situated at the local level. Apart from energy provision, there also seem to be promising routes for local economic development. A study on Scottish wind farmers demonstrates that RE can constitute a means to diversify and future-proof the farmers' business. However, in some cases, farmers fear the obstacles of economic risk and transaction costs and, therefore, compensate this by reducing the turbine size and renting land to developers. Thereby, these opportunities would be 'at risk of being co-opted by large-scale energy companies, which are better able to negotiate the growing complexities and risks of turbine development' (Sutherland & Holstead, 2014, p. 102). Economic and further obstacles related to size are also mentioned in a Finnish study on various kinds of RE: insufficient information and availability of professional services, lacking profitability of small-scale energy sales and the cost of production systems (Varho et al., 2016). An American case study on an on-farm biogas production explained this shutdown by the underestimation of technical problems and operating costs, overestimation of financial returns and low RE credit price (Wang et al., 2021). Finally, the obstacles of two case studies in South Africa on smaller-scale solar energy concern several of the previously mentioned dimensions, such as issues with battery management systems, an incoherent business model imposed by a large energy company, bureaucratic obstacles, and growing pains concerning cohesion within the concerned community (Bloem et al., 2021).

Thus, existing literature points to a series of obstacles for the development of RE, among which there is the political dimension. Since this is generally specific regarding a given territory, the following section develops the Swiss political context in more detail.

Swiss Governmental Policies and Goals

Annually assessed by the Federal Office of Energy, three approaches can be identified in the Swiss context for the substitution of fossil fuels: a purely electric system with battery storage (EBS), a hydrogen-based system (HYS) and a system using synthetic hydrocarbons (HCR). The EBS is the most energy-efficient method; however, this requires seasonal electricity storage to meet year-round energy needs. Using batteries for this is currently expensive and impractical due to production limits, and expanding pumped hydropower would have significant environmental impacts. The HYS allows for underground hydrogen storage to balance seasonal demand, but it needs infrastructure development. The HCR demands the largest photovoltaic (PV) field but leverages existing infrastructure (Züttel et al., 2022). Otherwise, the heating and mobility sectors, responsible for nearly half of domestic greenhouse gas emissions, are transitioning, which is leading to increased electricity demand (Bucher et al., 2019). Relatively, Switzerland's energy policies are designed to promote sustainability and reduce dependence on fossil fuels and nuclear energy. As a matter of fact, the 'Stratégie énergétique 2050' is a pivotal framework aiming for climate neutrality by 2050.[2] Key components of this strategy include the enhancement of energy efficiency, the development of

[2]https://www.bfe.admin.ch/bfe/en/home/policy/energy-strategy-2050.html/ (retrieved on 18 June 2024).

RE sources and the gradual phasing-out of nuclear energy sources. This strategy builds upon previous initiatives, for example, Energy Perspectives 2035, which sets ambitious targets to comprehensively transform the country's energy landscape. This consists notably of incentives for RE projects, stringent regulations to curb emissions and support for technological innovations. For instance, the government offers subsidies and tax incentives to encourage the adoption of RE technologies in both residential and industrial sectors (Züttel et al., 2022).

RE Production in Switzerland

Switzerland's RE portfolio is diverse, with significant contributions from hydropower, solar, wind and biomass energy. Hydropower remains the cornerstone, providing approximately 68% of the country's electricity. This represents an important source of revenue for public bodies, in particular in the mountainous regions (Gaudard et al., 2014). This focus is due to the country's abundant water resources, which offer a reliable and sustainable energy source. In recent years, the government and private sector have heavily invested in PV systems, leading to a significant increase in solar power capacity. Solar energy not only supplements the energy mix, however, it also reduces dependency on hydropower during dry seasons. Albeit less prevalent than hydropower and solar, wind energy is gaining traction. Thus, several wind farms have been established, primarily in mountainous regions where wind conditions are more favourable. Finally, biomass energy also contributes to Switzerland's RE mix. This alludes to energy generated from organic materials such as agricultural waste, wood and biogas. Biomass energy supports both electricity generation and heating applications, thereby enhancing energy security and reducing greenhouse gas emissions (Gaudard et al., 2014).

After the nuclear accident in Fukushima and the Swiss Federal Council's and parliament's landmark decision to successively replace nuclear power by RE sources (Díaz et al., 2017), several studies examined what the 'optimal' energy mix could be for Switzerland (Dujardin et al., 2017). In 2021, domestic energy production relied on three main pillars: hydropower plants (62%), nuclear power plants (29%), and conventional power plants and renewable energies (9%). Simultaneously, the share of oil and gas of the gross energy consumption still approaches 50%.[3] These figures show that the need to develop further RE is still strong if the political goal of zero net emissions target is to be met by 2050,[4] especially with the ongoing closure of nuclear power plants. Among the RE sources with development potential, PV, wind power, hydropower, geothermal power and biofuel are the most discussed methods (Kahl et al., 2019; Kienast et al., 2017).

---

[3]Swiss Confederation – Energy – Facts and Figures (admin.ch); consulted in June 2024.

[4]Swiss Confederation – What is the Energy Strategy 2050? (admin.ch); consulted in June 2024.

Apart from the issue of absolute production capacity, the annual distribution is another central issue for Switzerland. Indeed, the energy deficit is particularly important in winter. According to Kahl et al. (2019), this winter deficit could be reduced by up to 50% through the installation of PV at high altitudes, which means in the Swiss Alps. Yet, the production of renewable electricity often 'collides with provisioning, regulating and the cultural services of the landscape' (Kienast et al., 2017, p. 397). Based on a conflict assessment opposing RE sources, such as wind, PV, forest biomass, and six competing landscape services (nutrition and materials; aesthetics; physical and experiential interactions; heritage and symbolic content; water and liquid flows; lifecycle maintenance, habitat and gene pool protection), Kienast et al. (2017) consider that biomass from forests and PV placed/installed on rooftops are the least socially conflicting RE sources; however, PV on open, marginal and scrubland would be totally unfeasible. In fact, wind has a higher conflict potential.

The 'NIMBY' (not-in-my-backyard) syndrome also concerns RE in Switzerland. A study by Rudolf et al. (2014) demonstrates that Swiss people changed their attitude towards nuclear power plants after the Fukushima accident, whereas their preferences for other energies, such as RE, only changed marginally. A comparative study between Switzerland and Germany shows that the attitude towards geothermal energy is influenced by its proximity. Fearing seismicity, the public generally prefers projects situated in remote areas, although geographical proximity to consumers would increase their viability (Knoblauch et al., 2019). Similarly, a comparative study between Switzerland and Austria reveals that a majority of respondents would be willing to invest small sums in RE, among which are a large group of 'urban wind energy enthusiasts'. However, a significant part of these potential investors are reticent to nearby wind installation (Broughel & Hampl, 2018, p. 722).

Unsurprisingly for a federal state, such as Switzerland, the local context matters. First, values related to energy policy that exist at the local level differ compared to those communicated at the cantonal (regional) and national levels. At the local level, the promotion of energy production is seen as a means for local development, whereas at the cantonal level, the empowerment of the regional government in the field of energy policy implementation is emphasised. Finally, the value communicated at the federal level consists of the promotion for a national-level 'greener' environmental agenda (Díaz et al., 2017). Second, there are differences at the local level. The local context is framed by such aspects as politics and cultures, which plays a crucial role regarding acceptance of RE projects (Schumacher & Schultmann, 2017). For instance, regarding the rate of solar PV uptake, Hirt et al. (2021) identified nine clusters of municipalities, out of which solar PV uptake is greater in the case of clusters characterised by high agricultural and innovation activities, as well as higher education institution density. Furthermore, the roles played by different local actors also have an important impact. A comparative study of Switzerland, Germany and Austria reveals that citizens rate local scale opportunities related to distributed energy systems higher than the challenges; yet, they also consider that the responsibility for the energy system transition is the responsibility of the national government and large supply utilities rather than for municipalities and households (Seidl et al., 2019). Still regarding the role played by various actors, a study on higher degrees of regional energy autarky sees an important role for administrations and civil society actors at the local level in initialising and developing projects in order to ensure their acceptance and implementation (Müller et al., 2011). Also, Hirt et al. (2021, p. 1) consider that 'different local actors, such as local authorities, energy companies, and devoted citizens, can accelerate PV uptake using various strategies based on local specificities'. Consequently, they suggest developing context-specific strategies to promote PV uptake.

The Landscape of Swiss Energy Companies

In Switzerland, energy production is shaped by governmental policies and proactive initiatives of energy companies, often in near-monopolistic positions, which drive the transition towards more sustainable and resilient system (Mühlemeier, 2019). The foundational legislative framework, which is rooted in the 1990 Energy Article of the Federal Constitution, includes the Energy Act, CO_2 Act, Climate and Innovation Act and Electricity Supply Act.[5] While challenges exist, the opportunities for innovation and growth in the RE sector are substantial. Hence, Switzerland's journey towards climate neutrality by 2050 may serve as a model for other nations aiming to balance energy needs with environmental stewardship.[6] We hereby explore the current state of Swiss energy companies, focussing on the challenges and opportunities for the industry.

In recent years, Swiss energy companies have played a critical role in the nation's energy transition. For instance, major players such as Axpo, Alpiq and BKW have been substantively involved in various segments of the energy market, from generation and distribution to innovative energy solutions. Mainly, these companies seek to invest heavily in RE projects and smart grid technologies in order to enhance efficiency and reliability. Axpo, for instance, is a leader in hydropower and wind energy. The company has expanded its operations beyond Switzerland, contributing to RE projects across Europe. Another key player, BKW, is notable for its investments in solar energy and its comprehensive approach to integrating RE into the national grid. The company's initiatives include developing decentralised energy systems and promoting electric mobility, thus aligning with Switzerland's broader energy strategy (Crettenand, 2012; Dietsche & O'Sullivan, 2021; Hettich & Kachi, 2022). Most Swiss energy companies have a regional or a local anchorage. They operate in a monopolistic regime, viewing the network within their activity zone and in a market-based regime regarding energy production and supply (Mühlemeier, 2019). Data in our possession, which was generated from the base of a publicly available list[7] concerning energy-producing

[5]https://www.uvek.admin.ch/uvek/en/home/energy/energy-policy.html (retrieved on 18 June 2024).

[6]https://www.uvek.admin.ch/uvek/en/home/energy/energy-policy.html (retrieved on 18 June 2024).

[7]https://www.strom.ch/fr (retrieved on 18 June 2024).

companies, show a predominance of private companies in the Swiss energy sector, followed by autonomous public companies and non-autonomous public companies. It is an open question as to what extent this legal status plays a role in the production of RE. The majority of companies are small and large enterprises, comprising of over two-thirds of the total. Medium enterprises also form a significant portion, while micro-enterprises represent the smallest share.

Despite significant strides made by the country, several challenges remain for energy companies. As mentioned earlier, the primordial one is the balance between energy production and environmental conservation. If one considers hydropower projects, the ecological impact on river ecosystems is always at stake. Similarly, wind farms often face opposition due to their visual impact on the landscape and the noise produced (Huber et al., 2017; Spiess et al., 2015). Another challenge dwells in the intermittency of RE sources such as solar and wind. To address this, Swiss energy companies are investing in energy storage solutions and smart grid technologies with the hope of gaining more stability and reliability in the energy supply. On average a 25% increase in seasonal storage is required for a fully renewable, balanced system (Dujardin et al., 2017). All these challenges must not obscure the numerous opportunities available for growth and innovation. In particular, advances in technology, improved power storage and efficiency, not to mention Switzerland's strong research and development sector, support continuous improvements in the energy sector. The transition to RE also offers economic opportunities, including job creation in the green energy sector and the potential for the country to become a leader in RE technology exports (Hettich & Kachi, 2022).

Data and Methodology

As mentioned in the introduction, two major questions are at the core of this research. First, what are the strategies of the Swiss energy-producing companies regarding the production of renewable energies, and to what extent do they vary according to the companies' size and legal form? In order to answer these questions, annual reports from all Swiss energy-producing and -distributing companies for the year 2022 were used. Indeed, annual reports are a useful source because they usually mention information about produced energy and future plans, thus what is considered here as strategy. Annual reports were identified based on the member list of the Swiss Association of Electricity Companies.[8] This list is constituted of 408 members (state: end of January 2024). According to the association's director, about 600 energy companies exist in Switzerland, and those who are members of the association represent more than 90% of all produced, transported, traded and sold electricity from/in Switzerland. Thus, in the first step, all 408 members were screened regarding the fact whether they produce and distribute electricity, with a result of 177 companies. Then, annual reports were looked for on the respective companies' websites. 105 annual reports were identified and

[8]Adhésion | AES (strom.ch).

built the basis of this analysis. When analysing these reports, particular attention was paid to the current and planned energy production by source. Thus, if a company only bought and resold RE, without producing at least part of its sales, it was not considered in the study. In case of doubt concerning this producing characteristic or the type of RE produced, the company's website was additionally consulted. Furthermore, RE sources were only considered when the production sites were situated in Switzerland. Therefore, for instance, if wind energy was only produced abroad, it was not considered in the study. Finally, the size in terms of number of collaborators (whenever available in full-time equivalent [FTE] numbers), as well as the legal status of all analysed companies was determined based on the given annual report and/or the website.

The second research question concerns the types of obstacles met by Swiss energy companies regarding the development of RE. This question was examined by semi-structured interviews with six CEOs, each time covering a small and a large company of the three considered legal statuses, which means public non-autonomous company (which is a formal part of a given public administration), public autonomous company (which follows public law but has increased autonomy) and private company (which follows private law). In addition, interviews were also conducted with two experts from Swiss energy companies. They were interviewed concerning current strategies regarding RE production as well as internal and external obstacles they meet regarding the implementation of their strategies.

Empirical Results

Energy Companies' Strategies for Renewable Energies

Three types of energy sources are clearly the most popular among all 105 examined companies: PV, hydropower and district heating (see Fig. 1.1). About 74% sell or plan to sell energy produced from their own PVs. It is important to note that the concerned volumes vary considerably between individual companies. They range from a small installation on a roof of a municipality-owned building to very important surfaces in the Alps. The percentage of companies involved in hydropower production (70%) is also extremely high; this is, on one hand, because of the prevalence of numerous Swiss dams, lakes and rivers. On the other hand, it is also because even companies which do not have direct access to water bought significant parts of hydropower-producing companies. The third most popular energy source is district heating, although it is not an energy source as such, but depends on current sources, such as woodchips or heat from waste incineration plants, it is often mentioned by companies as being 'renewable' (because woodchips come from local forests) or CO_2-neutral (because the waste is incinerated in any case). However, some companies also admit that they still partly use fossil sources to produce heat and underline their willingness to change this source towards purely renewable or CO_2-neutral sources. Interestingly, almost half of all companies (45%) also suggest installation services for solar panels to public and/or private customers. Thus, they contribute to the decentralised

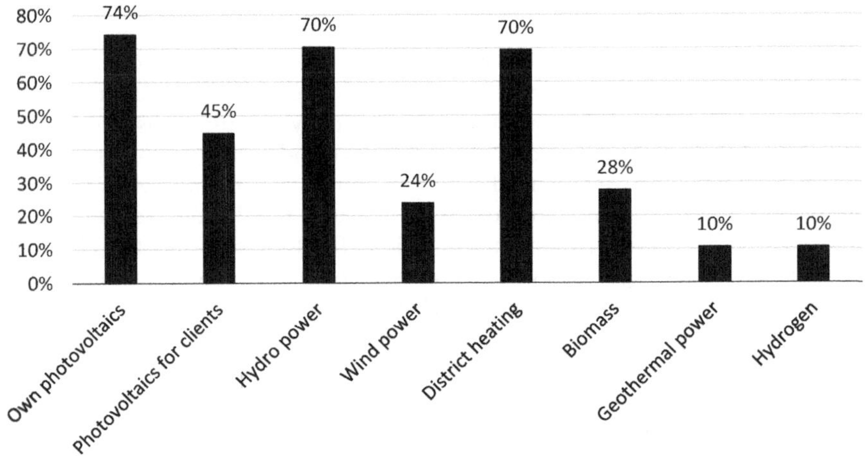

Fig. 1.1. Strategies for Renewable Energy by Source. *Source*: This figure is established by the authors based on the analysis of the energy enterprises' annual reports (obtained via Mitgliedschaft | VSE).

production of energy. Energy based on biomass (28%) and wind power (24%) are also increasingly mentioned as a desired or existing source, whereas geothermal power (10%) and hydrogen (10%) only play a marginal role.

An analysis by company size (see Fig. 1.2) shows that the large enterprises (more than 250 FTE employees) produce or plan to produce the different energy sources more often than smaller companies, except for district heating, where medium-sized enterprises (51–250 FTE) are strongest. Generally, it seems that the smaller a company, the less it is willing or able to produce RE. Nevertheless, between 43% and 71% of analysed small (11–50 FTE) and micro enterprises (1–10 FTE) are active in the production of RE based on PV, district heating and/or hydropower.

Finally, it can be observed that the type of produced energy also varies to some extent according to the companies' legal status (see Fig. 1.3). First, all 14 public non-autonomous companies (which are part of a given public administration) produce or plan to produce own solar energy. They are also more active regarding installation services for clients, geothermal power and biomass than autonomous public or private companies. There are only very weak differences between public non-autonomous and autonomous companies regarding hydro power and district heating, yet an important difference regarding biomass, which is very weakly developed among the 32 public autonomous companies. Finally, the share of the 52 private companies producing RE is the smallest for every kind of energy source, except for geothermal power (slightly stronger than public autonomous companies) and district heating (the same level as the two other types).[9]

[9]Due to the small number (only five companies), the legal status of 'cooperation' was not integrated in this analysis as an own category.

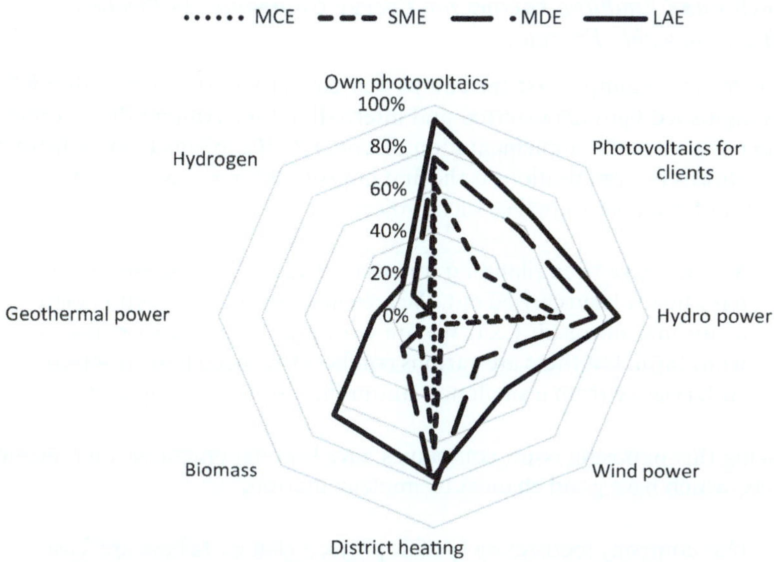

Fig. 1.2. Type of Energy Source by Company Size. *Source*: This figure is established by the authors based on the analysis of the energy enterprises' annual reports (obtained via Mitgliedschaft | VSE).

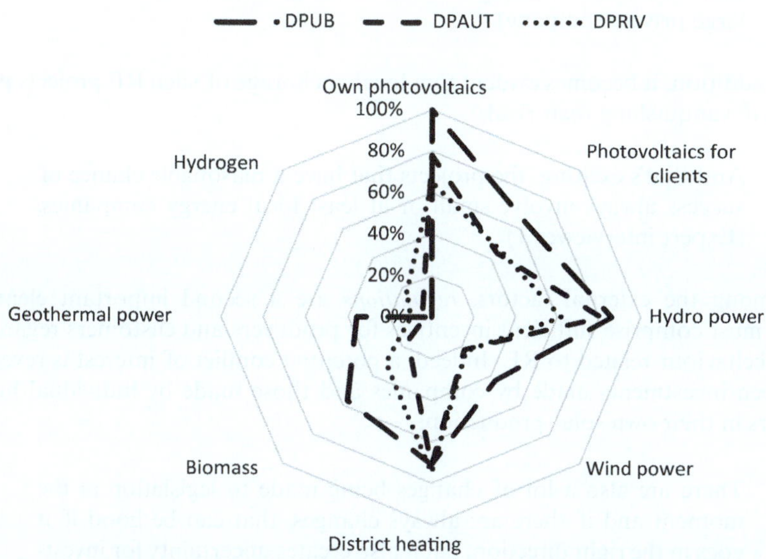

Fig. 1.3. Type of Energy by Legal Status. *Source*: This figure is established by the authors based on the analysis of the energy enterprises' annual reports (obtained via Mitgliedschaft | VSE).

Obstacles and Enabling Factors for Energy Companies to Produce Further Renewable Energies

Factors having an impact on the companies' capacity to develop further RE can be distinguished between external and internal factors. Among the external factors, *opposition* to the implementation of concrete RE plants coming from individual citizens or organisations is the first important type of obstacle. Companies need a lot of patience to realise such projects:

> Yes, we have been planning for over 10 years. A feasibility study has already been carried out. We are currently in the structure plan as an interim result (…). We are working very hard to realise a wind farm, but there are various conflicts that need to be resolved. (Interviewee from a small non-autonomous public company)

Facing this opposing issue, companies have become pragmatic and favour the projects, which have good chances of implementation:

> Our company focusses on specific projects that we believe are feasible in the foreseeable future. That is one of our principles. (…) We are talking about relatively small capacities that we are building up. (…) And it has taken us since 2008 to get this project through. That's why I'm so reluctant to discuss the really big projects of the future. Because I simply say that the litmus test for Switzerland is that we are now realising the projects we have. (Interviewee from a large private company)

In addition, it becomes evident that local anchorage of such RE projects plays a role in vanquishing their rivals:

> And that's exciting, the projects that have a reasonable chance of success always involve small or at least local energy companies. (Expert interviewee 1)

Among the external factors, *regulations* are a second important element. They must comprise sufficient incentives for producers and customers regarding their behaviour related to RE. Indeed, a potential conflict of interest is revealed between investments made by companies and those made by individual house owners in their own solar production:

> There are also a lot of changes being made to legislation at the moment and if there are always changes, that can be good if it goes in the right direction, but it also creates uncertainty for investments, and we have a lot of long-term investments to make in these areas. And then, of course, the consumer behaviour of customers today is also changing, which is also a factor that makes it very difficult to assess (…). Legislation is required to find solutions so

> that investments can still be made in the energy transition on the one hand, but that they and the security of supply are also paid for, on the other. [House owners have increasingly their own solar production, but] as a backup, everything still has to be available as redundancy. If my solar system doesn't work, the grid has to be there. That has to be paid for somehow. (Interviewee from a large non-autonomous public company)

One interviewee also points out the necessary *support coming from customers and citizens* concerning the development of RE:

> The energy transition is in competition with nature conservation and climate protection. This doesn't apply to every project, but to many, otherwise there simply won't be the corresponding increase in energy that we need. (...) This also has the corresponding price effect, and this must of course also be supported. This will also apply when it comes to speed in terms of expansion versus design, trees that we still want to plant in the city, i.e. the design of the surface structure, there are also competing effects here. In other words, if you want to be fast, you need the right support. These external factors are definitely extremely important. At the end of the day, of course, these are all elected institutions, so you need the backing of the voters, i.e. the citizens, otherwise it won't work. (Interviewee from a large autonomous public company)

A last external factor, namely *technology*, is not perceived as an obstacle; however, it is a potentially facilitating factor for the development of RE:

> Technology is certainly a factor. There is probably more than what we are using at the moment, but of course it will continue to develop, which is a good thing. There will definitely be one or two solutions that are not yet on our radar that will help us. (Interviewee from a large private company)

The first internal factor for energy companies, which has an impact on the development of RE, concerns the firm's *investment strategy*. Indeed, investment in RE represents a certain risk, which from the companies' point of view must be mitigated. Therefore, investments are not only made in Switzerland but also abroad and RE sources are chosen according to the topographic possibilities:

> We were given an amount to invest and if you want to build plants in Switzerland, you can't do it on this scale and that's why we took a stake, also to diversify the risk. I mean, you can put xy million into a single plant and it either goes well or badly, but it's a high risk. If you have shares in a whole park for xy million, which is also diversified with wind, water and solar, then you simply have fewer risks. (...) Politically, it is more difficult to sell when you invest in electricity

> production abroad. We have a bit of a problem with the argumentation there. And of course, we would prefer domestic production, which is always better now with solar, but hydropower is almost exhausted and biogas plants are also very cumbersome (...) Switzerland is simply too dense today and what is left that is not built on is simply mountains and other nature worth protecting that should also be preserved. I don't think you can make such comparisons. Wind production, for example (...) there [in Germany] is really less of a problem. They simply have space, and I just don't see it in Switzerland. (...) And there is also an optimal location for everything. (...) I think you also have to recognise that you can't do everything at every location, because otherwise the money is simply not well invested. (Interviewee from a large non-autonomous public company)

Furthermore, regarding investment strategies, several interviewees also pointed out the importance related to a company's concrete situation in terms of energy production and available funding:

> The starting position really shouldn't be underestimated. It's easy if you already have a good starting position that goes in the direction that is now politically desired. Then it's also easier, I mean companies that don't have a stake in nuclear power plants now, they applaud and say, yes wonderful, that doesn't stress me (...). And also, the issue of financial resources. So can I afford the conversion, the investments, because my owner also gives me the money, quite frankly, so that's another point. It just goes hand in hand with the political will. (Expert interviewee 2)

> For larger projects, this is simply a question of capital that small companies cannot afford, except for a little photovoltaics, but even alpine photovoltaics are relatively large investments for small companies. (Expert interviewee 1)

A second internal factor consists of available *human resources*. Indeed, several interviewees point to its crucial current and future importance in the development of RE:

> We have the expertise purely in terms of our ability to develop projects. The question is whether we have enough of these competences and capacities if we want to achieve the major growth that our strategy in Switzerland actually requires. Not really, we need to expand them. We also lack the resources to be able to realise this at this pace in terms of grid expansion. We're having a hard time thinking about how we can get more people there. And also, whether we might need less expansion. Local intelligence, local optimisation, more local consumption of energy, fewer long transport routes. (Interviewee from a large private company)

Indeed, all interviewees agree that *innovations* are a necessary factor regarding the energy transition, be it for the development of RE, energy efficiency or the grid. Last, but not least, interviewees also underline the important role played by the *internal political support* or *pressure* regarding the development of RE, especially regarding public companies.

Conclusion

The types of external and internal factors which influence Swiss energy companies in their RE production, such as those observed in the present study, are similar to the general obstacles identified in previous studies on Switzerland and other countries. Among the external factors, legal opposition from individual citizens or organisations due to the will to protect the landscape (Kienast et al., 2017) or their personal environment (Broughel & Hampl, 2018; Knoblauch et al., 2019) is a well-known phenomenon in Switzerland; the importance of regulations was already highlighted by a Polish study (Bednarek et al., 2023). The necessity to master technology was already underlined by a Chinese study (Wu et al., 2021). Finally, the crucial role of support coming from the local population was also already described in Swiss studies (Schumacher & Schultmann, 2017).

In the future, an external factor which could potentially increase in importance is the acceptance and adoption of higher energy prices by customers due to increased RE production (and more expensive nuclear energy). Indeed, the energy crisis which hit many European countries, including Switzerland, in 2022, was a harbinger for potential future challenges in case of higher energy prices. Indeed, low-income households suffered from the sudden increase which, in addition, varied according to the energy company. Thus, should the Swiss energy market become more liberalised in the coming years, Swiss energy companies would have to fight a hard battle for their customers, which is currently not necessary due to their (quasi-)monopoly at the local level.

Moreover, several of the internal factors already showed up in scientific literature but were refined thanks to the present study. Energy companies must obey an economic logic (Sutherland & Holstead, 2014) and, therefore, integrate risk reflections, which follow an economic rather than a political priority, for example, production abroad instead of within the country, and also may lead to the renouncement of further RE production because of the related and high investment costs incurred by the development of completely new RE sources. As noted by previous studies (Zhao et al., 2014), available human resources play a crucial role for the development of RE; however, innovation may also help. Finally, a specific factor was identified for public energy companies, where the support and/or pressure coming from local political authorities which is also important for RE development. Indeed, the quantitative analysis of energy companies' strategies shows that the share of public companies aiming at the development of any kind of RE source is higher than the share of private companies. We interpret this finding as the result of higher political pressure for the development of RE.

Size also seems to play a role. As shown by the analysis of the companies' strategies, the smaller an enterprise, the less it is willing or capable to invest in the development of RE. Thus, does the development of RE require a critical mass? A considerable part of the observed micro and small firms prove that they are able to produce RE based on PV, hydropower and district heating. Furthermore, successfully implemented RE projects are often the result of cooperations between large and small local companies. These findings are in line with those made by previous Swiss studies showing that the local context, either for spatial (Kienast et al., 2017) or social (Hirt et al., 2021) reasons, plays a non-negligeable role. In other words, if there is political will, there is a path towards more RE, simply with differences in terms of types of RE produced due to the spatial characteristics of a local environment. For instance, PV on rooftops is a socially accepted solution (Kienast et al., 2017) and sizeable in order to control related costs. Yet, if critical mass is not necessarily an obstacle, an important question to be raised is why do a majority of approximately 600 Swiss energy companies not produce any RE at all? Thus, there seems to remain quite some potential at a local scale for further RE development.

Finally, it must be mentioned that the companies' challenges related to RE not only concern their production capacity, but also technical and economic issues. On the one hand, they have to find technical solutions for their grid, when private houseowners produce significantly more solar energy than the volume needed by consumers; therefore, investments in the grid are unavoidable. On the other hand, the increasing share of private houseowners who are producing their own energy, decreases companies' sales volumes. Thus, a new type of competitor is emerging. Increasing this competition are especially large- and middle-sized firms, as well as non-autonomous public companies, which are numerous in offering new services related to the installation of PV. Given that such a service accelerates the development of the 'new competitor', it may seem paradoxical that companies themselves are sustaining this. It can be hypothesised that they offer this service for economic and/or political reasons. However, it is clear that, in the long term, energy companies will have to rethink their business model.

The present study has shed light on the strategies of Swiss energy companies, especially regarding the influence of varying internal and external constraints as well as size and legal status. Obviously, this study also has several limits. First, although a certain diversity was assured by the choice of the interviewees, a higher number of interviewees could have enlarged the types of identified constraints. Second, annual reports are indeed a rich source of information, however, due to different formats, not all of them necessarily contain exhaustive data concerning strategic issues, therefore, in some cases, certain strategic ambitions might not have been identified in a thorough manner.

The obtained results call for more research. First, it would be interesting to analyse RE strategies of all 600 Swiss energy companies, including those which currently do not themselves produce RE. Will these companies continue to buy their energy from other Swiss or foreign companies, or will they start developing their own production? Second, can patterns regarding size and legal status also be observed in other, especially federal countries or are they specific to Switzerland? Finally, how will energy companies position themselves in the future in the increasingly decentralised energy market, and what kind of business models will they develop and implement?

References

Bednarek, A., Klepacka, A. M., & Siudek, A. (2023). Development barriers of agricultural biogas plants in Poland. *Ekonomia i Srodowisko/Economics and Environment*, *84*(1), 229–258. https://doi.org/10.34659/eis.2023.84.1.528

Bloem, S., Swilling, M., & Koranteng, K. (2021). Taking energy democracy to the streets: Socio-technical learning, institutional dynamism, and integration in South African community energy projects. *Energy Research & Social Science*, *72*, Article 101906. https://doi.org/10.1016/j.erss.2020.101906

Broughel, A. E., & Hampl, N. (2018). Community financing of renewable energy projects in Austria and Switzerland: Profiles of potential investors. *Energy Policy*, *123*, 722–736.

Bucher, D., Buffat, R., Froemelt, A., & Raubal, M. (2019). Energy and greenhouse gas emission reduction potentials resulting from different commuter electric bicycle adoption scenarios in Switzerland. *Renewable and Sustainable Energy Reviews*, *114*, Article 109298.

Crettenand, N. (2012). *The facilitation of mini and small hydropower in Switzerland: Shaping the institutional framework (with a particular focus on storage and pumped-storage schemes)* [PhD thesis]. EPFL.

Díaz, P., Adler, C., & Patt, A. (2017). Do stakeholders' perspectives on renewable energy infrastructure pose a risk to energy policy implementation? A case of a hydropower plant in Switzerland. *Energy Policy*, *108*, 21–28. https://doi.org/10.1016/j.enpol.2017.05.033

Dietsche, D., & O'Sullivan, M. (2021). *Enthusiasm based on wrong expectations: BKW's failed transition to nuclear energy production (1970–1990)* [Master's thesis]. Université de Genève.

Dujardin, J., Kahl, A., Kruyt, B., Bartlett, S., & Lehning, M. (2017). Interplay between photovoltaic, wind energy and storage hydropower in a fully renewable Switzerland. *Energy*, *135*, 513–525.

Gaudard, L., Romerio, F., Dalla Valle, F., Gorret, R., Maran, S., Ravazzani, G., Stoffel, M., & Volonterio, M. (2014). Climate change impacts on hydropower in the Swiss and Italian Alps. *Science of the Total Environment*, *493*, 1211–1221.

Hettich, P., & Kachi, A. (2022). *Swiss energy governance: Political, economic and legal challenges and opportunities in the energy transition*. Springer Nature.

Hirt, L. F., Sahakian, M., & Trutnevyte, E. (2021). What socio-technical regimes foster solar energy champions? Analysing uneven photovoltaic diffusion at a subnational level in Switzerland. *Energy Research & Social Science*, *74*, Article 101976.

Huber, N., Hergert, R., Price, B., Zäch, C., Hersperger, A. M., Pütz, M., Kienast, F., & Bolliger, J. (2017). Renewable energy sources: Conflicts and opportunities in a changing landscape. *Regional Environmental Change*, *17*, 1241–1255.

IEA. (2023). *Switzerland 2023 – Energy policy review*. https://www.iea.org/reports/switzerland-2023

Kahl, A., Dujardin, J., & Lehning, M. (2019). The bright side of PV production in snow-covered mountains. *Proceedings of the National Academy of Sciences of the United States of America*, *116*(4), 1162–1167. https://doi.org/10.1073/pnas.1720808116

Kienast, F., Huber, N., Hergert, R., Bolliger, J., Moran, L. S., & Hersperger, A. M. (2017). Conflicts between decentralized renewable electricity production and landscape services – A spatially-explicit quantitative assessment for Switzerland. *Renewable & Sustainable Energy Reviews*, *67*, 397–407. https://doi.org/10.1016/j.rser.2016.09.045

Knoblauch, T. A. K., Trutnevyte, E., & Stauffacher, M. (2019). Siting deep geothermal energy: Acceptance of various risk and benefit scenarios in a Swiss-German cross-national study. *Energy Policy*, *128*, 807–816. https://doi.org/10.1016/j.enpol.2019.01.019

Mühlemeier, S. (2019). Dinosaurs in transition? A conceptual exploration of local incumbents in the Swiss and German energy transition. *Environmental Innovation and Societal Transitions*, *31*, 126–143.

Müller, M. O., Stämpfli, A., Dold, U., & Hammer, T. (2011). Energy autarky: A conceptual framework for sustainable regional development. *Energy Policy*, *39*(10), 5800–5810. https://doi.org/10.1016/j.enpol.2011.04.019

Rudolf, M., Seidl, R., Moser, C., Krütli, P., & Stauffacher, M. (2014). Public preference of electricity options before and after Fukushima. *Journal of Integrative Environmental Sciences*, *11*(1), 1–15. https://doi.org/10.1080/1943815X.2014.881887

Schumacher, K., & Schultmann, F. (2017). Local acceptance of biogas plants: A comparative study in the trinational Upper Rhine Region. *Waste and Biomass Valorization*, *8*(7), 2393–2412. https://doi.org/10.1007/s12649-016-9802-z

Seidl, R., von Wirth, T., & Krütli, P. (2019). Social acceptance of distributed energy systems in Swiss, German, and Austrian energy transitions. *Energy Research & Social Science*, *54*, 117–128.

Spiess, H., Lobsiger-Kägi, E., Carabias-Hütter, V., & Marcolla, A. (2015). Future acceptance of wind energy production: Exploring future local acceptance of wind energy production in a Swiss alpine region. *Technological Forecasting and Social Change*, *101*, 263–274.

Sutherland, L. A., & Holstead, K. L. (2014). Future-proofing the farm: On-farm wind turbine development in farm business decision-making. *Land Use Policy*, *36*, 102–112. https://doi.org/10.1016/j.landusepol.2013.07.004

Tabi, A., & Wüstenhagen, R. (2017). Keep it local and fish-friendly: Social acceptance of hydropower projects in Switzerland. *Renewable and Sustainable Energy Reviews*, *68*, 763–773.

Thaler, P., & Hofmann, B. (2022). The impossible energy trinity: Energy security, sustainability, and sovereignty in cross-border electricity systems. *Political Geography*, *94*, Article 102579. https://doi.org/10.1016/j.polgeo.2021.102579

Varho, V., Rikkonen, P., & Rasi, S. (2016). Futures of distributed small-scale renewable energy in Finland – A Delphi study of the opportunities and obstacles up to 2025. *Technological Forecasting and Social Change*, *104*, 30–37. https://doi.org/10.1016/j.techfore.2015.12.001

Wang, Q. B., Thompson, E., Tweedy, A., O'Leary, M. L., & Crossman, W. W. (2021). Potentials and obstacles for community anaerobic digesters in the United States: Evidence from a case study in Vermont. *Renewable & Sustainable Energy Reviews*, *137*, Article 110434. https://doi.org/10.1016/j.rser.2020.110434

Wu, Y. N., Liu, F. T., He, J. M., Wu, M., & Ke, Y. M. (2021). Obstacle identification, analysis and solutions of hydrogen fuel cell vehicles for application in China under the carbon neutrality target. *Energy Policy*, *159*, Article 112643. https://doi.org/10.1016/j.enpol.2021.112643

Zhao, Z. Y., Tian, Y. X., & Zillante, G. (2014). Modeling and evaluation of the wind power industry chain: A China study. *Renewable & Sustainable Energy Reviews*, *31*, 397–406. https://doi.org/10.1016/j.rser.2013.12.022

Züttel, A., Gallandat, N., Dyson, P. J., Schlapbach, L., Gilgen, P. W., & Orimo, S.-I. (2022). Future Swiss Energy Economy: The challenge of storing renewable energy. *Frontiers in Energy Research*, *9*, Article 785908.

Chapter 2

Stakeholder Engagement as Policy Instrument for Green Innovation and Development: A Study of Nigeria's Government Engagement with Educators

Cathérine Enorédia Odorige[a,b] *and Osakue Stevenson Omoera*[c]

[a]*Department of Organizational Development and Communication Science, Institute of Social Sciences, University of Dunaújváros, Dunaújváros, Hungary*
[b]*Women Researchers Council (WRC), Azerbaijan State University of Economics (UNEC)*
[c]*Department of Theatre and Film Studies. Faculty of Humanities, Federal University of Otuoke, Otuoke, Nigeria*

Abstract

Purpose: Nigeria is very active on the international scene in the global quest to curb carbon dioxide (CO_2) emissions, participating in the frameworks and ratification of agreements reached on the worldwide scene on climate change. This invites curiosity about policy initiatives with stakeholders on the home front. The critical role of education in promoting sustainable development, with the potential to foster the necessary behavioural changes to improve people's capacity to address environmental and developmental challenges, warrants this study.

Need for the study: Development communication establishes that proper development can be accessed through stakeholders' engagement. We assess the Nigerian government's commitment to sustainable development from the lenses of its engagement with stakeholders in education.

Methodology: Using a mixed research method, comprising a quantitative survey among educators and qualitative interviews of school proprietors, principals and management staff of privately owned elementary and high schools, as well as education inspectors, the researchers ascertain the levels

Sustainable Development and Green Innovation: Managing Risk through Interdisciplinary Approaches and Policy Strategies, 19–35

Published under exclusive licence by Emerald Publishing Limited
doi:10.1108/978-1-83608-462-420251002

of government engagement with players in this sector on the topic of sustainable development in Nigeria.

Findings: Results show relatively minimal engagement with the sector practitioners, implying that lack of policy initiatives and interpretation can negatively impact education actors' approach to addressing climate change from concerned individuals within the educational sector.

Practical implication: Given the widespread acknowledgement that sustainable development is unattainable without concrete government commitment, the current situation is hampering progress.

Keywords: Schools; greenwashing; sustainability; students; green innovation; educators; development communication

JEL codes: Q56; H53

1. Introduction

Nigeria is one of the 197 parties to the United Nations Framework Convention on Climate Change (UNFCCC), established in 1994 to combat desertification. It also stands out among countries that have ratified the Kyoto Protocol adopted on 11 December 1997, the only document that has emerged from the UNFCCC Process that imposed binding limits on the emission of greenhouse gases. The most populous country in Africa is also a signatory to the Paris Agreement on Climate Change adopted by 196 parties at the Conference of Parties (COP 21) in Paris in December 2015. At the conference, global players moved away from doubt about the impact of climate change on the environment, whereby many had engaged in what scholars refer to as the dialogue of the deaf, where diverse perspectives prevented an early consensus on what approaches to take on sustainable development (Runnalls & Cosbey, 1992; Schmitz, 2017; Scoones et al., 2015). The primary goal of the agreement is the planned limitation of global warming to 1.5°C. Global partnership is an accountability tool for measuring sustainable development growth indicators. A primary task of COP is the review of national communications and emission inventory submitted by parties that reflect their action of the Nationally Determined Contribution (NDC).

The place of bilateral and multilateral alliances in driving climate change policies has been emphasised (Schmitz, 2017). Parties to the convention revealed their NDC and agreed to be updated every 5 years. Nigeria unveiled its NDC in the 2015 convention on climate and updated it in 2021. Under the Paris Agreement, Nigeria's NDC is expected to unconditionally reduce carbon emissions by 20% and 45% with international support by 2030 (Oche, 2020). This has attracted scholarly reactions about the potential and major obstacles to actualisation (Dioha & Kumar, 2020; Ogbonna et al., 2023; Okoh, 2020; Unruh, 2000). Dioha and Kumar (2020), through a TIMES-Nigeria model, uncovered four mitigation scenarios in Nigeria's NDC: increased renewable penetration, energy efficiency improvements and fuel switching, with the residential sector having the highest potential for reduced energy demand, while the power sector, with potential for CO_2 emission mitigation, should be the focus. This is relatable to individual efforts to provide electricity to homes due to the country's failure to deliver stable electricity to its teeming population, where only 55.5% of the over 230 million people have access to the national grid, and Nigeria's less diversified economic dependence on fossil fuel places it among the carbon lock-in economies. A path-dependency process driven by technological and institutional increasing return to scale (Unruh, 2000). Ogbonna et al. (2023) present a ratio of 4.1 as a barrier against the potential of realising the NDC.

Education is highlighted as one of the key institutional frameworks listed for green development, including others, like legal system, multistakeholder participation, ecological compensation, scientific and technological innovation, regional cooperation and other institutional paths (Liang et al., 2022). Hence, a need to exfoliate Nigeria's government sustainability investment and engagement with education and educators. Educators are at the core of providing the needed behavioural changes across institutions through enlightenment and awareness creation. An invitation to cooperate with educators will enable a holistic engagement with the population that will match Nigeria's federal government's recent bravado on global warming and sustainability. The African continent is the least polluting in terms of CO_2 emissions globally; Nigeria still ranks fourth in Africa, in terms of pollution, coming behind Algeria, Egypt and South Africa (Ayompe et al., 2020). This is not a testimonial of highly improved green solutions in terms of energy solutions and production but rather of the low industrialisation of the 'African giant' compared to its status as the most populous country in Africa. Nigeria is called an energy giant because it has remarkable deposits of crude oil, gas, ignite and coal connected to fossils. It is also potentially endowed with renewable energy resources like solar, wind, biomass, hydropower and wood (Oyedepo, 2012). This study examines efforts to redirect national perspectives to renewable energy solutions via engagement with educators.

2. Critical Perspectives in Sustainable Education Development

Sustainable education development has attracted several scholarly perspectives in Nigeria. Before the sustainability awareness discourse, education was not without challenges, but the sustainability discourse has highlighted the myriad of issues around education in Nigeria. Bearing that the current global warming challenges were brought about by behaviour and education through every known corridor will be instrumental in reversing behaviours to develop sustainability-savvy citizens and leadership. From the lens of Nigeria's current challenges, Adaja and Olajide (2022) highlight the security challenges bedevilling the nation now and the need for stakeholder initiatives and engagement. The duo points to education as the most fundamental empowerment for human sustainability regarding socio-economic, socio-political and socio-cultural development. The yearning for more economic, technological and environmental development in Africa, Nigeria inclusive, cannot be sufficiently attained unless there is effective peace education and continuous engagement of critical stakeholders in the society. Nwalutu (2014), Ekwueme et al. (2016) and Edet and Beyin (2018) advocate a reorientation of grassroots education that takes into perspective a system that originates from the people's culture. Ekwueme et al. (2016) claim that knowledge, skills, attitudes and values are necessary to shape a sustainable future and make judgements and choices in favour of a sustainable lifestyle. Academic freedom as the vehicle for the expansion and discovery of new ideas of knowledge transmits and preserves culture developed in the learner's independent judgement of an environment free from external control and domination. They aver that converse to the traditional way of teaching, education for sustainable development means adopting a more holistic approach to education to create a better world for this generation and future generations (Ekwueme et al., 2016).

Boyi (2014) focusses on gender inequality and infrastructural deficiency. Ilechukwu et al. (2014) argue that education must be seen as a human right to achieve sustainable holistic development. They contend that a disconnect exists between education and development in Nigeria and make a case for education for sustainable development as the critical path to Nigeria's sustainable development, citing the present system as dysfunctional perpetuating and deepening poverty and underdevelopment. Tadoro and Smith (2009, p. 369) describe development as a matter of input and output, and education is fundamental to the broader notion of expanding human capabilities that is the fulcrum of development. They further point to education as playing a key role in the ability of a developing country to absorb modern technology and develop the capacity for self-sustaining growth and development (Tadoro & Smith, 2009). The central role of education in development was the focus in 1990 in Thailand by the World Conference on Education for All. The participants from around the world numbered up to 1,100 (UNESCO, 1990). In Senegal, 10 years later, the participants discovered that many countries were far from reaching the goal set out in 1990 (Peppler-Barry & Fiske, 2000). Aberu and Lawal (2022), however, decry the gross understudy of education as a potential factor in determining sustainable development in Nigeria, which could also mean a disconnect between the government's showing on the world stage and educational stakeholder connection for sustainable development.

3. Methodology

This study adopted a mixed methodology. We applied a quantitative survey questionnaire to interrogate workers across the academic landscape and qualitative interviews of proprietors of private elementary and high school institutions in one of the states in Nigeria. The respondents are domiciled in the western, eastern and southern parts of Nigeria and the capital city of Abuja, which is in the north. Their response to the state of origin also showed that they are from the middle belt (north central) down to the southern parts of Nigeria. This is to avoid generalisations that could indicate different results in the core northern part of the country. The interviews were conducted predominantly with proprietors from private elementary and secondary schools in South Nigeria. This is justified and representative because private schools in Nigeria represent over 60% of elementary and high school education providers (Omoera & Adegoriola, 2021). We also interviewed education inspectors from both the Federal Ministry of Education and the State Ministry of Education. Getting accurate data on the difference in the number of private/public schools in Nigeria was challenging for two primary reasons. Nigeria's education is on the concurrent list of the *Nigerian Constitution*, which spells that both the federal and state governments can legislate on education. It is the primary jurisdiction of the Federal Ministry of Education the unity schools, while the various states can legislate on education within their territory. So, they collect data relevant to their operational jurisdiction. The Universal Basic Education Council (UBEC) was introduced in 1999 by the federal government of Nigeria. It is a reform mechanism for providing access to and ensuring the quality of basic education in Nigeria. UBEC provides a point of convergence and the information on their website at the time of conducting this research shows a total of 91,252 for private schools and 79,775 for public schools.[1] The proliferation of private schools in Nigeria is mostly due to the state's failure to provide access to education for its teeming population and quality education (Angwaomaodoko, 2024; Härmä, 2013; Njoku & Adeyemi, 2013; Omoera & Adegoriola, 2021). The second reason is highlighted in Härmä (2013), that many schools are operating without state approval. This means that they are not captured on the state radar, which is both dangerous for education and an impediment to data collection.

3.1. Research Results: Demographic Data of Respondents

Table 2.1 shows the survey language as English. This is because it is Nigeria's official language, following her colonisation by the British. The country is both culturally and linguistically diverse. Having around 400 languages excluding dialects with the three major tribes' languages as possible official but usually only in spoken terms, English remains the language for official correspondence and education. The questionnaire was distributed online, and the response was voluntary. First shared on a social media platform of Nigerian teachers, an independent platform for engagement among educators. It was, however, distributed to other school's platforms for increased response, due to an initial slow response.

Table 2.2 shows the gender distribution of respondents with females dominating with a total of 65%; the number typifies the teaching profession, especially at the elementary and high school levels as female-dominated, which confirms Nigeria as a society where gender roles are professionally defined.

The age distribution in Table 2.3 shows that over 80% of respondents are young, a testimonial of Nigeria's workforce population being young.

About 70% of respondents have at least a first degree as shown in Table 2.4, a relatively educated community of teachers.

Table 2.5 shows that 80% of respondents in private sector employment, which is a testimonial of the present state of education in Nigeria, where the private sector has overtaken the government in education service provision.

[1]https://ubec.gov.ng/school-directory/.

Table 2.1. Parameters of Questionnaire Collected in Nigeria.

Online data collected	5 November 2023 to March 2024
Language of the questions/answers	English language
Number of respondents	174

Source: Authors' compilation.

Table 2.2. Gender Distribution.

Male in percentages	35
Female in percentages	65

Source: Authors' compilation.

Table 2.3. Age Distribution.

Age (years)	Data in Percentages
18–24	1.7
25–34	39.1
35–44	40.2
45–54	12.1
55 and above	6.9

Source: Authors' compilation.

Table 2.4. Highest Educational Qualification.

Qualification	Percentage (%)
High school certificate	1.7
National certificate of education (NCE)	9.2
Bachelor's degree	70.7
Master's degree	14.4
PhD	3.4

Source: Authors' compilation.

Table 2.6 shows the departments in the field of education in which respondents were domiciled. This variable was necessary to show the cross-section of actors across the education field who took part in the research.

Fig. 2.1 reveals more familiarity with sustainable development, followed by global warming which are the latest buzzwords on sustainability. A possible reason why respondents will be less familiar with the term millennium development is that they may have been too young during the era of millennium development,

Table 2.5. Domain of Employment.

Public	19.5%
Private	80.00%

Source: Authors' compilation.

Table 2.6. Fields of Employment.

Academic	69.0%
Non-academic	17.85
Both	3.4%
School proprietor	2.3%
Others	8.4%

Source: Authors' compilation.

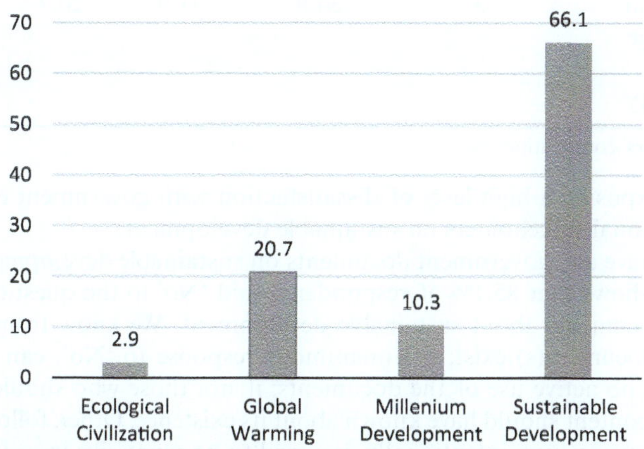

Fig. 2.1. Familiarity with Terms. *Source*: Authors' compilation.

or the momentum then has not reached the crescendo that sustainable development has attained presently.

Questions in Table 2.7 show the Likert scale psychographic responses that highlight evidence of levels of dissatisfaction with the lack of engagement with sector players.

The response to 'How satisfied are you about… engagement, correspondence, resource provision, and inspection?' shows a higher number of respondents either very dissatisfied, dissatisfied or neutral. A total of these (very dissatisfied, dissatisfied and neutral) to the questions on the Likert scale table comes to a range of 86% to 71%, meaning that satisfactory levels are between 14% and 29%, which is

Table 2.7. Satisfaction with Governmental Engagement with Education Stakeholders in … (%).

Likert scale / Question	1 – *Very dissatisfied*	2 – *Dissatisfied*	3 – *Neutral*	4 – *Satisfied*	5 – *Very satisfied*
…engagement with educators	3.7	45.2	37.8	13.3	0.7
…correspondence with educators	3.7	41.5	38.5	15.6	1.5
…resource provision to aid in teaching	3.7	36.3	37	20	3.7
…instruments to aid Sustainable Development behaviours	5.2	37.8	28.9	20.7	8.9
…supervision of knowledge transfer on Sustainability	3.7	34.8	31.9	20.7	9.6

Source: Authors' compilation.

quite low, exposing a high level of dissatisfaction with government engagement with educational stakeholders on sustainable development.

Do you have any government documents on sustainable development?

Fig. 2.2 shows that 85.1% of respondents said 'No' to the question of being aware of documents about sustainable development. We know from our study that these document(s) exist; the unanimous response to 'No', can only mean that there is no active use of the documents; if not those who should be implementing its content should have known about its existence. Other, follow-up questions in the survey were intentionally designed to be expressive in ways that elicit respondents to share their understanding of sustainable development transfer in the schools and innovative strategies that can address challenges of climate change and sustainability, which we refer to as 'bottom-up steps'. Clusters of responses show some real-time innovative responses that address present issues to the educational curricula and system, these responses were also confirmed in the interview with school proprietors. Some bottom-up steps are such that schools design curricula that directly address the disconnect between education and development (Ilechukwu et al., 2014). Technical courses are taught to encourage entrepreneurship and self-employment like welding and fabrication, tailoring and fashion design, catering, and event management. Others are initiatives that address challenges of global warming, like teacher/student partnerships on tree planting, competitive programmes for innovations to address sustainable development, and innovations on recycling with emphasis on biogas and developing solar systems and batteries.

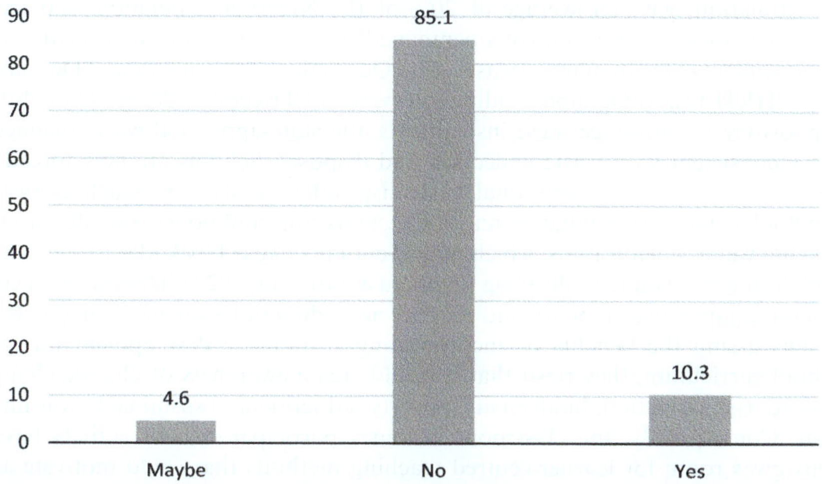

Fig. 2.2. Educators' Awareness of Existing Documents for Sustainable Development Education. *Source*: Authors' compilation.

4. Discussion of Findings

The interview respondents demonstrated knowledgeability in their field. First, Mrs Obeahon of Medna Group of Schools, a chemist by profession interviewed on 16 November 2023, gave a vivid implication of Nigeria's present non-discrete use of the earth's resources. She elaborated on the transition that has taken place already. She noted that it is the present epoch of the Holocene from the first epoch of the Pleistocene. She cited examples of the impact of some unregulated chemicals in producing insecticides, adversely affecting the environment and human health. This leads to excessive heat and flooding in the case of the environment and the case of human health leads to an increase in cancer-related ailments. She emphasised that we must take practical steps to reverse this trend. One statement that stood out for all interviewees is a lack of government commitment to teaching the behavioural changes that should support a sustainable thinking culture in Nigerian students. Interviewees admit that the paperwork is enormous with several topics on sustainable development in the school curriculum shared by the government ministry for education; however, the instruments and directives for actual implementation are nonexistent or ridiculously minimal. On a scale of 1–10, implementation is rated '1' (HRH Ogunbor). Knowledge sharing in sustainable development is dependent on the teacher's or school management's level of awareness and commitment to sustainability. A lack of structured training for the trainers/teachers to unlearn lifestyles that negatively impact the environment and learn more sustainable attitudes for a sustainable future will mean their inability to transfer such knowledge to their pupils and students.

Proper waste management, as a key indicator of a country's intentionality to be more sustainable cited as a challenge, Obeahon (11 November 2023) by way of estimation, gave an average of 20% of the Nigerian population who manage waste properly. Respondents bemoaned the lack of visible instruments that show students how to manage waste (Mrs Odumah, online interview, 9 December 2023; HRH Osaro Ogunbor, online interview, 11 December 2023). Though the schools try to introduce these instruments, the state-appointed waste managers are inconsistent with waste collection and disposal. Schools are now forced to resort to the same unconventional waste disposal methods they preach against in the books, like burning that increases CO_2 emissions and pouring waste into the flowing water when it rains, which may eventually cause blockades to the canals and drainages leading to flooding (Omoera & Guanah, 2022). This creates a considerable gap between theory and practice according to Ekwueme et al. (2016).

Discussing the benefits of incorporating sustainable development into the school curriculum, they posit that it would create awareness of climate change, disaster risk reduction, biodiversity, poverty reduction and sustainable consumption. Consequently, the classroom becomes participatory and activity-based. This gives room for learner-centred teaching methods that could motivate and empower the learners to change their behaviours and act for sustainable development. The knowledge acquired could help the learners to be able to relate what they learn in the classroom to their real-life activities. They will increasingly be able to take the lead in changing behaviours and adopting sustainable lifestyles. Regardless of the challenges, the school proprietors did refer to some bottom-up initiatives. First is the initiative to use solar-powered energy generation to run the schools; this attracts substantial financial investment. The erratic power supply from the Nigerian Power Holding Company, depicts a situation where only 55.5% of the population is connected to the national grid, with an average of 8 hours a day access to electricity. Power can be obstructed without prior notice. This means that learning can be obstructed at any time.

The initiative to introduce solar power both creates a more seamless learning environment and reduces air and noise pollution since they do not have to resort to fossil fuel generating sets to alternate the erratic power supply; this thus reduces air pollution and is compliant with sustainable energy-generating future. The school sources only 10% of its power utilisation from the national grid. Secondly, to address unemployment, which has become the bane of school leavers and graduates in Nigeria with a high unemployment rate of 33.3% in the fourth quarter of 2020. Yvonne Odumah of Havilah Land Academy (interviewed on 9 December 2023), shared a technical learning curriculum that fights unemployment and a form of poverty alleviation with sustainable education in key skills areas such as welding and fabrication, tailoring and fashion design, catering, and event management that support entrepreneurial income generation that directly lands students in employment after school, boycotting the unemployment phase.

The failings of the Nigerian government in infrastructural development have negatively affected education. This has led to the proliferation of private schools in Nigeria. Many studies have shown these privately owned educational facilities are motivated by a variety of reasons with profit-making as the highest impetus for people getting involved in education (Angwaomaodoko, 2024; Härmä, 2013; Njoku & Adeyemi, 2013; Omoera & Adegoriola, 2021). With profiteering as the bane of the market economy, one would expect that the government educational inspectorate department will be very active in inspecting and regulating the activities of these private schools. Unfortunately, Samuel Amakeme (in an interview on 29 April 2024) while responding to this question of how the relevant education ministry or agency supervises the privately owned schools, noted the issues of policy somersaults, lack of political will and corruption as the chief drawbacks in the supervisory function. However, the school proprietor respondents (Obeahon, Ogunbor and Odumah) expressed disappointment at the lack of inspection from the state directorate. Though an inspection visit can put the private school proprietors at several risks, such as being forced to commit more resources to certain areas like insisting on qualified staffing, and laboratory improvement, being fined for noncompliance, or worst case, being shut down due to issues of standardisation. Yet the respondents would rather have this engagement that puts them on their toes and helps them improve than a situation of no engagement. The respondents decried this lack of inspection, which they felt would have been an opportunity for engagement to address common concerns. The lack of inspection is why many schools can, in broad daylight, be operating without approval (Härmä, 2013).

5. Is This a Case of Greenwashing?

As much as we would like to exercise restraint in categorising the government's inability to match its global showing with policy implementation of the sustainability narrative as greenwashing, the results give it away as such. When we examine it from the greenwashing window from scholarly perspectives. Alluding to sustainability is the new norm of public relations, propaganda and corporate social responsibility. Customers' and clients' global warming and environmental risk awareness have put many companies on their toes. Customers are looking to patronise companies whose activities are compliant and have an active role in stemming the tide of global warming. Greenwashing, as a phenomenon, arises from companies' need to 'resolve' the trade-off between the increasing importance of environmental compliance and their genuine supportable efforts towards this objective (Bernini & LaRosa, 2024). Al Gore, former US Vice President, environmental activist, and Nobel Laureate, presented greenwashing as 'confusing and often misleading claims about sustainability benefits' that 'is a "rising threat" that could derail climate progress' (*Sky News*, 2021; cited in Nygaard & Silkoset, 2022). Kolcava (2023) seeks a top-down government regulation due to the shallowness of corporate sustainability commitment, which is a case of greenwashing. The question here and now is: What if the government is the culprit? Organisations faced with new institutional demands usually respond symbolically (Zhang et al., 2023).

Williams (2024) describes greenwashing as British Petroleum's (BP) investment of 570,000 pounds in advertisements with messages promoting their involvement in renewable energy, targeting UK social media users after making 7 billion pounds in profits in the second quarter of 2022 due to the global energy crisis. A Public Relations (PR) tactic, used to package a company, or its products look environmentally friendly. He therefore defines it as an 'optics' strategy of organisations wanting to improve their image while maintaining a business-as-usual approach.

Tateishi (2017, p. 370) summarises greenwashing as 'the selective disclosure of positive information about a company's environmental or social performance, without full disclosure of negative information on these dimensions, to create an overly positive corporate image'. Cooperative miscommunication, according to Montgomery et al. (2023), is an elusive end to greenwashing. The lack of engagement with education stakeholders and the correlation between policy documentation and actual implementation for a sustainable Nigerian future. We ascribe the government's global display a case of clientelism (Kitschelt, 2002; Piattoni, 2001; Roniger, 2004) that has been identified as a 'strategy for the acquisition, maintenance, and the aggrandisement of political power' (Piattoni, 2001, p. 2) and as a barrier to the development of democracy and the rule of law (Krygier & Czarnot, 1999; Sajó, 1998) discussed a new wave of corrupt practices in post-communist East and Central Europe. Synonymous with the practice of political actors in Africa who tend to ground local legitimacy by seeking international approval through partnering in global issues to convey a message to possible opposing forces that they have global recognition.

6. Educational Stakeholders' Engagement for Sustainable Development

Engaging with stakeholders is no longer an option for organisations and governments; the option is when and to what extent engagement should be. In today's global village and social media and AI-mediated communication possibilities, that help to isolate engagement challenges, the assumption of top-down interaction with stakeholders can only present an unseriousness in collaboration. The UN Millennium Development Goals emphasise the importance of exploring different scalable communication that should pull down such characteristics of vertical communication that are the presumptions that the sender holds all the necessary knowledge for ongoing communication for development, that only the sender has information that the receiver does not have, and because the message is sent through channels holding codes common to the sender and the receiver that the message has been effectively communicated Gálvez and Casanova (2019, p. 12). The interview results put a hole in these assumptions because the respondents are themselves experts in their field and are keeping a close watch on the unfolding scenarios of global warming and the impact of climate change on the environment.

Development communication experts emphasise the failures of vertical top-down propagandist communication in achieving the goals of development (Colle, 2008; Gumucio-Dagron, 2001, 2008; Mefalopulos, 2008; Servaes, 2008), among many others. Childers advocates that

> if you want development to be rooted in the human beings, who have to become the agents of it as well as the beneficiaries, you have got to enable them to communicate with each other and back to the planners in the capital city.

The respondents from this research show a population who are knowledgeable about issues of global warming and sustainable development, however, they feel left out of the scheme of things both in regulation, providing input, and being supported to develop knowhow for stemming global warming and becoming sustainability savvy. The challenges of global warming today are institutionalised deficiencies that depend on unsustainable development modules that have impacted the ozone layer. Of all institutions, the educational sector is key in helping us unlearn old ways and innovate new technologies to make our future more sustainable. Excluding the education sector as a stakeholder is tantamount to groping in the dark about our sustainable future (Awamleh et al., 2024; Humbatova et al., 2024; Inder et al., 2022; Li et al., 2024).

7. Recommendations

The statement credited to the immediate past president of Nigeria, Mohammadu Buhari, about the so-called *resilience of the Nigerian people* has more to do with people taking steps to find solutions to their everyday problems in the face of little or no help from the government. This research has revealed a group of stakeholders who understand the need to come up with solutions to global warming and a way to solve the long-standing challenges of infrastructural decay that impede progress in the educational sector like others. The interviewees and respondents are keen to see Nigerian education responding to the global needs for sustainable development and are ready to play their role if only the government will cooperate by putting tools in place for a sustainability-driven work structure to achieve educational goals in the 17 sustainable development goals, which is to ensure inclusive and equitable quality education and promote lifelong learning opportunities for all. The strategic place of education is at the core of supporting the unlearning and learning lifestyle that supports sustainable development. We share here some of the recommendations proposed by the interviewees and respondents and others we see as necessary from our engagement in this study:

(a) Policy documents related to sustainability must be made available across multiple communication channels to stakeholders in the education field. Stakeholders comprise the Ministry of Education and the Inspectorate of Education staff. Proprietors, principals and other management staff in the schools' Academic and non-academic staff of schools, parents and students. It can be tailored to the needs and understanding of a particular group. The place of channel preferences in organisational communication alerts us to the need to use all available channels just like in change management. An alert from the quote by Bernard Shaw that the biggest error in communication is the imagination that it already took place when it hasn't should be a guide in sharing the policy document.
(b) Structured training workshops for teachers to help them understand the discourse of sustainable development will help them to improve on their teaching methods.
(c) Continuous platforms for engagement among stakeholders are needed.

(d) Frequent scheduled and unscheduled inspections from the directorate of inspection to the schools are needed.
(e) Synergies of brainstorming among industry players in a participatory format which according to communication for development scholars is the way to get people to contribute and claim ownership of a project to prevent the project from failing, also prevent a lack of understanding of the process/project because clarity would have been established through stakeholder participation.
(f) Understanding the role of education and the cascading effect of attitudinal changes should increase engagement with stakeholders.
(g) Financial support and motivation for stakeholders should not be taken for granted.

The theoretical framework of this study is the importance of communication for development with stakeholder engagement as pivotal to growth and development. The recommendations above are just a tip on how to create a compass for engagement with education stakeholders. Opening communication channels with stakeholders will unravel the potential of groups to contribute to ongoing discourse on sustainable development.

8. Conclusion

This research focussed on investigating stakeholder engagement from one of the key institutional frameworks for green solutions to global warming. Though a non-representative cluster of investigation, it is significant enough to unravel awareness of government commitment to ensuring that educational stakeholders are carried along to give societal interpretation to the sweeping changes that ought to be taking place due to the reverse trajectory that sustainability commands. The results from this study have exposed Nigeria's government agency in chasing shadows with a global show of commitment to sustainable development without concrete stakeholders' engagement with the educational sector. The research nonetheless has also shown a group of ready partners in the education field who are committed to reversing the trend of global warming. Strategic engagement by the government with the educational sector to reverse the unsustainable decay in society by inspiring educational skills development that will set Nigeria on the part of grassroots awareness of global warming challenges. The Nigerian government needs to quit 'acting' and get down to the real business of stakeholder engagement for sustainable development. Scholars insist that there cannot be actual sustainable development growth in a country without strategic government policy, regulation, monitoring, motivation and subsidisation, which are currently missing on the Nigerian stage. Unless the government reaches out to stakeholders for engagements that will make the education sector and other sectors relevant to sustainability key partners in the drive towards sustainable development, the fraudulence of a global show-off will soon be too glaring to cover up.

References

Aberu, F., & Lawal, Y. O. (2022). The relationship between education and sustainable development in Nigeria. *Journal of Public Administration, Finance and Law, 11*(24), 7–16. https://doi.org/10.47743/jopafl-2022-24-01

Adaja, O., & Olajide, O. E. (2022). *Peace education, community engagement and sustainable development in Nigeria*. Sahel Publishers (pp. 68–86).

Angwaomaodoko, E. A. (2024). An analytical study of the proliferation of private schools in Nigeria. *Path of Science: International Electronic Scientific Journal, 10*(9), 10–17.

Awamleh, F. T., Alarabiat, Y. A., & Bustami, A. N. (2024). Enhancing sustainable development through international performance indicators: The role of business intelligence techniques. *Challenges in Sustainability, 12*(3), 203–218.

Ayompe, L. M., Davis, S. J., & Egoh, B. N. (2020). Trends and drivers of African fossil fuel CO_2 emissions 1990–2017. *Environmental Research Letters, 15*(12), Article 124039. https://doi.org/10.1088/1748-9326/abc64f

Bernini, F., & La Rosa, F. (2024). Research in the greenwashing field: Concepts, theories, and potential impacts on economic and social value. *Journal of Management and Governance, 28*, 405–444. https://doi.org/10.1007/s10997-023-09686-5

Boyi, A. A. (2014). Education and sustainable national development in Nigeria. Challenges and the way forward. *International Letters of Social and Humanistic Sciences, 3*(2014), 65–72.

Colle, R. D. (2008). Threads of development communication. In J. Servaes (Ed.), *Communication for development and social change*. Sage. https://doi.org/10.4135/9788132108474.n7

Dioha, M. O., & Kumar, A. (2020). Exploring the energy system impacts of Nigeria's nationally determined contributions and low-carbon transition to mid-century. *Energy Policy, 144*, Article 111703. https://doi.org/10.1016/j.enpol.2020.111703

Edet, P. I., & Beyin, U. T. (2018). Education for sustainable development in Nigeria and other developing nations. *British Journal of Education, 6*(5), 41–51.

Ekwueme, C. O., Ekon, E. E., & Ezenwa-Nebife, D. C. (2016). Education for sustainability through academic freedom. *Global Journal of Educational Research, 15*, 23–30. https://doi.org/10.4314/gjedr.v15i1.3

Gumucio-Dagron, A. (2001). *Making waves stories of participatory communication for social change*. Rocky Feller Foundation.

Gumucio-Dagron, A. (2008). Vertical minds versus horizontal cultures: An overview of participatory processes and experience. In J. Servaes (Ed.), *Communication for development and social change* (pp. 68–81). Sage.

Härmä, J. (2013). Access or quality? Why do families living in slums choose low-cost private schools in Lagos, Nigeria? *Oxford Review of Education, 39*(4), 548–566. https://doi.org/10.1080/03054985.2013.825984

Humbatova, S. I., Hajiyeva, N., Fodor, M. G., Sood, K., & Grima, S. (2024). The impact of economic growth on the ecological environment and renewable energy production: Evidence from Azerbaijan and Hungary. *Journal of Risk and Financial Management, 17*(7), Article 275.

Ilechukwu, L. C., Njoku, C. C., & Ngwuozor, F. O. (2014). Education and development disconnect in Nigeria: Education for sustainable development (ESD) as the 21st century imperative for Nigeria's national transformation, sustainable development and global competitiveness. *Journal of Economics and Sustainable Development, 5*(23), 44–56.

Inder, S., Sood, K., & Grima, S. (2022). Antecedents of behavioural intention to adopt internet banking using structural equation modelling. *Journal of Risk and Financial Management, 15*(4), Article 157.

Kitschelt, H. (2002). Popular dissatisfaction with democracy: Populism and party systems. In Y. Mény & Y. Surel (Eds.), *Democracies and the populist challenge*. Palgrave Macmillan. https://doi.org/10.1057/9781403920072_10

Kolcava, D. (2023). Greenwashing and public demand for government regulation. *Journal of Public Policy*, *43*, 179–198. https://doi.org/10.1017/S0143814X22000277

Krygier, M., & Czarnota, A. (1999). *The rule of law after communism. Problems and prospects in East and Central Europe*. Taylor and Francis Group/Routledge.

Li, Q., Wu, H., Zhang, B. Q., Dong, Z. H., & Ling, T. (2024). Safety system study of gas stations based on preliminary hazard analysis and fault tree analysis. *Journal of Engineering Management and Systems Engineering*, *3*(3), 149–163.

Liang, J., Bai, W., Li, Q., Zhang, X., & Zhang, L. (2022). Dynamic mechanisms and institutional frameworks of China's green development: An analysis from the perspective of collaboration. *Sustainability*, *14*(11), Article 6491. https://doi.org/10.3390/su14116491

Mefalopulos, P. (2008). *Development communication sourcebook: Broadening the boundaries of communication*. World Bank.

Montgomery, A. W., Lyon, T. P., & Barg, J. (2023). No end in sight? A greenwash review and research agenda. *Organization & Environment*, *37*(2), 221–256. https://doi.org/10.1177/10860266231168905

Njoku, A. C., & Adeyemi, A. A. (2013). Disparities in public and private pre-primary and primary schools' enrolments, classrooms and teachers in Nigeria: Implications for access and educational management. *International Journal of Development and Management Review*, *8*(1), 246–255.

Nwalutu, M. O. (2014). Basic education and sustainable development in the era of globalization: Does Nigeria mortgage her future in accepting international assistance for her primary education projects? In *Counterpoints – Emerging Perspectives on 'African Development': SPEAKING DIFFERENTLY* (Vol. 443, pp. 157–178). Peter Lang AG. http://www.jstor.org/stable/42982054

Nygaard, A., & Silkoset, R. (2022). Sustainable development and greenwashing: How Blockchain technology information can empower green consumers. *Business Strategy and the Environment*, *32*(6), 3801–3813. https://doi.org/10.1002/bse.3338

Oche, A. (2020). Comparative analysis of green bond regimes in Nigeria and China. *Journal of Sustainable Development Law and Policy*, *11*(2), 160–184. https://doi.org/10.4314/jsdlp.v11i1.8

Ogbonna, C. G., Nwachi, C. C., Okeoma, I. O., & Fagbami, O. A. (2023). Understanding Nigeria's transition pathway to carbon neutrality using the multilevel perspective. *Carbon Neutrality*, *2*, Article 24. https://doi.org/10.1007/s43979-023-00065-5

Okoh, A. I. S. (2020). An analysis of Nigeria's nationally determined contribution (NDC) in the transition to low carbon economy. *Open Journals of Social Science and Humanities (OJSSH)*, *1*(1), 42–60. https://openjournalsnigeria.org.ng/pub/ojssh20200104.pdf

Omoera, O. S., & Adegoriola, A. M. (2021). Bridging the information gap to keep educators healthy: Health insurance awareness and actions by private school employees in Nigeria. *The Journal of Development Communication*, *32*(2), 1–14. http://jdc.journals.unisel.edu.my/ojs/index.php/jdc/article/view/205

Omoera, O. S., & Guanah, J. S. (2022). Climate change induced flash floods in Federal Capital Territory, Abuja, Nigeria: Media shaping awareness? *Przegląd Krytyczny/Critical Review*, *4*(1), 1–18. https://doi.org/10.14746/pk.2022.4.1.5

Oyedepo, S. O. (2012). Energy and sustainable development in Nigeria: The way forward. *Energy, Sustainability and Society*, *2*, Article 15. https://doi.org/10.1186/2192-0567-2-15

Peppler-Barry, U., & Fiske, E. B. (2000). *World education forum 26-28 April 2000 Dakar, Senegal, final report*. Retrieved October 10, 2025, from https://unesdoc.unesco.org/ark:/48223/pf0000121117

Piattoni, S. (Ed.). (2001). *Clientelism, interests, and democratic representation: The European experience in historical and comparative perspective*. Cambridge University Press.

Roniger, L. (2004). Political clientelism, democracy, and market economy [Review of Le clientélisme politique dans les sociétés contemporaines; Poor People's Politics: Peronist Survival Networks and the Legacy of Evita; Clientelism, Interests, and Democratic Representation: The European Experience in Historical and Comparative Perspective, by J.-L. Briquet, F. Sawicki, J. Auyero, & S. Piattoni]. *Comparative Politics*, *36*(3), 353–375. https://doi.org/10.2307/4150135

Runnalls, D., & Cosbey, A. (1992). *Trade and sustainable development: A survey of the issues and a new research agenda* (pp. 11–13). International Institute for Sustainable Development. https://www.iisd.org/system/files/publications/trade_and_sd.pdf?q=sites/default/files/publications/trade_and_sd.pdf

Sajó, A. (1998). Corruption, clientelism, and the future of the constitutional state in Eastern Europe. *East European Constitutional Review (spring)*, *7*(2), 37–46.

Schmitz, H. (2017). Who drives climate-relavant policies in the rising powers? *Journal of the New Political Economy*, *22*(5), 521–540.

Scoones, I., Leach, M., & Newell, P. (Eds.). (2015). *The politics of green transformations*. Routledge/Earthscan.

Servaes, J. (Ed.). (2008). *Communication for development and social change*. Sage.

Tateishi, E. (2017). Craving gains and claiming "green" by cutting greens? An exploratory analysis of greenfield housing developments in Iskandar Malaysia. *Journal of Urban Affairs*, *40*(3), 370–393. https://doi.org/10.1080/07352166.2017.1355667

Todaro, M. P., & Smith, S. C. (2009). *Economic development* (10th ed.), Pearson Education Limited.

UNESCO. (1990). *World conference on education for all. 5th to 9th March 1990, Jomtien, Thailand*. Retrieved October 10, 2024, from https://unesdoc.unesco.org/ark:/48223/pf0000085625

Unruh, G. C. (2000). Understanding carbon lock-in. *Energy Policy*, *28*(12), 817–830.

Williams, J. (2024). Greenwashing: Appearance, illusion and the future of 'green' capitalism. *Geography Compass*, *18*(1), Article e12736. https://doi.org/10.1111/gec3.12736

Zhang, K., Pan, Z., Janardhanan, M., & Patel, I. (2023). Relationship analysis between greenwashing and environmental performance. *Environment, Development and Sustainability*, *25*(8), 7927–7957. https://doi.org/10.1007/s10668-022-02381-9

Chapter 3

Green Finance and Sustainable Development: A Bibliometric Review

Niluka Rajakaruna[a], *Hiranya Dissanayake*[a] *and Anuradha Iddagoda*[b]

[a]*Department of Accountancy, Faculty of Business Studies and Finance, Wayamba University of Sri Lanka, Kuliyapitiya, Sri Lanka*
[b]*Management Science Unit, Faculty of Applied Sciences, University of Sri Jayewardenepura, Nugegoda, Sri Lanka*

Abstract

Purpose: This study seeks to thoroughly examine the literature surrounding green finance and sustainable development, aiming to delineate the existing landscape of publications in this field.

Need for the study: This study on green finance and sustainable development is needed to consolidate existing knowledge, identify gaps and provide insights for policymakers, investors and researchers aiming to advance environmentally sustainable economic practices.

Methodology: The analysis of 410 documents from the Web of Science database, spanning 2007–2024, seeks to identify influential contributors to green finance and sustainable development. The researchers use descriptive-analytical methods such as trend, author, country and keyword analysis alongside advanced techniques like thematic maps and co-word analysis to map the landscape and pinpoint research gaps in this field.

Findings: The study highlights a significant rise in articles on green finance and sustainable development between 2007 and 2024, originating from 67 countries with notable contributions from China, Pakistan and India. Common keywords such as 'renewable energy', 'China', 'green bonds' and 'sustainable finance' underscore prevalent themes. Identified research gaps include areas like 'renewable energy', 'climate finance' and 'human capital',

Sustainable Development and Green Innovation: Managing Risk through Interdisciplinary Approaches and Policy Strategies, 37–66

doi:10.1108/978-1-83608-462-420251003

suggesting a need for exploration into the relationship between green finance and sustainable development.

Practical implications: The study provides policymakers with insights into key research trends, aiding targeted investment and policy formulation for environmental sustainability. It also fosters interdisciplinary collaborations among researchers, accelerating innovation towards global sustainability goals.

Keywords: Sustainable development; green finance; Web of Science; Biblioshiny co-word analysis; thematic maps; co-citation

JEL codes: O13; Q5; Q56

Introduction

Green finance refers to the financing of investments that provide environmental benefits (D. Zhang et al., 2019). Green finance also refers to 'sustainable finance', 'environmental finance', 'climate finance' and 'green investment'. Green finance integrates financial services and products with sustainability, including lowering commercial pollution, managing the environment, improving sanitation and conserving natural resources (C. Z. Li & Umair, 2023). As the global concern for environmental conservation, climate change and sustainable development has emerged, policymakers and researchers have recently shifted their focus to green finance (Akomea-Frimpong et al., 2022). Based on the definition of sustainable development provided by Daly (2006). It has two forms: utility sustainability and physical throughput sustainability. Utility sustainability pertains to the doctrine that states that the welfare or happiness (utility) of future people should not be worse than that of current people, again or more simply, the average welfare of people in the future generation must be equal to or better than that of the present generation. Physical Throughput Sustainability refers to the flow of resources around the economy, from nature, through the economy, and back to nature, whose rate cannot be reduced. The flows in the ecosystem should continue to be sustained; they maintain the stock or the natural wealth so that the future generation will not be deprived of enjoying the benefits the current generation is enjoying from this ecosystem. Throughput can be defined as the total resource usage by the community at any given time or a given timescale, such as per capita resource use by the community multiplied by the community's population. Thus, the financial sector is an influential factor in economic growth. Therefore, even if the team has relatively fewer finances at its disposal, it should implement efficient management systems to provide significant productivity (Afzal et al., 2022). Green finance is crucial for sustainable development as it addresses environmental and climate change issues by directing capital towards environmentally sensitive projects. It also facilitates the principles of good banking and investments for sustainability (Rahman et al., 2023). Literature on green finance and sustainable development should be studied to evaluate strategies and new approaches to financing environment-friendly projects, prevent incorrect decisions, and contribute to the global progress of sustainable initiatives. It helps to understand how economic processes relate to the preservation of the environment, which is a critical factor in solving significant problems in the modern world.

To the best of the authors' knowledge, there are very few bibliometric analyses performed on this area of research or literature review of green finance and sustainable development, as Krastev and Krasteva-Hristova (2024) conducted a bibliometric analysis on 'Challenges and Trends in Green Finance in the Context of Sustainable Development' by considering the publications between 2016 and 2024. The researchers have used the Scopus database to search for the documents for this study. To fill that gap, the current study used the Web of Science database for this analysis and considered the total number of publications from 2007 to 2024. Web of Science could be more appropriate for searching and analysing open-access resources at the publication level (Pranckutė, 2021). Y. Zhang et al. (2024) conducted a review study on 'The Impact of Green Finance on High-Quality Economic Development'. It is purely focussed on a systematic analysis rather than a bibliometric analysis. Besides these studies, many bibliometric studies can be found about green finance, but all those studies are connected with other subject areas. Hoang et al. (2023) conducted a study on 'green finance in the banking industry'. Mashari et al. (2023) studied 'Alignment of Green Finance and Carbon Trading', etc. The current study aims to address research gaps by collecting data from 2007 and employing advanced analytical methods. Lotka's Law and Co-occurrence analysis will be applied to assess the reliability and distribution patterns of publications in the dataset, thereby enhancing the quality assessment of the bibliometric analysis. In addition, this study used thematic maps and trending topics to investigate main themes and research topics to be explored by future researchers.

The study utilised bibliometric analysis and content analysis techniques to investigate a series of research questions regarding green finance and sustainable development:

RQ1. What is the trend of publications related to green finance and sustainable development?

RQ2. Who are the most cited pioneer authors on green finance and sustainable development?

RQ3. Which journals dominate green finance and sustainable development?

RQ4. What is the total number of articles based on countries and international collaboration on green finance and sustainable development?

RQ5. What are the relevant author keywords relating to green finance and sustainable development?

RQ6. Which publications and papers on green finance and sustainable development have the most significant citation impact?

Methodology

This study also performs a bibliometric analysis to explore the development of the Green Finance and Sustainable Development research. According to the descriptions of statisticians and mathematicians that include (Garfield, 1955) this technique employs various other mathematical instruments and statistical methods to analyse and scour articles and books, among other published documents. Bibliometric statistics are applied for the explanation of scientific research methodologies and features of a particular discipline (Bouyssou & Marchant, 2011; De Bakker et al., 2005; Dissanayake et al., 2023). Through bibliometric analysis, the history of a particular field is explained, its current status elucidated, and potential future trends explained to the researchers (Bilal et al., 2022; Durieux & Gevenois, 2010).

In conducting the analysis, articles and papers were sourced from reliable bibliographic databases, particularly the Web of Science. Specific search terms targeted articles that addressed issues concerning Green Finance and Sustainable Development. The Web of Science database was selected because it includes indexed, international, interdisciplinary and scholarly articles (Dissanayake et al., 2022; Schotten et al., 2017). They were extracted based on recent publications to ensure the capture of current trends in the Green Finance and Sustainable Development literature in the last decade.

Boolean operators were used in the search, and 'green finance' was used with 'Sustainable development' to increase the literature coverage while utilising the truncation symbol. This study integrates data extraction using systemic review with a bibliometric analysis approach (Amarathunga et al., 2024). Preferred Reporting Items for Systematic reviews and Meta-Analyses (PRISMA) framework, which is depicted in Fig. 3.1, illustrates the data extraction phase (Page et al., 2021). Articles were further narrowed down based on the language of the article (English), the type of the article (peer-reviewed), and the particular area of study.

Bibliometric data collection entailed identifying basic publication-related features like publication year, authors, journal names, keywords and numbers of citations. The information gathered is processed by the bibliometric software tools, particularly Biblioshiny, for further analysis. This tool can be used to visualise citations, conduct co-word analysis, and find the key authors and core works in Green Finance and Sustainable Development.

Findings

Trend Analysis

Fig. 3.2 illustrates the trend analysis of the number of articles containing the terms 'green finance' and 'sustainable development' from 2007 to 2023, indicating the growth of interest in the field. During the first phase of the research activity, the years between 2007 and 2016 were characterised by low numbers of publications and infrequent articles (for instance, one publication in 2007, two in 2010, one in 2014 and one in 2015). This period indicates the initial concern and need for research in the given space, which can be attributed to low knowledge of green finance and sustainable development as a novel field of study and practice.

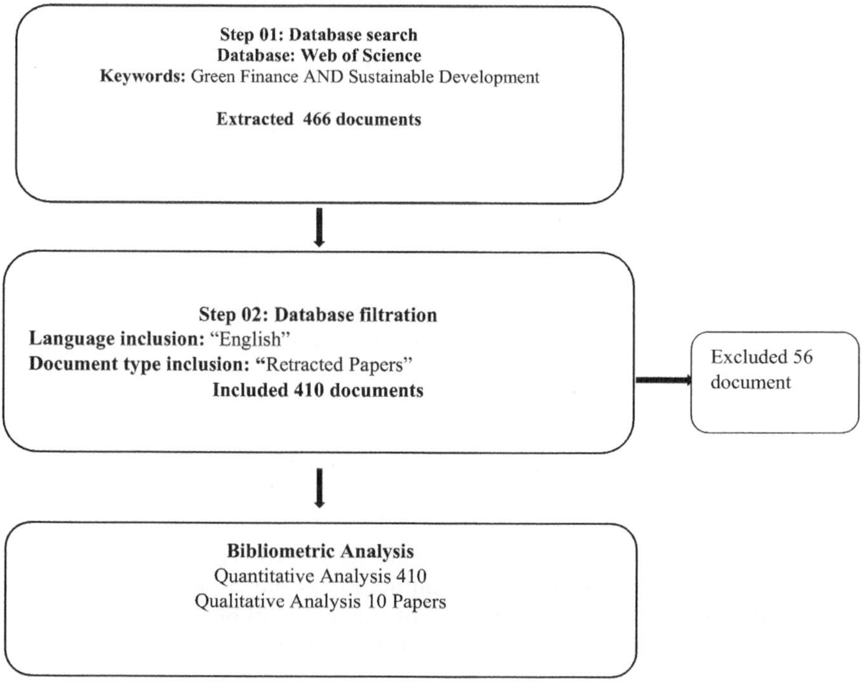

Fig. 3.1. Prisma Framework. *Source*: Constructed based on the PRISMA framework.

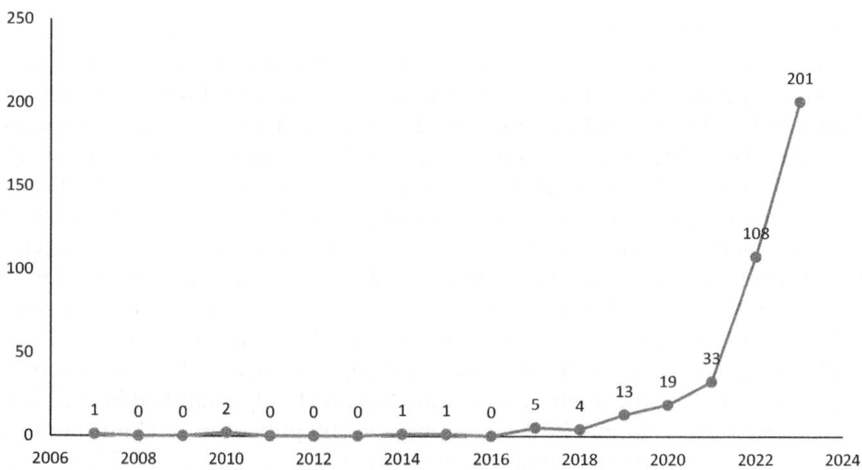

Fig. 3.2. Trend Analysis. *Source*: Authors' calculations.

The trends reveal that from 2017 to the following year, there was a slight increase in the number of articles published yearly. The publication count increased to five articles in 2017; the same trend was seen in 2018 and a higher surge in 2019. Specifically, there were 13 articles in 2019, while the production of articles reached 19 articles in 2020. This trend has increased substantially in 2021 with 33 articles and then sharply increased in 2022 to 108, ultimately culminating in 2023 with 201 articles. This exponential growth, especially in recent years, aims to advance sustainable development and green finance globally due to rising awareness of environmental issues and policies and the urgency for climate change studies and sustainable solutions. The significant increase in published articles shows that green finance and sustainable development have emerged as substantial fields of research and discussion, which respond to the scholars' and policymakers' rising interest.

Author Analysis

Lotka's Law, or the inverse square law of scientific productivity, states that the number of authors who have published *n* papers equals 1/*n*21/*n*2 (Lotka, 1926). Lotka Law of the database is illustrated in Table 3.1. This means a few authors contribute many publications, while the majority contribute only a few. The provided data reflect this principle: most authors (944 out of 1,057) have written only one document, representing 89.31% of the total authors. In contrast, only a few authors have high productivity, with just one author writing 12 documents, constituting a mere 0.09% of the total.

This distribution demonstrates the classic pattern predicted by Lotka's Law, where the scientific community's output is heavily skewed. Most researchers contribute a limited number of papers, while a few are highly prolific. Such patterns are typical in academic and research settings, emphasising the significant contributions of a small core of highly productive authors. This output concentration among a few key researchers underscores their critical role in advancing knowledge and driving scientific progress.

In assessing bibliometric data, an author analysis depicted in Table 3.2 showcases the various researchers who have significantly impacted green finance and sustainable development. The author with the highest score is Taghizadeh-Hesary F, with an *h*-index of 9 and a *g*-index of 12, indicating high productivity and citation rates. Analysing the publications, since 2019, Taghizadeh-Hesary F holds 12 publications in leading peer-reviewed journals, which have been cited 993 times, thus contributing significantly to the knowledge base. This is followed by Abbas J with an *h*-index of 5 and a *g*-index of 5, having published five articles and receiving 606 citations since 2022. Interestingly, Abbas J has a high *m*-index of 1.667, implying growth and influence in the amount of work in a relatively small period.

Other authors include Yoshino N and Najam H, whose *h*-index is 3 and has excellent citation influence. Yoshino N, who began as early as 2019, has received 462 citations in 3 of the publications, while Najam H only published in 2022 but has garnered 330 citations in the same number of publications. Contributions from Rasoulinezhad E and Umair M also have the same *h*-index of 2 have also supported this study greatly, where Rasoulinezhad E gained 325 citations and

Table 3.1. Lotka Law.

Documents Written	No. of Authors	Proportion of Authors
1	944	0.89309366
2	81	0.07663198
3	23	0.0217597
4	5	0.00473037
5	3	0.00283822
12	1	0.00094607

Source: Constructed based on Biblioshiny software.

Table 3.2. Author Analysis.

Author	*h*-index	*g*-index	*m*-index	TC	NP	PY-start
Taghizadeh-Hesary F	9	12	1.500	993	12	2019
Abbas J	5	5	1.667	606	5	2022
Yoshino N	3	3	0.500	462	3	2019
Najam H	3	3	1.000	330	3	2022
Rasoulinezhad E	2	2	0.667	325	2	2022
Umair M	2	2	1.000	285	2	2023
Mohsin M	3	4	1.000	255	4	2022
Managi S	3	3	0.500	240	3	2019
Keeley Ar	2	2	0.333	210	2	2019
Tolliver C	2	2	0.333	210	2	2019

Source: Authors' calculations.

Umair M had 285 citations, respectively, but since they are newly published in 2022 and 2023, respectively; therefore, they have a latest contribution.

Source Analysis

Bradford's Law of Scattering describes how articles on a specific subject are distributed across scientific journals (Brookes, 1977). This analysis of sustainability and environmental science journals divides the data into three zones based on their article frequency. Zone 1 comprises a small number of core journals such as *Sustainability*, *Environmental Science and Pollution Research*, *Resources Policy*, and *Renewable Energy*, which collectively contribute 136 articles. These core journals are highly productive and central to the field, as predicted by Bradford's Law.

Zones 2 and 3 illustrate the dispersion of relevant articles across a broader range of journals. Zone 2 includes journals like *Frontiers in Environmental Science* and

Journal of Cleaner Production, which collectively account for a significant but lesser number of articles than Zone 1. Zone 3 contains numerous journals, each contributing only one article, indicating a long tail of less frequent contributors. This distribution pattern aligns with Bradford's Law, emphasising the concentration of significant research output in a few core journals while the remainder is spread thinly across many less prolific sources. This insight aids in identifying key journals for comprehensive literature searches and effective resource allocation in research.

The findings from the source analysis of the bibliometric data in Table 3.3 detail the positions and importance of different journals in green finance and sustainable development. At the top of this list is the established *Renewable Energy* journal; it has a productivity and citation impact *h*-index of 16 and a *g*-index of 25, which published 25 articles with 911 total citations since 2022, indicating a relatively recent involvement in the field. Next is *Resources Policy*, which is ranked with an *h*-index of 15 and a *g*-index of 29, thus having gradually a wider range of citations. It has been cited 850 times in 29 publications since 2021, proving that it is timely and has been widely cited by scholars in a relatively short time.

Other notable journals are *Sustainability* with an *h*-index of 13 and a *g*-index of 27, with 782 citations and 46 published articles since 2020, which is evidence of the significant contribution in the field spearheaded the discourse on sustainable development. *Journal of Cleaner Production* and *Environmental Science and*

Table 3.3. Source Analysis.

Source	*h*-index	*g*-index	*m*-index	TC	NP	PY-start
Renewable Energy	16	25	5.333	911	25	2022
Resources Policy	15	29	3.750	850	29	2021
Sustainability	13	27	2.600	782	46	2020
Journal of Cleaner Production	10	12	2.500	578	12	2021
Energy Economics	8	11	2.667	487	11	2022
Environmental Science and Pollution Research	9	21	2.250	462	36	2021
Finance Research Letters	1	2	0.167	365	2	2019
Energy Efficiency	1	1	0.333	241	1	2022
Economic Analysis and Policy	6	8	1.500	233	8	2021
Business Strategy and the Environment	5	6	0.833	225	6	2019

Source: Constructed based on Biblioshiny software.

Pollution Research also have high impact factors; they have an *h*-index of 10 and 9. *Journal of Cleaner Production* has 578 citations with 12 publications, and the *Environmental Science and Pollution Research* has 462 citations that include 36 publications, which showcase the increased usage of these novel journals in environmental research since their establishment in 2021.

This list of journals and their applicability reveal that tackling global sustainability has emerged as an intricate process requiring a multi-pronged strategy, which is good news for the growth of this essential scholarly niche.

Country Analysis

The country-wise bibliometric analysis of green finance and sustainable development shown in Table 3.4 depicts the effects of involvement and varying extent in global nation-states. China has the highest total publications and citations scores, with an average score of 19.3 citations per article. However, focussing specifically on the quantity of 556 published articles, it only revealed a moderate impact per article based on the average citations. However, Japan appears to have a notably low average, with only 31 publications across all categories but an average citation of 115. This indicated the prominence of Japanese-based research in this area but a lower output of articles.

This analysis underscores the diverse geographical contributions to green finance and sustainable development research. Countries like China and India are leading in volume, reflecting their significant academic and policy interest in sustainability issues. Meanwhile, nations such as Japan, Pakistan and Turkey, though producing fewer publications, are making highly influential contributions, as evidenced by their high average citations per article. This highlights the importance of quality and impact over sheer quantity in advancing the global discourse on

Table 3.4. Country Analysis.

Country	TP	TC	Average Article Citations
China	556	4,653	19.3
Japan	31	1,038	115.3
Pakistan	46	571	51.9
Turkey	7	268	67
India	34	220	18.3
United Kingdom	20	205	25.6
Australia	12	201	40.2
Vietnam	19	136	19.4
Indonesia	7	133	44.3
United States	31	64	12.8

Source: Constructed based on Biblioshiny software.

sustainability. The data also suggest the potential for increased collaboration and knowledge exchange between high-output countries and those with high-impact research, fostering a more integrated and practical global approach to addressing sustainability challenges.

Keyword Analysis

According to the applied keyword analysis of publications on green finance and sustainable development, it was established that some keywords are more essential in this research field and are interconnected (see Table 3.5). According to the Author Keyword frequency analysis results, the term 'Green Finance' is the most used keyword in this research area that is 266 occurrences. This could be because it is probably one of the central and most inclusive ideas here, encompassing many different types of financial strategies for promoting environmentalism. After this, the term 'sustainable development' is used 110 times to underline the

Table 3.5. Author Key Word Frequency Analysis.

Words	Occurrences
green finance	266
sustainable development	110
renewable energy	39
China	38
green bonds	26
sustainable finance	20
sustainability	16
green economy	15
sustainable development goals	15
climate change	14
bibliometric analysis	11
environmental sustainability	11
environmental regulation	10
financial development	10
carbon neutrality	9
energy efficiency	9
carbon emissions	8
COVID-19	8
ESG	8
green innovation	8

Source: Constructed based on Biblioshiny software.

latter's significance within the context. The fact that the term 'renewable energy' has been coined 39 times speaks about the sector's role in transitioning to cleaner models and proves the interest in the topic.

Thus, the keyword search analysis gives a coherent picture of the important clusters of topics related to the sphere of green finance and sustainable development. It emphasises the importance of financial instruments and the role of regulation in attaining sustainability, the works of such countries as China, and the persistence of the goals related to international sustainability. New concepts have emerged since the seminal documents' publication, suggesting that the field is constantly developing; the effect of relatively recent global events can also be observed in the current literature. Consequently, this analysis helps to emphasise that green finance and sustainable development involve more than one dimension – these comprise environmental, economic and social dimensions.

The word cloud analysis, the most frequently used keyword for green finance and sustainable development, depicts the most frequently used terms and concepts in this area of research (see Fig. 3.3). The term 'green finance' is noted most often; it is mentioned 266 times, expressing its subject significance. After that, the next most often used term is 'sustainable development', which occurred 110 times, showing the term's significant role in defining the research themes. Other mentioned terms were 'renewable energy' (39), 'China' (38) and 'green bonds' (26), which point to respondents' concerns with clean energy, purchases from China and the advances of sustainable bonds. Terms like 'sustainable finance', 'sustainability' and green finance 'green economy' point to the financial/economic strategy of the discourse, whereas 'climate change', 'environmental sustainability' and 'environmental regulation' highlight the financed/economic strategy of the discourse. The occurrence of 'carbon neutrality', 'energy efficiency' and 'carbon emissions' relates to certain tactics and results of sustainability endeavours. Also, using the term 'COVID-19' signals the effects of the pandemic on this sector. In general, cloud analysis can quickly reveal the key message of Green Finance and Sustainable Development (GFSD) research, which forms a broad and complex picture of the continuous development of the field.

Fig. 3.3. Word Cloud. *Source*: Constructed based on Biblioshiny software.

Thematic Analysis

The thematic map (Fig. 3.4) visually represents the major research themes within the dataset. The analysis and understanding of the interconnectedness of green finance and sustainable development keywords are also presented based on some leading or prominent clusters. Each cluster represents a distinct theme, with the size of the nodes indicating the frequency of keyword occurrences and the proximity of nodes representing the strength of their co-occurrence relationships. Seven clusters are identified in the thematic map and divided into four quadrants.

The top right-hand corner of the thematic map includes highly relevant and highly developed motor themes. This consists of two clusters, namely green finance and human capital; the largest and most dominant cluster, namely the 'green finance' cluster, contains an extensive range of terms, while the term 'green finance' itself was used 266 times, indicating its core importance within the scholarly literature (C. Z. Li & Umair, 2023; Rasoulinezhad & Taghizadeh-Hesary, 2022; Taghizadeh-Hesary & Yoshino, 2019). Indeed, this cluster consists of words like 'sustainable development', which is mentioned 110 times, 'renewable energy' 39, and 'China' 38, which reflect the presence of financial foundations to develop sustainable finance and the intensified Chinese involvement in the sphere. Other terms in this group include 'environmental regulation', 'carbon neutrality' and 'energy efficiency', which connect finance with various forms of regulation and/or certain environmental objectives.

The bottom right-hand corner of the thematic map includes highly relevant and low-developed themes, known as basic themes. This cluster includes green bonds and financial development. 'Green Bonds' where the key term 'Green Bonds' is used 26 times, and the betweenness centrality is 782 (Ilić et al., 2019;

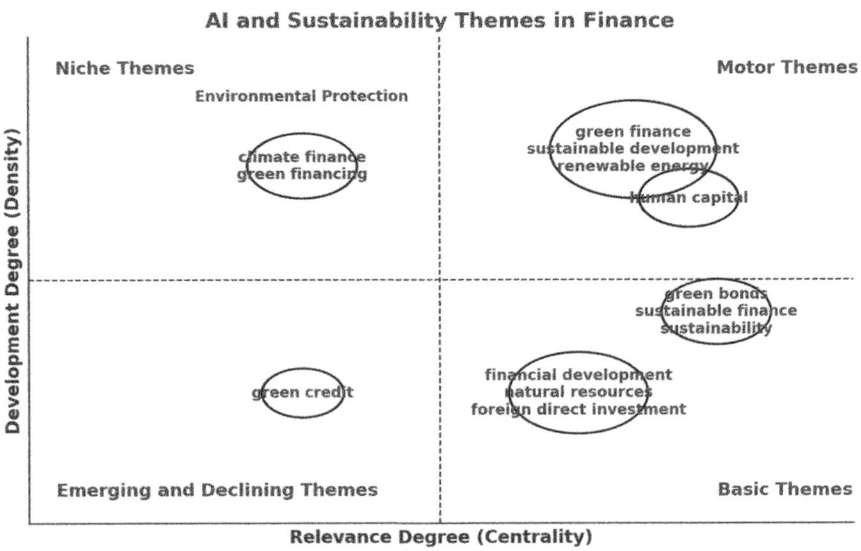

Fig. 3.4. Thematic Map. *Source*: Constructed based on Biblioshiny software.

Tolliver et al., 2021; Zioło et al., 2023). Some of the keywords belonging to this cluster include sustainable finance, sustainability and the green economy, where there are 20, 16 and 15 hits, respectively, and dramatically underlined the role of the financial tools for the support of sustainability initiatives. At the same time, the appearance of the phrases 'sustainable development goals' (15) and 'climate change' (14) within this cluster indicates the correspondence of green bond research to further general international sustainability initiatives and combating climate change. This cluster focusses on the role of green financial actions involving the manipulation of appropriate financial instruments to support the process of the internationalisation of sustainable development and combating global environmental issues.

The 'financial development' group includes such words as 'financial development' (10), 'natural resources' (7) and 'FDI' (6), suggesting the relations between financial progress and the use and management of non-renewable resources (Ibrahiem & Sameh, 2022).

The top left-hand corner of the thematic map includes low-relevant and highly developed niche themes. There are two clusters, namely environmental protection and climate finance. In the environmental protection cluster, there are phrases such as 'environmental protection' (5) and 'environmental pollution' (5), and it is set on the environmental aspect and regulation (Xu et al., 2023). Climate finance cluster includes climate financing and green financing (Y. Liu & Xia, 2023).

Bottom left-hand corner of the thematic map included low-relevant and low-developed themes, which are known as emergent or declined themes. This includes one cluster known as green credit (GC) (K. Zhang & Zhou, 2022).

Co-word Co-occurrence Analysis

The co-word occurrence analysis provided in Fig. 3.5 categorises different nodes (keywords) into clusters based on their interrelationships and significance in the dataset. Here's a summary of the key findings:

Cluster 1: Core Concepts in Green Finance and Sustainability

These are basic concepts consisting of 'green finance', 'renewable energy', 'sustainability', 'climate change' and 'environmental sustainability'. Among these, the node with the highest betweenness centrality is 'green finance', which, therefore, serves as the main connector. It is also worth mentioning that the word 'China' also belongs to this cluster since it concerns a country actively participating in discussions regarding green finance and sustainability (K. H. Wang et al., 2022).

Cluster 2: Current New Approaches and Technologies

Some of the key terms in this cluster are 'sustainable development', 'green bonds', 'sustainable finance', 'green economy' and 'carbon emissions'. The centrality of 'sustainable development' is very high, thus indicating that it is a bridge between many of the other terms. Other topics included in this cluster are also relatively

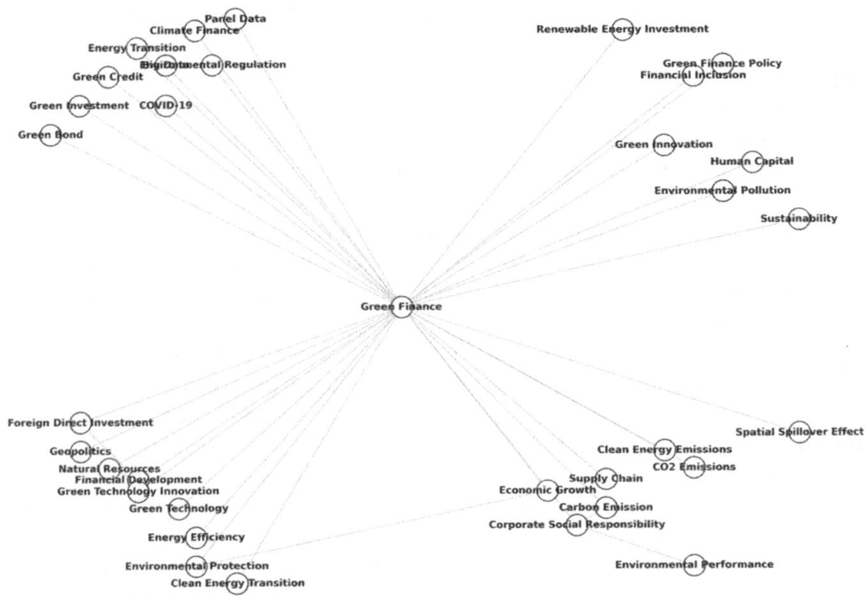

Fig. 3.5. Word Co-occurrence Network. *Source*: Constructed based on Biblioshiny software.

new and include 'COVID-19' and 'digital finance', which speaks about their increasing significance (Ilić et al., 2019; Tolliver et al., 2021; Zioło et al., 2023).

Cluster 3: Financial Mechanisms

This cluster is most focussed on financial aspects being 'green investment', 'GC' and 'financial development' nodes, implying the financial measures used to fund these GC (K. Zhang & Zhou, 2022).

Cluster 4: Natural Resources and Investments

Natural resources not only give property rights to investors but also invest in them.

It comprises two categories, one of which is 'natural resources', and the other one is 'foreign direct investment', stressing the connection between resource governance and investment movements. According to the calculations, the betweenness centrality of 'natural resources' is significant, pointing to its prominence in the green finance conversation. Research studies advise for enhancement of the national natural tax law, fostering green investment and environmentally conscious policies to keep check on carbon emissions (Qadri et al., 2023; Y. Shen et al., 2021).

Cluster 5: Spatial Dynamics

A number of words, such as 'spatial spill-over effect' and 'carbon emission', can be classified under this category, which suggests that the focus of green finance activities will be the geographical and environmental factors (Awamleh et al., 2025; Guo et al., 2022; Humbatova et al., 2024; Inder et al., 2022; Q. Li et al., 2024; Y. Wan et al., 2023).

Cluster 6: Policy and Regulation

The policy and regulation of the field focus on the formation and management of hydrogen-compatible power generation systems. 'Green finance policy' is the term in this cluster that provides significance to the regulatory concern in moving towards green finance. Green finance policies are the policies related to green finance that should seek to enhance the efficient achievement of new green solutions, support the advancement of green solutions, promote increased green capital investments, and lastly, maximise the possibility of green business transactions (Capasso et al., 2019; X. Liu et al., 2023; Z. Liu, Tang, et al., 2023; M. Shen et al., 2024).

Cluster 7: General Environmental Concerns

There is only one node in this cluster that is connected to the term 'Environment' hence, broader environmental issues (Q. Wan et al., 2022).

Cluster 8: Financial Constraints

'Limited funding' refers to the problems of obtaining capital for initiatives aimed at sustainability (Clark et al., 2018).

Cluster 9: Economic Growth

'Green economic growth' is the approach to the process of economic growth in which attempts are made to combine the economic aims with the environmental goals. Green Economic Growth (GEG) is generally considered to be 'an environmentally sustainable economic development method without damaging the environment and natural resources' (Z. Liu, Xu, et al., 2023, p. 1329).

Cluster 10: Analytical Methods

'DEA' (data envelopment analysis) is in favour of emphasising the assessment of efficiency of various green finance activities (Z. Liu, Xu, et al., 2023). The analysis reveals that 'green finance' is the most central concept, serving as a hub that connects various themes related to sustainability, technological innovation, financial mechanisms and policy regulations. Emerging trends like digital finance and the impact of COVID-19 also indicate the evolving landscape of green finance (Jain et al., 2023; Manta & Napoleon, 2017).

These clusters give a clear understanding of the various subfields and the thematic relationships within the green finance and sustainable development research field, revealing that this research domain is complex and interdisciplinary.

Trend Topics

Discussion of Trend Analysis in Environmentally Sustainable Aspect and Finance is depicted in Fig. 3.6. The analysis of the provided data gives certain trends in different spheres of research connected with environmental sustainability and finance. This way, each of the topics reveals the pattern of interest and activity in the given years and demonstrates the evolutionary character of sustainability consideration.

Investments

The topic of investments to sustainability was rather infrequent and most significantly discussed between 2019 and 2020. Even though this keyword only has a frequency rate of 3, the analysis shows that there is a keen emphasis on investments during this time, implying that certain incidences or studies must have provoked this topical discussion (Taghizadeh-Hesary & Yoshino, 2019). Sustainable investment is defined by the Global Sustainable Investment Review (2018) as the integration of environmental, social and governance (ESG) factors in investment decision-making (Alliance, 2019; Talan & Sharma, 2019). In other words, sustainability investments refer to the process of using funds to buy securities in projects or firms that embrace sustainable activities and are friendly to the environment. This supports the hypothesis that there is increasing concern about linking profitability with sustainable and ethical standards.

Low-carbon Economy

The low-carbon economy is considered as a slowly but constantly progressing research topic starting from the year 2018 with the expected peak in 2023. As

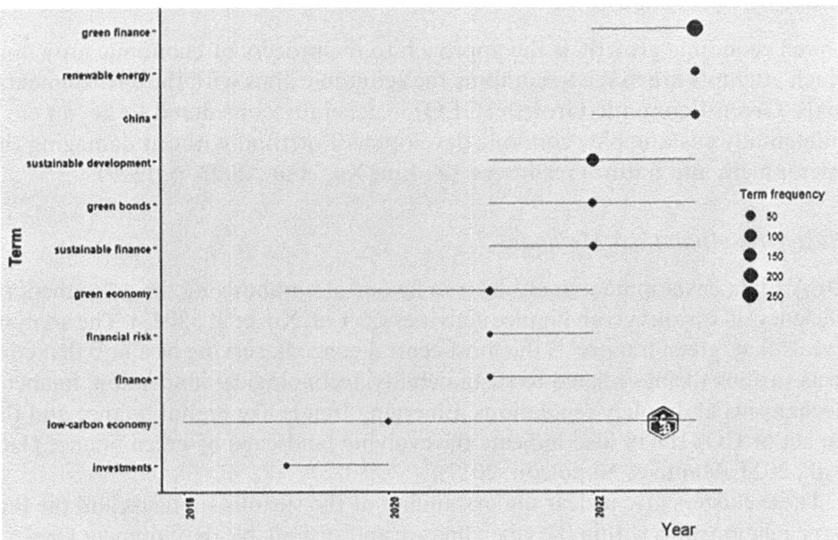

Fig. 3.6. Trend Topics. *Source*: Constructed based on Biblioshiny software.

with the previous topic, there is a consistent interest in this topic with a frequency of 6, which implies focus on the global efforts to lower carbon emission. The low-carbon economy includes concepts and measures intended to avoid the release of carbon dioxide into the atmosphere with regard to climate change issues and the availability of cleaner energy sources (Ramon Lugo-Morin & Bergman, 2021).

Green Economy

Concerning the green economy, aiming at promoting economic activity while reducing harm to the natural environment, its popularity increased between 2019 and 2022. Having a frequency of 15, this topic details times when fiscal strategies started to shift to sustainable practices. Green economy has been defined by UNEP (2011) as one that results in improved 'well-being and social equity, while significantly reducing environmental risks and ecological scarcities'. Green economy can be simply defined as being low-carbon, resource-efficient and socially inclusive (Loiseau et al., 2016; UNEP, 2011). Green economy entails activities that incorporate economic improvement with environmental conservation in order not to have any trade-off between development and protection of the environment.

Finance and Financial Risk

Over the course of the year, two subjects appeared in published research: general finance and financial risk related to sustainability, with both subjects reaching a frequency of 3 in the year 2022. Perhaps these topics received the attention of researchers due to the conditions prevailing in the market and the appearance of new types of financial instruments. Research in these areas studies the ways in which financial systems and risk management practices can instantiate sustainability principles while financial markets themselves are consistent with environmental objectives (Valaskova et al., 2018).

Sustainable Development

Sustainable development was the most frequently mentioned concept, used 110 times, and has been seamlessly integrated from January 2021 to December 2023. This high level of interest is well evidenced by the importance of formulating policies and researching sustainable long-term environmental goals (He & Yan, 2020). Sustainable development is defined by the Brundtland report as a 'development that meets the needs of the present without compromising the ability of future generations to meet their own needs' (World Commission on Environment and Development, 1987). Sustainable development is a process that helps people to live well and stay healthy without harming the ability of future generations to meet their needs and wants. This balances three major areas as the economy, society, and the environment.

Green Bonds

The frequency of green bonds, which are primarily project-establishment finance tools focussed on environmentally sustainable projects, rose from $2021 to $2023, with a frequency of 26. It emerged due to their increasing role as a means of financing sustainable development through areas such as the financing of renewable energy, green transportation, amongst other areas (Ilić et al., 2019; Tolliver et al., 2021; Zioło et al., 2023).

Sustainable Finance

ESG criteria embedded in the provision of any form of financial service used in making a business or investment decision from the field of sustainable finance has been detected from 2021 to 2023 with a frequency of 20. This trend deals with the consideration of sustainability in the decision-making of investments, particularly with a focus on financial returns that are sustainable and positive for the environment and society (Swiss Sustainable Finance, 2018).

Green Finance

Green finance emerged as more popular, with a total frequency of 266, and featured in emergentist trends in both 2022 and 2023. This study area deals with permanent and early maturity investments, especially in visible operations such as environmental and efficient carbon emission decrease, energy efficiency, and biodiversity (C. Z. Li & Umair, 2023; Rasoulinezhad & Taghizadeh-Hesary, 2022; Taghizadeh-Hesary & Yoshino, 2019). This clearly shows how important green finance is in facilitating the funding of projects that combat climate change and cases of environmental degradation.

Renewable Energy

As seen in the graph, renewable energy, which reached its highest frequency of 39 in 2023, represents the current efforts and developments towards the shift to renewable energy sources. This area of research comprises the utilisation of renewable energy where inventions such as wind, solar, hydro and other solutions are used to serve power needs to increase the use of fossil energy and render a negative impact on global climate change (Xiong & Dai, 2023; L. Zhang et al., 2022).

China's Role

The most frequently used source country is China, with a total of 38, which attracted attention in 2022 and was intensively discussed in 2023. China may receive a lot of attention due to its key role in shaping the global sustainable development agenda. Studies in this domain focus on the analysis of the policies of China with regard to the environment, green technology and innovation and their relevance to the sustainable development agenda (den Elzen et al., 2016; Z. X. Zhang, 2010).

The focus of the analysis also increases and develops various aspects of sustainability, especially in green finance, sustainable development and renewable energy sources. These trends indicate that more future research and developmental policy endeavours are likely to focus on the above areas, based on the premise that they are valuable tools in realising sustainable development objectives in different parts of the world. The focus on and growing interest in these topics demonstrate the states' intentions to implement sustainable development principles within economic and financial practices to meet the climate change and environmental crisis.

Critical Review of Literature

This section discusses the 10 highly cited documents published from 2007 to 2023, focussing on green finance and sustainable development research. Hence, Taghizadeh-Hesary and Yoshino (2019) researched the 'How to promote private initiative in green finance and investment'. Regarding the shortcomings that have been mentioned, the respondents felt that this study fills in those gaps by presenting two applied frameworks that fall under the theoretical frameworks of green finance and investment according to project size. The two theoretical frameworks were the Credit Guarantee Scheme, returning spill-over tax, distributed ledger technologies (DLTs) and social spending. The goal was to encourage non-state actors to invest in and finance green projects. They discovered that financial institutions and investors did not actively participate in the provision of green energy projects because they believed that investing in green energy would yield poorer returns than in other sources of energy and that it was an extremely risky enterprise. The model presented in this study includes credit guarantee schemes and spill-over effect return tax because of the large-scale green projects, such as large-scale solar farming and hydroelectric power. These measures are used to maximise the rate of return on these significant green projects while minimising high risks and fluctuations. The study showed how the organisation explained the integration of DLTs into the present hometown investment trust (HIT) structure in the context of its solar and wind energy green projects, particularly those deemed relatively small for HIT financing. As a result, the private sector was able to participate in green finance and investment with greater efficacy, accountability and openness about money. This was made possible by DLTs, which also managed and decreased risk. As was previously said, the model that was put up included every decision-related aspect of the investor's dilemma. The latter is that the HIT investors received a larger return because only projects with better prospects and credit scores that the assessors for HIT found acceptable were allowed to invest in the green funds. Hence, the involvement of the project assessor in the development of this scheme was quite pertinent.

Rasoulinezhad and Taghizadeh-Hesary (2022) studied the 'Role of green finance in improving energy efficiency and renewable energy development'. This study examined the relationship between CO_2 emissions, energy efficiency, the green energy index (GEI), and green finance among the 10 main providers of green finance using the regression influence on the Stochastic Impacts by Regression on Population, Affluence, and Technology (STIRPAT) model. Because of this, this study possesses the qualities listed below, which distinguish it from previous research in the following ways. Initially, the coefficients were computed using the green finance, green energy and energy efficiency causal models mentioned above. Second, it examined the global causal relationship between the factors concerning the leading proponents of green finance. Yes, there were advancements in the field of knowledge, but these were merely the fundamental results. The third section of the chapter examined the empirical model for the GEI, which included a variety of developed green energy resources that were analysed using the Principal Component Analysis (PCA) technique. Fourth, the STIRPAT approach was used to advance estimation, making it a prominent analysis method in energy economics that takes the environment into account. The study's result demonstrated that green bonds can be used to fund renewable energy initiatives and significantly lower CO_2 emissions. As a result, it might be claimed that these factors had little relationship in the short term throughout the same era. In light of this, governments must employ long-term policies to promote private sector participation in funding environmentally friendly initiatives that promote green energy and economic growth. This policy may have been relevant during and after the COVID-19 period when green projects were more tested in terms of financing.

C. Z. Li and Umair (2023) researched the 'Does green finance development goals affect renewable energy in China?'. This study investigated how green financing and renewable energy sources in China contributed to sustainable development. The given research used the method of panel cointegration and causality modelling to investigate the sources of renewable energy development in China from 2005 to 2020. The result portrayed how good it is to embrace green finance development and the role of the private sector in the development of local and global economies. Trademark registrations increased by 0.487% and financial development filings by 0.144% for every 1% increase in renewable energy sources. The degree of private sector participation increased by 0.032%, while trademarks and patents increased by 0.057%. With moderation made on investment, trade and human development, these relationships existed. Several robustness tests supported the findings. The study's empirical evidence provided policymakers and environmentalists with valuable insights for creating and implementing environmental projects with long-term financial advantages. This study also encountered challenges. Hence, the limitations of this study were as follows. First, it covered a number of publicly publicised energy enterprises, which restricted the scope for the acquisition of instances of a greater sample using enhanced data-gathering procedures. Second, it left out the sum of green finance investments and specified only three investment segments of renewable energy. Third, whereas the study evidenced that Green Governance has calming impacts, it failed to account for the natural resource exploration or the investment in green sources of energy, thus limiting generalisability. Thus, further work that would help alleviate these limitations will prove helpful in this discipline.

Furthermore, X. Wang and Wang (2021) examined the impact of green finance on the upgrading of China's regional industrial structure from the perspective of sustainable development. This article used the grey correlation model to systematically capture the relationship between China's green finance system and the evolution of industrial structure, based on data collected between the 2008 and 2020 fiscal years. In order to improve the industry's structure, the system Generalized Method of Moments (GMM) model was applied to test the degree and indications of green finance. The primary analytical variable for each province was the share of GC to Gross Domestic Product (GDP), which represents the scale of green finance, whereas the explanatory variable was industrial structure upgrading (IS1). The government expenditure level, served as the control in this study. Green finance was found to have the largest positive coefficient with the output value in the primary, secondary and tertiary industries, according to the statistics. In order to support the development of the quick expansion and the improvement of the industrial pattern, Chinese green finance accounted for the greatest percentage of the tertiary industry. Regression coefficients for human capital, R&D innovation capability, openness level, government spending, and urbanisation level were all positive univariately, suggesting that improving these variables has a significant positive influence on the modernisation of the industrial structure. An examination of the impact of green finance on the modernisation of the industrial structure revealed a significant regional disparity and centralisation, which represent the imbalances in the state. With statistically positive coefficients, the eastern region's parameter estimations were greater and significantly higher than those of the middle and western regions. Based on this, the study has reviewed the policy countermeasures for green finance, including fostering the establishment of green financial operations, enhancing foreign exchange and collaboration in the field of green finance, and enhancing the development of green technology innovation (GTI).

In addition to the above, Jiakui et al. (2023) conducted a study on 'Green technological innovation, green finance, and financial development and their role in green total factor productivity: Empirical insights from China'. This study is evaluated in light of the scope index of green finance development. Given that the industry dominates its financial sector, it examined how driving forces like green finance, financial development and GTI affected the green total factor productivity (GTFP) of 28 Chinese provinces between 2011 and 2021 using non-parametric DEA and the DEA-DDF (Data Envelopment Analysis-Directional Distance Function) method. The empirical findings showed that GTFP, green finance and financial development have increased, indicating a shift in economic activity towards a structure that is more inventive, efficient and sustainable. Second, there's no denying that with the rise in GTI, the green output increased. Third, financial development, GTI and green financing all had a greater overall and significant impact on green production; these effects were typically seen from the standpoint of provenance, where there was a higher degree of financial development and green finance. Last but not least, the sector's suitable application of environmentally friendly and sustainable practices strengthened green finance, GTI and financial development for green production. China's environmental and green finance agenda benefits from the policy implications of the empirical findings found in this study. One of the few early studies to link green finance, GTI and financial development for green technology into a literature study was this one. Still, a number of restrictions were applied. However, other factors were omitted, such as environmental regulations, technological advancements, foreign investment, and their relationships to GTFP. All of these should be taken into account in further research to build on them. Further developing the idea of green productivity and recovery measures would also be aided by broadening the research's scope in terms of time or geography, as well as by analysing the experiences of other nations, such as Sweden, Germany and the United States.

Moreover, Zahoor et al. (2022) conducted a study on 'Clean energy investment and financial development as determinants of environmental and sustainable economic growth: evidence from China'. This study validates the finding that investments in clean energy have a positive relationship with financial development for environmental sustainability and overall economic growth. It does this by analysing manufacturing value-added assessments and using urbanisation as a moderator for the entire 1970–2016 period. Long-term estimates for the empirical estimates are obtained using multiple regressions using completely modified least squares, dynamic least squares, resilient least squares and unit root tests of structural breaks. The findings showed that while supporting China's economic growth, investments in clean energy also decreased CO_2 emissions and the country's environmental impact. According to the analysis, China's degree of urbanisation and the focussed net worth enhancement of manufacturing had a positive possibility of having a beneficial impact on CO_2 release, the balance of ecological footprints and the growth of the country's economy. Additionally, this study, like previous studies of a similar nature, reaffirmed that investments in clean energy had a positive economic impact on the environment at the expense of industrial value addition, urbanisation, and financial development, on the other hand, had a negative impact on the environment.

Hafner et al. (2020) conducted research on 'Closing the green finance gap – A systems perspective'. Among the findings were policy studies designed to raise legislators' awareness of the challenges associated with increasing green investment in energy structures. Using a web search that provided guidance on what kind of keywords to use in the search engine, the policy reports were found. Furthermore, the subsequent standards were utilised to determine which policy papers should be included: Having been established in 2009, Written by groups comprising multiple stakeholders, either public or private, and published by an organisation based in a developed nation, provided that it made explicit reference to the obstacles facing large-scale investments in clean energy and infrastructure. In so far as policy uncertainty and the financial system's terrible short-termism rank among the main deterrents to investing, it further supported the findings. This indicates that it was determined that the barriers that were identified resulted in the development of a structure that incorporates non-linearity, lock-in and path dependency. Concerning the above suggestion, which calls for developing a policy discourse for the policy stream from a systems theory perspective and expanding or creating a sustainable investment vehicle as a more tenable short-term intervention while waiting to develop a long-term policy intervention from a systems theory point of view.

Madaleno et al. (2022) researched 'A step forward on sustainability: The nexus of environmental responsibility, green technology, clean energy, and green finance'. The objective of this work was to investigate the relationship between green technology, clean energy, green finance and environmental accountability using daily data from 31 July 2014 to 12 October 2021 and the core concept of a new symmetry test. Because the data were oscillating periodically, the adoption of this time-varying technique was both realistic and effective. Green finance, clean energy, environmental responsibility and green technology were found to have bi-causality, but not during the research time. During the COVID-19 era, all of these factors dropped and completely vanished. These findings were obtained using the recursive evolving and rolling window techniques. Furthermore, the causal association between green finance and clean energy was generally not very strong, with the exception of a few specific instances far from the figure, particularly during the start of COVID-19. However, the results of the variance and causality tests showed that although there were good outcomes as soon as clean energy was included in the study, the relationship between clean energy and green financing took a bit longer to develop. There was a clear demand for clean energy finance; therefore, green finance investment was initiated and scaled again. Consequently, the study raised the imperative of formulating and developing a more ambitious approach towards raising ecological engagement and green finance by funding green technology for smooth energy conversion and achieving sustainable development goals.

Tolliver et al. (2021) studied the 'Green Innovation and Finance in Asia'. Your new undetectable content: therefore, this article's purpose was to promote green innovation and finance as the primary markers of improved Sustainable Economy (SE) in the most developed Asian nations. As a result, the article has attempted to present and explore the most recent evolving strategies in China, Japan, South Korea and India, in addition to activities and developments at the company and national levels. In particular, it was believed that the trends in green patent registration were crucial to understanding how green innovation will affect sustainable development. In addition, two common green finance instruments, green bonds and green foreign direct investment, were used with general ESG transparency at the business level to assess the input component of numerous green supporting innovations for sustainable development. The study revealed which degree of green innovation and financing was increased to support Asia's growing need for a sustainable economy. There were increased rates of green patents as well as patent rights. Consistent growth rates were observed in green bond registrations in China, South Korea, Japan and other countries. Since the middle of the 1980s, Japan has been one of the countries that file for patents on environmentally sound technologies the most frequently. China and South Korea have also been working to improve pollution-related green patents to meet the market need for environmentally safe products. These increases may primarily be attributed to government measures that demonstrated how these encouraged such initiatives. More institutions have recently begun to issue green bonds; since 2015, China has issued most of these bonds, with development banks and major financial businesses in South Korea and Japan still issuing them. However, compared to

Western nations, even Asian nations like South Korea and Japan appeared to have drawn less green foreign direct investment. Furthermore, China and South Korea saw a greater rise in environmentally adjusted multifactor production than the industrialised nations. Thus, in the sampled nations of China, South Korea and Japan, the majority of large-revenue enterprises showed a positive correlation between their revenue growth and the publication of ESG information. The findings of this study pave the way for future scholars to investigate green innovation and finance in Asia and around the world. Other studies may have looked into the relationship between firm success in developing Asian economies and the sharing of ESG information, even without future data. Furthermore, the study may have focussed on the investment's success by, for example, figuring out the ESG rating of certain companies, given the abundance of information available on green bonds and foreign direct investment.

D. Zhang et al. (2022) explored 'Does green finance counteract the climate change mitigation: Asymmetric effect of renewable energy investment and R&D'. To investigate the hypothesis on the contribution of digital and green finance to environmental protection, the authors report that they used quantitative regression analysis with data analysis on the economies of the G20 countries in the financial years 2008–2018. Given the formulation of the primary research question about the relationship between the use of Renewable Energy (RE), green funding, and carbon emissions, quantile regression was used for regularity analysis. Along with energy consumption and trade, GDP, R&D and Foreign Direct Investment (FDI) were employed to refine the results and construct statistical controls. In general, CO_2 emissions were decreased by green finance, investments in renewable energy and technological improvement; nevertheless, certain variables like trade, FDI, energy use and economic growth raised CO_2 emissions. The analysis led the authors to suggest the following measures that policymakers can take to further green financing, financial digitisation and the development of the carbon trading market. The explanation went into detail on how access to renewable energy consumption could reduce environmental pollution, with the primary drawback being the expense associated with producing renewable energy. Regarding the authors' recommendations, they advised that for future work, more effort should be devoted to the advancement of more methods for constructing green financial measures.

Conclusion

This bibliometric analysis has helped in scanning the existing literature and gaining an exhaustive and concise idea about the research domain of Green Finance and Sustainable Development. Thus, it provides a meaningful understanding of academic discussions' development and current state in the given field by analysing trends, seminal works and developing themes.

The trend analysis shows that the number of publications related to green finance and sustainable development increased dramatically between 2007 and 2023. The first years of publication were characterised by fluctuating rhythms, probably due to the area's development stage. Specifically, the number of publications increased starting in 2017, though a steeper rise is observed from 2019. This peak illustrates the increasing trend of globalisation because of environmental conservation, policies and academic interest issues. Some well-recognised authors like Taghizadeh-Hesary F and Abbas J are also involved in the work, clearly showing their *h*-index value and citation counts. These are the key authors working in the field regarding the issue and bearing the works of Yoshino N and Najam H. The most productive and cited journals that belong to this area are *Renewable Energy*, *Resources Policy* and *Sustainability*. China has become the leading country due to the frequency of publications. However, there are other countries like Japan, Pakistan and Turkey where there are fewer publication outputs, but the many citations per article prove the countries' prominence in their research. The variations in geographical inputs are evidence of the international focus of research on green finance and sustainable development with regard to the inputs of both advanced and developing countries. Many keywords are identified in the keyword location analysis, but two major subjects can be extracted: 'Green Finance' and 'Sustainable Development'. Meanwhile, the other frequently used terms are 'renewable energy', 'China' and 'green bonds' as the field has multiple aspects.

The findings indicate several avenues for future research. The findings indicate several avenues for future research. Due to the interaction and interlinkage between green finance and sustainable development, interdisciplinary research that entails environmental science, economics, and policy is crucial. The topics such as 'carbon neutrality', 'energy efficiency' and 'COVID-19 effect on sustainability' trends have emerged. Subsequent research should advance in these areas to conform to fresh global issues. More research should be conducted from such regions as this will bring more diverse approaches to sustainability. Country cooperation can help magnify the knowledge sharing and development of new ideas. In addition, there is room for future research on green finance linked with digitalisation to achieve sustainable development. Thus, research is needed into the role and implications of green bonds and other sustainable finance instruments for increasing the effectiveness of sustainable goals. Further research should be conducted concerning green finance, sustainability and financial literacy in the framework wherein the improvement of the level of financial literacy helps the advancement of sustainable investment practices and, subsequently, the advancement of green finance initiatives (Thilakarathna & Rajakaruna, 2022).

Finally, this bibliometric analysis reveals that research in green finance with a focus on sustainable development is continually expanding and rapidly developing. More publications, more representations of authors and countries, and dissimilar thematic focus areas prove that this field has been playing a critical role in solving sustainability issues worldwide.

The study is important to policymakers, especially in identifying major trends in research areas of interest to formulate relevant policies supporting environmental conservation. The study identifies these trends in achieving the goal, enabling proper resource management and addressing the major environmental problems. Also, it strengthens interdisciplinarity among the researchers by connecting scholars and linking up different fields, enhancing innovations in the quest to attain sustainable development goals. It builds on and strengthens the notions of synergy that exist in singular studies and encourages detailed and creative ways of solving myriad environmental problems.

References

Afzal, A., Rasoulinezhad, E., & Malik, Z. (2022). Green finance and sustainable development in Europe. *Economic Research/Ekonomska Istrazivanja*, *35*(1), 5150–5163. https://doi.org/10.1080/1331677X.2021.2024081

Akomea-Frimpong, I., Adeabah, D., Ofosu, D., & Tenakwah, E. J. (2022). A review of studies on green finance of banks, research gaps and future directions. *Journal of Sustainable Finance and Investment*, *12*(4), 1241–1264. https://doi.org/10.1080/20430795.2020.1870202

Alliance, G. (2019). *Global sustainable investment review* 2018. https://apo.org.au/node/228331

Amarathunga, B., Khatibi, A., & Talib, Z. M. (2024). Work readiness and trending avenues for future studies: A systematic literature review and bibliometric analysis. *Higher Education, Skills and Work-Based Learning*, *14*(5), 1087–1105. https://doi.org/10.1108/HESWBL-10-2023-0280

Awamleh, F. T., Shwawreh, S., Al-Kharabsheh, S. A. I., & Alzghoul, A. (2025). The integration of renewable energy adoption in sustainability practices for sustainable competitive advantage in Jordanian SMEs. *Challenges in Sustainability*, *13*(1), 135–145.

Bilal, B., Hysa, E., Akbar, A., Yasmin, F., Ur Rahman, A., & Li, S. (2022). Virtual learning during the COVID-19 pandemic: A bibliometric review and future research agenda. *Risk Management and Healthcare Policy*, *15*, 1353–1368. https://doi.org/10.2147/RMHP.S355895

Bouyssou, D., & Marchant, T. (2011). Ranking scientists and departments in a consistent manner. *Journal of the American Society for Information Science and Technology*, *62*, 1761–1769. https://doi.org/10.1002/asi

Brookes, B. C. (1977). Theory of the Bradford law. *Journal of Documentation*, *33*(3), 180–209. https://doi.org/10.1108/EB026641

Capasso, M., Hansen, T., Heiberg, J., Klitkou, A., & Steen, M. (2019). Green growth – A synthesis of scientific findings. *Technological Forecasting and Social Change*, *146*, 390–402. https://doi.org/10.1016/J.TECHFORE.2019.06.013

Clark, R., Reed, J., & Sunderland, T. (2018). Bridging funding gaps for climate and sustainable development: Pitfalls, progress and potential of private finance. *Land Use Policy*, *71*, 335–346. https://doi.org/10.1016/J.LANDUSEPOL.2017.12.013

Daly, H. E. (2006). Sustainable development – Definitions, principles, policies. In M. Keiner (Ed.), *The future of sustainability* (pp. 39–53). Springer. https://doi.org/10.1007/1-4020-4908-0_2

De Bakker, F. G. A., Groenewegen, P., & Den Hond, F. (2005). A bibliometric analysis of 30 years of research and theory on corporate social responsibility and corporate social performance. *Business and Society*, *44*(3), 283–317. https://doi.org/10.1177/0007650305278086

den Elzen, M., Fekete, H., Höhne, N., Admiraal, A., Forsell, N., Hof, A. F., Olivier, J. G. J., Roelfsema, M., & van Soest, H. (2016). Greenhouse gas emissions from current and enhanced policies of China until 2030: Can emissions peak before 2030? *Energy Policy*, *89*, 224–236. https://doi.org/10.1016/J.ENPOL.2015.11.030

Dissanayake, H., Dissabandara, D., Perera, K., & Ajward, A. R. (2023). Research trends in corporate governance index: A bibliometric analysis. *IUP Journal of Corporate Governance*, *22*(1), Article 5.

Dissanayake, H., Iddagoda, A., & Popescu, C. (2022). Entrepreneurial education at universities: A bibliometric analysis. *Administrative Sciences*, *12*(4), Article 185. https://doi.org/10.3390/ADMSCI12040185

Durieux, V., & Gevenois, P. A. (2010). Bibliometric indicators: Quality measurements of scientific publication. *Radiology*, *255*(2), 342–351. https://doi.org/10.1148/radiol.09090626

Garfield, E. (1955). Citation indexes for science. *Science*, *122*(3159), 108–111. https://doi.org/10.1126/SCIENCE.122.3159.108

Guo, C. Q., Wang, X., Cao, D. D., & Hou, Y. G. (2022). The impact of green finance on carbon emission – Analysis based on mediation effect and spatial effect. *Frontiers in Environmental Science*, *10*, Article 844988. https://doi.org/10.3389/FENVS.2022.844988/BIBTEX

Hafner, S., Jones, A., Anger-Kraavi, A., & Pohl, J. (2020). Closing the green finance gap – A systems perspective. *Environmental Innovation and Societal Transitions*, *34*, 26–60. https://doi.org/10.1016/j.eist.2019.11.007

He, C., & Yan, G. (2020). Path selections for sustainable development of green finance in developed coastal areas of China. *Journal of Coastal Research*, *104*(SI), 77–81. https://doi.org/10.2112/JCR-SI104-014.1

Hoang, Y. H., Cương, L. N. K., Hà, N. T. T., Thư, L. P. K., Thư, V. A., & Yến, L. K. (2023). Green finance in banking industry: A systematic literature review using bibliometric analysis. In *Proceedings of the 11th international conference on emerging challenges: Smart business and digital economy 2023 – ICECH 2023*. Atlantis Press International BV. https://doi.org/10.2991/978-94-6463-348-1_18

Humbatova, S., Foziljonov, I., & Panahova, G. (2024). Corporate carbon footprint: Evaluating environmental risks and incentives in the era of climate finance. *Journal of Environmental Assessment Policy and Management*. https://doi.org/10.1142/S1464333224500121

Ibrahiem, D. M., & Sameh, R. (2022). Financial development and natural resources nexus in Egypt: The role of clean energy sources and foreign direct investment. *International Journal of Energy Sector Management*, *16*(4), 680–703. https://doi.org/10.1108/IJESM-04-2021-0003

Ilić, B., Stojanovic, D., Djukic, G., Ilić, B., Stojanovic, D., & Djukic, G. (2019). Green economy: Mobilization of international capital for financing projects of renewable energy sources. *Green Finance*, *1*(2), 94–109. https://doi.org/10.3934/GF.2019.2.94

Inder, S., Sood, K., & Grima, S. (2022). Antecedents of behavioural intention to adopt internet banking using structural equation modelling. *Journal of Risk and Financial Management*, *15*(4), Article 157.

Jain, R., Kumar, S., Sood, K., Grima, S., & Rupeika-Apoga, R. (2023). A systematic literature review of the risk landscape in Fintech. *Risks 2023*, 11(2), Article 36. https://doi.org/10.3390/RISKS11020036

Jiakui, C., Abbas, J., Najam, H., Liu, J., & Abbas, J. (2023). Green technological innovation, green finance, and financial development and their role in green total factor productivity: Empirical insights from China. *Journal of Cleaner Production*, *382*, Article 135131. https://doi.org/10.1016/j.jclepro.2022.135131

Krastev, B., & Krasteva-Hristova, R. (2024). Challenges and trends in green finance in the context of sustainable development – A bibliometric analysis. *Journal of Risk and Financial Management*, *17*(7), Article 301. https://doi.org/10.20944/preprints202406.0232.v1

Li, C. Z., & Umair, M. (2023). Does green finance development goals affects renewable energy in China. *Renewable Energy*, *203*, 898–905. https://doi.org/10.1016/J.RENENE.2022.12.066

Li, Q., Wu, H., Zhang, B. Q., Dong, Z. H., & Ling, T. (2024). Safety system study of gas stations based on preliminary hazard analysis and fault tree analysis. *Journal of Engineering Management and Systems Engineering*, *3*(3), 149-163.

Liu, X., Zhao, T., & Li, R. (2023). Studying the green economic growth with clean energy and green finance: The role of financial policy. *Renewable Energy*, *215*, Article 118971. https://doi.org/10.1016/J.RENENE.2023.118971

Liu, Y., & Xia, L. (2023). Evaluating low-carbon economic peer effects of green finance and ICT for sustainable development: A Chinese perspective. *Environmental Science and Pollution Research*, *30*(11), 30430–30443. https://doi.org/10.1007/S11356-022-24234-8/TABLES/7

Liu, Z., Tang, Y., Wilson, J., Tao, X., Lv, B., Wang, Z., Xu, Y., Zhang, Z., Zhang, Y., & Zhao, W. (2023). Influence of government attention on environmental quality: An analysis of 30 provinces in China. *Environmental Impact Assessment Review*, *100*, Article 107084. https://doi.org/10.1016/J.EIAR.2023.107084

Liu, Z., Xu, J., Wei, Y., Hatab, A. A., & Lan, J. (2023). Nexus between green financing, renewable energy generation, and energy efficiency: Empirical insights through DEA technique. *Environmental Science and Pollution Research*, *30*(22), 61290–61303. https://doi.org/10.1007/S11356-021-17092-3/FIGURES/4

Loiseau, E., Saikku, L., Antikainen, R., Droste, N., Hansjürgens, B., Pitkänen, K., Leskinen, P., Kuikman, P., & Thomsen, M. (2016). Green economy and related concepts: An overview. *Journal of Cleaner Production*, *139*, 361–371. https://doi.org/10.1016/J.JCLEPRO.2016.08.024

Lotka, A. J. (1926). The frequency distribution of scientific productivity. *Journal of the Washington Academy of Sciences*, *16*(12), 317–323.

Madaleno, M., Dogan, E., & Taskin, D. (2022). A step forward on sustainability: The nexus of environmental responsibility, green technology, clean energy and green finance. *Energy Economics*, *109*, Article 105945. https://doi.org/10.1016/j.eneco.2022.105945

Manta, O., & Napoleon, P. (2017). The virtual currency and financial blockchain technology. Current trends in digital finance. *Studii Financiare (Financial Studies), Centre of Financial and Monetary Research "Victor Slavescu"*, *21*(3), 45–49. https://openurl.ebsco.com/EPDB%3Agcd%3A3%3A10779795/detailv2?sid=ebsco%3Aplink%3Ascholar&id=ebsco%3Agcd%3A126014924&crl=c

Mashari, D. P. S., Zagloel, T. Y. M., Soesilo, T. E. B., & Maftuchah, I. (2023). A bibliometric and literature review: Alignment of green finance and carbon trading. *Sustainability (Switzerland)*, *15*(10), Article 7877. https://doi.org/10.3390/su15107877

Page, M. J., McKenzie, J. E., Bossuyt, P. M., Boutron, I., Hoffmann, T. C., Mulrow, C. D., Shamseer, L., Tetzlaff, J. M., Akl, E. A., Brennan, S. E., Chou, R., Glanville, J., Grimshaw, J. M., Hróbjartsson, A., Lalu, M. M., Li, T., Loder, E. W., Mayo-Wilson, E., McDonald, S., … Moher, D. (2021). The PRISMA 2020 statement: An updated guideline for reporting systematic reviews. *The BMJ*, *372*, Article N71. https://doi.org/10.1136/BMJ.N71

Pranckutė, R. (2021). Scopus and Web of Science stands out for systematic reviews, offering comprehensive coverage across disciplines, including journals, conferences, and patents. *Publications*, *9*(1), Article 12.

Qadri, S. U., Shi, X., Rahman, S. ur, Anees, A., Ali, M. S. E., Brancu, L., & Nayel, A. N. (2023). Green finance and foreign direct investment–environmental sustainability nexuses in emerging countries: New insights from the environmental Kuznets curve. *Frontiers in Environmental Science*, *11*, Article 1074713. https://doi.org/10.3389/FENVS.2023.1074713/BIBTEX

Rahman, M. H., Rahman, J., Tanchangya, T., & Esquivias, M. A. (2023). Green banking initiatives and sustainability: A comparative analysis between Bangladesh and India. *Research in Globalization*, *7*(August), Article 100184. https://doi.org/10.1016/j.resglo.2023.100184

Ramon Lugo-Morin, D., & Bergman, M. (2021). Global future: Low-carbon economy or high-carbon economy? *World 2021*, 2(2), 175–193. https://doi.org/10.3390/WORLD2020012

Rasoulinezhad, E., & Taghizadeh-Hesary, F. (2022). Role of green finance in improving energy efficiency and renewable energy development. *Energy Efficiency*, *15*(2), 1–12. https://doi.org/10.1007/S12053-022-10021-4/TABLES/11

Schotten, M., el Aisati, M., Meester, W. J. N., Steiginga, S., & Ross, C. A. (2017). A brief history of Scopus: The world's largest abstract and citation database of scientific literature. In F. J. Cantu-Ortiz (Ed.), *Research analytics* (pp. 31–58). Auerbach Publications. https://doi.org/10.1201/9781315155890-3

Shen, M., Ma, N., & Chen, Q. (2024). Has green finance policy promoted ecologically sustainable development under the constraints of government environmental attention? *Journal of Cleaner Production*, *450*, Article 141854. https://doi.org/10.1016/J.JCLEPRO.2024.141854

Shen, Y., Su, Z. W., Malik, M. Y., Umar, M., Khan, Z., & Khan, M. (2021). Does green investment, financial development and natural resources rent limit carbon emissions? A provincial panel analysis of China. *Science of the Total Environment*, *755*, Article 142538. https://doi.org/10.1016/J.SCITOTENV.2020.142538

Swiss Sustainable Finance. (2018). *What is sustainable finance?* https://www.jstor.org/stable/pdf/resrep22000.4.pdf

Taghizadeh-Hesary, F., & Yoshino, N. (2019). The way to induce private participation in green finance and investment. *Finance Research Letters*, *31*, 98–103. https://doi.org/10.1016/J.FRL.2019.04.016

Talan, G., & Sharma, G. D. (2019). Doing well by doing good: A systematic review and research agenda for sustainable investment. *Sustainability 2019*, *11*(2), Article 353. https://doi.org/10.3390/SU11020353

Thilakarathna, M. D. N., & Rajakaruna, G. K. N. P. (2022, November 10). Impact of financial literacy on investment decisions of individual investors in the Colombo stock exchange. In *8th Symposium of Accountancy and Finance Research (SACFIRE 2022)* (pp. 16–20). Department of Accountancy, Faculty of Business Studies and Finance, Wayamba University of Sri Lanka.

Tolliver, C., Fujii, H., Keeley, A. R., & Managi, S. (2021). Green innovation and finance in Asia. *Asian Economic Policy Review*, *16*(1), 67–87. https://doi.org/10.1111/AEPR.12320

UNEP. (2011). *Towards a green economy: Pathways to sustainable development and poverty eradication*. Sustainable Development Knowledge Platform. https://sustainabledevelopment.un.org/index.php?page=view&type=400&nr=126&menu=35

Valaskova, K., Kliestik, T., Svabova, L., & Adamko, P. (2018). Financial risk measurement and prediction modelling for sustainable development of business entities using regression analysis. *Sustainability 2018*, *10*(7), Article 2144. https://doi.org/10.3390/SU10072144

Wan, Q., Miao, X., & Afshan, S. (2022). Dynamic effects of natural resource abundance, green financing, and government environmental concerns toward the sustainable environment in China. *Resources Policy*, *79*, Article 102954. https://doi.org/10.1016/J.RESOURPOL.2022.102954

Wan, Y., Sheng, N., Wei, X., & Su, H. (2023). Study on the spatial spillover effect and path mechanism of green finance development on China's energy structure transformation. *Journal of Cleaner Production*, *415*, Article 137820. https://doi.org/10.1016/J.JCLEPRO.2023.137820

Wang, K. H., Zhao, Y. X., Jiang, C. F., & Li, Z. Z. (2022). Does green finance inspire sustainable development? Evidence from a global perspective. *Economic Analysis and Policy*, *75*, 412–426. https://doi.org/10.1016/J.EAP.2022.06.002

Wang, X., & Wang, Q. (2021). Research on the impact of green finance on the upgrading of China's regional industrial structure from the perspective of sustainable development. *Resources Policy*, *74*, Article 102436. https://doi.org/10.1016/j.resourpol.2021.102436

World Commission on Environment and Development. (1987). *Our common future*. Springer Netherlands. https://doi.org/10.1007/978-94-007-0753-5_441

Xiong, Y., & Dai, L. (2023). Does green finance investment impact on sustainable development: Role of technological innovation and renewable energy. *Renewable Energy*, *214*, 342–349. https://doi.org/10.1016/J.RENENE.2023.06.002

Xu, L., Liu, Y., Zhang, B., & Xiang, B. (2023). Study on the impact of green finance on low carbon development of manufacturing industry from the perspective of multidimensional space: Evidence from China. *Environmental Science and Pollution Research*, *30*(17), 50772–50782. https://doi.org/10.1007/S11356-023-25690-6/METRICS

Zahoor, Z., Khan, I., & Hou, F. (2022). Clean energy investment and financial development as determinants of environment and sustainable economic growth: Evidence from China. *Environmental Science and Pollution Research*, *29*(11), 16006–16016. https://doi.org/10.1007/s11356-021-16832-9

Zhang, D., Mohsin, M., & Taghizadeh-Hesary, F. (2022). Does green finance counteract the climate change mitigation: Asymmetric effect of renewable energy investment and R&D. *Energy Economics*, *113*(June), Article 106183. https://doi.org/10.1016/j.eneco.2022.106183

Zhang, D., Zhang, Z., & Managi, S. (2019). A bibliometric analysis on green finance: Current status, development, and future directions. *Finance Research Letters*, *29*, 425–430. https://doi.org/10.1016/j.frl.2019.02.003

Zhang, K., & Zhou, X. (2022). Is promoting green finance in line with the long-term market mechanism? The perspective of Chinese commercial banks. *Mathematics* 2022, *10*(9), Article 1374. https://doi.org/10.3390/MATH10091374

Zhang, L., Berk Saydaliev, H., & Ma, X. (2022). Does green finance investment and technological innovation improve renewable energy efficiency and sustainable development goals. *Renewable Energy*, *193*, 991–1000. https://doi.org/10.1016/J.RENENE.2022.04.161

Zhang, Y., Jiang, Y., Chen, D., & Zhang, C. (2024). Literature review on the impact of green finance on high-quality economic development. *Advances in Economics and Management Research*, *10*(1), Article 65. https://doi.org/10.56028/aemr.10.1.65.2024

Zhang, Z. X. (2010). China in the transition to a low-carbon economy. *Energy Policy*, *38*(11), 6638–6653. https://doi.org/10.1016/J.ENPOL.2010.06.034

Zioło, M., Bąk, I., Spoz, A., Oesterreich, M., Niedzielski, P., & Raczkowski, K. (2023). Relationship between sustainable development and financial development from the perspective of the European green economy. Fuzzy approach. *Frontiers in Environmental Science*, *11*, Article 1244119. https://doi.org/10.3389/FENVS.2023.1244119/BIBTEX

Chapter 4

The Role of Technology, AI, ML and DLT in Sustainable Finance and a Green Economy

Kushtrim Gashi and Luan Vardari

University "Ukshin Hoti" Prizren, Republic of Kosovo

Abstract

Purpose: The purpose of this research is to explore how new technologies, such as DLT (distributed ledger technology), ML (machine learning) and AI (artificial intelligence), can support green economic growth and sustainable finance.

Need for the study: Awareness of environmental challenges highlights the importance of using technology to support and promote sustainable financial practices. Therefore, this study, among other things, aims to explore this importance by analysing how AI, ML and DLT can contribute to continuously improving innovation and efficiency in various sustainable finance projects.

Methodology: This study uses a literature review technique to examine technology use, sustainable finance, and the transition to a sustainable economy. To achieve this goal, qualitative interviews were conducted with professionals in the fields of sustainability, technology and finance to explore different practices and identify different strategies for developing the future of the finance industry.

Findings: Based on the findings of previous studies, AI, ML and DLT play an important role in improving risk management, increasing transparency and simplifying procedures that serve to make decisions in the sustainable finance sector. The transformation to a green and sustainable economy can be more straightforward if it relies on the ability of these important technologies to

Sustainable Development and Green Innovation: Managing Risk through Interdisciplinary Approaches and Policy Strategies, 67–89

Published under exclusive licence by Emerald Publishing Limited
doi:10.1108/978-1-83608-462-420251004

incorporate some ESG (environmental, social and governance) considerations into organisations' plans for potential investments.

Practical implications: The study's findings will help software developers, financial institutions and policymakers promote and strengthen sustainable development. Furthermore, the use of technology, especially advances in AI, ML and DLT, offers various valuable perspectives for those engaged in the transition to more environmentally friendly financial practices, contributing to creating a more sustainable global economy.

Keywords: Sustainable finance; technology adoption; artificial intelligence; machine learning; distributed ledger technology; green economy; environmental, social and governance

JEL codes: Q58; G32; G23; O32

Introduction

Since various studies are needed to address several environmental challenges to promote economic growth, the close connection between technology and sustainable finance has recently attracted much attention from studies in this field. Sustainable finance, which includes ESG factors in financial decision-making processes, is considered a fundamental basis for aligning financial operations with long-term environmental sustainability objectives (United Nations Environment Programme Finance Initiative [UNEP FI], 2018). In addition to other advantages, emerging technologies such as AI, ML and DLT provide modern tools and techniques that help improve and develop financial procedures and help make valuable organisational decisions in general (Demirkan & Delen, 2013; Zhou, 2021). Numerous studies in this field, which have been developed by explicitly evaluating the valuable effects of these technologies on the growth and development of sustainable finance and the green economy in general, underline the importance of these technologies in many directions. For example, the study by Zhou (2022) supports this impact, according to which the effective use of digital finance, among others, is very closely linked to technological advances, as it is considered to help promote economic development in general, but in particular helps in the development and advancement of the green economy and sustainable development, among others. Tang et al. (2023) also supports this influence, stating that he sees digital banking as a key component that promotes green and sustainable practices and as a solution to various financial issues.

On the other hand, according to Zhou (2022), digital money and technological advances promote economic growth, green economy and sustainable development. According to Tang et al. (2023), digital finance promotes business innovation in green technologies and thus helps to overcome various financial constraints. Han et al. (2023) also emphasises the importance of digital finance in increasing the efficiency of green development, especially in developed countries.

In addition, according to Fan et al. (2023), AI and Deep Learning (DL) can improve sustainability in areas such as renewable energy, environment and health and energy management in various buildings. These and many other studies from the field of finance highlight the transformative importance of these technologies in promoting and developing sustainable finance and a green economy.

Although many studies acknowledge the transformative potential of these technologies, a complete and empirically based exploration of the true potential of these technologies is still lacking. Thus, through an in-depth analysis of academic studies and industry reports, an overview of the current state of the transformative potential of these technologies is provided, where, among other things, trends and various reviews are identified that encourage new models for more profound research in this field. Among the studies that highlight the potential of these technologies is the study developed by Puschmann and Leifer (2020), according to which the integration of technology in green finance has significant transformative potential in the way financial institutions assess and overcome risks, allocate capital and direct their investments from environmental projects (Puschmann & Leifer, 2020). Furthermore, technologies such as AI and ML enable the analysis of large amounts of data, identifying new patterns and predicting trends with high accuracy (Bosshardt, 2019). Furthermore, DLT offers highly secure and transparent transactions, increasing accountability and trust in many financial institutions (Lacity & Hansen, 2018). All of these aforementioned innovations, among others, have great potential to improve and develop the operations of organisations, especially in reducing costs, which contributes to increasing financial sustainability (Habisch et al., 2019).

Background of Study

In recent years, societies have paid great attention to the field of sustainable finance development and the great potential that technology is considered to have in this field as they continue to face various challenging environmental issues and constantly seek new ways to balance environmental conservation with economic growth (UNEP FI, 2018). According to Clark et al. (2015), this new strategy is crucial in incorporating ESG considerations into the decision-making process for sustainable investments, as the development of the green economy is greatly aided by technological advances such as AI, ML and DLT. Furthermore, banking and insurance organisations continue to widely and effectively use multimedia technologies, especially audio, visual and other animated films, which are greatly helping the development of these industries (Vardari et al., 2023). Introducing new digital solutions has become easier and more feasible due to these technologies' significant contributions, especially to financial inclusion and organisational efficiency. Deloitte (2020) claims that these developments in AI, ML and DLT encourage innovation in the financial industry. Large volumes of data, for example, can be examined using AI and ML algorithms, finding different patterns to more accurately predict future trends in this field (Bosshardt, 2019). However, blockchain provides very secure platforms for developing these financial transactions, which helps improve accountability and build trust in many financial institutions (Lacity & Hansen, 2018). Among other things, it has been seen as very important to understand the background and current conditions of these financial and technical advancements as it is considered to create opportunities to facilitate the exploration of new approaches and the role that technology plays in the growth and development of sustainable finance. According to Habisch et al. (2019), opportunities can be created for developing financial systems and new approaches for developing innovations of these technologies that help direct potential investments from various environmental projects by harmonising sustainable finance with technology together. Moreover, this procedure continuously faces many challenges, including complicated legislation, privacy concerns and other technological barriers (Demirkan & Delen, 2013).

Objectives of Study

This research aims to investigate how AI, ML and DLT technologies can support sustainable finance and the growth of a green economy by examining and evaluating data from previous research. Another objective is to review the current status of sustainable finance and identify the most important current problems and methods in this field. This study also sheds light on how technological advances have the potential to be used in various sustainable finance initiatives. Exploring the application of technologies such as AI, ML and DLT in sustainable finance frameworks is another objective, where through case studies and various theoretical assessments, this chapter examines different models and approaches and highlights how they have the potential to improve and develop approaches to sustainable finance and increase organisational efficiency. The chapter also aims to assess how integrating these technologies into the green economy would impact the consideration of various opportunities and resolution of issues related to their use to advance sustainable development objectives. The study also aims to provide stakeholders with practical recommendations in this area. Therefore, these recommendations are taken into consideration to support decision-making and continuously promote the integration of valuable sustainable financial practices driven by these modern technologies to facilitate the transition to a green economy.

Structure of Chapter

This chapter aims to provide more valuable information on the relationship between AI, ML and DLT technologies and explore practical ways to connect them with sustainable finance. The first half of the chapter describes a general overview of the evolution of sustainable finance and how these technologies have the potential to advance, transform and develop this crucial field. Furthermore, the chapter provides an important basis for setting goals that include, among other things, assessing the latest developments in sustainable finance and analysing how these technologies work and the ways in which they can impact a green economy. Initially, the chapter begins with a review of the literature in this field, followed by a methodological section describing the procedure for collecting and analysing data. Finally, a section is dedicated to summarising the various findings on this topic in a general way. Furthermore, after a discussion that bridges the gap between theory and practice in the sector, the chapter concludes with a summary of the analysis findings and suggestions for further study on the role of these technologies in sustainable finance.

Overview of Literature

A continuous effort has been made to investigate the possible links between these technologies and sustainable finance through a literature review in order to present different methods, which provide in-depth information about the various opportunities and challenges in this field and in some way it is thought to improve and develop innovation for a more sustainable future. This research in this field aims to consolidate the many different results on the harmonisation of these technologies and sustainable finance, providing opportunities to develop sound theoretical foundations and practical applications in the real world. Among the studies from this field, Clark et al. (2015) consider the harmonisation of ESG aspects in financial decision-making as a fundamental criterion of sustainable finance. Also, studies developed in the last 5 years, such as those of Bosshardt (2019) and Deloitte (2020), show that AI, ML and DLT technologies have incredible transformative and developmental potential, especially in increasing transparency, developing efficiency and improving accountability in financial systems. In addition, studies by Habisch et al. (2019) highlight the role of blockchain in promoting responsible investment practices, while Lacity and Hansen (2018) highlight many opportunities for improving outsourcing in financial business processes. According to Vergara and Agudo (2021), FinTechs have the potential to impact the overall sustainability of financial institutions, which can thus pave the way for facilitating and encouraging sustainable innovation.

In addition to the various benefits these technologies can bring, they contribute to addressing potential gaps and development opportunities, which pave the way for innovations and modern solutions in the field of sustainable finance. The literature review highlighted that financial technologies, such as blockchain and AI, can also support low-carbon and climate-resilient investments in addition to creating opportunities to facilitate sustainable financial practices (Nassiry, 2019). Furthermore, AI and ML significantly contribute to sustainable development in important industries such as renewable energy and the healthcare sector (Fan et al., 2023). Among others, the digital finance revolution, through FinTech, InsurTech and blockchain, makes valuable contributions to the transformation and development of financial services, which, as a result, are considered to have a significant impact on the development of a more sustainable economy (Puschmann, 2020).

Definition of Key Concepts

Studies by Uecke (2012) and Strickland explore the impact of defining key concepts and facilitating understanding in their respective fields. On the one hand,

Uecke mainly focusses on innovation, technology transfer and entrepreneurship in science and industry, while Strickland applies this methodology to studying history. Karlöf (1993) extended this idea to the business sector, underlining the importance of clarity and understanding concepts to improve practice and learning in different fields. However, in the context of technology, Gandhi and Gandhi (2022) characterise the advancement of AI, ML and DLT as rapidly evolving technologies with significant promise in many sectors, including the financial and healthcare industries. McCarthy demonstrates that while DL uses neural networks to improve analysis and decision-making, AI and ML focus primarily on the capacity of computers to learn from data. In addition, these technologies are still widely used in various industries, especially in healthcare, where they are mainly used for the detection and treatment of various diseases, while in the financial industry, they are used to develop the efficiency of various operations and to perform various challenging analyses (Erpolat Tasabat & Aydin, 2021; Yazdani et al., 2023).

Technologies such as AI, ML and DLT are considered essential for sustainable finance in many ways, as they help, among other things, foster innovation and advance the economy and the environment in general. Sustainable finance, among other things, includes ESG considerations when determining which potential investments should be made in order to allocate financial resources for the creation and development of projects that, among other things, promote sustainable growth and reduce the level of risks related mainly to climate change (UNEP FI, 2020). In this regard, these technologies are still considered crucial for the development of a green economy in particular and for the promotion of global sustainability in general.

From the exploration of numerous studies in this field, it is observed that the important contribution that AI, ML and DLT technologies provide has been emphasised, in particular, the opportunities they offer in promoting sustainable finance and the growth and development of a green economy, using a variety of research methodologies (Chen et al., 2012; El-Zoghdy et al., 2013; Sulaksana, 2023). Sulaksana (2023) claims that big data analysis using AI and ML algorithms can provide opportunities to identify many trends, valuable patterns and potential risks mainly related to sustainability indicators and environmental problems. Thus, financial institutions can benefit from this capability, as it can help them make better investment decisions, considering ESG concerns. Another important component is considered risk management, where, according to El-Zoghdy et al. (2013), AI-powered systems can assess potential environmental risks that are relevant to potential investments, such as the effects of climate change, resource shortages or regulatory changes in this area. According to Chen et al. (2012), ML models can predict the different financial effects of potential risks, enabling different investors to minimise as efficiently as possible and cope with any difficulties that may be encountered. Another important area in which these technologies have a decisive effect is the efficient allocation of resources. According to El-Zoghdy et al. (2013), AI-supported systems offer the opportunity to assess potential environmental risks, which mainly relate to potential investments, such as the potential consequences of climate change, insufficient resources or even changes made to the legislation in this area. According to Chen et al. (2012),

ML models offer the opportunity to predict the different financial consequences of potential risks in a way that allows different investors to reduce as effectively as possible and address any challenges that may arise. According to Sulaksana (2023), DLT can help reduce intermediaries to enable transparent and economical transactions. In addition, peer-to-peer trading of sustainable assets, such as carbon credits and green energy certificates, is mainly enabled by blockchain-powered platforms, which encourage the best possible allocation of resources within the green economy in general. These innovative technologies, among other things, also help improve reporting and accurate measurement of impact in this way. According to El-Zoghdy et al. (2013), these technological solutions help in the collection, accurate analysis and publication of sustainability data in such a way that they allow investors to track the social accurately and, at the same time, environmental effects of their investments. Moreover, according to Chen et al. (2012), AI and ML algorithms, among other things, also help in the automation of the assessment of ESG performance criteria in such a way that they increase responsibility and make sustainable finance more transparent.

Technologies such as AI, ML and DLT are considered essential in encouraging the development of innovation and sustainable finance and, on the other hand, encouraging the approximation of a green economy. Financial institutions have the opportunity to use these technologies for development purposes, in particular, to make fairer judgements, improve the management of potential risks most logically, to allocate resources in the most effective way and at the same time to constantly assess how these investments will have an impact on further social development and environmental sustainability in general. According to Berensmann (2016), green finance is considered a fundamental part of sustainable finance, as it directs funds towards initiatives that improve the environment, help achieve the Sustainable Development Goals (SDGs) and encourage sustainable behaviour in general. Among other things, green finance includes many industrial, social and economic aspects; as such, it requires significant government support to be successfully implemented. However, several issues, including knowledge gaps and the acquisition of environmental externalities, are still considered to hinder the mobilisation of funds for various green initiatives. According to Armintasari (2021), by effectively managing ESG risk and aligning with net-zero emission pledges, financial institutions have various options, including changing their organisational operations towards sustainability in general. Therefore, to provide a more comprehensive approach to sustainable development, financial and organisational operations should be aligned with sustainability goals (Armintasari, 2021).

Historical Development

Integrating technologies such as AI, ML and DLT with sustainable finance and the green economy reflects continuously changing progress. This process has highlighted these technologies' transformative impact in encouraging innovation, sustainability and efficiency, particularly in the banking industry and in promoting a greener economy. Various studies, such as those by Zhou (2022) and Liu et al. (2021), highlight the impact of financial technology on improving green finance and contributing to economic growth. Another study by Fan et al. (2023) argues that digital finance has a significant impact on fostering green technological innovations and, as a result, contributes to solving various financial problems of businesses. Another study by Puschmann (2020) describes the opportunities technologies such as FinTech, InsurTech and blockchain have in creating a sustainable digital financial ecosystem, explicitly addressing the energy, banking and transport industries.

Research in developed countries by Han et al. (2023) and Fu et al. (2022) highlights that digital finance and digital commerce, both together, have the potential to contribute, among other things, to environmentally friendly development and sustainability. According to Yang (2020), FinTech has an important role in reducing credit risk and continuously improving regulations for green finance, while according to Zhilkina et al. (2022), there are potential negative impacts, such as high energy consumption associated with the use of information technologies. Thus, the evolution of sustainable finance is considered to have moved from ethical and fair investments to the full inclusion of ESG factors in financial decision-making (Archer, 2019). One of the main reasons for these developments is the increased involvement of the private sector in all industries, especially in the banking industry (Sredojević, 2021). However, different industries face various obstacles and barriers, including potential legal ambiguities and a lack of transparency in various processes (Korytsev, 2022). Despite these obstacles, it is increasingly evident that the importance of implementing a new paradigm of corporate financing that includes, among other things, ESG components is also growing. This development, among other things, highlights the importance of technology and ESG in shaping a sustainable financial future, in addition to addressing current problems and seizing opportunities for progress, development and innovation (Agârbiceanu, 2021).

From simple data gathering to implementing several sophisticated decision-making systems powered by AI and other blockchain-supported transaction platforms, the role of technology in sustainable finance and the green economy has evolved. Integrating sustainability is becoming more and more crucial as these significant financial practices change in tandem with the quick advancement of technology, especially to maintain long-term stability and to support environmental preservation and general social well-being (Green & Wachter, 2005; Hawley & Williams, 2000; Schoenmaker, 2020). The importance of technology in sustainable finance and the green economy will continue to develop rapidly, beginning with basic data collecting and progressing to the implementation of sophisticated decision-making systems backed by AI and other blockchain-enabled transaction platforms. Because sustainability fosters environmental conservation on the one hand and enhances social well-being on the other, as these financial practices jointly contribute to technological advancements, it is becoming more and more recognised as essential to preserving long-term stability (Green & Wachter, 2005; Hawley & Williams, 2000; Schoenmaker, 2020).

Most of the underpinnings for sustainable finance come from the ethical and Socially Responsible Investing (SRI) movements of the early 20th century. These initiatives gained momentum in the late 20th and early 21st centuries due to various factors, including increased awareness of social and environmental concerns, regulatory reforms, and growing expectations for ethical investing practices (Green &

Wachter, 2005; Hawley & Williams, 2000). Technology initially made the collection and continuous dissemination of ESG data more manageable. However, integrating these data into sustainable finance continues to be a work in progress. As a result, due to the advances and developments being made in AI and ML, this role of technology has progressively grown over time to include data analytics, effective risk monitoring and various decision support systems (Schoenmaker, 2020). However, it is claimed that current developments in AI and ML have improved sustainable finance by making it possible to analyse massive data sets and identify possibilities and hazards associated with ESG. These technologies have increased risk modelling accuracy and empowered investors to make educated decisions that support sustainability objectives (Liu et al., 2021; Zhou, 2022). Furthermore, the deployment of DLT, especially blockchain, is considered to have created opportunities to improve efficiency and increase the security level of many financial activities, which at the same time has made them more transparent (Fan et al., 2023; Puschmann, 2020). Thus, the creation of ESG data platforms, the widespread application of tradable tools serving for AI-supported sustainability data analysis, the implementation of carbon trading systems based primarily on blockchain, and the incorporation of ML algorithms that measure and report impact are considered notable examples, demonstrating these technological advances in sustainable development (Fu et al., 2022; Han et al., 2023; Schoenmaker, 2020).

Theoretical Framework

Several recent studies have examined the function and significance of AI, ML and DLT technologies in sustainable finance and a green economy. Zhou (2022) highlights the application of this technology in the growth of the economy, green economy and sustainable development, with a focus on digital finance and technological innovation. Liu et al. (2021) also highlights the noteworthy function of financial technology in advancing green finance, especially in a regional context. Fan et al. (2023) provides evidence of the positive effects of digital finance on firms' green technological innovation, focussing on financing costs and financial flexibility. Vishwakarma (2023) highlights the role of green financing in encouraging high-quality development, especially in India's e-economy. The theoretical foundations guiding the study of digital finance and sustainable technology include the strategic alignment of resources emphasised by the resource-based view, such as human resource management practices and organisational culture, to foster innovation in Small and Medium-sized Enterprises (SMEs) (Gashi, 2024a). In addition, the quality management framework is critical for understanding how quality management techniques enabled by digital finance improve business performance and operational efficiency in poor countries (Gashi & Bibiqaj, 2024). These studies highlight the potential of technology to promote sustainable finance and a green economy.

Based on studies that strongly emphasise these technologies, four main theoretical frameworks emerge that explore the role of technology in the green economy and sustainable finance. According to technological determinism, technological developments are considered significant influences that also affect human behaviour and promote society's general growth (Gujral, 2023). Innovations such as DLT,

ML and AI create opportunities for financial practices to change this way. Better resource management has become possible due to these developments, which also help measure impact (Matsepe & van der Lingen, 2022). Advocates broadly claim that technologies such as chain-based carbon trading systems and AI-powered ESG research tools have the potential to enhance sustainability significantly (Gujral, 2023). Therefore, how various institutions create opportunities to contribute to organisational behaviour is generally considered the main emphasis of institutional theory (Hemanand et al., 2022). According to Vardari et al. (2023), this emphasis mainly emphasises how industry standards and legal requirements can facilitate the adoption of these valuable and necessary technical advances in sustainable finance.

In order to align their data management procedures with ESG reporting criteria, financial institutions are increasingly encouraged to continuously implement solutions that are mainly oriented towards AI and ML (Hemanand et al., 2022). To achieve sustainable results, the concept emphasises how necessary it is to achieve a balance between adopting technological advances and respecting institutional norms and expectations in general (Vardari et al., 2023). On the other hand, the diffusion of innovation theory is another valid theory that explains how new technologies can be embraced and spread continuously within a social system (D'Orazio & Valente, 2019). This theory focusses on several factors likely to influence the acceptance of these technological advances in sustainable finance, such as perceived benefits, complexity of implementation and the ability to align with existing practices. This theory also states that social networks and other organisational characteristics are essential, especially for promoting and adopting new technologies in this important sector (Hoff, 2012).

On the other hand, another theory that offers a comprehensive approach to this problem is systems thinking, which examines the many potential complex connections between environmental, social and economic systems (Vardari & Jusufi, 2023). According to this theory, the necessity to adopt these integrated approaches is mainly emphasised by the foreseeable outcomes and potential systemic problems associated with adopting technologies by the financial sector such as DLT, AI and ML (Tang et al., 2023). As a result, issues that mainly include algorithmic bias, privacy risks and potential system defects have the opportunity to be resolved as effectively as possible (Wang, 2022). These theoretical frameworks can help researchers and practitioners make sense of different dynamics, such as technological innovations, regulatory impacts, adoption processes and systemic effects in the pursuit of sustainable development. Furthermore, integrating these perspectives can help advance and develop green economics and sustainable finance in sectors as diverse as marketing, tourism and healthcare (Zhou, 2022).

Digital Finance, Technological Innovation and Green Technology

Digital finance has significantly impacted economic growth by helping to improve financial inclusion and operational efficiency. Mobile payments, blockchain and digital banking have consistently played a fundamental role in expanding access to financial services, especially in various marginalised regions. Thus, through practical examples and case studies, it explores how digital finance has increased access to financial services while making a significant contribution to economic development and the promotion of sustainable behaviours.

Application of Digital Finance in Economic Development

Integrating AI in the financial industry and technological innovations, in general, are considered very important factors driving change. According to the OECD (2021), the increased availability of data in the financial services sector is helping to accelerate the adoption of AI in a way that brings innovation and efficiency to operations. As a result, this integration affects the acceleration of economic growth, as it affects the increase in access and efficiency of financial services. More specifically, multimedia technologies, such as sound, graphics, animations and full-motion videos, continue to contribute to developing the banking sector, various financial services and the insurance market. These advances are helping to achieve strategic goals such as improved fraud detection and enhanced analysis of financial data through methods of ML and deep learning alongside the application of robotic process automation (Vardari & Jusufi, 2023; Vardari et al., 2023).

Blockchain technology has proven revolutionary, especially in the insurance industry, where it speeds up claims processing and improves fraud detection capabilities (Sood et al., 2022). Beyond improving operational efficiency, blockchain technology offers significant cost savings in administrative operations. Digital public infrastructure (DPI), which includes digital identity, payment and data exchange networks, has proven critical during disasters such as the COVID-19 pandemic. Marskell et al. (2024) emphasise that DPI enables fast and secure emergency cash transfers and online services transactions, increasing economic resilience and financial inclusion across all sectors.

AI and fintech technologies in digital finance are essential in accelerating economic growth. According to Liu et al. (2024), AI helps automate financial transactions and creates opportunities by providing personalised services, reducing financial challenges and promoting overall economic growth globally. According to Nassiry (2018), fintech integrations, such as mobile payments and wealth management, offer opportunities to increase and develop efficiency and enable the expansion of access to financial services in a way that affects key sectors of the economy. Also, according to Grabner-Kräuter et al. (2021), corporate social responsibility plays an important role, especially in improving job satisfaction, and thus creates a favourable environment for economic growth, helps retain talent and highlights the tremendous social benefits of ethical business practices for long-term development.

The World Bank (2024a) reports that digital finance has played a fundamental role in economic growth by improving and developing sectors such as health, education and agriculture in developing countries through significant digital infrastructure. In this way, this infrastructure supports connectivity and data-driven services, which are essential for development in these sectors. Specifically, the World Bank (2024b) makes several recommendations, including comprehensive digitalisation combined with climate action, as it considers that it provides opportunities for improving financial inclusion and encouraging economic progress in low- and middle-income countries. Consequently, digital finance is essential for economic growth as it uses various technologies, such as blockchain and AI, to increase efficiency and improve access to financial services (Schmucki & Matthews, 2024). These technologies also contribute significantly to global economic growth by strengthening economic sustainability, expanding diverse perspectives for financial inclusion and promoting sustainable financial habits.

Role of Technological Innovation in Green Economy

Technological developments are considered essential for a sustainable future because they create opportunities for changes in the global economy to make it more environmentally conscious and sustainable in general. Digital solutions offer increased efficiency and create opportunities to incorporate sustainability into economic operations in the new era due to technological advances (Liu & Stemmler, 2024). In this regard, information technology is constantly outpacing global economic growth in helping to integrate these latest technologies into other industries. Among other things, this has helped increase operational efficiency and created valuable opportunities to support environmentally friendly practices. OECD (2021) predicts that the financial sector will increasingly use AI and big data because they are important in gaining a competitive advantage through sustainable practices. These technologies present other valuable opportunities for accurate environmental monitoring, renewable energy system optimisation and more reasonable resource allocation. Furthermore, digital infrastructures such as multi-tenant data centres and Internet Exchange Points (IXPs) offer opportunities to expand and improve access to digital services, which reduces operational costs and carbon emissions (Minges, 2024).

Blockchain and DLT are considered two examples of technologies that have the potential to transform and develop financial transactions and advance and increase transparency in many projects related to green finance. Nassiry (2018) claims that because these technologies help to meet global climate obligations continuously, they are considered essential, especially in creating the possibility of issuing green bonds and, on the other hand, in coordinating investments with sustainable development objectives. According to Tyagi et al. (2023), AI, among other things, is considered to have a vital role, especially in environmental and health management, but also in increasing sustainable performance measurements, while according to OECD (2021), AI has a crucial role, especially in its contribution to reducing potential climate risks and in creating opportunities to increase the harmonisation capacity of organisations in general. Thus, the inclusion of AI, ML, DLT and other digital technologies in the green economy and sustainable finance is considered to be of great importance as they harmonise and align their goals to address these important global environmental issues (Nassiry, 2018; OECD, 2021; Tyagi et al., 2023). According to Liu and Stemmler (2024), these advances, among others, can increase operational efficiency and create a solid foundation for fair and sustainable development. Furthermore, these technologies will play a crucial role, especially in creating a future where environmental conservation and economic growth will be closely linked as long as different players continue to create and implement these digital solutions (Minges, 2024).

Positive Impact of Digital Finance on Innovation

Digital finance encourages innovation in various sectors, using advanced technologies such as AI, ML and DLT in their organisational operations. These technologies play a fundamental role in the transformation and development of financial services and in creating opportunities to expand financial inclusion and economically empower various marginalised communities. According to the OECD (2021), AI is, among other things, revolutionising wealth management, providing opportunities for big data analysis and optimising various investment strategies (Awamleh et al., 2024; Humbatova et al., 2024; Inder et al., 2022; Li et al., 2024).

The harmonisation of digital finance with human resource management on the one hand and organisational culture on the other is considered to be encouraging continuous innovation in small- and medium-sized enterprises, especially in developing countries (Gashi, 2024a). This strategic harmonisation creates opportunities for improving the efficiency of various operations and increasing customer satisfaction in a way that helps SMEs maintain competitiveness and develop important management processes. In addition, digital finance is offering significant benefits to organisations in developing countries in that it provides opportunities for providing infrastructure for various necessary technologies to increase the possibility of being more competitive globally (Gashi, 2021). This involvement is considered to be helping organisations increase their operations' capacities and expand their market, developing and promoting innovation in the industry and overall economic development. The integration of blockchain and big data analysis has brought about important innovative models of insurance services, which have enabled improved risk management and the protection of their customers (Kaswan et al., 2022). These technologies enable insurers to, among other things, provide personalised services, as well as create and develop closer relationships with their customers through transparent transactions and data-based insights. According to the World Bank (2024a), digital finance enhances innovation by facilitating secure and efficient transactions, contributing to economic development and achieving the SDGs. As a result, digital banking is becoming a catalyst that transforms and encourages innovation in various economic sectors (OECD, 2021; World Bank, 2024a). Integrating AI, ML, DLT and other digital innovations improves efficiency in various organisational operations, supporting inclusive growth and thereby contributing to achieving the SDGs (Gashi, 2024a; Kaswan et al., 2022). These advances and developments are shaping a future where financial services can be accessible, transparent and sustainable (World Bank, 2024b).

Alleviating Financial Constraints through Digital Finance

The incredible intensity of technological developments such as AI, ML and DLT is helping digital finance overcome potential financial barriers and improve and develop economic sustainability. In this way, digital finance plays a fundamental role, especially in financial constraints, expanding financial inclusion and creating and developing long-term economic growth. According to OECD (2021), portfolio managers and various corporate investors are increasingly using AI, ML and big data analysis to develop financial strategies and continuously improve access to more affordable financial services for all. Digital finance, among others, is also bringing benefits to developing countries, especially for SMEs, as it creates opportunities for improving and developing management practices to increase business performance, operational efficiency and customer satisfaction (Gashi & Bibiqaj, 2024). As a result, digital finance has the potential to support economic development and sustainability in general by creating opportunities to reduce financial challenges and supporting SMEs to compete in global markets.

Furthermore, digital finance, among other things, also offers important opportunities to address various challenging economic issues, especially in challenging economic times, in a way that contributes to simplifying the financing process for SMEs and also affects the acceleration of various potential transaction processes (Yadav et al., 2023). Regarding the European Union's Digital Operational Sustainability Act, blockchain technology is essential as it enables increased sustainability and makes operations more efficient regarding digital financial systems (Grima et al., 2021). Among other things, these technologies also offer valuable opportunities to improve the flexibility and reliability of transactions. Since it is essential for expanding access for many marginalised individuals, reducing inequality and promoting sustainable economic growth, digital finance is also a potent tool, especially for democratising financial services (OECD, 2021). Furthermore, AI-powered impact investing and climate risk modelling are increasingly being enabled by digital finance, resulting in more prudent financial decisions informed by many important environmental issues (Schmucki & Matthews, 2024). This strategy, among other things, encourages and develops core sustainability objectives and, conversely, supports investments primarily consistent with climate sustainability. Moreover, consequently, digital finance plays a crucial role, particularly in reducing potential barriers and financial hardship, creating opportunities for expanding the potential for financial inclusion and fostering long-term economic growth (Gashi & Bibiqaj, 2024; OECD, 2021; Yadav et al., 2023). Thus, using technologies such as AI, ML, DLT and blockchain, digital finance creates power for the development of SMEs, promoting digital entrepreneurship and strengthening economic sustainability (Grima et al., 2021; Schmucki & Matthews, 2024). Moreover, as digital banking evolves, it will continue to be an important catalyst for innovation, financial inclusion and achieving the SDGs, shaping a sustainable and inclusive global economy (OECD, 2021; World Bank, 2024a).

AI and DL in Driving Sustainability Across Sectors

AI and ML are transforming many industries, particularly sustainability and renewable energy. Thus, technologies such as AI, ML and DLT play a fundamental role in improving these sustainable practices in various sectors, especially regarding sustainable energy. As a result, combining these technologies offers opportunities to transform the financial industry, encouraging more responsible practices in various businesses. Financial advisory platforms are adopting high-intensity technologies such as blockchain and ML algorithms to create opportunities for increased operational efficiency and security and to continuously promote a sustainable approach in their daily operations (Gashi, 2024b).

Potential of AI and DL in the Renewable Energy Sector

AI and ML technologies also play a fundamental role in improving and developing energy management systems in smart buildings, as they are considered to increase energy efficiency and continuously promote sustainability (Tyagi et al., 2023). These developments are fundamental to transforming into greener methods of energy consumption. According to Minges (2024), the Information and Communication Technology (ICT) sector plays an important role in promoting the adoption of sustainable energy, as it uses the power of large companies to strengthen renewable energy markets, especially in developing economies. In this way, governments can support this transformation by creating a favourable investment climate and financial incentives for energy-efficient data centres to ensure the most effective use of AI and DL in the sustainable energy sector. Given that various analytical and predictive models supported by AI create opportunities that help optimise energy production, also contribute to increasing grid stability and facilitate the integration of renewable energy sources, according to Liu et al. (2024), AI and DL-based technologies offer opportunities to revolutionise the sustainable energy market. These advances and developments also demonstrate the potential of AI to create opportunities to support a green economy and are considered entirely consistent with the SDGs. In addition, given that AI and DL also have the potential to create opportunities to increase grid resilience and improve efficiency in energy production, the World Bank (2024a) considers them as technologies that are creating continuous development, especially in the sustainable energy sector. This presents additional opportunities to accelerate the global transition towards sustainable energy sources. AI can also revolutionise renewable energy by creating opportunities to optimise energy use, improve grid stability and enable many preventive repairs that can be made to infrastructure, claim Verbeek and Lundqvist (2021).

Furthermore, AI-based technologies are essential for accelerating the adoption of renewable energy sources and transitioning to a more sustainable economy. According to Taghizadeh-Hesary and Hyun (2022), the application of AI and DLT in green finance is recommended, as they not only expand the potential for improvements in operational efficiency but also help increase the accountability and transparency of various transactions. These technologies, essential for achieving the SDGs, not only open the doors for financial institutions to become more decentralised but also provide valuable alternatives, especially for risk management and promote continued support for green financing projects. Therefore, due to continued advances in AI and ML, there are many chances to transform sustainability in various industries, especially in renewable energy (Tyagi et al., 2023; Verbeek & Lundqvist, 2021). Therefore, these technologies are continuously supporting sustainable development by creating opportunities to enhance and develop energy management strategies on the one hand and by developing advanced analytics on the other, as well as developing valuable models that help predict and increase operational efficiency (Liu et al., 2024; World Bank, 2024a). Due to its potential to create opportunities for significantly improving sustainable development, AI and ML advances are considered valuable for various international initiatives that preserve the environment and economic sustainability (Taghizadeh-Hesary & Hyun, 2022).

AI and DL Innovations in Sustainable Environmental Management

The use of AI and ML in the ecological management of healthcare is considered to play a crucial role, especially in the conservation of biodiversity and the sustainability of the ecosystem in general, as it creates valuable opportunities for predictive data analysis and real-time monitoring (Tyagi et al., 2023). According to the World Bank (2024b), these technologies have a fundamental role, especially for intelligent energy management systems of buildings, as they create valuable opportunities to continuously monitor and develop adaptive strategies that serve energy use, which contribute to reducing the impact on the environment, especially in urban environments and create opportunities to save energy significantly. Furthermore, AI and DL have a crucial role, especially in creating valuable opportunities to support environmental and health management to make allocating resources more optimal and generate valuable opportunities that help reduce any potential environmental effects (Schmucki & Matthews, 2024). Verbeek and Lundqvist (2021) assert that accurate diagnosis of the problem, creation of models that help predict potential environmental effects and effective use of a variety of resources can lead to significant advances and developments, especially in environmental and human health management.

AI and DL technologies are essential, especially in their contribution to optimising energy consumption patterns in the context of smart buildings, as they offer valuable opportunities that encourage sustainability and lower carbon footprints (Tyagi et al., 2023). Marskell et al. (2024) argue that because DPI provides real-time analytics and fosters applicable data sharing, it also significantly contributes to more environmentally sustainable practices, creating more efficient energy use opportunities. Liu et al. (2024) argue that using AI and DL for intelligent building energy management offers significant opportunities to reduce the carbon footprint and offer profitable potential to increase building efficiency. In this way, AI-powered solutions are steadily advancing important sustainability goals in urban infrastructure by aiding in real-time data analysis for preventive maintenance planning, continuous monitoring of building performance and overall modification of energy use. According to the World Bank (2024), AI and DL significantly impact energy management in smart buildings, namely by creating opportunities for improving sustainability and energy efficiency through continuous real-time monitoring and predictive maintenance. Thus, AI and ML technologies generate valuable opportunities, especially in optimising energy management in smart buildings and in advancing sustainability in general, using resources efficiently and implementing and developing innovative environmental management techniques in general (Liu et al., 2024; Tyagi et al., 2023; Verbeek & Lundqvist, 2021). Thus, these technologies make a valuable contribution, particularly in achieving global sustainability goals, and create valuable opportunities to reduce overall environmental impacts (Schmucki & Matthews, 2024; World Bank, 2024b).

Conclusion

The revolutionary importance of technologies such as AI, ML and DLT in the promotion and continued development of sustainable finance and the green economy is highlighted at the end of this chapter. The chapter explores how these valuable developments are changing the financial landscape at large, creating opportunities to encourage environmental sustainability and opening the door to more equitable and inclusive economic growth.

Summary of Key Points

The impact of advanced technologies such as AI, ML and DLT on sustainable finance and the opportunities for the transition to a green economy is examined in this chapter. Through real-time data analysis, exploration of personalised services and increasing transaction speed, these technologies are continuously improving and developing access, increasing efficiency and improving transparency in many financial institutions in such a way that they are promoting and developing valuable, more sustainable financial practices. Thus, they are offering valuable opportunities, which serve, among other things, to increase environmental sustainability but also to improve and develop operations to accelerate the transition to more environmentally friendly economic structures in general (Sood et al., 2022; Tyagi et al., 2023). The integration of blockchain and AI has greatly improved and developed organisational processes in a way that has reduced emissions and continuously encouraged valuable, sustainable practices in many industries. These developments are also essential for the continuous improvement and development of intelligent energy management of buildings, anticipating potential climate risks and encouraging the expansion of green financing. To optimise energy use, improve and develop the stability of the grid in general and create opportunities to help meet valuable global sustainability goals, solutions driven by technologies such as AI, for example, offer valuable opportunities to analyse data in real-time (Liu et al., 2024; Schmucki & Matthews, 2024).

By enabling underserved groups to access banking services, credit, and investment opportunities, these valuable technologies are considered essential, especially for advancing financial inclusion. Digital finance, supported by AI and DLT, also strengthens economic sustainability and reduces inequalities. At the same time, digital infrastructure plays an important role, especially in reducing the digital divide and creating opportunities to maximise climate benefits while limiting digital emissions through clear policies and investments (World Bank, 2024b). Thus, AI and related technologies support financial and energy systems and create opportunities to promote sustainable resource management in a way that encourages innovation for a more equitable and sustainable economy (Liu et al., 2024; Schmucki & Matthews, 2024). Through comprehensive regulations and the integration of these technologies into sustainable practices, these developments and innovations make a significant contribution to meeting the global SDGs (Tyagi et al., 2023; World Bank, 2024b).

Directions for Future Research

Future research should focus primarily on more comprehensive studies that create opportunities to analyse the longer-term economic, environmental and social impacts of AI, ML and DLT in the field of sustainable finance. The results from these studies would create opportunities to determine their sustainability and scalability while promoting environmental protection and economic development in general (Kaswan et al., 2022; Yadav et al., 2023). Therefore, it is essential to design and build valid and appropriate regulatory frameworks that create additional opportunities to balance innovation with potential risk management. Therefore, these frameworks pave the way for broader adoption in general and create opportunities to help secure the potential long-term advantages of these valuable technologies (Schmucki & Matthews, 2024).

The chapter aimed to provide clear and consistent guidance for the more ethical application of AI, ML and DLT in financial markets. These guidelines should, among other things, provide additional opportunities to address important issues that arise in various organisational processes, such as data accessibility, the extent to which a given model is correct, and potential obstacles and difficulties that arise as a result of regulatory issues in order for sustainable finance to adopt them more broadly (Schmucki & Matthews, 2024). Thus, implementing various interdisciplinary approaches that integrate blockchain, AI, ML, DLT and IoT, among others, can pave the way for new avenues that create opportunities to support continuous development and increase sustainability in many industries. Therefore, close and substantial collaboration is needed in this area of study to identify the most valuable synergies and practices that are scalable and support and continuously advance environmental sustainability and overall economic success. As the shift towards more ethical and inclusive AI practices in sustainable finance progresses, it is essential to create opportunities to address these ethical issues (Schmucki & Matthews, 2024; Yadav et al., 2023). As a result, these AI solutions considered adequate for sustainable finance can be multiplied so that their impact will expand internationally, opening up more valuable opportunities to use these best practices and those that are more favourable globally (Kaswan et al., 2022). Thus, the chances of developing sustainable finance and helping to create a green economy depend heavily on technical advances such as AI, ML and DLT. In order to fully utilise these technologies, develop and improve economic growth and development, create opportunities to address global issues and meet environmental sustainability objectives, the analysis developed in this chapter considers it essential to continue research, increase cooperation and implement innovative policies in this area (Tyagi et al., 2023; World Bank, 2024b).

References

Agârbiceanu, S. M., & Păun, T. (2021). The need for a paradigm shift in finance: Sustainable corporate finance. *Management of Sustainable Development*, *13*(1), 33–38. https://doi.org/10.54989/msd-2021-0006

Archer, M. (2019). Sustainable finance. In E. Wohl (Ed.), *Oxford bibliographies: Environmental science*. Oxford University Press. https://doi.org/10.1093/obo/9780199363445-0117

Armintasari, F., & Ramdlaningrum, H. (2021). *Sustainable finance to foster green recovery post COVID-19 pandemic*. https://repository.theprakarsa.org/publications/353999/sustainable-finance-to-foster-green-recovery-post-covid-19-pandemic

Awamleh, F. T., Alarabiat, Y. A., & Bustami, A. N. (2024). Enhancing sustainable development through international performance indicators: The role of business intelligence techniques. *Challenges in Sustainability*, *12*(3), 203–218.

Berensmann, K., & Lindenberg, N. (2016). *Green finance: Actors, challenges and policy recommendations* [Briefing Paper No. 23/2016]. German Development Institute/Deutsches Institut für Entwicklungspolitik (DIE).

Bosshardt, W. (2019). Artificial intelligence and machine learning in finance: Market developments and financial stability implications. *Financial Stability Review*, *23*, 59–69.

Chen, H., Chiang, R. H. L., & Storey, V. C. (2012). Business intelligence and analytics: From big data to big impact. *MIS Quarterly*, *36*(4), 1165–1188. https://doi.org/10.2307/41703503

Clark, G. L., Feiner, A., & Viehs, M. (2015). From the stockholder to the stakeholder: How sustainability can drive financial outperformance. *Journal of Sustainable Finance & Investment*, *5*(4), 215–233.

D'Orazio, P., & Valente, M. (2019). The role of finance in environmental innovation diffusion: An evolutionary modelling approach. *Journal of Economic Behavior & Organization*, *162*, 417–439. https://doi.org/10.1016/j.jebo.2018.12.015

Deloitte. (2020). *Sustainable finance: Guiding principles for financial institutions*. https://www2.deloitte.com/us/en/insights/industry/financial-services/sustainable-finance-guiding-principles-for-financial-institutions.html

Demirkan, H., & Delen, D. (2013). Leveraging the capabilities of service-oriented decision support systems: Putting analytics and big data in the cloud. *Decision Support Systems*, *55*(1), 412–421.

El-Zoghdy, S. F., Nofal, M., Shohla, M. A., & El-Sawy, A. A. (2013). An efficient algorithm for resource allocation in parallel and distributed computing systems. *International Journal of Advanced Computer Science and Applications*, *4*(2), Article 040238. https://doi.org/10.14569/ijacsa.2013.040238

Erpolat Tasabat S., & Aydin, O. (2021). Deep learning. In Q. H. Do (Ed.), *Advances in computational intelligence and robotics book series* (pp. 171–196). IGI Global. https://doi.org/10.4018/978-1-7998-3238-6.ch008

Fan, Z., Yan, Z., & Wen, S. (2023). Deep learning and artificial intelligence in sustainability: A review of SDGs, renewable energy, and environmental health. *Sustainability*, *15*(18), Article 13493. https://doi.org/10.3390/su151813493

Fu, H., Huang, P., Xu, Y., & Zhang, Z. (2022). Digital trade and environmental sustainability: The role of financial development and ecological innovation for a greener revolution in China. *Economic Research/Ekonomska Istraživanja*, *36*(2), 1–19. https://doi.org/10.1080/1331677x.2022.2125889

Gandhi, V. C., & Gandhi, P. P. (2022, April 7–9). *A survey – Insights of ML and DL in health domain* [Paper presentation]. 2022 International conference on sustainable computing and data communication systems (ICSCDS), Erode, India. https://doi.org/10.1109/icscds53736.2022.9760981

Gashi, K. (2021). The relationship between SME's organizational culture and training and development as a human resource management practice. *Journal of Global Policy and Governance*, *10*(2), 139–161. https://doi.org/10.14666/2194-7759-10-2-008

Gashi, K. (2024a). Strategic integration of organizational culture and HRM practices: A catalyst for quality management. In E. İ. Şahin & M. Kıdıryüz (Eds.), *Proceedings of the 12th international scientific researches conference* (p. 462). Çukurova.

Gashi, K. (2024b). The future of Robo-advisors in management. In S. Gupta, S. Taneja, V. Kumar, E. Ozen, & L. Vardari (Eds.), *Robo-advisors in management* (pp. 35–56). IGI Global. http://doi.org/10.4018/979-8-3693-2849-1.ch003

Gashi, K., & Bibiqaj, A. (2024). The role of quality management in improving the performance of SMEs in developing countries. In N. Demir (Ed.), *Proceedings of the international congress on scientific research-X* (p. 1494). June 25–27, 2024 (Vol. 1, p. 351). IKSAD Publishing.

Grabner-Kräuter, S., Breitenecker, R. J., & Tafolli, F. (2021). Exploring the relationship between employees' CSR perceptions and intention to emigrate: Evidence from a developing country. *Business Ethics, the Environment & Responsibility*, *30*, 87–102. https://doi.org/10.1111/beer.12291

Green, R. K., & Wachter, S. M. (2005). The American mortgage in historical and international context. *Journal of Economic Perspectives*, *19*(4), 93–114. https://doi.org/10.1257/089533005775196660

Grima, S., Kizilkaya, M., Sood, K., & ErdemDelice, M. (2021). The perceived effectiveness of blockchain for digital operational risk resilience in the European Union insurance market sector. *Journal of Risk and Financial Management*, *14*, Article 363. https://doi.org/10.3390/jrfm14080363

Gujral, R. K. (2023). Determinants of FinTech and Internet of Things for technological disruption: A new-age sustainable and comprehensive outlook. *Research Review International Journal of Multidisciplinary*, *8*(3), 141–149. https://doi.org/10.31305/rrijm.2023.v08.n03.016

Habisch, A., Czerny, A. I., & Hoepner, A. G. F. (2019). Responsible investment in blockchain and other distributed ledger technologies. In D. L. K. Chuen & R. H. Deng (Eds.), *Handbook of blockchain, digital finance, and inclusion: Cryptocurrency, FinTech, InsurTech, regulation, ChinaTech, mobile security, and distributed ledger* (pp. 603–617). Elsevier.

Han, Y., Li, Y., & Wang, Q. (2023). Digital finance, environmental regulation, and green development efficiency of China. *Frontiers in Environmental Science*, *11*, Article 1131058. https://doi.org/10.3389/fenvs.2023.1131058

Hawley, J. P., & Williams, A. T. (2000). *The rise of fiduciary capitalism: How institutional investors can make corporate America more democratic*. University of Pennsylvania Press.

Hemanand, D., Mishra, N., Premalatha, G., Mavaluru, D., Vajpayee, A., Kushwaha, S., & Sahile, K. (2022). Applications of intelligent model to analyze the green finance for environmental development in the context of artificial intelligence. *Computational Intelligence and Neuroscience*, *2022*, 1–8. https://doi.org/10.1155/2022/2977824

Hoff, P. H. (2012). *Greentech innovation and diffusion*. Gabler Verlag Wiesbaden. https://doi.org/10.1007/978-3-8349-3601-1

Humbatova, S. I., Hajiyeva, N., Fodor, M. G., Sood, K., & Grima, S. (2024). The impact of economic growth on the ecological environment and renewable energy production: Evidence from Azerbaijan and Hungary. *Journal of Risk and Financial Management*, *17*(7), Article 275.

Inder, S., Sood, K., & Grima, S. (2022). Antecedents of behavioural intention to adopt internet banking using structural equation modelling. *Journal of Risk and Financial Management*, *15*(4), Article 157.

Karlof, B., & Gilderson, A. J. (1993). *Key business concepts: A concise guide*. Routledge.

Kaswan, K. S., Dhatterwal, J. S., Sharma, H., & Sood, K. (2022). Big data in insurance innovation. In K. Sood, R. K. Dhanaraj, B. Balusamy, S. Grima, & R. Uma Maheshwari (Eds.), *Big data: A game changer for insurance industry* (Emerald Studies in Finance, Insurance, and Risk Management, pp. 117–136). Emerald Publishing Limited. https://doi.org/10.1108/978-1-80262-605-620221008

Korytsev, M. A., & Morozov, S. A. (2022). Institutional development of sustainable finance: Its potential and current limitations. *Journal of Economic Regulation*, *13*(4), 125–137. https://doi.org/10.17835/2078-5429.2022.13.4.125-137

Lacity, M. C., & Hansen, D. L. (2018). Blockchain for business process outsourcing. In F. X. Olleros & M. Zhegu (Eds.), *Research handbook on digital transformations* (pp. 397–410). Edward Elgar Publishing.

Li, Q., Wu, H., Zhang, B. Q., Dong, Z. H., & Ling, T. (2024). Safety system study of gas stations based on preliminary hazard analysis and fault tree analysis. *Journal of Engineering Management and Systems Engineering*, *3*(3), 149–163.

Liu, Y., & Stemmler, H. (2024). The digital sector drives innovation, growth, and job creation. In World Bank (Ed.), *Digital progress and trends report 2023* (pp. 23–44). International Bank for Reconstruction and Development/The World Bank. https://doi.org/10.1596/978-1-4648-2049-6

Liu, Y., Boy, H. C., Khurana, S., & Sinha, A. (2024). Artificial intelligence: Revolutionary potential and huge uncertainties. In World Bank (Ed.), *Digital progress and trends report 2023* (pp. 85–106). International Bank for Reconstruction and Development/The World Bank. https://doi.org/10.1596/978-1-4648-2049-6

Liu, Z., Song, J., Wu, H., Gu, X., Zhao, Y., Yue, X., & Shi, L. (2021). Impact of financial technology on regional green finance. *Computer Systems Science and Engineering*, *39*(3), 391–401. https://doi.org/10.32604/csse.2021.014527

Marskell, J., Marin, G., & Varghese, M. (2024). Digital public infrastructure: Transforming service delivery across sectors. In World Bank (Ed.), *Digital progress and trends report 2023* (pp. 67–83). International Bank for Reconstruction and Development/The World Bank. https://doi.org/10.1596/978-1-4648-2049-6

Matsepe, N. T., & van der Lingen, E. (2022). Determinants of emerging technologies adoption in the South African financial sector. *South African Journal of Business Management*, *53*(1), Article e2493. https://doi.org/10.4102/sajbm.v53i1.2493

Minges, M. (2024). Digital infrastructure: There is a continual need for upgrading and greening. In World Bank (Ed.), *Digital progress and trends report 2023* (pp. 45–64). International Bank for Reconstruction and Development/The World Bank. https://doi.org/10.1596/978-1-4648-2049-6

Nassiry, D. (2018). *The role of fintech in unlocking green finance: Policy insights for developing countries* [ADBI Working Paper Series No. 883]. Asian Development Bank Institute. https://www.adb.org/publications/role-fintech-unlocking-green-finance

Nassiry, D. (2019). The role of Fintech in unlocking green finance. In J. Sachs, W. Woo, N. Yoshino, & F. Taghizadeh-Hesary (Eds.), *Handbook of green finance* (pp. 1–22). Springer. https://doi.org/10.1007/978-981-10-8710-3_27-1

OECD. (2021). *Artificial intelligence, machine learning and big data in finance: Opportunities, challenges, and implications for policy makers.* https://www.oecd.org/finance/artificial-intelligence-machine-learning-big-data-in-finance.htm

Puschmann, T., & Leifer, L. (2020). *Sustainable digital finance: The role of FinTech, InsurTech and blockchain for shaping the world for the better*. University of Zurich and Stanford University. https://doi.org/10.5167/uzh-199615

Schmucki, P., & Matthews, O. (2024). *The use of AI in sustainable finance. Insights: ESG and sustainability*. KPMG Switzerland.

Schoenmaker, D. (2020). Sustainable finance. In J.-F. Morin & A. Orsini (Eds.), *Essential concepts of global environmental governance* (2nd ed., pp. 253–254). Routledge. https://doi.org/10.4324/9780367816681-103

Sood, K., Kaur, B., & Grima, S. (2022). Revamping Indian non-life insurance industry with a trusted network: Blockchain technology. In K. Sood, R. K. Dhanaraj, B. Balusamy, S. Grima, & R. Uma Maheshwari (Eds.), *Big data: A game changer for insurance industry* (Emerald Studies in Finance, Insurance, and Risk Management, pp. 213–228). Emerald Publishing Limited. https://doi.org/10.1108/978-1-80262-605-620221014

Sredojević, S., & Sredojević, D. (2021). Sustainable finance: Evolution or revolution in the banking sector. *Bankarstvo, 50*(2), 114–131. https://doi.org/10.5937/bankarstvo2102114s

Sulaksana F. D. (2023). Green financing: One effort achieving sustainable development. *Banking and Management Review, 11*(2), 1592–1603. https://doi.org/10.52250/bmr.v11i2.562

Taghizadeh-Hesary, F., & Hyun, S. (Eds.). (2022). *Green digital finance and sustainable development goals* (Buchreihe: Economics, Law, and Institutions in Asia Pacific). Springer Nature Singapore.

Tang, D., Chen, W., Zhang, Q., & Zhang, J. (2023). Impact of digital finance on green technology innovation: The mediating effect of financial constraints. *Sustainability, 15*(4), Article 3393. https://doi.org/10.3390/su15043393

Tyagi, P., Grima, S., Sood, K., Balamurugan, B., Özen, E., & Thalassinos, E. (Eds.). (2023). *Smart analytics, artificial intelligence and sustainable performance management in a global digitalised economy* (Contemporary Studies in Economic and Financial Analysis, Vol. 110B). Emerald Publishing Limited. https://doi.org/10.1108/S1569-37592023000110B017

Uecke, O. (2012). Definition of key concepts. In O. Uecke (Ed.), *How to commercialize research in biotechnology?* (pp. 62–83). Gabler Verlag. https://doi.org/10.1007/978-3-8349-4134-3_3

United Nations Environment Programme Finance Initiative (UNEP FI). (2018). *The positive impact of sustainable finance*. https://www.unepfi.org/fileadmin/documents/The_Positive_Impact_of_Sustainable_Finance_17_07_2018.pdf

Vardari, L., & Jusufi, S. (2023). Evolution of multimedia banking and technology acceptance theories. In S. Grima, K. Sood, B. Rawal, B. Balusamy, E. Özen, & G. G. G. Gan (Eds.), *Intelligent multimedia technologies for financial risk management: Trends, tools and applications* (pp. 29–42). Institution of Engineering and Technology. http://doi.org/10.1049/PBPC060E_ch2

Vardari, L., Koro, E., & Ozen, E. (2023). *Intelligent multimedia technologies for financial risk management: Trends, tools and applications*. Institution of Engineering and Technology. https://doi.org/10.1049/pbpc060e

Verbeek, A., & Lundqvist, M. (2021, June). *Artificial intelligence, blockchain and the future of Europe: How disruptive technologies create opportunities for a green and digital economy* [Main Report]. Innovation Finance Advisory, part of the European Investment Bank's advisory services. European Commission, European Investment Bank. https://doi.org/10.2867/126279

Vergara, C., & Agudo, L. (2021). Fintech and sustainability: Do they affect each other? *Sustainability, 13*(13), Article 7012. https://doi.org/10.3390/su13137012

Vishwakarma, N. (2023). An analytical study of India's roadmap to e-economy. *International Journal of Creative Research Thoughts, 11*(7), 899–706. https://ijcrt.org/papers/IJCRT2307694.pdf

Wang, H. (2022). Research on the role and mechanism of digital finance in improving the performance of industrial green innovation. *Geofluids, 2022*(4), 1–13. https://doi.org/10.1155/2022/1698827

World Bank. (2024a). *Digital development*. Retrieved June 17, 2024, from https://www.worldbank.org/en/topic/digitaldevelopment/overview#1

World Bank. (2024b). *Green digital transformation: How to sustainably close the digital divide and harness digital tools for climate action*. Climate Change and Development Series. World Bank. https://doi.org/10.1596/978-1-4648-2002-1

Yadav, U. S., Sood, K., Tripathi, R., Grima, S., & Yadav, N. (2023). Entrepreneurship in India's handicraft industry with the support of digital technology and innovation during natural calamities. *International Journal of Sustainable Development and Planning, 18*(6), 1777–1791. https://doi.org/10.18280/ijsdp.180613

Yang, X. (2020). FinTech in promoting the development of green finance in China against the background of big data and artificial intelligence. In *4th international seminar on education innovation and economic management (SEIEM 2020)* (pp. 130–133). https://doi.org/10.25236/seiem.2020.034

Yazdani, A., Costa, S., & Kroon, B. (2023). Artificial intelligence: Friend or foe? *Australian and New Zealand Journal of Obstetrics and Gynaecology*, *63*(2), 127–130. https://doi.org/10.1111/ajo.13661

Zhilkina, A. N., Zhilkin, O. N., & Bondarovich, E. P. (2022). Green finance and information technology: Contradictions and cooperation. *Vestnik Universiteta*, *4*, 137–145. https://doi.org/10.26425/1816-4277-2022-4-137-145

Zhou, S. (2021). Artificial intelligence, machine learning, and financial markets. *Journal of Economic Surveys*, *35*(2), 421–457.

Zhou, Y. (2022). The application trend of digital finance and technological innovation in the development of green economy. *Journal of Environmental and Public Health*, *2022*(3), 1–8. https://doi.org/10.1155/2022/1064558

Chapter 5

Greening the Future: A Comprehensive Approach to Sustainable Development

Fisnik Morina, Duresa Kilaj and Aulonë Cenaj

Faculty of Business, University "Haxhi Zeka", Peja, Republic of Kosovo

Abstract

Purpose: This chapter analyses and explains a comprehensive approach to sustainable economic development based on environmental issues in a global context.

Need for the study: The effect of globalisation on the global economy and the dynamics of the international business environment in terms of economic and environmental challenges have influenced the need to study these global environmental and economic challenges as well as the necessity of providing a development strategy on a scientific basis to give concrete recommendations for creating a stable economic environment and an innovative approach in the field of green economy.

Methodology: The scientific method applied in this chapter includes a qualitative approach based on comparative analysis and critical analysis of scientific literature. Another qualitative approach this study uses provides case studies and SWOT (strengths, weaknesses, opportunities and threats) and PESTLE (political, economic, social, technological, legal and environmental) analysis, where sustainable development policies and the green economy are critically examined.

Findings: This study's findings identify challenges and opportunities in sustainable economic development and the necessity for many countries to develop effective economic strategies and policies to achieve sustainable progress in terms of meeting the ESG (environmental, social and governance) standards.

Sustainable Development and Green Innovation: Managing Risk through Interdisciplinary Approaches and Policy Strategies, 91–126

Published under exclusive licence by Emerald Publishing Limited
doi:10.1108/978-1-83608-462-420251005

Practical implications: This study's practical implications are that the governments of many different countries worldwide must develop adequate and innovative policies to use natural resources efficiently, and these countries allocate as much internal and external funds as possible for the advancement of new technologies in the fields of green economy and environmental protection.

Keywords: Sustainable development; green economy; environmental policies; development policies; environmental challenges; natural resources; technology; innovation

JEL codes: Q01; Q56; O13

1. Introduction to Sustainable Development

Sustainable development is a concept that includes a process that fulfils all of the present generation's needs and, through the abilities of future generations, influences their fulfilment. Sustainable development underscores the equilibrium between economic progress, environmental protection and social equality, which positively impacts the utilisation of natural resources in various countries' economies. Government economic policies in countries worldwide that aim to advance sustainable development must integrate ecological principles with the best economic, social and environmental practices. Such integration leads to a safe and sustainable future for all humanity globally.

Implementing sustainable development policies that address the problems and difficulties brought about by climate change, the need to protect biodiversity, and the reduction of natural resources is significant in solving and mitigating these challenges. The climate changes that have occurred in recent years at the global level pose a substantial risk to all ecosystems and the global population. Such a risk necessitates that the governments of various countries around the world and international environmental organisations take urgent action and coordinate their environmental policies to reduce greenhouse gas emissions. Such an action will positively influence the promotion of best practices in sustainable ecological development and efficient energy use. These sustainable development practices can affect the careful management of natural resources in different countries' economies. Good and effective management will ensure that limited natural resources are available to future generations. In the coming decades, the preservation of functional ecosystems will largely depend on biodiversity protection, which is considered a critical factor in functionalising sustainable ecosystem services.

Through this study, we aim to provide a comprehensive approach to integrating sustainability rules or norms in the risk management process. Such comprehensive integration offers a theoretical and practical framework that promotes effective risk management and contributes positively to sustainable development. In recent decades, many countries around the world have encountered difficulties in managing environmental issues. Therefore, the governments of these countries and international ecological organisations must coordinate their actions and provide an innovative solution to reduce the degradation of the environment in which we live. This scientific chapter aims to analyse how environmental policies and strategies have influenced the effective management of risk and the implementation of sustainable projects that impact a country's economic development. Global warming, ecological degradation and climate change have negatively affected sustainable economic development and overall well-being at the global level, also influencing the urgent need to integrate sustainability policies into environmental risk management. Such a development strategy is relevant and critical for international environmental organisations that, through an effective policy on environmental issues, promote protection and optimal and efficient use of the lifespan of natural resources. Through effective environmental policies, these international organisations aim to minimise the impact of negative factors that degrade the environment and ensure a balanced level between the behaviour of the human factor and the environment (Awamleh et al., 2024; Li et al., 2024).

Perdan (2004), in his study, has analysed sustainable development and policies and strategies that affect the environment. The study examined the impact of economic and demographic factors on environmental management. The author analysed excessive consumption within the framework of economic factors and considered population growth as a variable within the framework of demographic factors. It is worth noting that economic and demographic factors also significantly impact the development of environmental policies and the design of appropriate strategies to promote environmental protection and biodiversity. In this study, the author emphasises that environmental degradation is at a high level in several countries in the world due to the economic activities of industrial production and the environmental impact not very well controlled by the government and relevant institutions in the field of environment and ecology. Therefore, due to the environmental consequences of industrial activities, developing environmental policies and strategies has become indispensable in effectively managing environmental challenges and problems. According to the study by Vare and Scott (2007), society in general needs a comprehensive approach to educating the younger generations about sustainable development and the importance of economic, social and environmental well-being. Niţoi et al. (2021) look at the roles of regional governance in sustainable development and suggest that actions that affect the economic, ecological and social aspects of regional development should be put first. Minh et al. (2016) analyse factors influencing the sustainable development of coffee production in Dak Lak province, Vietnam, including capital, labour and land as key factors for coffee productivity and agricultural practice improvement. In his study, Reimers (2021) argued for the role and impact of universities in advancing knowledge about the green economy and increasing the population's general awareness about climate change. Therefore, universities at the global level should invest as much as possible in training academic staff to teach the green economy and innovations in this field so that university education affects the advancement of knowledge about the environment and changes human behaviour towards the environment

(Humbatova et al., 2024; Inder et al., 2022). Such an integration of the field of green economy in all study programmes in universities around the world will positively affect sustainable development and the successful implementation of many development projects in the field of green economy.

These studies have practical implications regarding sustainable development factors and the critical aspect of managing global environmental challenges. The scientific findings of these studies provide precise guidelines for public policies, agricultural practices and education that will positively affect sustainable development and prepare society to face environmental challenges and problems that may arise due to climate change. Perdan (2004), in his study, has analysed a significant and critical issue related to demographic issues: the challenges resulting from population growth and excessive consumption. The study by Perdan (2004) emphasises that in many different countries, it is necessary to draft and implement specific policies that meet the population's current needs in terms of national income and consumption, not to burden future generations to meet their requirements. The advancement of knowledge about sustainable development and the green economy is also emphasised in the study of Vare and Scott (2007), who attach great importance to higher education institutions' role in increasing human awareness about environmental protection and biodiversity. Higher education through study programmes in the field of green economy and integrating this discipline into the higher education curriculum can contribute significantly to advancing knowledge about the green economy.

Meanwhile, Niţoi et al. (2021) emphasise the great importance of local governments in developing concrete economic plans for environmental protection and improving the quality of life at the local level. Through this study by these authors, it is emphasised that local governments have an essential influence on the implementation of adequate economic and development policies to create a favourable business environment for the successful implementation of new innovative projects in the field of green economy. In their study, Minh et al. (2016) highlight the importance of factors that affect sustainable production. Also, the recommendations of this study encourage reflection that all policymakers create appropriate agricultural policies by subsidising agricultural technology and that an investment in this agricultural machinery enables more efficient use and management of the resources available to agricultural producers. Proper management of resources will affect the level of environmental impact that agricultural production has on the environment. Reimers (2021) argues that climate change and the challenges arising from environmental degradation should be addressed through public policies especially educational policies. Universities, through their study programs, should play a key role in promoting green knowledge to raise awareness among future generations and to better prepare them in managing global environmental challenges. These studies offer valuable insights into global policies and practices that promote sustainable development.

This study contributes to risk management and sustainable development by offering a new perspective on integrating sustainability principles. It provides an advanced theoretical framework and practical recommendations for different economic and social sectors. This study addresses current challenges and contributes to creating a more sustainable and equitable future for all by assisting organisations in adopting more sustainable practices. Its focus and structure emphasise the importance of sustainable development in a global context and serve as a guide for practitioners and policymakers seeking to incorporate sustainability into their risk management practices.

1.1. The Originality and Novelty of the Study

The originality and novelty of this study consist of a comprehensive approach that addresses all aspects of sustainable development, with special emphasis on environmental issues. This chapter scrutinises current literature and case studies worldwide, elaborating on the findings of the literature review and case studies. It employs a critical and argumentative approach to evaluate the significance of other authors' research and its practical implications. This chapter employs SWOT and PESTLE analyses to examine the impact of sustainable development policies on the green economy and the economic growth of various nations. This chapter links theoretical and practical aspects to integrate all risk management principles into sustainable development and the green economy. A detailed explanation of these sustainability risk management rules will provide readers and stakeholders with new ideas on how to promote effective management of environmental risks and, through effective management, contribute positively to sustainable economic growth.

1.2. Relevance of the Study

This study provides a comprehensive analysis of contemporary trends in sustainable development, linking these trends to the needs of various countries worldwide in promoting the green economy through a comparative approach. In recent years, numerous governments worldwide have grappled with challenges and difficulties stemming from environmental issues, global warming, climate change, and other phenomena that economic activity can impact. To easily face these challenges, the governments of different countries need to implement expansionist policies through an integrated approach to their financial and environmental policies. The integration of ecological policies entails the effective management of potential pollution risks. This study aims to underscore the pressing necessity for various nations to establish economic and environmental policies that encourage decreased natural resource consumption, safeguard biodiversity, and allocate resources towards modern, efficient technologies. These policies facilitate adopting improved practices and protective products and underscore the significance of current global trends. This study's case studies and recommendations offer a practical approach to designing public and agricultural policies at the local and central levels and enhancing the education level on environmental and green economy issues in educational institutions. Such a comprehensive approach consists not only of increasing economic and environmental sustainability but also of the more efficient management of all the challenges faced by society in general due to environmental pollution.

1.3. Objectives and Research Questions

The main objective of this chapter is to provide a comprehensive approach to issues related to sustainable development and the green economy. This chapter will provide a comparative and integrative analysis focussing on environmental issues and the impact of economic phenomena on the environment. The results of this study aim to identify the challenges that different countries face in risk management for sustainable development, as well as to offer as many practical recommendations as possible on how to design the most effective strategies and policies that will positively affect the economies of these countries and the improvement of the living environment.

- **Research Questions**:

1. What are the main obstacles and opportunities in sustainable development and the green economy?
2. How can we integrate sustainability concepts into the risk management process to promote sustainable development?
3. What are the optimal strategies and guidelines for the responsible use of natural resources and the promotion of environmentally friendly technology and practices?
4. How can we synchronise the efforts of countries and international organisations to decrease the release of greenhouse gases and save biodiversity?

These objectives and research questions provide an overarching framework for our study of how governments in different countries address environmental and economic issues. However, this study aims to provide concrete recommendations through case studies, aiding in managing environmental and financial risks globally.

2. Integration of Economic, Social and Environmental Factors in Sustainable Development

Considering the economic, social and environmental challenges and difficulties that the global society faces in contemporary times, the need for studies in sustainable development and green economy is very significant. The complex nature of environmental and economic issues stems from these challenges different countries face. Therefore, such studies contribute positively to the interconnection of practical aspects of environmental and financial problems. The integration of economic–environmental policies and strategies affects sustainable development in the long term, and such a model of the implementation of economic and environmental policies will solve environmental problems as a whole and not cause other issues that bring a domino effect on the environment.

Such integration of economic–environmental policies and strategies in different countries aims to achieve a balance in adapting the requirements for sustainable economic growth and biodiversity protection. Such an approach to financial and environmental policies and strategies will minimise inequalities and discrimination in society in economic, social and ecological aspects. Combining these aspects will contribute positively to sustainable economic growth, and such an integrated approach will benefit society. Also, the integration of economic, social and environmental elements in the public policies and strategies of different countries at the global level will be achieved to protect natural resources for future generations.

Such a mode of implementing policies and strategies in these countries will ensure greater effectiveness in managing sustainable development challenges and protecting the living environment. These economic and environmental policies should include coordinating all the mechanisms that ensure the effective allocation of resources, the reduction of environmental pollution, the reduction of greenhouse gas emissions and the protection of biodiversity, which aims to improve the society's standard of living and social well-being. In the coming years, all countries should focus their economic strategies on innovation and technological development of international projects that will influence the creation and operationalisation of the best practices of sustainable development. The development of such a plan at the national level will also positively affect the macroeconomic level by generating new jobs in the green economy and circular economy fields.

Developing these national strategies includes integrating economic, social and environmental aspects that require the involvement of many actors and stakeholders. Such an extensive involvement of actors in the design and development of these strategies at the macro level will ensure greater sustainability in the long term for the economic growth of these countries. The stakeholders that should be involved in the design of these strategies are governments, civil society, the private sector, the scientific community and higher education institutions. Such inclusiveness of key actors helps to increase efficiency and effectiveness in the measures that will be taken in this area, and the contribution of these stakeholders to these policies will ensure the sustainability of these economic objectives in the long term.

According to scientific studies that have been carried out in the field of sustainable development, modern society nowadays faces a large number of challenges, and these challenges require urgent management. Therefore, integrating various factors such as education, industrial security, inclusion in the labour market and economic, social and environmental factors significantly impacts the achievement of sustainable development and economic growth objectives. In recent years, many scientific studies have been carried out that have analysed sustainable development and ESG factors from different perspectives. These scientific studies provide good empirical evidence on the best economic, social and environmental practices that can positively affect sustainable development. Given the substantial influence exerted by higher education institutions, governments, civil society, the private sector, and other relevant stakeholders, the advancement of green innovation and the enhancement of financial performance in businesses across diverse economies are closely linked to university-level education in the green economy, inclusive labour market participation, industrial safety, and a combination of economic, social, and environmental determinants.

Various scientific studies' empirical findings have emphasised the importance of economic strategies that include an integrated approach to ESG factors in sustainable development. Implementing such comprehensive strategies influences the promotion of equal opportunities for education, the integration of the best practices of businesses in green business activities, and the increase of safety standards in the workplace. In his study, Segovia Hermoza et al. (2023) analysed the correlation between university education, labour market dynamics, and industrial security regarding sustainable development. In this study, the author, through empirical results, has argued that good cooperation and coordination between stakeholders (educational institutions, private sector and government) for integrated education in the field of green economy will influence students to be more qualified for the labour market. Such an approach will ensure higher safety standards and transparency in the workplace. Through such an approach, the governments of different countries can quickly achieve progress in sustainable development and improve the economic and social well-being of life. In their study, Morina and Dinaj (2024) analysed the impact of ESG factors on the performance of investment portfolios in international financial markets. This study emphasises that companies at the global level that manage to have high ESG ratings tend to have better economic performance, stability in their financial and capital investments, and better management of effective financial risk. A high rating in the field of ESG enables companies to have better financial sustainability in the long term and to be able to attract more institutional capital.

According to Wang et al. (2023), the evaluations and high ratings of independent agencies for companies in the field of ESG influence to a great extent the growth and advancement of green innovations of these businesses. A high ESG rating influences many companies to develop innovative projects in green entrepreneurship. In this study, the authors emphasise that businesses that do not have bad financial conditions and limited financial resources and, in general, private companies have more opportunities to access funds dedicated to green innovations. So, through innovative projects in ESG, these businesses can have better financial performance in the long term.

According to a study carried out on China's economy by Tan and Zhu (2022), it is emphasised that the ESG assessment carried out by independent agencies not only encourages corporations to implement innovative projects in the field of green economy but also improves to a considerable extent the activities of social responsibility of enterprises and creates greater access to finance. According to this study, it is estimated that the high rating of businesses for ESG factors has a significant impact on green innovative activities, and primarily, such a phenomenon can be observed at a time when legal and regulatory requirements are very rigorous about the environment and competition in the relevant industry.

In recent years, scientific studies in ESG assessments have emphasised the importance of university education, labour market dynamics and demands, workplace safety, industrial control, and best practices for developing ESG factors. Segovia Hermoza et al. (2023), through his study, emphasises the great importance of higher education institutions' development of study programmes in the field of green economy. These study programmes enable students to gain new knowledge about the green economy field; also, these students are more qualified for the labour market through these programmes. The advancement of university education for future generations on the green economy and ESG factors has the effect of promoting more industrial safety and higher standards in the labour market. In their study, Morina and Dinaj (2024) emphasise that different companies that invest in international financial markets should focus on sustainable investments to improve their long-term financial performance. Also, to achieve excellent financial performance, these companies must strengthen the ESG regulations that raise awareness of the companies' business activities regarding the environment. Wang et al. (2023), through their study, have reflected the great importance that ESG assessments have for businesses and their incentive for green innovative activities. Such ESG assessment by independent agencies creates many opportunities for companies with financial constraints to develop innovative green projects successfully. Tan and Zhu (2022) make recommendations that all environmental laws and regulations in different countries should be strengthened, and governments should have stricter requirements for other companies so that the managers of these companies advance their education and knowledge about the field of green economy and through this to achieve better financial performance through innovative green projects. Such a strategy at the macro level ensures the financial stability of all businesses in different sectors of the real economy. It positively affects the generation of greater profits for these companies.

3. Global Environmental Challenges and Ecological Stability

In recent years, many countries have faced significant environmental challenges, including global warming, soil and living environment pollution, soil degradation, climate change, biodiversity loss, ample water and air pollution, etc. Therefore, the governments of different countries are obliged to develop environmental policies and strategies in the coming years that require rigorous legal regulation so that the adverse effects of the loss of biodiversity and ecological pollution are at a lower level. Global warming remains one of the biggest environmental challenges globally. This global warming is a result of climate change and is a consequence of the increase in the emission of greenhouse gases. As a result of the adverse effects of the rise in climate change, we also have an increase in the level of the seas and other negative consequences that have caused environmental phenomena to an extreme level.

The continuous growth of the population at the global level, urbanisation, globalisation and the excessive productive activity of enterprises in various industries have negatively affected land degradation. This degradation is a consequence of the human factor's ineffective management of natural resources, causing poor utilisation of agricultural land and increasing the probability that the phenomenon of erosion and desertification will occur with high frequency on the land. The appearance of erosion on agricultural lands increases the risk of a decline in the capacity of the land to support human life and the use of agricultural land for food production and raw materials for many other agricultural products.

Nowadays, the world is facing significant environmental challenges that affect daily life, and the management of these challenges requires urgent government intervention to understand how different factors affect the environment where we live. Ecological challenges that are increasingly complex and impact the global environment are global warming, land degradation, loss of biodiversity and land degradation. In this chapter, the PESTLE analysis will be used, which is a very suitable qualitative method to analyse political, economic, social, technological, legal and environmental factors in a structured way and through a comprehensive approach. The purpose of this qualitative analysis is to identify the factors that influence ecological pollution, to identify the main environmental challenges at the global level, and to give specific recommendations in terms of strategy and which steps should be taken to minimise their harmful effect. The recommendations derived from the PESTLE analysis are from a strategic perspective and will influence the ecological promotion of sustainable development. Table 5.1

Table 5.1. PESTLE Analysis of Global Environmental Challenges and Ecological Stability.[a]

The PESTLE Factor	Major Environmental Challenges	Strategic Recommendations
Political	The main environmental challenges in the political context are climate change, global warming and ineffective and insufficient ecological policies	A strategy to minimise the risks of climate change is the design and implementation of rigorous environmental policies. From a political point of view, international cooperation should be increased to reduce the emission of greenhouse gases
Economic	The main environmental challenges in the economic context are the high cost of advanced technologies in green innovations and the low volume of investments in renewable energy sources	Strategic steps include continuously promoting investments dedicated to clean energy and green innovations. In terms of economic factors, more funds seem to be given through subsidies to companies that implement sustainable practices
Social	The main environmental challenges in the social context are population growth, increasing urbanisation and insufficient awareness of environmental issues	From a strategic point of view, citizen education on environmental protection should be increased. From a social point of view, it is recommended that more sustainable practices be encouraged in everyday life

Table 5.1. (*Continued*)

The PESTLE Factor	Major Environmental Challenges	Strategic Recommendations
Technology	The main environmental challenges in the technological context are the application of old polluting machines and technologies in various industries and the low implementation of green innovations in multiple sectors of the economy	It is recommended that a strategy of investments be implemented in the research and development of advanced technologies in the green economy and increased improvements in energy infrastructure
Legal	The main environmental challenges in the legal context are the lack of strict ecological protection laws and their weak implementation	The legal strategies recommend that we focus on strengthening environmental protection laws and regulations and on effectively implementing these laws
Environmental	The main environmental challenges at the global level are loss of biodiversity, land degradation and water and air pollution	From a strategic point of view, all countries should take initiatives to improve the soil's quality and preserve biodiversity. Also, it is necessary to strictly monitor people's behaviour in relation to water and air to reduce their pollution

Source: Data processing by authors (2024).

[a]The PESTLE analysis was elaborated based on the report's data on the global environment forecast by the United Nations Environment Programme (UNEP, 2019).

presents the following categories of the PESTLE analysis: the PESTLE factors, the description of the leading environmental challenges at the global level, and the specific strategic recommendations on how to face and manage these ecological challenges.

Global warming is one of the leading environmental challenges worldwide, and various ecological policies are primarily related to economic factors. A concrete case is the strategic policies of different countries in the world to reduce exposure to the risks of environmental pollution and take measures to reduce the emission of greenhouse gases. Such an ecological policy requires investments in advanced environmental technologies, green innovations and renewable energy. Legal and regulatory frameworks should be provided in many countries to promote green investments. This way, all companies and investors are stimulated to invest in the green economy. If these states, through their environmental policies, do not promote these investments, companies have high costs for their involvement in innovative green projects. Governments that support businesses and investors through subsidies in the purchase of sustainable technologies and green innovations enable the economy of these countries to have sustainable economic development in the long term and affect the improvement of biodiversity.

Raising the population's awareness about their behaviour towards the environment and the application of new technologies has a highly positive and significant correlation in practical terms. The advancement of the education of the younger generations about environmental issues and the increase in the citizens' awareness affect the probability that the demand for sustainable products and services will increase. A trend of increasing this probability affects incentives for green innovations and investments in advanced renewable energy technologies. We have connected a practical case with citizens' awareness about the harmful effects plastic products can bring to our environment. So, suppose consumers become aware of these environmental consequences caused by plastic. In that case, consumers also demand more ecological products, influencing the increase of investments in production technologies that pack sustainable products. These investments are necessary to improve the environment and increase the population's awareness of their behaviour about the environment and biodiversity.

Reducing air and water pollution requires all countries globally to implement strict environmental protection laws to overcome these environmental challenges much more quickly. However, it should be borne in mind that each country's ecological laws must be applied strictly, fairly and without discrimination. Such implementation affects the legal effect of these environmental laws and increases their effectiveness. Applying ecological laws efficiently affects the preservation of the environment and biodiversity. It also creates equal treatment for all enterprises because it prevents unfair competition, especially from companies that do not respect international environmental standards. Strict environmental laws affect the protection of biodiversity and enable the improvement of our planet from significant ecological degradation caused by human factors. Rigorous and effective enforcement of environmental legislation is essential for preserving ecosystems and creating a sustainable and healthy environment for the entire global population.

Within the PESTLE analysis, we have a vital connection between political and legal factors. Governments of different countries should strengthen their respective legislations to effectively implement various environmental policies to protect the environment and biodiversity. Suppose the government of a country implements an environmental policy that aims to reduce greenhouse gas emissions in the atmosphere. In that case, this government seems to have the capacity to monitor and control whether this environmental law is being implemented effectively through its mechanisms and whether all companies comply with the rules established under this law. Another important interrelationship in this PESTLE analysis is between economic and environmental factors. As a result of the inaccurate assessment of environmental costs in different financial models, many companies, when they decide to invest in green technologies and innovations for renewable energy, have very high costs. If external environmental prices, such as pollution and degradation of various natural resources, are high, then in these economic models, a financial framework can be created that focusses on green investments and sustainability practices.

In recent years, the scientific literature in the economic and social fields has given great importance to sustainable management practices and environmental policies. In this part of the chapter, the findings of various scientific studies that explored the ecological challenges faced by different countries in the world, as well as the principles of environmental economy management and natural resource management, will be analysed. According to Tanveer et al. (2023), employees in the hotel industry have significant challenges in implementing sustainable practices in the circular economy and investing in green innovations in the tourism sector. Human resources in this sector have a lack of knowledge related to environmental regulations and the preservation of biodiversity, the implementation of corporate social responsibility in the development strategies of tourist agencies, and the need for employees in this sector of the economy to advance their professional capacities and competencies in the management of sustainable development and green innovations.

Setioningtyas et al. (2022) have analysed the correlation between the green economy and sustainable development goals in their study. In this study, as an object of analysis, there were also obstacles and various economic factors that affect the implementation of environmental policies in developed and developing countries. The study's findings emphasise that one of the main challenges in ecological economics is the lack of financial resources, the lack of investment in green technologies and innovations and the need for development policies and strategies that affect the sustainable development of these countries. The efficient management of these environmental challenges affects economic growth, preservation of biodiversity, management of natural resources and protection of the environment in general. In this study, it is estimated that increasing citizens' awareness of their behaviour towards the environment affects the achievement of sustainable development goals.

According to Bretschger and Pittel (2020), there is a high correlation between a country's economic system and its ecological environment. Such a significant connection is an excellent scientific basis for future scientific research that will be carried out in the field of natural resource management and green economy. The development of new theories and advanced empirical studies affects the increase in the efficient and fair use of natural resources in the economies of different countries. So, the higher the level of scientific research in the economy of natural resources, the more the effectiveness of the sustainable use of natural resources increases. In their study, Demidova et al. (2021) assessed ecological security and its impact on sustainable development in the countries of the Euro-Asian Economic Union. In this study, several mixed quantitative methods were applied, the primary purpose of which was to analyse the impact of human capital on the ecological security of the countries of this region. The quantitative methods used in this study are structural analysis, logical, econometric–statistical and comparative models. The results of this study show a very high correlative relationship between socioeconomic indicators and the variability that appears in the level of ecological security in most of the countries of the Euro-Asian Economic Union region.

According to Acheampong and Opoku (2023), environmental degradation and economic growth in different countries have a very high correlation. This meaningful correlative relationship between environmental degradation and economic growth helps to analyse how the increase in environmental pollution affects the economic development of different countries. In their study, these authors used a data panel of 140 countries, and it turns out that environmental pollution has a modest effect on economic growth. The study's findings highlight a significant correlation between economic growth, greenhouse gas emissions and the ecological footprint. According to this study, it is recommended that improving public health, increasing foreign direct investment, and technological investment in green innovations are ways in which environmental degradation can have a prolonged effect on economic growth or a minimal impact. The scientific literature of recent years offers significant findings about global ecological challenges and opportunities for solving these challenges related to global warming, climate change, biodiversity conservation and natural resource management. In their study, Tanveer et al. (2023) analysed employees' role in promoting best practices of green innovations and sustainable management. The scientific research carried out by Tanveer et al. (2023) emphasises the significant strategic role that employees have in increasing green innovations and promoting sustainable management practices, while the study of Setioningtyas et al. (2022) analyses the impact of economic, financial and technological factors on sustainable development and through this study-specific recommendations are given for the management of regulatory obstacles faced by the governments of different countries in the world. Bretschger and Pittel's (2020) and Demidova et al.'s (2021) studies have emphasised the importance of an integrated approach to global environmental challenges and socioeconomic factors' impact on the ecological security of different countries. These scientific studies highlight the importance of human capital and education as one of the main factors in promoting sustainable practices. Successfully implementing sustainable practices in the green economy and enforcing environmental laws are critical in addressing global environmental challenges and promoting sustainable economic development.

4. Economic Imperatives of Sustainable Development

Sustainable development investment projects are a catalyst for economic growth and the generation of new jobs in various countries worldwide. These projects include investments in renewable energy and green infrastructure, which improve resource efficiency and positively reduce environmental pollution. The effective management of natural resources has a positive effect on the productivity of various manufacturing industries and the attraction of foreign direct investments with particular emphasis on the green economy. Sustainable development investments encourage the development of green innovations in multiple sectors of a country's economy and create new markets. These investments include the advancement of green technologies that affect economic diversification and increase financial stability in the long term.

Economies of different countries are trying to integrate sustainable management practices into their development policies and strategies. However, these global economies constantly face various challenges that affect the progress achieved for sustainable development objectives. The main factors that cause limitations for these global economies in implementing sustainable management practices are the high costs of green technologies and the excellent resistance of various sectors of the economy that are reluctant to change from traditional practices. However, implementing these sustainability principles brings long-term benefits to the economies of these countries, affecting the reduction of energy costs and improving public health. Reducing energy costs brings positive effects not only on environmental stability but also on sustainable economic development. Strengthening environmental policies and developing well-planned economic strategies influence the added economic value of sustainability and increase international cooperation between countries to more effectively manage global ecological challenges.

According to the study of Holden et al. (2016), the economies of different countries in the world need the development of a sustainability model based on meeting the aggregate requirements of the population, ensuring economic well-being, ensuring social equality and respecting environmental rights. The successful implementation of this sustainability model and the fulfilment of these factors argue that these are the economic priorities of sustainable development for each country, and these factors also set limits on human behaviour towards the environment. These economic priorities of sustainable development also define the limitations of the financial activities of companies in different sectors of the real economy and challenge the traditional models of sustainable development. In their study, Chaturvedi (2024) analyse the complex issues of sustainable development in the economies of different countries in the world, and these economic dilemmas are related to the challenges associated with the use of natural resources and the level of environmental degradation. These authors propose solving these global ecological challenges through increased investment in green innovations and advanced sustainability technologies. An excellent solution to these environmental challenges can be achieved by strengthening ecological laws and political interventions regulating environmental issues.

Mensah (2019) studied the correlation between the environment, economy and society about the principles of sustainable development. Exploring the correlations between these variables is important because the design and development of strategic environmental policies in different countries must consider the relationship between the environment, economy and society. All policymakers and decision-makers must consider the connections between these factors to increase people's awareness of their behaviour about the environment and the preservation of biodiversity. The study by Cheah and Cheah (2003) criticise traditional development models, arguing that these models are based on economic aspects that create inequality and do not affect long-term sustainability. Through this study, these authors recommend that different countries' governments develop advanced alternative models that ensure transparency and ethics and are more sustainable in the long term. Integrating the elements of ethics, transparency and social equality affects the fulfilment of the needs of the majority of the population at the global level. Developing these alternative models also positively affects the reduction of economic and social inequalities in all global population groups.

The studies analysed in this part of the chapter have significantly contributed to sustainable development because they help policymakers and other stakeholders better understand the strategic priorities of sustainable development policies in different countries. Through their study, Holden et al. (2016) have developed a model that emphasises the strategic priorities of sustainable development, where the model mainly focusses on human needs, social equity and environmental rights issues. The advancement of new development models in sustainable management has positive effects on current economic policies at the global level because it challenges traditional models and influences the optimisation of sustainable development goals that are related to ESG principles. Chaturvedi (2024) emphasise that increasing investments in green technologies and encouraging innovations in the green economy affect the promotion of sustainable economic development and create a reasonable basis for solving global environmental challenges related to climate change. According to this study, it is estimated that the government has a crucial role in the policy development of ecological issues that will affect the effective management of natural resources and create a secure future for biodiversity and the global population. Mensah (2019), in his study, argues that the environment, economy and society are critical factors that support the sustainable development of a country. The scientific research that will be developed in the future related to the strategic priorities of sustainable development should focus more on the research of ethical and social considerations in economic policies and the promotion of transparency and social justice in the entire population. These scientific studies should develop new models integrating green technologies in different industry sectors to successfully manage economic inequalities and social justice challenges.

5. Policy Frameworks for Sustainable Development

Different countries at the global level during the last few years have been designing and implementing various environmental and economic policies for sustainable development that aim to manage the global ecological challenges resulting from climate change as effectively as possible. These environmental and economic policies include measures related to reducing carbon dioxide emissions, reducing adverse effects resulting from global warming and protecting biodiversity.

Such environmental and monetary policies will positively influence the creation of a stable ecological balance in the long term that will provide a reasonable basis for optimising natural resources at the global level. The main goal of these environmental and economic policies is to encourage different countries to use alternative renewable energy sources, such as the sun and wind, to reduce dependence on fossil resources while simultaneously affecting the reduction of environmental pollution. The financing of international projects by the governments of these countries and global financial institutions for the next few years in the field of circular economy will play a vital role in reducing waste and increasing the use of recyclable materials. Promoting effective natural resource management policies will positively affect the protection of ecosystems that are estimated to be critical from environmental pollution and affect sustainable global economic development.

The main goal of public economic policies and strategies is to ensure effective management in all sectors of the real economy in a country and also to achieve this effective management; it is necessary to analyse the effectiveness of these public policies and strategies from the point of view of economic well-being and living standard growth. These policies and financial strategies are effective when they positively affect the fulfilment of sustainable development goals. A concrete example that can be analysed from the point of view of the effectiveness of economic policies and strategies is the health sector, precisely healthcare policies. So, healthcare policies aim to improve the access and quality of healthcare services to protect the environment and preserve biodiversity and public health in a country. Suppose the government of a country makes capital investments in improving and advancing the healthcare infrastructure. In that case, such investments will increase awareness among the population about prevention services. Such a factor will positively affect the reduction of health costs in the long term and significantly improve healthcare institutions' work productivity. Through national education strategies, educational institutions in different countries should promote the inclusion and equal access to education of all population groups to contribute positively to developing sustainable skills for the green economy and, simultaneously, are more qualified for the labour market through these skills. In the framework of these educational policies at the national level in the various countries of the world, international projects that support the advancement of knowledge in the field of technology and the increase of professional skills in the green economy and innovation should be included. Through such educational policies and their integration with social protection policies, it is possible to ensure the inclusion of population groups without discrimination. Such an integration of educational and social policies will affect the reduction of inequalities and the advancement of social cohesion. So, effective policies and strategies for environmental, economic, academic and social issues will increase social security and support for the unemployed through various social programmes to create a global, equal and sustainable society.

In their research, Dhali et al. (2023) find that a solid legal framework and effective implementation of this legislation in the oil and gas sector will positively affect the achievement of sustainable development goals. In this study, the authors have used a qualitative methodology through the comparative approach by analysing the legislation of Bangladesh and Nigeria. The study's findings show that although these two countries have made considerable advances in the legal aspect in terms of sustainable development, the legislation of these countries still needs to be improved to achieve the goals of sustainable development in the energy sector. Through this study, these two countries should develop significant reforms in their legislation on environmental and energy issues to ensure these laws' suitability by the European Commission's requirements for sustainable development.

In their research, Bekun et al. (2021) have analysed the impact of international tourism, foreign direct investment, electricity production and urbanisation on sustainable economic growth in the five countries that have the most sustainable economies (China, Turkey, India, the United States and Indonesia). The econometric findings of this study show a positive correlation between foreign direct investment and the level of income for the economies of these developed countries. This positive correlation between Foreign Direct Investment (FDI) and the level of income in the economies of these countries exists because these foreign direct investments influence the attraction of new capital, contemporary technology and the bringing of expertise from different countries. These factors positively affect the economies of these countries through increased productivity and an increase in the general income level. In this study, the authors also investigated the curve of environmental Kuznets and the halo effect of foreign direct investment on environmental issues. Because foreign direct investments in the economies of these countries bring the halo effect through the improvement of the ecological standard, technologies and management practices in the host country, then in this study, it is recommended that the governments of these countries undertake concrete actions to promote sustainable economic growth through foreign direct investments in the field of green economy and clean technologies.

According to the analysis made by Tomai et al. (2024), all stakeholders in environmental and sustainable development issues must be informed about all the necessary steps to follow during a transition process. Therefore, each firm must create a conceptual framework to explain in detail these steps, starting from presenting the problem, formulating concrete actions, and evaluating them to take concrete measures to improve sustainability practices. Conceptual frameworks developed by businesses should include best sustainability practices through an integrated approach that will positively influence company leadership and policymaking in terms of sustainable development. This integrated approach of these companies to improving sustainability practices includes the evaluation phase of systemic challenges, the design of the mission, vision and strategies in the function of sustainability and the implementation of political actions undertaken by the company's leadership. According to Filho et al. (2024), higher education institutions in their study programmes should include and promote more innovatively the concepts of sustainable development and the fulfilment of learning expectations of their academic programmes. The study programmes' objectives should also incorporate scientific research and contemporary teaching. These institutions of higher education need to develop an integrated approach by applying new teaching and scientific research methods and tools so that all study programmes succeed in dealing with the concepts of sustainable development. The study results note a gap in the scientific literature regarding the appropriate tools that should be applied to integrate sustainable development goals in the study programmes of higher education institutions. Therefore, these authors propose designing an international framework to help universities include sustainable development goals in university programmes. This global framework should consist of the institutional aspects, main themes, structure and individual issues that need to be considered to implement a successful integration of the sustainable development goals in university programmes.

6. Technological Innovations and Green Solutions

Nowadays, the development of technology and green innovations are among the main factors influencing the improvement of environmental performance, reducing environmental degradation, and reducing the adverse effects on the environment resulting from industrial activities. Ecological and biodiversity degradation comes from greenhouse gas emissions, energy consumption and hazardous waste. In many countries, reducing environmental pollution and preserving biodiversity requires more investments in modern technologies to reduce greenhouse gas emissions and positively affect efficient and sustainable energy consumption. Governments must develop environmental policies and strategies that support and promote green investments that will positively impact the protection of the environment and biodiversity. These green investments include investments in efficient energy management systems, green innovations and advanced technologies that will enable the benefit of electric energy from alternative sources. The evolution of artificial intelligence through environmental data analysis enables all stakeholders and companies to manage environmental resources better and apply the best sustainability practices. Business and industrial processes that apply innovative artificial intelligence systems have positively affected these industries by eliminating some externalities to the environment and biodiversity.

Economies of developed countries have implemented many considerable investment projects in technology and green innovations, which have preserved the environment and biodiversity from degradation and ongoing climate change. These green investments enable the economies of different countries to implement the best environmental policies in sustainable development, which will improve environmental pollution and more efficient management of the ecosystem. Wind and solar energy as alternative renewable energy sources result from continuous investments in advanced environmental and energy technologies. An increase in renewable energy sources brings positive effects, such as reducing dependence on fossil resources and environmental degradation. Green innovations affect the advancement of new methods of recycling waste and other waste materials. Such an effective waste management process will affect the improvement of natural resource management in the economies of different countries. Investments in green technologies and innovations affect not only the protection of the environment but also the creation of a strong base of sustainability in the economies of different countries worldwide.

Saqib and Usman (2023) argue a high positive correlation between the green economy, strict rules set by energy regulatory agencies, technological innovations and zero carbon emissions. This correlation is valid for the US economy and China because these two countries have made deep reforms in environmental and energy policies to ensure carbon emissions at the lowest possible levels. The scientific results of this study show that continuous investments in technological innovations and the growth of green activities in the economies of these two countries have a significant adverse effect on the probability of carbon emissions in these two countries in the future. These long-term forecasts argued by this study will serve as a good reference for the governments of these two countries to harmonise their environmental and energy policies according to the results derived from this study. Therefore, these environmental policies and strategies should promote and encourage green innovations and increase green economy activities to achieve zero carbon emission targets.

In their conclusion, Lai and Shi (2020) argue that investments in green innovations and the advancement of modern technologies that reduce carbon emissions are a new segment for sustainable development in the economies of many countries globally. Therefore, future scientific research in the environment, energy and economy focusses on analysing the correlative links between economic factors, environment and energy policies. As evidenced by advanced scientific methodologies, these future scientific researchers will use the interdisciplinary approach to develop new theories. The scientific results of these studies will be a good reference base for policymakers to solve various environmental challenges and address the complex environmental problems presented by ecological pollution and biodiversity loss. These scientific studies suggest that each country should promote green innovations for sustainable economic, environmental and energy development. Fulfilling these sustainable development objectives requires integrating new approaches of modern technologies and innovations in the field of green economy.

According to Ozkan et al. (2023), investments in green innovations and advanced environmental technologies will increase the probability of reducing Turkey's carbon footprint by influencing sustainable economic development and improving environmental quality from industrial activities in Turkey. Through this study, the authors emphasise that the Turkish government must implement more rigorous environmental policies to control energy consumption in this country so that in the future, it can take efficient measures to reduce the level of environmental degradation resulting from climate change. Economic and ecological policies in Turkey should focus on developing various government programmes that will influence the promotion of green investments in the Turkish economy. Through multiple subsidies, these government programmes will help companies in different sectors of the economy to invest in green projects for sustainable economic development and conservation of biodiversity.

According to the scientific results of the study by Li et al. (2023), the construction sector in the Chinese economy is characterised by a significant level of investment in green innovations. These green investments in this sector of the economy will significantly influence the reduction of carbon emission levels and positively reduce exposure to environmental risks. The econometric results of this study highlight a significant nonlinear relationship between green innovations and carbon emissions in the Chinese economy. This nonlinear correlation is statistically significant and has an exponential trend. It is worth noting that this nonlinear correlative relationship largely depends on the level of implementation of environmental policies in China. So, environmental regulations in China must be rigorous and fully implemented to maximise the positive impact of green innovations on carbon dioxide emissions. Investments in green innovations in China will affect the exponential growth of the carbon dioxide emission level, and such a ratio shows a significant nonlinear correlation.

7. Case Studies and Best Practices in Sustainable Development

In recent years, the world has been facing various environmental, social and economic challenges that affect the population's daily life at the global level, and these challenges are becoming more and more complex and complicated to solve.

As a result of these difficulties arising from environmental, social and economic challenges, for many international organisations and governments of different countries, the issue of sustainable development has become a primary objective of their national policies in terms of environmental, economic and social issues. This part of the chapter will analyse some case studies that have successfully implemented the best sustainability practices and created a more sustainable living environment. Through these case studies, concrete examples will be taken from the practices of different countries to investigate how other companies have successfully implemented their strategies in terms of sustainable development. In these case studies, concrete cases will be explained that will include companies and projects from different fields that, through their strategies, have positively influenced the fulfilment of sustainable development goals. A SWOT analysis will also be offered in this part of the chapter. The advantages, shortcomings, opportunities and risks will be analysed for all these companies that implement sustainable development practices and projects in different fields. Through this analysis, the best sustainability practices considered success stories are identified, and specific recommendations for implementing development strategies in the field of sustainability are offered.

This part of the chapter will review the literature on the best sustainability practices that have been successfully implemented in the economies of different countries worldwide. Then, we will focus on three specific case studies and show a success story in implementing the best practices of sustainable development. According to the study by Hannan (2015), the poverty level and the successful implementation of green economy projects largely depend on how effectively ecosystems are managed and how sustainable they are. Therefore, governments in different countries should set the main objectives in their development policies and strategies at the national level, such as increasing the standard of living, improving economic well-being and reducing expenses for family economies and businesses. Such economic progress has positive effects on all groups of society and has financial benefits for all companies in various sectors of the economy at home and abroad. The development of entrepreneurial projects in the field of green economy should support economic growth in all sectors of the industry, the generation of new jobs, the reduction of the poverty level and the increase of the social well-being of the population. All these macroeconomic objectives for the government of a country are achieved in parallel by preserving the ecosystem and biodiversity and reducing environmental degradation. To successfully achieve all these macroeconomic objectives, it is more important to emphasise that the governments of different countries in the world must develop concrete policies and strategies at the national level to support the green economy and international trade. This study provides a convincing argument for all policymakers and stakeholders that the green economy requires effective management to positively impact poverty levels, improve living standards, and increase economic and social well-being for all groups without demographic discrimination.

The study by Bustum (2015) argues that the development of ecotourism is a significant factor that affects sustainable economic development. By generating new jobs in the ecotourism sector, the country's poverty level is significantly reduced. The population in a country with a lower income and a lower standard of living through the development of ecotourism can maximise the social, economic and environmental benefits for these special population groups. It is worth noting that this correlation between the development of ecotourism and the reduction of poverty is not a direct causal relationship because it requires the integration of policies and economic strategies that must be effectively implemented to achieve positive results in reducing poverty. As part of the study, several countries have been analysed regarding how they have developed ecotourism and various international projects in the green economy field that positively impact a country's sustainable development. A concrete country considered to be a success story for the development of ecotourism is South Africa, which, through projects developed in the ecotourism sector, has created cooperation between the formal and informal sectors in the economy of this country. This cooperation, specifically between the hospitality and artisanal production sectors, has brought great economic, social and environmental benefits to all communities living in different areas of South Africa. So, ecotourism in this country has enabled the increase of cooperation between these two sectors, where all the households that deal with handicraft products have had the opportunity to supply these products to the various businesses in the tourism and hotel sectors. Through this study, we can observe that if the ecotourism sector develops in a country and we successfully integrate policies and economic strategies that support the development of this sector, then the government of a country, through such a policy, improves the economic situation of the country and helps special groups of the population that have lower incomes.

Following this chapter, we will analyse another very successful case study in Austria that shows the role of higher education institutions in developing international projects that offer innovative solutions for the green economy and sustainable development of a country. In 2014, the Technical University of Vienna established the mobility laboratory in Austria to provide a project where all universities and other stakeholders can collaborate and develop various innovative ideas in the field of green economy. The stakeholders involved in this mobility lab are industry, businesses, government, regulatory agencies, non-governmental organisations and citizens. All these stakeholders, in cooperation with universities in Austria within this laboratory, cooperate to offer innovative solutions in the field of green economy. Through this laboratory, all stakeholders, especially Austrian citizens, have actively participated in the realisation of green projects and in developing new innovative ideas in the field of green economy. Through this mobility laboratory, the Austrian government has created a sustainable public–private partnership financing model that integrates the active involvement of all stakeholders in developing innovative ideas in the green economy. In general, the project of creating the mobility laboratory in Austria has influenced the advancement of the implementation of the best sustainability practices and has served as a model for other European countries to develop similar laboratories that enable the solution of complex environmental problems and provide green solutions. The integration of all stakeholders in this project means that cooperation between the different communities is achieved to offer as many new innovative green ideas as possible to solve the various environmental challenges that may result from climate change (OECD, 2023).

The SUSBINCO (Sustainable Binders and Coatings) project in Finland is very successful in the green economy and sustainable development field. This project was an innovative idea developed by 18 partner institutions, including industrial organisations and research institutes in Finland and beyond. The main goal of this project was to create bio-alternatives based on materials used in different sectors of Finnish industry. This innovative project is financed by leading industrial companies and businesses in Finland and is led as a project by Åbo Akademi University in Finland. Through this project, it is intended that the Finnish economy offers an ecological solution for this country, positively affecting the reduction of dependence on fossil fuels. The results of this green project show that many Finnish industrial companies and businesses have developed bio-based ingredients based on the final products produced in various industry sectors. Also, through this project, the effects that can be caused by using chemical materials that do not contain toxic substances have been investigated to a large extent, and the environmental impact of the new biomaterials that this project has developed will have been tested. This project has produced much-needed scientific results for the needs and demands of the industry. Also, the universities involved have developed and disseminated these scientific results. Project SUSBINCO is a model of how industry, businesses, government and universities should collaborate to create new innovative green ideas that positively affect the management of global environmental challenges in the future. This project has positively impacted the Finnish economy because all the exporting companies involved have increased competition with foreign world markets, positively influencing economic growth and the generation of new jobs in various sectors of the Finnish economy. Green's high implementation success and sustainability rank Finland as one of the leading countries in the world in terms of implementing sustainability best practices and green innovations (OECD, 2023).

The Ørsted company was founded in 1972 in Fredericia, Denmark, and is one of the largest multinational companies in the energy sector in Denmark. This company is a case study in this chapter because it is considered a very successful business model that has transformed how electricity is produced by implementing the best practices of sustainable development and a green economy. This transformation involves the production model of clean energy from a process that has been based on fossil fuel sources. In recent years, the Ørsted company has been estimated to be a global leader in benefiting from clean energy and meeting sustainable development goals in the Danish economy. In 2008, the management of this company decided to change its strategy regarding how electricity would be produced. In their development strategies for energy efficiency, the company decided to focus on renewable sources of energy efficiency, such as solar and wind. Therefore, the company has invested a lot in technologies that benefit clean energy in recent years. These investments have enabled this company to replace the old machines, mainly applied to the benefit of energy from sources such as coal. With these gigantic investments that this global company has made in the benefit of clean energy from the sun and wind, the largest offshore wind parks have been built. These offshore wind energy investments have been made within the Hornsea 1 project in Great Britain; according to energy and environmental experts, it is estimated that this project will build the largest park in the world, which uses offshore wind as an open energy source. The transformation of this Danish company in obtaining energy from fossil sources to clean energy from the sun and wind has turned out to be one of the most profitable and successful projects in managing global challenges caused by climate change. This project has influenced the significant decrease in the emission of greenhouse gases with particular emphasis on carbon dioxide, and since 2006, this decrease in carbon emission has been reduced by 80%. By 2025, Ørsted aims to be a leading company in the energy sector as it tends to zero carbon emissions. This transformation process of this Danish company is a success story in implementing good sustainability practices because renewable energy from clean alternative sources such as solar and wind has ensured that this company has a very high reputation globally but also brings significant benefits in economic and environmental terms. The strategies developed by the Ørsted company are a good reference point for all other global companies in the energy sector because, through well-planned and sustainable investments, a transformation of energy production from fossil to renewable sources can be successfully achieved (Ørsted, 2023).

The following will analyse the case of Singapore, which is estimated to be a model country that has created best practices of sustainability in water management, water security and the advancement of water system infrastructure. Singapore is one of the most prosperous states, and it has developed very efficient policies for advancing the wastewater system and recycling. Government policies and strategies for environmental issues in Singapore are oriented towards the development of an integrated system for water management in all urban and rural areas in this country. This system includes recycling wastewater, sustainable use of natural resources and modernising the water supply network. Wastewater management and its recycling process in Singapore is done through an efficient system called NEWater that uses sophisticated technologies to treat and purify wastewater. After this process, this system enables disinfection with ultraviolet rays, and through this process, an efficient system for recycling wastewater has been created. The NEWater water management system in Singapore has created a sustainable model for producing clean water and meets all the needs of households and businesses in Singapore. Also, it is worth noting that this water management system has ensured a reliable supply for all residents of Singapore. Managing wastewater in Singapore through recycling and converting it into clean water is a very safe and reliable process for public health. According to international water quality standards, it is subject to all filtration and disinfection processes. This water is primarily used to meet all industrial requirements during production in various industry sectors in Singapore.

The local government in the city of Singapore has allocated a large part of the budget for capital investment for the construction and advancement of water infrastructure. Investments in water infrastructure include the construction of water tanks, new equipment for water purification and the advancement of the drainage system for controlling surface water and running water. Advances in water system infrastructure and wastewater recycling have contributed to creating sustainability in water supply and meeting all the needs of various industries in Singapore. This wastewater recycling project has influenced the protection of natural resources in Singapore because this country has implemented adequate policies and strategies for protecting natural resources. Efficient management and protection of natural resources have been realised through capital investments in sophisticated technologies for controlling and monitoring water quality according to international standards. Through this project, the Government of Singapore has effectively managed wastewater, and the importance of developing an integrated strategy for recycling wastewater in other countries is also emphasised. So, this integrated approach includes investments in advanced technologies and greater cooperation of relevant institutions to develop policies to protect biodiversity, preserve water quality, and efficiently manage natural resources. Singapore's economy has greatly benefitted from this wastewater recycling project because, through a sustainable water supply, all business activities in various sectors of the economy are supported, the quality of life is increased, more capital investment is stimulated, and a model is advanced in global water management (PUB, Singapore's National Water Agency, 2017).

This part of the chapter will analyse the last case study related to the Rodale Institute in Pennsylvania, United States. This American institute is one of the main leaders in organic and sustainable agriculture in the United States and globally. The Rodale Institute was founded in 1947 and, as a scientific institution, has developed a successful strategy in promoting the best practices applied in organic agriculture. These practices have been promoted through research projects and educational campaigns that have served as a very good guide for US farmers. Through innovative scientific projects in organic agriculture, the Rodale Institute has developed new and advanced techniques for testing organic farming methods. These methods include the application of organic or green manures, crop rotation and biological management of natural pests. This institute has developed new strategies to increase the production of healthy and safe food for the entire American population. The projects applied by this American institute are focussed on developing methods for soil conservation and increasing soil quality to produce healthy food without using pesticides and chemical fertilisers.

The development of new production methods in organic agriculture has dramatically influenced the growth of food production in the United States according to international quality standards in organic agriculture. In addition to increasing the production of healthy and organic food at the macroeconomic level, the Rodale Institute has also contributed positively to local economic development. This positive impact on the local American economy is emphasised through increased living standards for rural families and increased incomes for American farmers. So, these farmers have had an increase in demand for organic products, which has helped them reach greater in the American markets and beyond. In terms of sustainability, the Rodale Institute has influenced, through organic agriculture application projects, to significantly reduce the exposure of the environment to the adverse effects that may result from organic agriculture products. These adverse effects of organic farming on the environment include soil erosion and environmental degradation from various agricultural chemicals.

The success of the projects carried out by the Rodale Institute in the United States shows that organic agriculture is beneficial and profitable for families and businesses, with a particular emphasis on farmers. So, through this organic farming model, the idea has been promoted that all farmers, not only in the United States but also in other countries of the world, can follow the best practices and experiences of sustainability and increase the residents' awareness about the benefits that the consumption of organic foods brings. The Rodale Institute, through the model developed in organic agriculture, has positively influenced the economic development of the United States through the diversification of the agricultural economy and the increase of employment and export in the markets of organic products. The model developed by this American institute has positively influenced the effective management of natural resources and increased the quality of the environment and agricultural land. This organic agriculture model will be a good reference model for other countries developing organic agriculture projects (Rodale Institute, 2021).

Fig. 5.1 presents the SWOT analysis for all companies implementing sustainability practices. This analysis explains the strengths, weaknesses, opportunities and threats these companies face in implementing the best practices of sustainable development. One of the main strengths of companies that implement sustainability practices is the improvement of reputation or good name in the industry in which that company operates. Implementing these best practices of sustainable development will improve the market's image, attract more consumers and

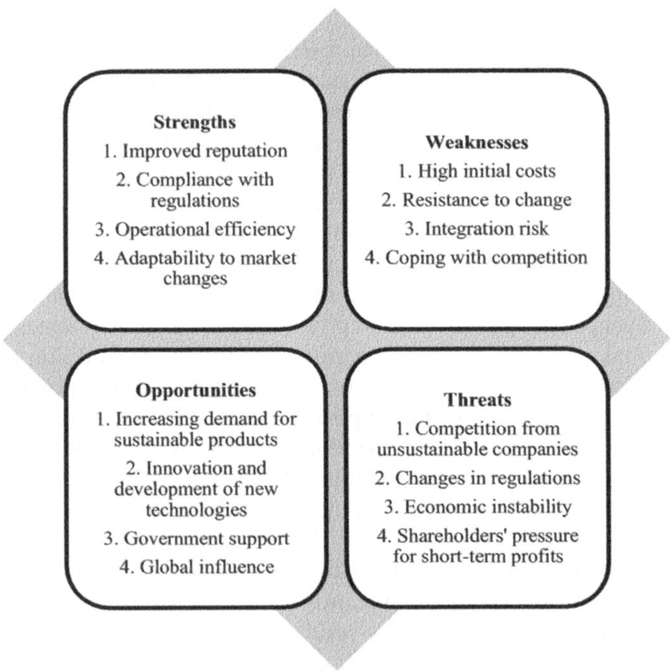

Fig. 5.1. SWOT Analysis for Companies Implementing Sustainable Development Practices. *Source:* The Global Risks Report (World Economic Forum, 2023).

increase their involvement in the market. A better reputation in the market also influences the attraction of more investors interested in investing in sustainable projects because they are considered profitable.

When companies in various industries and sectors of the economy implement these sustainability practices, they have a higher level of compliance with environmental policies and regulations. A higher level of this harmonisation between the companies' development strategies and ecological rules reduces the risk of various sanctions. These companies are evaluated as successful in implementing these sustainability practices and have higher efficiency and adaptability to market changes. These sustainability practices influence companies in the more efficient management of the resources they have available, influencing the reduction of operating costs and positively impacting the increase of profitability in the long term. Because the global market is dynamic due to rapid changes, companies that successfully implement these sustainability practices are well prepared to manage these changes and will likely be less exposed to market risks.

Among the weaknesses of companies that implement sustainable practices, the high initial costs, exposure to integration risk, resistance to changes, and challenges from the competition have been identified. Companies that implement sustainable development practices at the initial stage have high costs due to the investments that must be made in green technologies, and this high level of costs causes difficulties in identifying sources of short-term financing. These companies must be well prepared to face obstacles from internal and external factors in the business environment where they operate. Integrating these sustainability practices into all business activities presents a complex challenge for managers, and in some cases, these difficulties are a consequence of internal factors. Therefore, these companies must design an adequate strategy for integrating sustainability practices into business operations to avoid encountering internal obstacles. As internal factors, there is also resistance to changes resulting from implementing sustainable development practices. This internal resistance mostly comes from individuals who have experience with more traditional practices and resist learning more contemporary work practices, which positively affect their performance and the company's. In the framework of the external factors of the business environment, it is a challenge to face the competition and precisely for the price level. Companies that do not implement sustainable practices can compete in the market with lower price levels, and this part greatly influences the creation of competitive advantages for companies that successfully implement sustainable development practices.

Opportunities for companies that implement sustainable development practices include the increase in demand for green products, the promotion of innovation and the development of new technologies, support from the government and various international organisations, and influence on global markets. Considering that we have increased awareness of the green economy and sustainable development in recent years, the demand for green products and services has also increased. Such an increase in demand for these products and services is a perfect opportunity to develop many businesses in the field of sustainability and generate new jobs, as well as to create new professions that require this knowledge in the labour market. Since green products and services need to be supported by new technologies and innovations, these companies must invest in these technologies, and this investment can create a competitive advantage in the market compared to new companies. Also, such a competitive advantage encourages the growth and development of business activity through green products and services. Since as a weakness in this SWOT analysis, we identified the high level of initial costs for these companies that implement sustainability practices, then as their opportunity are subsidies for various government programmes and incentives that international organisations can support, can help these companies to easily afford these costs and manage their financial resources more efficiently. Global policies and European Union policies focus on sustainable development and the green economy to successfully manage the various environmental challenges that result from climate change. Therefore, these companies that successfully implement these sustainable practices have many opportunities to improve and advance their position in global markets and attract more international investment.

According to the SWOT analysis, several threats have been identified that may endanger companies that implement sustainability practices in their business activities. These threats are competition from companies that do not implement these sustainability practices, changes in laws and regulations, economic instability or lack of stability, and pressure from shareholders to obtain higher returns from their financial investments in short-term periods. Companies operating in the same industry or economic sector and others that need to implement these sustainable practices can compete in the market with lower prices, which creates pressure on the profit margin. Therefore, lower prices are considered a threat to companies that implement sustainable practices. In this situation, these companies must be cautious about how external factors are managed and what marketing strategy to apply to mitigate the pressure from competition. Rapid and unexpected changes in government laws and regulations are sometimes considered a shock because these changes affect the immediate cost increase resulting from implementing sustainability practices. So, these costs can be derived from changing environmental laws requiring rapid adaptation to legal requirements. When a country's economy is in recession or we have an economic crisis, many companies estimate that green investments are excessive and can be postponed to future periods because they cause high and unaffordable business costs during economic decline. Another threat for these companies is the shareholders' focus on short-term profits, and such an investment strategy of these shareholders negatively affects the development of sustainability practices. Shareholders' focus on short-term profits hinders the successful implementation of sustainability practices because long-term profits are required and create more significant exposure to various financial and macroeconomic risks.

8. Community and Stakeholder Engagement in Sustainable and Green Activities

Sustainable development and green economy policies largely depend on the level of engagement of the community and stakeholders in various sectors of the economy and industry. Successfully developing these policies requires the involvement and increased role of the community and stakeholders in green policies and sustainability. This active role of the community and stakeholders is essential because it is easier to identify all the fundamental needs that society has, build greater trust between the main actors, and increase the level of implementation of these policies since we have a more comprehensive approach to the development of sustainable and green policies. Such integration of the community and all interested parties makes the decision-making more effective and makes these decisions more stable in terms of their importance and implementation in society. Integrating the community and stakeholders in sustainable development policies means that all actors involved in these issues have achieved a higher level of harmonisation between interests and values. Raising the standard and effectiveness of green policies largely depends on community and stakeholder engagement for sustainable development and a green economy. This increase in the quality and standard for implementing these development policies relies on the commitment of the stakeholders because new innovative ideas can be developed that contribute positively to the success of these green policies.

In their research, Stocker et al. (2023) find that increasing the quality of corporate sustainability reporting and effective management of environmental issues and green policies largely depends on the involvement and integration of stakeholders in sustainability issues. The participation of stakeholders in the company's sustainability-related issues should be realised through a model that integrates three types of strategies. These stakeholder integration strategies are the information strategy, the response strategy and the sustainability involvement strategy. The scientific findings of this study from an analysis of 119 sustainable development reports in the energy industry of 40 different countries show that the inclusion strategy is the most adequate and effective method that has influenced the increase in the standard and quality of green and sustainability policies in these countries. So, even though stakeholder involvement strategies in sustainability policies are of higher quality, these strategies must be more appropriate and compatible with the companies analysed in this study. These companies have involved stakeholders in simpler forms, such as information strategy through sustainability reports where stakeholders are informed about periodic issues without participating in in-depth analysis. Through this study, a matrix has been proposed that develops models and modalities for integrating the stakeholder involvement strategy in sustainability practices to improve performance and increase quality standards in corporate reporting.

Nonet et al. (2023) argue that many countries must develop adequate policies to achieve the objectives of the United Nations 2030 Agenda for Sustainable Development. This study emphasises that in some countries, the involvement of the community and interested parties in sustainable activities and the development of green policies has influenced achieving the objectives set according to the 2030 Agenda. To be completed, these objectives require an active commitment to all relevant actors in the field of sustainability and the full integration of green policies with development strategies for environmental issues. However, it is worth noting that full involvement of all interested parties and a focus on practical strategy are challenging because all private companies implementing sustainable practices encounter significant obstacles to creating collaborations based on shared principles. To overcome and solve these difficulties for private companies, the needs of the sectors of the economy must be harmonised, the strategic objectives must be specified, and the way stakeholders understand operational perceptions must be analysed. According to the analysis done by Henriques et al. (2023), there is a positive correlation between quality standards of non-financial reports and stakeholder involvement in the paper sector in Spain and Portugal. According to the empirical findings of this study, it is emphasised that Spanish and Portuguese companies in the paper sector that have correctly followed all international reporting standards of consistency and integrity of accounting information give more importance to relations with the community and stakeholders. These enterprises in the paper sector have higher levels of information on economic, social and environmental issues that must be presented in sustainability reports and that influence the increase in the quality of the reports.

In their study, Zikargae et al. (2023) argue that increasing economic and social well-being in Ethiopia's rural areas depends mainly on stakeholders' involvement in green policies and sustainable development projects under the United Nations 2030 Agenda. This active engagement of stakeholders in various green and sustainable projects also affects the increase of environmental security in rural settlements in Ethiopia. The empirical results of the thematic analysis have identified three critical concepts for the active role of stakeholders in sustainability issues. The key concepts identified are consultation, cooperation and partnership, which are estimated to be essential factors that positively influence the engagement of stakeholders in sustainable development policies in Ethiopia. Through this study, it is recommended that all non-governmental organisations and civil society, in general, apply work methods based on good faith and promote cooperation between different stakeholders to ensure long-term sustainability in various community projects.

9. Assessing the Impact and Efficiency of Sustainable Development Strategies

The evaluation of how long-term environmental, economic and social goals have been achieved in a country by the 2030 Agenda of the United Nations is realised through evaluating the impact and efficiency of different sustainable development strategies. The evaluation of the effects and efficiency of sustainable policies and strategies is done through analytical methods that enable the measurement of specific results and the classification of scientific findings considered relevant for making consistent decisions in sustainable development. The analytical techniques used to evaluate the impact and effect of sustainable strategies in a country's economy are statistical analyses, qualitative analyses, and the evaluation of the life cycle of products and services. Statistical analyses are econometric methods that apply quantitative data. Economic measurements evaluate the impact and efficiency of policies and strategies on a country's economy. Also, statistical analysis considers the environmental impact of a country's economic and industrial activity. Through these coefficients, the type of impact is correctly assessed.

Qualitative analyses mainly evaluate the perceptions and opinions of stakeholders from different perspectives, enabling the identification of critical concepts and qualitative information derived from experiences and discussions with these stakeholders. In the framework of qualitative assessments, in-depth interviews, and focus groups can be organised with experts in the economy, environment and other related fields to analyse their perceptions and opinions regarding the effectiveness of sustainable policies in economic development and environmental protection in general. One of the most necessary methods for companies in various sectors of the economy and industry to assess the environmental impact of products and services is the life cycle assessment method. So, through this method, qualitative and quantitative measurements can be made for all phases of a product and service life cycle. These measurements start from the source of raw materials and continue to the last stage of the life cycle, waste disposal. The comparative method of the life cycle identifies which stage is the most critical and the need to take measures to improve the negative effects on the environment.

According to Angrisani et al. (2023), environmental sustainability assessment must be realised through a methodological approach that applies information and communication technology to model the ecological impact of different companies' economic and industrial activity. In recent times, environmental sustainability measurement systems have advanced. They must apply automation in production processes and advanced technologies such as the Internet of Things, artificial intelligence, big data and cyber-physical systems. Applying these advanced technologies in sustainable environmental measurements creates a more accurate, more reliable measurement system. It affects the increase in the quality of the confidence in the results to achieve the fulfilment of the objectives of sustainable development.

The study conducted by Sarker et al. (2021) points out that the most advanced and accurate models that help in the process of making effective sustainability decisions by industrial managers are the balanced scorecard (BSC) and fuzzy multiple criteria decision making (FMCDM). Evaluating the efficiency of sustainable policies and strategies is more accurate and reliable when integrating these two methods, which are applied to making different decisions by industrial managers. BSC is a method that evaluates the overall performance of companies based on key indicators of the green economy and ESG factors. This method also evaluates progress achieved in the context of sustainable development objectives related to economic, social and environmental issues. FMCDM is the second method applied to assess sustainability and the impact of ESG factors on the performance of organisations that implement sustainability best practices. This method is part of the theory of information and mathematics that, according to fuzzy logic, treats information related to the impact of economic, social and environmental factors on the performance of different organisations. The information generated by this method facilitates industrial managers in making effective decisions that benefit the company and the environment. So, both methods present potent tools for managers in different enterprises to make efficient decisions.

Popescu et al. (2021) argue that investment funds should improve and advance their sustainability assessment methods so that these assessments are more accurate and reliable and also avoid greenwashing, which represents a practice where investment funds do not reflect the actual environmental impact they have on sustainable development. Through this study, the authors emphasise that scientific methods focussed on sustainability should also be a priority for investment fund managers to evaluate the impact of investments in achieving sustainability objectives. Using these methods based on scientific research ensures more excellent reliability, validity and transparency in the results, which will reflect the effects that investments have on sustainable development. Mengistu and Panizzolo (2023) emphasise the importance of industrial sustainability indicators used to evaluate the performance of small- and medium-sized enterprises in different sectors of the economy. These indicators are efficient and valuable because they evaluate economic benefits, productivity, social sustainability and natural resource efficiency. The results of this study show that the indicators of industrial sustainability are reliable, and through them, the confidence in measurements related to the sustainability assessment in Small and Medium Enterprises (SMEs) increases. These indicators of SMEs' industrial sustainability include economic, environmental and social indicators. Economic indicators include energy costs, market, production level, return on investments, etc. Within the framework of ecological indicators, the level of carbon dioxide emission, water consumption, energy efficiency and waste management should be evaluated. Within the framework of social indicators, working conditions, employee satisfaction, community engagement stakeholders, etc., should be evaluated. All these indicators help small and medium enterprises improve their performance in these areas and advance in meeting sustainable development objectives according to the 2030 Agenda.

10. Conclusions and Recommendations

Sustainable development in many countries around the world requires governments to draft concrete policies that integrate economic, social and environmental factors into these policies to more efficiently manage the environmental challenges that many countries around the world are facing due to climate change, such as global warming, environmental and biodiversity degradation, etc. Globalisation has influenced many countries worldwide to address the economic and environmental challenges they have faced recently. These effects of globalisation have increased the demand for governments of many countries worldwide to draft and implement effective development policies and strategies to promote a green economy and the rational and sustainable use of natural resources.

According to the SWOT and PESTLE analysis findings, appropriate environmental policies significantly affect technological innovations and the reduction of greenhouse gas emissions in the economies of many countries worldwide. Therefore, the successful design and implementation of these environmental policies will positively affect the growth of green innovations and innovative projects in green entrepreneurship. An important issue worth highlighting from this study is that including knowledge about the green economy in university programmes is a key factor that will increase awareness and change the individual's behaviour towards the environment and biodiversity. Enriching the university curriculum with courses in the green economy field will positively affect future generations. Considering the global environmental challenges, coordination between states and international organisations is essential to solve the problems that are related to environmental degradation and to promote sustainable development.

Considering the various environmental challenges different countries face, we recommend that governments undertake several reforms integrating economic and environmental policies to protect the environment and biodiversity. These economic and environmental policies should be integrated through an adequate strategy that ensures the optimal and sustainable use of natural resources and reduces dependence on non-renewable sources of electricity. These government policies should promote innovative technologies in the green economy by increasing national and international funds dedicated to developing green technologies that will promote efficiency and sustainability in all sectors of the economy and industry. Education for sustainable development and the green economy also significantly change human behaviour towards the environment. Therefore, universities should invest as much as possible in preparing and advancing academic staff for teaching in the field of the green economy, as well as offering courses in university programmes in the field of the green economy. An increase in university education for the green economy will positively affect human behaviour towards the environment. It will enhance the capacity to manage future global environmental challenges arising from the behaviour of the primary factor.

In the international aspect, all countries should coordinate their environmental and strategic policies in reducing greenhouse gas emissions. Therefore, these countries should cooperate to decide on binding standards through environmental strategies to protect the environment and influence the reduction of environmental degradation. Setting clear standards through international coordination will positively affect the reduction of greenhouse gas emissions. A key factor for the success of economic and environmental policies in preserving the environment and biodiversity is local policies that should focus more on implementing innovative projects that positively affect sustainable regional economic development. Therefore, in many countries, better coordination of economic and environmental policies is needed to manage the resources available better and improve the livelihoods and economic well-being of different communities. Through this chapter, we also recommend that applying SWOT and PESTLE analyses should be integrated into decision-making policies to identify the challenges and opportunities facing the global economy and the environment in general today. Incorporating such analyses and decision-making techniques into economic and environmental policies and strategies will ensure a more straightforward identification of future strategic activities that can be undertaken and will positively impact sustainable development. These recommendations aim to support governments, relevant institutions in the economic and environmental fields, international organisations, the private sector, businesses and other stakeholders in decision-making and taking concrete steps to ensure a sustainable and secure future for young generations.

References

Acheampong, A. O., & Opoku, E. E. O. (2023). Environmental degradation and economic growth: Investigating linkages and potential pathways. *Energy Economics, 123*, Article 106734. https://doi.org/10.1016/j.eneco.2023.106734

Angrisani, L., Arpaia, P., D'Arco, M., De Benedetto, E., Esposito, A., Imbó, M., & Tedesco, A. (2023). Measurement sustainability: A first methodological step for its modeling and assessment. *Measurement, 209*, Article 112539. https://doi.org/10.1016/j.measurement.2023.112539

Awamleh, F. T., Alarabiat, Y. A., & Bustami, A. N. (2024). Enhancing sustainable development through international performance indicators: The role of business intelligence techniques. *Challenges in Sustainability, 12*(3), 203–218.

Bekun, F. V., Adedoyin, F. F., Lorente, D. B., & Driha, O. M. (2021). Designing policy framework for sustainable development in Next-5 largest economies amidst energy consumption and key macroeconomic indicators. *Environmental Science and Pollution Research, 29*(11), 16653–16666. https://doi.org/10.1007/s11356-021-16820-z

Bretschger, L., & Pittel, K. (2020). Twenty key challenges in environmental and resource economics. *Environmental and Resource Economics, 77*, 725–750.

Bustum, T. (2015). *Towards green and inclusive prosperity – Building green economies that deliver on poverty reduction Annex: Case studies: Inclusive green economy and ecotourism as an approach for poverty reduction*. The United Nations Development (UNDP).

Chaturvedi, S. (2024). The economics of sustainable development: Challenges and solutions. *Educational Administration: Theory and Practice, 30*(5), 9061–9067. https://doi.org/10.53555/kuey.v30i5.4497

Cheah, H.-B., & Cheah, M. (2003). Doing the right thing: Incorporating the ethical imperative into the sustainable development process. In J. B. Kidd (Ed.), *Corruption and governance in Asia* (pp. 225–250). Palgrave Macmillan.

Demidova, S., Balog, M., Chircova, T., Kulachinskaya, A., Zueva, S., Akhmetova, I., & Ilyashenko, S. (2021). Development of methodology and assessment of ecological safety of the EAEU and CIS regions in the context of sustainable development. *Economies, 9*(3), Article 100. https://doi.org/10.3390/economies9030100

Dhali, M., Hassan, S., & Subramaniam, U. (2023). Comparative analysis of oil and gas legal frameworks in Bangladesh and Nigeria: A pathway towards achieving sustainable energy through policy. *Sustainability, 15*(21), Article 15228. https://doi.org/10.3390/su152115228

Filho, W. L., Frankenberger, F., Salvia, A. L., Azeiteiro, U., Alves, F., Castro, P., Will, M., Platje, J., Lovren, V. O., Brandli, L., Price, E., Doni, F., Mifsud, M., & Ávila, L. V. (2021). A framework for the implementation of the sustainable development goals in university programmes. *Journal of Cleaner Production, 299*, Article 126915. https://doi.org/10.1016/j.jclepro.2021.126915

Hannan, E. (2015). *Towards green and inclusive prosperity – Building green economies that deliver on poverty reduction. Annex: Case studies: Sustainable Ecosystems Management for poverty reduction and green economy*. The United Nations Development (UNDP).

Henriques, R., Gaio, C., & Costa, M. (2022). Sustainability reporting quality and stakeholder engagement assessment: The case of the paper sector at the Iberian level. *Sustainability, 14*(21), Article 14404. https://doi.org/10.3390/su142114404

Holden, E., Linnerud, K., & Banister, D. (2016). The imperatives of sustainable development. *Sustainable Development, 25*(3), 213–226. https://doi.org/10.1002/sd.1647

Humbatova, S. I., Hajiyeva, N., Fodor, M. G., Sood, K., & Grima, S. (2024). The impact of economic growth on the ecological environment and renewable energy production: Evidence from Azerbaijan and Hungary. *Journal of Risk and Financial Management, 17*(7), Article 275.

Inder, S., Sood, K., & Grima, S. (2022). Antecedents of behavioural intention to adopt internet banking using structural equation modelling. *Journal of Risk and Financial Management*, *15*(4), Article 157.

Lai, X., & Shi, Q. (2020). Green and low-carbon technology innovations. In C. M. Galanakis (Ed.), *Innovation strategies in environmental science* (pp. 209–253). Elsevier. https://doi.org/10.1016/B978-0-12-817382-4.00007-1

Li, X., Qin, Q., & Yang, Y. (2023). The impact of green innovation on carbon emissions: Evidence from the construction sector in China. *Energies*, *16*(11), Article 4529. https://doi.org/10.3390/en16114529

Li, Q., Wu, H., Zhang, B. Q., Dong, Z. H., & Ling, T. (2024). Safety system study of gas stations based on preliminary hazard analysis and fault tree analysis. *Journal of Engineering Management and Systems Engineering*, *3*(3), 149–163.

Mengistu, A. T., & Panizzolo, R. (2023). Metrics for measuring industrial sustainability performance in small and medium-sized enterprises. *International Journal of Productivity and Performance Management*, *73*(11), 46–68. https://doi.org/10.1108/ijppm-04-2022-0200

Mensah, J. (2019). Sustainable development: Meaning, history, principles, pillars, and implications for human action: Literature review. *Cogent Social Sciences*, *5*(1), Article 1653531. https://doi.org/10.1080/23311886.2019.1653531

Minh, H. T., Trang, D. T. N., & Chen, J. (2016). Input factors to sustainable development of coffee production in the Dak Lak Province. *Open Access Library Journal*, *3*(12), 1–10. https://doi.org/10.4236/oalib.1103187

Morina, F., & Dinaj, S. (2024). Strategic insights: How environmental, social, and governance factors shape portfolio investments. K. Citirati (Ed.), *8th FEB international scientific conference: Challenges in the turbulent economic environment and organizations' sustainable development* (Vol. 8, pp. 257–268). Univerzitetna založba Univerze v Mariboru. https://doi.org/10.18690/um.epf.5.2024.25

Niţoi, V. S., Chiriac, C., & Gîrtan, M. (2022, May 26–30). *Principles of modelling development processes at regional level* [Paper presentation]. Proceedings of the World Lumen Congress 2021, Iasi, Romania. https://doi.org/10.18662/wlc2021/53

Nonet, G. A., Gössling, T., Van Tulder, R., & Bryson, J. M. (2022). Multi-stakeholder engagement for the sustainable development goals: Introduction to the special issue. *Journal of Business Ethics*, *180*(4), 945–957. https://doi.org/10.1007/s10551-022-05192-0

OECD. (2023). *Unlocking co-creation for green innovation*. OECD Science, Technology and Industry Policy Papers. https://doi.org/10.1787/b887f436-en

Ørsted. (2023). *Uniting action on climate and biodiversity*. https://orsted.com/en/what-we-do/insights/white-papers/uniting-action-on-climate-and-biodiversity

Ozkan, O., Khan, N., & Ahmed, M. (2023). Impact of green technological innovations on environmental quality for Turkey: Evidence from the novel dynamic ARDL simulation model. *Environmental Science and Pollution Research*, *30*(28), 72207–72223. https://doi.org/10.1007/s11356-023-27350-1

Perdan, S. (2004). Introduction to sustainable development. In *Sustainable development in practice: Case studies for engineers and scientists* (1st ed., pp. 3–28). John Wiley & Sons Ltd.

Popescu, I., Hitaj, C., & Benetto, E. (2021). Measuring the sustainability of investment funds: A critical review of methods and frameworks in sustainable finance. *Journal of Cleaner Production*, *314*, Article 128016. https://doi.org/10.1016/j.jclepro.2021.128016

PUB, Singapore's National Water Agency. (2017). *Innovation in water Singapore. An R&D publication of PUB, Singapore's National Water Agency, 9*. https://www.pub.gov.sg/-/media/Images/Feature/Content-Pages/Resources/R-and-D/PUB_InnovationinWater_Issue9.pdf

Reimers, F. M. (2021). The role of universities: Building an ecosystem of climate change education. In P. Bentsen, S. Ho, K. Kesson, J. C. K. Lee, J. Lupele, G. Mannion, P. O'Riley, C. Reddy, & H. Whitehouse (Eds.), *Education and climate change* (pp. 1–44). https://doi.org/10.1007/978-3-030-57927-2

Rodale Institute. (2021). *40 year and counting. FST 40-year report*. https://rodaleinstitute.org/wp-content/uploads/FST_40YearReport_RodaleInstitute-1.pdf

Saqib, N., & Usman, M. (2023). Are technological innovations and green energy prosperity swiftly reduce environmental deficit in China and United States? Learning from two sides of environmental sustainability. *Energy Reports*, *10*, 1672–1687. https://doi.org/10.1016/j.egyr.2023.08.022

Sarker, M. R., Ali, S. M., Paul, S. K., & Munim, Z. H. (2021). Measuring sustainability performance using an integrated model. *Measurement*, *184*, Article 109931. https://doi.org/10.1016/j.measurement.2021.109931

Segovia Hermoza, M., Huamani Morales, K. L., Moreno Albuja, M. D. C., Espinosa, D., & Miranda Estévez, M. (2023). University education, labour inclusion and industrial safety: A comprehensive approach to sustainable development. *Journal of Namibian Studies*, *33*(S2), 3669–3676.

Setioningtyas, W. P., Illés, C. B., Dunay, A., Hadi, A., & Wibowo, T. S. (2022). Environmental economics and the SDGs: A review of their relationships and barriers. *Sustainability*, *14*, Article 7513. https://doi.org/10.3390/su14127513

Stocker, F., De Arruda, M. P., De Mascena, K. M. C., & Boaventura, J. M. G. (2020). Stakeholder engagement in sustainability reporting: A classification model. *Corporate Social Responsibility and Environmental Management*, *27*(5), 2071–2080. https://doi.org/10.1002/csr.1947

Tan, Y., & Zhu, Z. (2022). The effect of ESG rating events on corporate green innovation in China: The mediating role of financial constraints and managers' environmental awareness. *Technology in Society*, *68*, Article 101906. https://doi.org/10.1016/j.techsoc.2022.101906

Tanveer, M. I., Yusliza, M. Y., & Fawehinmi, O. (2023). Green HRM and hospitality industry: Challenges and barriers in adopting environmentally friendly practices. *Journal of Hospitality and Tourism Insights*, *7*(1), 121–141. https://doi.org/10.1108/jhti-08-2022-0389

Tomai, M., Ramani, S. V., & Papachristos, G. (2024). How can we design policy better? Frameworks and approaches for sustainability transitions. *Sustainability*, *16*(2), Article 690. https://doi.org/10.3390/su16020690

United Nations Environment Program. (UNEP). (2019). *Global environment outlook-Geo-6: Healthy planet, healthy people*. Cambridge University Press eBooks. https://doi.org/10.1017/9781108627146

Vare, P., & Scott, W. (2007). Learning for a change. *Journal of Education for Sustainable Development*, *1*(2), 191–198. https://doi.org/10.1177/097340820700100209

Wang, J., Ma, M., Dong, T., & Zhang, Z. (2023). Do ESG ratings promote corporate green innovation? A quasi-natural experiment based on SynTao Green Finance's ESG ratings. *International Review of Financial Analysis*, *87*, Article 102623. https://doi.org/10.1016/j.irfa.2023.102623

World Economic Forum. (2023). *The global risks report 2023*. https://www.weforum.org/reports/global-risks-report-2023/

Zikargae, M. H., Woldearegay, A. G., & Skjerdal, T. (2022). Assessing the roles of stakeholders in community projects on environmental security and livelihood of impoverished rural society: A nongovernmental organization implementation strategy in focus. *Heliyon*, *8*(10), Article e10987. https://doi.org/10.1016/j.heliyon.2022.e10987

Chapter 6

Imperatives of Social Marketing in the Context of Rural Entrepreneurship

George Abuselidze[a,b], Liudmyla Tarasovych[c], Maryna Yaremova[c], Tetiana Usiuk[c], Svitlana Lavrynenko[c] and Anna Slobodianyk[d]

[a]*Batumi Shota Rustaveli State University, Batumi, Georgia*
[b]*The University of Georgia, Tbilisi, Georgia*
[c]*Polissia National University, Zhytomyr, Ukraine*
[d]*National Aviation University, Kyiv, Ukraine*

Abstract

Purpose: The purpose of this study is to justify the necessity and advantages of using social marketing methods and programmes for the development of the national economy in general, with a special emphasis on rural entrepreneurship.

Need for the study: The study emphasises that implementing the marketing concept in social spheres is becoming increasingly relevant in solving current social problems in Ukraine, along with economic and political challenges. The study considers the concept of social marketing, which is based on the harmonious merger of public interests, consumer needs and profitability of business entities.

Methodology: The study's approach is founded on the theoretical underpinnings of management and the evolution of social marketing, as well as the accepted scientific standards of empirical research in economics.

Findings: The study outlines a novel approach to entrepreneurship that prioritises the integration of social and corporate problem-solving. These ideas are thought to help solve societal issues and guarantee the welfare of the general people.

Sustainable Development and Green Innovation: Managing Risk through Interdisciplinary Approaches and Policy Strategies, 127–146

doi:10.1108/978-1-83608-462-420251006

Practical implications: Since social marketing can be seen as a form of social administration, a specialised marketing strategy for businesses, a planned instrument for market economy regulation and a social policy tool, the practical significance of this research lies in its scientific validation of its application in rural entrepreneurship. Future studies will concentrate on creating both qualitative and quantitative standards for assessing the impact of social programmes and technology, followed by confirmation of the results.

Keywords: Marketing; social marketing; rural entrepreneurship; social innovation; financing

JEL codes: M31; O35; Q13; P25; R51; D25; E22

Introduction

Modern society is undergoing constant changes in socio-economic phenomena and processes, and the influence of both local and global social issues is becoming more and more noticeable. Developed economies use effective mechanisms to integrate socially oriented initiatives into their national development, contributing to overall social progress. Ukraine also acknowledges that it is a socially conscious state, with laws and their application intended to enhance the standard of living for its people. This commitment is enshrined in the main state document, the Constitution of Ukraine (Verkhovna Rada of Ukraine, 1996). Even though the focus on social progress has been defined, the real situation looks different. Particularly in rural regions, negative social patterns are becoming more prevalent. A major portion of the population has low living standards, poverty is pervasive, property inequality is high, social guarantees are limited, demographic transitions are unappealing, the labour market is unpredictable, and disadvantaged groups have little opportunity to engage in public life.

It is widely acknowledged that tackling social concerns and enhancing individuals' well-being are important tasks for government agencies and other non-governmental groups. However, to date, this approach has demonstrated its ineffectiveness in achieving the set goals and often does not lead to significant progress or development of society. Given the limitations of the issues under consideration and the available resources, this approach today demonstrates the inability to achieve the desired results and, sometimes, indicates the absence of significant progress or social development.

Understanding the intricate patterns of evolution of social processes in society is expanded by the establishment of a national socio-economic development plan and the implementation of mechanisms for the formulation, execution and enhancement of state regulatory policy. This involves social dynamics changing and the necessity of evaluating how elements of the external global economic environment, as well as living circumstances in the social and environmental spheres, directly affect the status of the economy.

The authors demonstrate that the disparity in market relations issues' regulatory frameworks is also common in the nation's agriculture industry. Under such circumstances, it is imperative to create novel systems for regulating social processes grounded on democratic ideals and civil society's fundamental values. This includes identifying social problems and justifying methods for solving them, as well as developing social skills in using technology to solve socially important problems among all stakeholders. The idea of social marketing encompasses all of this, and its requirements necessitate a thorough theoretical and methodological foundation. These days, this sophisticated idea doesn't necessarily result in linked models, mechanisms and useful technology.

In order to guarantee that social marketing is enough for full integration into the global economy, the research establishes the necessity of a scientific approach to problem-solving.

The main purpose of this study is to substantiate the importance of introducing social marketing technologies and programmes to promote national economic development, with a special emphasis on the development of rural entrepreneurship. Based on these conclusions, the study aims to identify approaches to improving the quality of life of citizens and ensuring social welfare in the period of post-war reconstruction of Ukraine.

The main objectives can be summarised as follows:

1. The core of social marketing as a cutting-edge marketing idea is revealed.
2. To explain a novel approach to entrepreneurship that places emphasis on resolving social issues and conducting business.
3. An explanation of the advantages of implementing social marketing initiatives and technology within the framework of rural entrepreneurship.

Literature Review

Many scholars from Ukraine and other countries have paid attention to the study of social marketing as a modern concept in the field of marketing. Kotler defined social marketing as 'understanding people and interacting with them effectively, leading to the adoption of new views. Changing your position leads to behavioural changes that affect the solution of social problems in which you are involved' (Kotler & Lee, 2005). Different scientific schools use different approaches to the interpretation of the term 'social marketing', and fundamental research in this area has also been conducted by scientists from abroad, such as Andreasen (2002), Brychkov and Domegan (2017), Layton (2017), Merritt et al. (2017), Truong and Dietrich (2018), White (2018), and others.

Numerous academics in Ukraine have concentrated their studies on social marketing throughout the last 10 years, especially in relation to the application of corporate social responsibility (CSR) concepts. Among them are Akimov (2009), Akimova et al. (2020), Awamleh et al. (2024), Li et al. (2024), Achkasova (2022), Belova and Gulka (2019), Lytvynchuk et al. (2021), Poltorak (2015), Sotnyk et al. (2018), Skydan et al. (2022), Abuselidze and Slobodianyk (2020), Shimko (2010), and others. Scientific studies on the use of marketing strategies in social entrepreneurship are published in publications by Kisil (2018), Knyazeva and Alekseenko (2021), Kolomiets et al. (2019), Kostyuk et al. (2018), Kravchuk et al. (2017), Levkivska and Levkovych (2017), Prutska (2019), Tkachuk et al. (2020), Abuselidze and Slobodianyk (2022), Abuselidze (2021b), Ostapchuk et al. (2023), Mohylevska et al. (2023), Abuselidze et al. (2023), and others.

To describe the concept of social marketing, researchers often use terms such as socially ethical, socially oriented, socially responsible, or community marketing. It is crucial to remember that none of these methods compromise the fundamental characteristics of the idea being studied. This is due to the fact that social marketing is intended to put social responsibility into reality and foster social harmony in society, which is a fundamental component of contemporary corporate practices.

Recently, scientific research in the field of social marketing has mainly focussed on three areas:

1. Classical marketing, which recognises the existence of exchange processes within social relations.
2. Socially oriented marketing, which outlines the elements and particulars of CSR.
3. The use of innovative technologies to promote socially important issues with the help of marketing tools and technologies in the process of solving social problems (Akimov, 2009; Knyazeva & Alekseenko, 2021; Tarasovych & Yaremova, 2021; Tarasovych et al., 2021).

This focus on using marketing methods and technology to address social issues highlights how novel and cutting-edge social marketing is as an idea. Through the efficient management of social changes and processes in a market society, it seeks to enhance the standard of living for both individuals and society at large.

Research Methodology

This study's central hypothesis is that social marketing programmes and technology may support the resurgence of rural entrepreneurship, which will ultimately support the post-war recovery of the national economy. The principles of marketing theory, along with a wealth of research findings from both local and international academics that examine the origins and evolution of social marketing in Ukraine and throughout the world, provide the theoretical and methodological foundation of the study.

To conduct this study, a combination of generally accepted and specialised research methods was used. In particular, the inductive–deductive method was used to comprehensively study, generalise and systematise the basic principles of marketing management in the context of its social orientation. This entails taking into account social marketing as a component of social management, a distinct type of marketing activity, a tool for social policy, and a way to regulate the market economy.

The results of the study on the etymological core of social marketing, as well as its fundamental concepts, attributes and criteria, were compared with the aid of the comparative analysis approach. It also helped to identify the distinctive features that distinguish traditional entrepreneurship from social entrepreneurship, the latter being determined mainly by the social mission of business entities, which is to create social value to meet public needs and simultaneously make a profit.

To construct a scientific perspective on social marketing, specifically to support its importance and use as a tool for fostering the growth of rural entrepreneurship, an operationalisation technique was used. This is accomplished by combining three elements in a pleasing way: 'public interests + consumer needs + business profitability'.

The discoveries pertaining to the etymological core of social marketing, as well as its fundamental principles and standards, were systematised and generalised with the aid of the comparative analysis approach. This approach allowed to identify the main differences between traditional entrepreneurship and social entrepreneurship, placing the main emphasis on the social mission of the enterprise in creating social value to address social needs and simultaneously making a profit.

To construct the scientific viewpoint of social marketing and to establish its importance as a tool for fostering the growth of rural entrepreneurship, the idea operationalisation approach was employed. This is accomplished by skilfully combining three essential elements: taking into account public interests, meeting consumer needs and achieving profitability for business.

This approach emphasises the importance of social marketing as an innovative concept aimed at improving the quality of life and social progress through effective management of social change in a market society.

An economic rationale for the implementation of several social marketing initiatives and technology in rural regions was shown using the monograph's methodology. Establishing company and community collaboration, corporate volunteerism, social investment, corporate philanthropy, socially meaningful marketing, corporate social marketing, and promoting a corporate charity mission were some of these methods. Programmes addressing social collaboration, environmental preservation and resource conservation, workplace health and safety, human development and ethical corporate practices were also taken into consideration. It was determined that this strategy was strategic for conducting business in rural regions.

The historical evolution of social marketing as a tool within the contemporary marketing paradigm in the social realm was examined using the economic and historical method.

The idea, goal, objectives and technology of social marketing were all taken into consideration using the structural–functional analysis technique. The role and significance of social marketing in commercial organisations' management systems were also clarified.

A grouping method was used to identify key regulatory and support institutions in the field of social marketing. This approach also allowed for the classification of social marketing stakeholders depending on their affiliation with the public or private sector, as well as with non-governmental civil society organisations.

The association between the degree of entrepreneurial development and the socio-economic changes that are now occurring in rural regions was discovered using the complementary technique. This made it feasible to ascertain the advantages of using entrepreneurship in the execution of social projects and initiatives because of its capacity to grow and establish a suitable resource base.

To systematise the results of the study and formulate conclusions, the methods of abstraction and concretisation were used, which allowed for a deeper understanding of the practical processes of using social marketing tools within rural entrepreneurship.

Both tabular and graphical approaches were used to depict the study's findings. This study's approach to social marketing research, which emphasises its function in fostering the growth of rural entrepreneurship, is what makes it distinctive. This method highlights the study's applicability and timeliness by integrating systemic and marketing viewpoints to identify the requirements for economic growth during Ukraine's post-war reconstruction.

Results and Discussion

The emergence of the concept of social marketing stems directly from the evolution of marketing, focussing on aligning marketing goals with solving social problems. The philosophies and objectives of social marketing are different from those of commercial marketing. While commercial marketing is aimed at creating value for paying customers and satisfying their needs in order to generate economic profit (usually by formulating and implementing a marketing strategy based on achieving predictable results in economic activity), social marketing adapts the principles of commercial marketing to specific projects. Its goal is to influence the behaviour of target audiences, empower them to make decisions, improve their well-being, contribute to the development of society or create valuable public goods.

The articulation and practical application of social marketing result from the harmonious integration of its main components and functional attributes: 'a function of social management + a unique form of marketing activity of business entities + a conscious tool for regulating the market economy + a social policy tool'. Therefore, the application of social initiatives and programmes for the good of society is the main focus of the social marketing philosophy. These projects and programmes cover various elements, including the necessary scientific and applied research, advertising efforts, product (service) marketing technologies, image formation, reputation management, etc.

The way the key elements interact results in the manifestation of social marketing's role. Among these is the role of social management, a special kind of marketing that businesses engage in. It is also a useful tool for social policy and a deliberate way to control the market economy. The main goal of social marketing is to influence the behaviour and awareness of target audiences, promote healthy decision-making, improve their quality of life and health and make a significant contribution to social progress.

Social marketing goes beyond the traditional marketing approach, focussing on the importance of addressing social issues and solving global challenges. This can cover a variety of areas, such as promoting environmental responsibility, fighting inequality, supporting public health, inclusiveness and other socio-cultural issues.

A coherent application of social marketing involves the implementation of a comprehensive strategy that includes a variety of elements, from research and analysis to advertising campaigns and partnerships. Its success lies in its ability to influence the values and perceptions of society, as well as to promote behavioural changes that lead to positive social transformations (Fig. 6.1).

Given the limited funding of social programmes by the state, which are primarily focussed on solving urgent problems during military conflicts, it is increasingly important to constantly increase investment to address social issues in Ukraine. Implementation of these transformations with a focus on social needs is a key prerequisite for the effective development of the rural economy in general and rural entrepreneurship in particular, which is an important component of the national economy. In recent years, in particular in the context of the transition from martial law to the post-pandemic crisis, the issue of social investment has received special emphasis.

This transition has led to the intensification of the activities of state institutions and public organisations, including the attraction of funds from foreign sources, to ensure social investment. At the same time, there has been a decline in entrepreneurial initiatives aimed at implementing social projects. Limitations of opportunities for adequate investment in the social sphere are explained by factors such as forced reduction of business activity, deterioration of economic performance or even termination of operations of enterprises. Three important organisations are in charge of regulating and assisting social media marketing in Ukraine: (1) public administration sector, (2) private sector and (3) non-profit sector (Table 6.1).

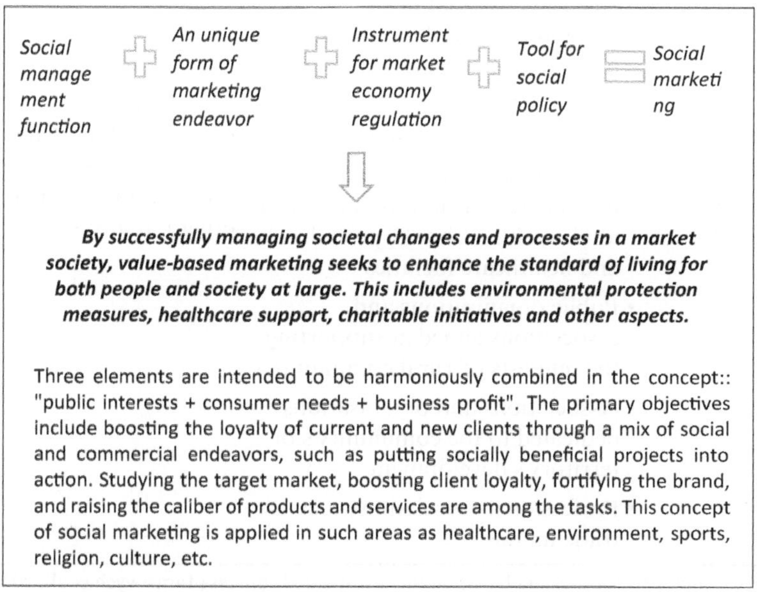

Fig. 6.1. Social Marketing Explication. *Source:* Compiled by the authors based on the investigated sources (Tarasovych et al., 2023).

Table 6.1. Participants in Social Marketing for the Growth of the Rural Economy.

Group of Stakeholders	Representatives of Stakeholders	Social Marketing Tools and Technologies
Public administration sector (local authorities)	• Local self-government bodies and their departments • Administrations and institutions at the district, regional and national levels • Scientific research institutions, state universities and colleges • Investors representing the state	Social standards, social payments, support for small- and medium-sized businesses
Private sector (business)	• Enterprises of all sizes, including large, small, medium and micro enterprises, as well as individual entrepreneurs • Financial institutions, such as banks, credit unions and others • Business associations, including chambers of commerce and industry and others • Agencies, associations of entrepreneurs and intermediaries that promote business support and development	Charity events, sponsorship, volunteering, social investments, socially oriented marketing, social cooperation, environmental and resource conservation activities, health and safety, and personnel development
Non-profit sector (civil society)	• Citizens' self-organisation groups • Educational, cultural and healthcare institutions at the local level, such as schools, pre-schools and healthcare facilities • Public organisations and associations aimed at supporting the interests of rural communities • Associations and organisations dedicated to the community's or territory's development • Professional associations such as trade unions	Charity, volunteering, social investments, grants, social cooperation and other initiatives

Source: Compiled by the authors based on the investigated sources (Tarasovych et al., 2023).

Over the past decade, investment in rural social infrastructure has reached a critical level. The upward trend in capital investments in this sector stopped in 2012, and since then they have decreased threefold to UAH 19 billion (Kisil, 2018). In recent years, the majority of these expenditures (up to 90%) have been directed primarily to housing construction, especially in peri-urban villages, while limited resources are allocated to trade, utilities, education, food and other important areas. This underscores the challenges faced by both the government and non-governmental organisations in addressing social issues of this magnitude, especially in the context of declining social development in rural areas. It is crucial to increase the role of entrepreneurship in the execution of social programmes and initiatives since this industry has a great deal of potential for growth and resource development. In this regard, social marketing serves as a powerful stimulant to quicken the launch and execution of marketing campaigns in the commercial sector.

The availability of services in many rural communities has decreased over time. Changing the population, public sector cuts, and the effects of global warming can all encourage local communities to step up and fill the void. One of the defining aspects of Smart Villages is the discovery and implementation of novel solutions to local concerns. According to the definition, Smart Villages 'use creative approaches to strengthen their resilience, building on existing assets and opportunities'. This includes new services that can serve as a catalyst for raising a village's standard of living.

Smart Villages innovate in a variety of ways, based on the possibilities and difficulties presented by their local settings. One of the main characteristics of Smart Village new amenities is that they are designed and implemented by several persons or groups. These include locals (internal stakeholders) as well as external players that provide help. In addition, the private sector can play a significant role. Private enterprises frequently display flexibility and creativity, which can enhance the supply of services to the community at large. Regardless of whether external stakeholders are engaged, development cannot occur without adequate capability and a solid organisational mechanism to carry it out.

Combining services can significantly improve service delivery efficiency. Small rural towns struggle to locate specialist staff and mobilise financial resources. As a result, innovative solutions are required to guarantee that these communities have access to a diverse range of activities.

Notably, the business sector is crucial to the revitalisation of rural areas, as demonstrated by its contributions to territorial communities' budgets and creation of an alluring investment climate, national food security, employment creation for rural residents, income growth, facilitation of access to social benefits, establishment of production and economic networks, and introduction of technologies to streamline logistical business processes. This significantly expands the opportunities for rural producers to add value to their goods, to develop and implement territorial development strategies, to brand and improve the image of territories, and so on. The confluence of these benefits and prospects within the context of rural entrepreneurship fosters the growth of human capital as an independent intangible asset, hence bolstering company and the entrepreneurial community (Fig. 6.2).

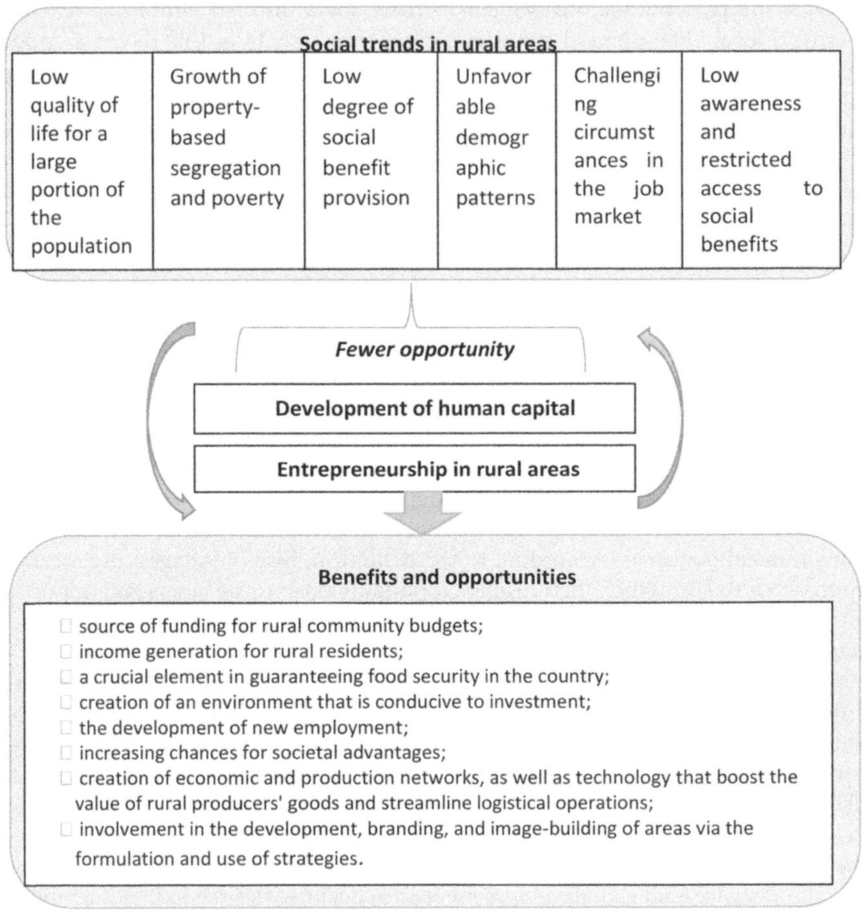

Fig. 6.2. An Explanation of Rural Social Changes and the Entrepreneurial Sector Using a Supplementary Methodology. *Source:* Compiled by the authors based on the investigated sources (Tarasovych et al., 2023).

Key characteristics of entrepreneurship include risk-taking, scalability, creativity, invention and financial independence. Generating profits, allocating them to founders, investors and shareholders, and preserving financial independence from outside financing sources are the key goals of conventional entrepreneurship. The existing state of the market, elements of the company's internal and external environments, the company's strengths and weaknesses, a lack of marketing knowledge, and mistakes made in marketing research and planning are some of the reasons that contribute to marketing risks. Aiming to maximise the ratio of projected profit to risk, effective marketing risk management should be grounded on prior qualitative and quantitative market research. Identifying possible risks, investigating and analysing them, evaluating them both qualitatively and statistically, implementing countermeasures to reduce or eliminate them, and measuring the success of these actions are all steps in the marketing risk management process.

The inclusion of social aspects and the use of social marketing represent modern challenges and voluntary initiatives for enterprises. Essentially, when entrepreneurship is aimed at solving social problems and meeting social needs, it can be defined as social entrepreneurship. In this case, social value and profit are generated simultaneously, and priority is given to the social mission, not just financial success. It is worth noting that social entrepreneurship is based on social engagement, not on the allocation of a share of profits to address social issues. For example, the fact that a certain share of profits is systematically allocated to social initiatives does not automatically make a business social. For initiatives in the area of CSR or socially responsible marketing, it is likely that tax incentives will be more appropriate (Abuselidze & Gogitidze, 2020).

Effective implementation of social projects requires the ability to make management decisions with a focus on social aspects. The primary elements of social marketing in the management system are identifying, shaping and satisfying the demands of the target audience as well as the development, execution and monitoring of social programmes meant to accomplish social goals and put certain workable measures into place. Fig. 6.3 provides an overview of the role of social marketing in the business management system.

Three main areas are the focus of social marketing initiatives and technology used in rural entrepreneurship: building beliefs, implementing social practices and creating a social product. It also includes a dual emphasis on prioritising a specific social problem and developing an effective solution for it. As a result, selecting the right social media programmes and technology for a certain company organisation becomes crucial.

The following social marketing methods are widely used in rural entrepreneurship:

1. *Implementation of the corporate charity concept*: companies use financial, in-kind and other corporate resources to draw attention to a specific social problem in society.
2. Marketing that is socially meaningful involves setting aside a portion of earnings to support charitable causes.
3. Companies that sponsor public relations or advertising initiatives that try to alter behavioural patterns in order to enhance social health, safety, the environment and community development are said to be engaging in corporate social marketing.
4. *Corporate philanthropy*: companies make donations to charitable organisations or finance events and projects through grants, gifts, etc.
5. Business and community partnerships: promotes territorial development management and implementation of social marketing in cooperation in a particular territory.
6. *Corporate volunteering*: involvement of employees in volunteer activities to support local public organisations and initiatives.

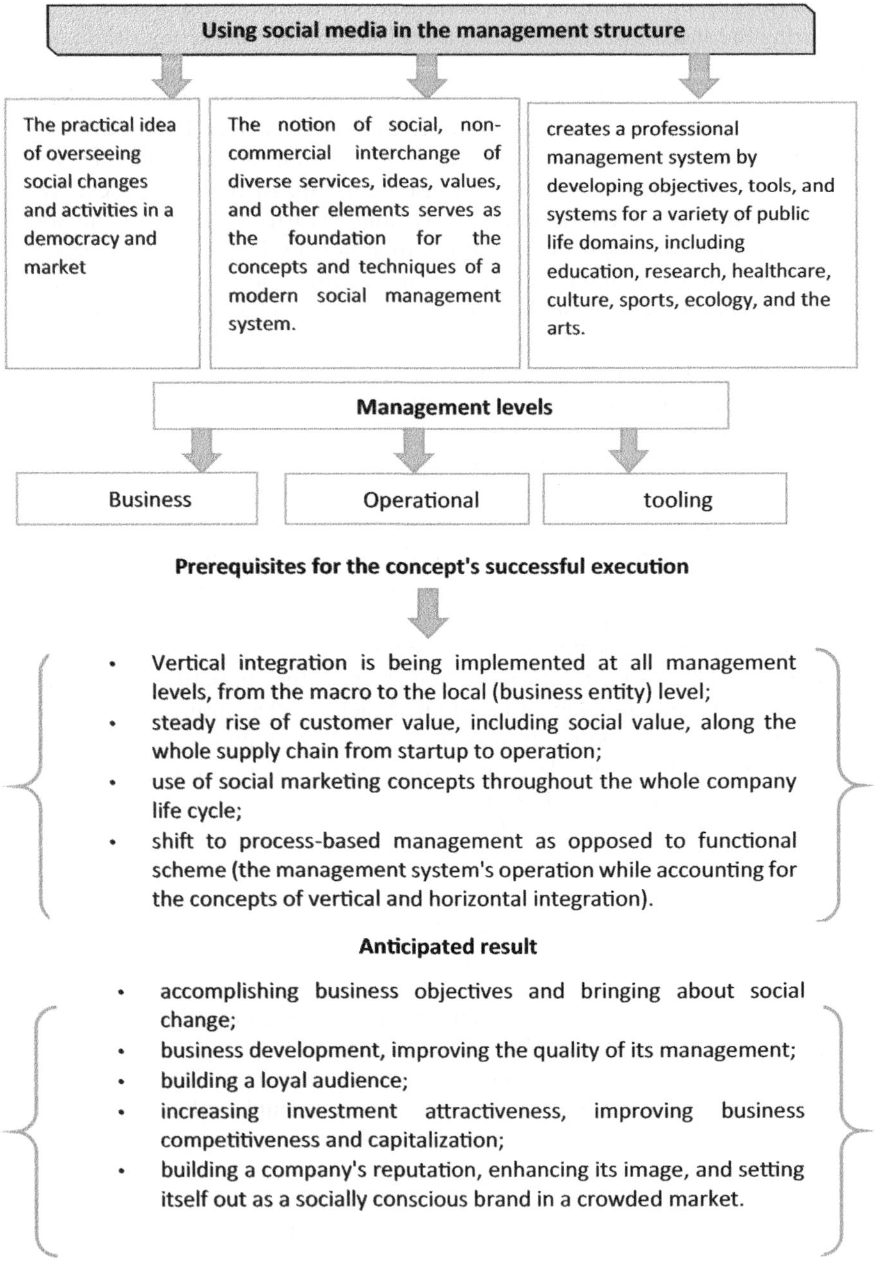

Fig. 6.3. Social Marketing's Place in Corporate Organisations' Management Systems. *Source:* Compiled by the authors based on the investigated sources (Tarasovych et al., 2023).

7. *Social investing*: businesses invest in and carry out initiatives to protect the environment and enhance the quality of life in the neighbourhood, typically through long-term collaborative projects.

Various social initiatives contribute to the development of entrepreneurship, including the following areas:

- *Personnel development*: this includes training, professional development, incentive compensation plans, social packages and the creation of favourable conditions for recreation and leisure.
- *Health and safety*: initiatives aimed at establishing and maintaining additional health and safety standards in the workplace.
- *Environmental protection and resource conservation*: initiatives aimed at reducing the negative impact on the environment.
- *Social collaboration*: involvement in the execution of social initiatives, assistance for socially disadvantaged populations, and sponsorship of regional cultural, athletic, and scientific events and organisations.
- *Integrity of business*: creation of favourable commercial relationships between all parties involved, including clients, partners and suppliers (Humbatova et al., 2024; Inder et al., 2022; Tarasovych & Yaremova, 2021; Tarasovych et al., 2021).

The use of social marketing tools and programmes is becoming an important strategic aspect of modern business management (Fig. 6.4).

The scope of Smart Villages policies can be quite vast. Social marketing programmes are frequently seen to focus on a variety of the wider characteristics and circumstances for rural development that necessitate cooperative rather than solo effort to accomplish meaningful change. According to the local circumstances and motive, these projects may highlight social, economic or environmental problems – or a combination of the three. There is no reason to deal with all that at once. On the contrary, long-standing challenges, such as the quality of rural services (e.g., health, education and transportation) and natural resource management (e.g., community water quality), continue to motivate locals to mobilise and act to enhance the quality of living (Abuselidze, 2021a). New methods and solutions can provide novel approaches to tackling these 'classic' rural concerns.

The rise of social marketing in Ukraine is linked to the usage of social media platforms, mostly by international businesses or well-known local firms that prioritise customer confidence and brand image. In Ukraine, social marketing strategies are most often implemented through sponsorship and charity, which are used to gain consumer trust and build loyalty. Also, recognised companies that are part of large financial and industrial groups traditionally emphasise their ability to be socially responsible.

Established in 2000, the Ukrainian Social Investment Fund (USIF) seeks to coordinate activities, draw in financial resources and boost the effectiveness of

Fig. 6.4. Programmes and Tools for Social Marketing in the Entrepreneurial Space. *Source*: Compiled by the authors based on the investigated sources (Shimko, 2010; Tarasovych et al., 2023).

social investments in Ukraine. The Fund is a non-profit organisation that carries out projects to build social infrastructure facilities and buy products, services and projects funded by money obtained from foreign technical assistance projects and Ukrainian economic and social development efforts. Numerous international financial institutions, including the United Nations Development Program, the Charles Stewart Mott Foundation, the Canadian International Development Agency, the International Renaissance Foundation, the Government of Sweden (Sida), the Government of Japan (Japan Social Development Fund [JSDF]), the World Bank, the European Union, the Government of Germany (Green Climate Fund [KfW]), the UK Government (Department for International Development [DFID]) and the Charles Stewart Mott Foundation, provide financial support for these initiatives (Table 6.2; Abuselidze & Gogitidze, 2020; Ministry of Reintegration of the Temporarily Occupied Territories of Ukraine, 2024; Tarasovych et al., 2023).

More than 1,200 microprojects have been successfully carried out in different Ukrainian local communities since the USIF was established. Repairing residential amenities, enhancing social and community infrastructure and strengthening local communities' ability to handle issues locally are the main goals of these initiatives. They also contributed to increasing the level of citizen engagement in decision-making and supported the creation of innovative models of social services, particularly for vulnerable groups.

Table 6.2. The USIF's Initiatives.

Donor	Funding Amount	Objective	Place of Implementation (Oblast)
Delivery of social services in the community			
JSDF through EBRD	USD 2.85 million	The goal of encouraging territorial communities' growth is to increase their capacity to offer citizens high-quality social services, increase access to communal and social infrastructure, and enhance services for the population's most vulnerable segments	Odesa Ternopil
Encouragement of the development of social infrastructure (USIF. VI)			
German Government through KfW	EUR 9 million	Implementation of projects to provide housing for veterans and improve the infrastructure of educational institutions	Dnipropetrovsk Zaporizhzhia Luhansk Kharkiv
Encouragement of the development of social infrastructure. Enhancement of basic health in rural areas (USIF. VII)			
German Government through KfW	EUR 14.45 million	Upgrading 40 healthcare facilities to improve the conditions of primary healthcare for more than 370,000 users	Dnipropetrovsk Donetsk Zaporizhzhia Luhansk Kharkiv
Encouragement of the development of social infrastructure (USIF. VIII)			
German Government through KfW	EUR 19.4 million	This will improve the conditions of primary health care in at least 12 primary and secondary health care facilities, as well as provide the necessary medical equipment to respond to Ukraine's needs and counteract COVID-19 and the negative effects of the pandemic	Poltava Zaporizhzhia Mykolaiv Vinnytsia Rivne Lviv Chernivtsi

(*Continued*)

Table 6.2. (*Continued*)

Donor	Funding Amount	Objective	Place of Implementation (Oblast)
EU4Skills: Ukraine's infrastructure for vocational education and training is being modernised			
European Union through KfW	EUR 19.4 million	The renewal of the vocational education system in Ukraine will help to increase the attractiveness of this type of education among young people and create an effective educational foundation. Skills in occupations that are in demand on the Ukrainian labor market will be prioritised	Poltava Zaporizhzhia Mykolaiv Vinnytsia Rivne Lviv Chernivtsi

Impact investing is a new type of investment that has grown rapidly in Ukraine in recent years. This type of investment is concentrated on initiatives that seek to produce favourable social, environmental and financial outcomes. Distinguishing impact investment from social entrepreneurship is crucial. The United Nations Development Programme states that three key tenets underpin impact investing: positive social and environmental effects, a responsible method of project evaluation, and financial viability (with returns that may be higher or lower than the market average) (Baranova, 2023). According to the Global Impact Investing Network (GIIN), which establishes four standards for impact investing, there are around USD 228 billion in total investments made in these kinds of initiatives worldwide (Table 6.3).

The evolution of Ukrainian society has a significant impact on international organisations through a variety of channels of communication with the government. The United Nations' socio-economic collaboration with domestic authorities is particularly diversified and needs to be improved in the following areas: creating a framework for predicting the generalisation of an efficient monitoring system to meet international targets for Ukraine's sustainable development; establishing a productive working relationship for the administration of projects and programmes; Enhancing Ukraine's collaboration with the Food and Agriculture Organization of the United Nations (FAO) and International Labour Organization (ILO) through pertinent cooperation initiatives is also crucial. To solve food, social and environmental challenges, Ukraine's cooperation with FAO is crucial, as agriculture has historically played a significant role in the country's economy. Receiving technical support for the growth of the agro-industrial complex is one of the main benefits of Ukraine's collaboration with FAO (Shpachuk

Table 6.3. Impact Investment Standards and Tenets.

Criteria	
A precise statement of a social/ environmental objective	The business strategy outlines the anticipated outcome
Return on investment	Long-term returns on investments should be expected
Profitability	The economic advantage and the social (environmental) outcome must be connected
Measure and assessment of effect (impact)	Essential for determining the extent to which societal goals have been met
Principles	
Profitability: the rate of return may be lower or greater than the average for the market	
Positively affecting the environment and society	
Evaluating project outcomes with a responsible mindset	

Source: Compiled by the authors based on results (European Union, 2024).

et al., 2023). Examples of these investments have been observed in a number of locations during the last 5 years, including Kyiv, Lviv, Odesa, Ivano-Frankivsk, and others. It is important to note that the business sector has played a key role in the realisation of these initiatives. Impact investment involves clearly articulating social or environmental goals. It is especially important to define the results of such corporate initiatives according to clear criteria and transparently inform the public about these results.

Conclusion

The modern trend of social marketing is still in its infancy in Ukraine, but it has enormous development potential. Social marketing is an innovative tool for inclusive rural development when it comes to addressing significant social issues and ensuring the welfare of the population as a whole. The social marketing tools, programmes and technology are used by all kinds of entrepreneurship; there are no notable differences between the ways in which each sort of firm runs. Therefore, given the same goal – the creation of economic and social advantages through the delivery of a synergistic impact – commercial companies should not be discriminated against when it comes to the opportunity to exploit rural or urban areas.

The demands of social marketing highlight the necessity of eschewing conventional methods and developing a fresh, original entrepreneurial model that successfully blends commercial with resolving social issues. Incorporating social responsibility into this new entrepreneurial approach helps create shared value that encompasses economic and social benefits, while benefiting businesses, consumers and society as a whole. It is crucial for businesses not only to make occasional investments in social projects or occasional charitable contributions to social causes but also to embed social responsibility in their daily business operations.

In entrepreneurship, social marketing is a unique and effective strategy for advancing the company, enhancing management effectiveness, using creativity to accomplish marketing objectives, and fostering social change. This approach helps to build a loyal audience, demonstrating the business's commitment to meeting its needs and solving complex social problems. Furthermore, it is a successful strategy for boosting capitalisation, being more competitive, and improving a company's image and reputation – particularly globally. This enables a company to differentiate itself in a competitive market as a socially responsible brand that promotes its brand and social values while investing in both its own success and the advancement of society.

References

Abuselidze, G. (2021a). Empirical investigation of healthcare financing and its influence on social security: Peculiarities, problems and challenges. *E3S Web of Conferences, 319*(3), Article 01030. https://doi.org/10.1051/e3sconf/202131901030

Abuselidze, G. (2021b). *Use of hedging instruments on example grain market* [Paper presentation]. 20th international scientific conference engineering for rural development proceedings, Jelgava, Latvia, May 26–28, 2021, pp. 1655–1662. https://doi.org/10.22616/erdev.2021.20.tf359

Abuselidze, G., & Gogitidze, I. (2020). Tax policy for business entities under the conditions of association with the European Union: Features and optimization directions. *E3S Web of Conferences, 166*(2), Article 13013. https://doi.org/10.1051/e3sconf/202016613013

Abuselidze, G., & Slobodianyk, A. (2020). Social responsibility of business and government in the conditions of the COVID-19 pandemic. *E3S Web of Conferences, 210*(2), Article 15016. https://doi.org/10.1051/e3sconf/202021015016

Abuselidze, G., & Slobodianyk, A. (2022). Marketing aspects of the key issues of agricultural machinery in the industrial enterprises. *Journal of Optimization in Industrial Engineering, 15*(1), 311–320.

Abuselidze, G., Talavyria, M., Vyshnivska, B., Bondarenko, L., Makedon, H., Kniazieva, T., & Salkova, I. (2023). The economic mechanism of marketing activity management of food enterprises. *E3S Web of Conferences, 371*, Article 05002. https://doi.org/10.1051/e3sconf/202337105002

Achkasova, O. (2022). Development of social entrepreneurship in Ukraine under martial law. *Economy and Society, 4*(32), 116–125. https://doi.org/10.32782/2524-0072/2022-37-40

Akimov, D. (2009). Social marketing: Subject and main types. *Journal of Sociology: Theory, Methods, Marketing, 1*, 186–203.

Akimova, L., Khomiuk, N., Bezena, I., Lytvynchuk, I., & Petroye, O. (2020). Planning of socio-economic development of the territories (experience of European Union). *International Journal of Management, 11*(4), 567–575. https://doi.org/10.34218/IJM.11.4.2020.054

Andreasen, A. (2002). Marketing social marketing in social change marketplace. *Journal of Public Policy*, *21*, 3–13.

Awamleh, F. T., Alarabiat, Y. A., & Bustami, A. N. (2024). Enhancing sustainable development through international performance indicators: The role of business intelligence techniques. *Challenges in Sustainability*, *12*(3), 203–218.

Baranova, N. (2023). *What is impact investing: We understand the terminology. Greenhouse of social technologies*. https://te-st.org/2017/09/12/impact-investment-terms/

Belova, T. G., & Gulka, V. I. (2019). Application of the concept of socially responsible marketing in enterprise activity. *Scientific notes of TNU named after V. I. Vernadskyi*, *30*(2), 82–85.

Brychkov, D., & Domegan, C. (2017). Social marketing and systems science: Past, present and future. *Journal of Social Marketing*, *7*(1), 74–93. https://doi.org/10.1108/JSOCM-10-2016-0065

European Union. (2024). *How does the EUnlocking project support social entrepreneurship?* https://euneighbourseast.eu/news/publications/how-does-the-eunlocking-project-support-social-entrepreneurship-2/

Humbatova, S. I., Hajiyeva, N., Fodor, M. G., Sood, K., & Grima, S. (2024). The impact of economic growth on the ecological environment and renewable energy production: Evidence from Azerbaijan and Hungary. *Journal of Risk and Financial Management*, *17*(7), Article 275.

Inder, S., Sood, K., & Grima, S. (2022). Antecedents of behavioural intention to adopt internet banking using structural equation modelling. *Journal of Risk and Financial Management*, *15*(4), Article 157.

Kisil, M. (2018). *Investments in the social sphere of the village decreased by three times*. Institute of Agrarian Economy. https://agropolit.com/news/10316-investitsiyi-u-sotsialnu-sferu-sela-zmenshilisya-utrichi-institut-agrarnoyi-ekonomiki

Knyazeva, T. V., & Alekseenko, I. M. (2021). Marketing strategy for the development of social entrepreneurship. *Problems of the Systemic Approach in Economics*, *1*(81), 86–92.

Kolomiets, H. M., Melentsova, O. V., Shtuchnyi, V. G., & Sushchenko, N. B. (2019). Transformations of marketing in the conditions of the digital economy: Imperatives and obstacles. *Business-Inform*, *9*, 362–369. https://doi.org/10.32983/2222-4459-2019-9-362-369

Kostyuk, O. S., Stepanyshyn, I. I., & Chytailo, M. B. (2018). Social and ethical marketing as a business strategy. *Economy and Society*, *14*, 395–401.

Kotler, F., & Lee, N. (2005). *Corporate social responsibility. How to do as much good as possible for your company and society*. Standart.

Kravchuk, N., Tarasovych, L., & Yaremova, M. (2017). Development of the socially-oriented economy in Ukraine: Prerequisites and strategic forecasting. *Baltic Journal of Economic Studies*, *3*(2), 66–72. https://doi.org/10.30525/2256-0742/2017-3-2-66-72

Layton, R. (2017). My search for meaning in marketing. *Journal of Historical Research in Marketing*, *9*, 217–243.

Levkivska, L., & Levkovych, I. (2017). Social responsibility in Ukrainian agriculture. *The Regional Issue Eastern Journal of European Studies*, *8*(1), 97–114.

Li, Q., Wu, H., Zhang, B. Q., Dong, Z. H., & Ling, T. (2024). Safety system study of gas stations based on preliminary hazard analysis and fault tree analysis. *Journal of Engineering Management and Systems Engineering*, 3(3), 149–163.

Lytvynchuk, I., Skydan, O., & Ivaniuk, O. (2021). Local governance and territorial development on the basis of GIS. *Management Theory and Studies for Rural Business and Infrastructure Development*, *42*(4), 422–433. https://doi.org/10.15544/mts.2020.43

Merritt, R., Kamin, T., Hussenöder, F., & Huibregtsen, J. (2017). The history of social marketing in Europe: The story so far. *Social Marketing Quarterly*, *23*, 191–301.

Ministry of Reintegration of the Temporarily Occupied Territories of Ukraine. (2024). *Ukrainian social investment fund*. https://minre.gov.ua/en/

Mohylevska, O., Sanchenko, O., Slobodianyk, A., Abuselidze, G., Romanova, L., & Filipovski, A. (2023). Marketing component of green technologies energy efficiency at traditional and renewable energy facilities. *IOP Conference Series: Earth and Environmental Science*, *1126*(1), Article 012020. https://doi.org/1755-1315/1126/1/012020

Ostapchuk, A., Karpenko, L., Abuselidze, G., & Chornenka, L. (2023). Management of marketing risks in sustainable development. *E3S Web of Conferences*, *371*(25), Article 05011. https://doi.org/10.1051/e3sconf/202337105011

Poltorak, V. A. (2015). Social marketing: Modern problems of development and application in educational, medical, cultural, territorial, charitable, ideological spheres of Ukrainian society. *Social Technologies: Current Problems of Theory and Practice*, *65*(66), 12–24.

Prutska, O. O. (2019). Financing of organic agricultural production in the context of impact investing. *Economics, Finance, Management: Topical Issues of Science and Practice*, *5*, 56–63.

Shimko, O. V. (2010). Social marketing as a tool of socio-economic development of society. *Proceedings of Series Economy*, *14*, 297–304.

Shpachuk, V., Hornyk, V., Kravchenko, S., Vizirov, B., Aleinikova, O., & Abuselidze, G. (2023). State policy of cooperation between countries and global institutions: Condition and prospects. *E3S Web of Conferences*, *371*(1), Article 05004. https://doi.org/10.1051/e3sconf/202337105004

Skydan, O. V., Yaremova, M. I., Tarasovych, L. V., Dankevych, V. Y., & Kutsmus, N. M. (2022). Possibilities of developing sustainable world by introducing bioeconomy: Global perspective. *Problemy Ekorozwoju*, *17*(1), 162–170. https://doi.org/10.35784/pe.2022.1.15

Sotnyk, I. M., Gavrilova, V. V., & Kovalenko, E. V. (2018). Social entrepreneurship as a tool for implementing global goals of sustainable development. *Actual Problems of the Economy*, *2*(200), 62–73.

Tarasovych, L., & Yaremova, M. (2021). Coherence of marketing imperatives for managing the development of socio-economic systems. *Scientific Horizons*, *24*(7), 81–89. https://doi.org/10.48077/scihor.24(7).2021.81-89

Tarasovych, L., Yaremova, M., Vlasenko, O., Shuliak, B., & Kotova, L. (2021). Formation of marketing concept of rural economic development. In B. Alareeni, A. Hamdan, & I. Elgedawy (Eds.), *The importance of new technologies and entrepreneurship in business development: In the context of economic diversity in developing countries* (Vol. 194, pp. 445–453). Springer. https://doi.org/10.1007/978-3-030-69221-6_33

Tarasovych, L., Yaremova, M., Usiuk, T., Lavrynenko, S., Slobodianyk, A., & Abuselidze, G. (2023). Social marketing: Imperatives for rural entrepreneurship. *E3S Web of Conferences*, *389*(4), Article 09049. https://doi.org/10.1051/e3sconf/202338909049

Tkachuk, V. I., Shvets, T. V., & Plotnikova, M. F. (2020). Strategic management of investments in the development of entrepreneurship of territorial communities. *Agroworld*, *24*, 13–21. https://doi.org/10.32702/2306-6792.2020.24.12

Truong, D., & Dietrich, T. (2018). Master's thesis research in social marketing (1971–2015). *Journal of Social Marketing*, *8*, 58–98.

Verkhovna Rada of Ukraine. (1996). *Constitution of Ukraine, 01.01.2020*. https://zakon.rada.gov.ua/laws/show/254%D0%BA/96-%D0%B2%D1%80.#Text

White, L. (2018). Social marketing in the Caribbean: Philosophy, programs, projects, and pedagogy. *Social Marketing Quarterly*, *24*, 35–44. https://doi.org/10.1177/1524500417752311

Chapter 7

Sustainability of Tourism and Regional Airports Based on Good and Less Good Practices

Peter Novoszath[a] *and Rovena Vangjel (Troplini)*[b]

[a]*University of Dunaujvaros, Hungary*
[b]*Aleksandër Moisiu University of Durrës, Albania*

Abstract

Purpose: In a regional context, Central-Eastern Europe and the Balkans rank among the least competitive and least developed in tourism and regional airport sustainability compared to other European nations.

Study objective: This study aims to showcase the practices of regional airports that have made significant strides towards enhancing sustainability.

Methodology: Our research analysed data from scientific publications, industry journals and corporate reports. We compared previous findings with the latest reports on sustainability from key organisations such as the World Economic Forum (WEF), the Airport Carbon Accreditation (ACA) Organization and the International Council of Airports Europe. Additionally, we included case studies from Budapest Airport, Tirana International Airport (TIA), AviAlliance Holding and the Vinci S.A. group in our final analysis.

Findings: The study highlights the core features of global sustainability efforts at regional airports, emphasising initiatives to reduce carbon emissions and improve sustainable operations.

Practical implications: This research's primary objective is to support regional airports in adopting and implementing sustainable practices, thereby improving environmental, social and economic outcomes in the aviation sector.

Sustainable Development and Green Innovation: Managing Risk through Interdisciplinary Approaches and Policy Strategies, 147–177

Published under exclusive licence by Emerald Publishing Limited
doi:10.1108/978-1-83608-462-420251007

Keywords: Airport carbon emission reduction; carbon-neutral airport accreditation; global sustainability standards for airports; international airport sustainability initiatives; regional airport sustainability strategies; socio-economic and environmental sustainability in aviation; sustainable tourism and travel development

JEL codes: Q54; Q53; L93; Q56; R42; O44; F64; L98; Q58; R11; Q01; R48; Q52; L83; Q57; Z32

List of acronyms

Acronym	Full form	Description
ACA	Airport Carbon Accreditation	Certification programme for reducing airport carbon emissions
ACI Europe	Airports Council International Europe	Association representing European airports
ATM	Automated Teller Machine	Anyone with a credit card or debit card can access cash at most ATMs
CIPP	Certified Information Privacy Professional	Certification for professionals in privacy management and compliance
CPA	Certified Public Accountant	A professional accounting designation
EASA	European Union Aviation Safety Agency	EU agency ensuring aviation safety and sustainability
EBIT	Earnings Before Interest and Taxes	Earnings before interest and taxes (EBIT) is a company's operating profit without interest expenses and income taxes
EBITDA	Earnings Before Interest, Taxes, Depreciation, and Amortization	Short for earnings before interest, taxes, depreciation, and amortization, is an alternate measure of profitability to net income. It's used to assess a company's profitability and financial performance.
ESG	Environmental, Social and Governance	Framework assessing sustainability and ethical impact of business operations
EU	European Union	Political and economic union of European countries
FAA	Federal Aviation Administration	US government body regulating civil aviation

Acronym	Full form	Description
GBP	Great British Pound	The pound sterling, or GBP, is the official currency of the United Kingdom
GDP	Gross Domestic Product	GDP is the total value of all finished goods and services produced within a country in a specific time period
GHG	Greenhouse Gas	Gases that contribute to the greenhouse effect, including CO_2 and methane
GRI	Global Reporting Initiative	Organisation providing sustainability reporting standards
IAPP	International Association of Privacy Professionals	Organisation focussed on advancing privacy policies and data protection globally
ICAO	International Civil Aviation Organization	UN specialised agency for global aviation standards and policies
ISO	International Organization for Standardization	Organisation that sets global standards across various industries
LED	Light-Emitting Diode	A LED or light-emitting diode is an electrical component that produces light when current passes through it. LEDs are semiconductor devices, light is produced when the electrons combine with the material used as the semiconductor.
PMP	Project Management Professional	A globally recognised certification for project managers
PSP Investments	Public Sector Pension Investment Board	Canadian Crown Corporation managing pension fund investments
SDGs	Sustainable Development Goals	UN goals for sustainable global development by 2030
TIA	Tirana International Airport	Main international airport of Albania
TTDI	Travel and Tourism Development Index	Index measuring competitiveness and sustainability of travel and tourism in various countries
VINCI	Vinci Airports	Global private airport operator
WEF	World Economic Forum	International organisation for public–private cooperation

1. Introduction

The sustainability of tourism and regional airports has become a critical issue in global efforts to combat climate change and promote sustainable development. In particular, the countries of Central-Eastern Europe and the Balkan regions face unique challenges and opportunities in enhancing the sustainability of their tourism and regional airports. These regions are among the least competitive and capable of development in terms of sustainability compared to other European countries, necessitating a focussed examination of best practices and areas needing improvement.

This study presents and analyses the practices of regional airports that have taken significant steps towards sustainability. It examines data from scientific publications, industry reports and company data to provide a comprehensive overview of these efforts. The study also compares these efforts with global standards and initiatives, particularly those outlined by the WEF, the ACA Organization and the International Council of Airports Europe.

Through detailed case studies of Budapest Airport, TIA, AviAlliance Holding and the Vinci S.A. group, this study highlights successful strategies and areas where further improvements are necessary. Budapest Airport has implemented a 'Green Airport Program', which includes measures such as reducing energy consumption, promoting the use of renewable energy and increasing electric mobility. On the other hand, TIA has achieved Level 2 'Reduction' accreditation under the ACA programme and has implemented modern waste management practices and energy efficiency improvements.

The findings indicate that while some regional airports have made commendable progress, there is still a significant need to adopt broader sustainability initiatives. Factors such as financial constraints, lack of awareness and infrastructural limitations often hinder the implementation of sustainable practices.

The ultimate goal of this study is to provide practical implications and recommendations that can help regional airports enhance their sustainability, reduce carbon emissions and contribute positively to the socio-economic and environmental well-being of their respective regions. In doing so, this study underscores the importance of adopting holistic and integrated approaches to sustainability that encompass environmental, social and economic dimensions.

This research aims to foster a deeper understanding of the complexities and imperatives of sustainable tourism and regional airport operations in the Central-Eastern European and Balkan regions by showcasing good practices and identifying less effective ones. The study also highlights the role of international cooperation and policy support in driving the sustainability agenda forward, advocating for a collaborative approach to overcoming these regions' challenges.

2. Literature Review

Numerous studies have explored the sustainability of regional airports and their influence on tourism. Karagkouni and Dimitriou (2022) highlight the critical need for environmental management plans at regional tourist airports. Budd et al. (2015) and Sreenath et al. (2021) stress the importance of adopting sustainable practices to minimise environmental impacts while enhancing economic and social benefits. Hellmeister and Richins (2019) emphasise the advantages of sustainability certifications in the tourism sector, including cost savings, increased revenue and improved reputation. Prather (2016) notes that over half of small airports have implemented at least one sustainable initiative. Similarly, Zan Ke et al. (2012) discuss how programmes like EarthCheck have successfully introduced holistic approaches to environmental management and carbon reduction in tourism. Serio et al. (2022) find that multi-year ecological transition programmes significantly enhance airport performance. Jordão (2009) examines top-performing airports with sustainability-focussed strategies.

Research specific to the Western Balkans highlights the complexities of sustainable tourism and airport management. Radnić et al. (2015) emphasise the importance of sustainable tourism, particularly in rural areas, and the role of local communities. Karagkouni and Dimitriou (2022) stress that environmental performance management is essential for regional airports, especially in tourist destinations. Radovanov et al. (2020) underscore the positive impact of sustainable tourism development on tourism services efficiency in the region. Sreenath et al. (2021) identify the importance of adopting new technologies to support airport sustainability initiatives.

Setiawan et al. (2018) demonstrate that improved airport performance can positively influence related sectors, such as water management, waste disposal, retail, accommodation and transport services. Conversely, Gaspari (2015) points out that hotels vary significantly in their commitment to sustainable practices. Dincer and Dincer (2013) highlight how the 'Visa-Free Balkans' initiative by Turkish Airlines increased tourism interest among Turkish citizens. Giurea et al. (2018) focus on sustainable food, beverage consumption and packaging criteria. Yordanov (2019) notes that the rise of low-cost airlines has significantly influenced the selection of tourist destinations.

In Albania, the sustainability of tourism and regional airports involves various stakeholders (Brokaj & Murati, 2014). While awareness of sustainable practices increases, challenges such as limited awareness and financial constraints persist (Gaspari, 2015). Brokaj and Murati (2014) conclude that sustainable tourism leads to guest satisfaction, stable business profits, regional growth, improved living standards and environmental protection. Carlucci et al. (2018) assert that market mechanisms, such as air transport privatisation and deregulation, can enhance regional airport sustainability and efficiency.

Albania's natural attractions, including the Adriatic Sea Coast and the Albanian Alps, offer significant opportunities for sustainable tourism development (Bajrami et al., 2015; Lushaj et al., 2012). Ciro and Toska (2021) note that local initiatives and private service providers often drive tourism development in the country. More significant government and private sector collaboration is needed to support sustainable tourism and regional airport operations.

Another critical aspect of sustainability involves greenhouse gas (GHG) emissions from airport activities. Studies in various countries, including South Korea (Song & Shon, 2012), Kazakhstan (Sarbassov et al., 2020) and Belgium (Boussauw & Vanoutrive, 2019), highlight the environmental impact of airports. Atasoy et al. (2021) identify CO_2 as the primary contributor to emissions at Hasan Polatkan Airport. Altuntas (2014) estimates an average carbon dioxide equivalent of 1,629 kg per landing and takeoff in Turkish airports. Yilmaz (2017) calculates a reduction of 177.90 tonnes per year in CO_2 emissions at Kayseri Airport following shorter landing and takeoff times. However, Albania lacks comprehensive studies on airport-related GHG emissions, presenting an opportunity for future research to address this gap.

3. Development of the Travel and Tourism Sustainability Index in an International Comparison

The competitiveness of tourist destinations has been a significant topic in academic research for over 30 years. In 2007, the WEF introduced the Travel and Tourism Competitiveness Index (TTCI) to assess and rank the world's top tourist destinations. The TTCI evaluates the factors and policies that enhance a destination's attractiveness and competitiveness in the global tourism market. This index is regularly featured in the *Travel and Tourism Competitiveness* journal and other publications. The Travel & Tourism Competitiveness Report, published every 2 years, evaluates the competitiveness of over 100 economies (currently 117). It examines the factors enabling sustainable development in tourism and those contributing most to a country's overall competitiveness in the sector (WEF, 2022). These assessments provide valuable insights for policymakers and industry stakeholders aiming to strengthen tourism performance and sustainability.

The *Travel & Tourism Development Report 2021* uses a comprehensive methodology that combines the latest statistics from international organisations with survey results from key industry leaders. The TTDI comprises 17 pillars, grouped into five sub-indices, encompassing 112 indicators (Fig. 7.1). Approximately two-thirds of the TTDI data set is derived from official statistics. At the same time, the remaining third is based on survey responses collected through the WEF's annual executive opinion survey. This survey captures qualitative or internationally

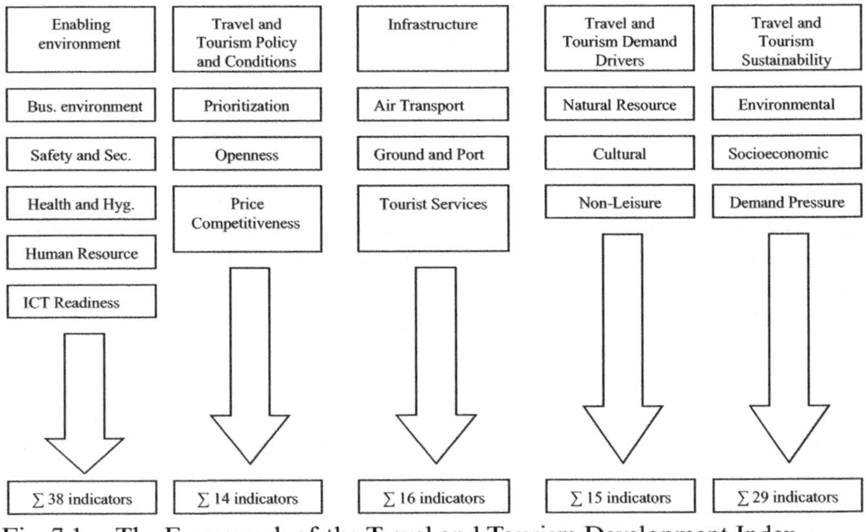

Fig. 7.1. The Framework of the Travel and Tourism Development Index (TTDI). *Source*: Author's edition on the basics of WEF (2022, p. 8).

comparable insights unavailable through standard country data. Each year, over 16,000 business leaders across the assessed economies participate, providing valuable perspectives on the key factors influencing the competitiveness and quality of travel and tourism.

4. Development of the Tourism and Travel Sustainability Index in An International Comparison

The sustainability sub-index evaluates the quality of tourism sustainability in an economy through three key pillars: environmental, socio-economic and demand-related factors.

1. *Environmental Sustainability (15 Indicators):* This pillar assesses the state and protection of a country's natural environment, which is vital for tourism. It measures factors such as natural resource vulnerability, environmental protection efforts and policies supporting sustainability. Indicators include water quality, pollution levels (air and sea), deforestation and species extinction risks. Public and private sector commitment to environmental preservation, including the protection of national parks and adherence to international environmental conventions, also plays a crucial role. Additionally, metrics on GHG emissions, the use of renewable energy, green infrastructure investment and climate adaptation readiness are critical for evaluating how a country addresses the long-term threat of climate change to tourism.
2. *Socio-economic Resilience and Circumstances (Seven Indicators):* This pillar captures an economy's socio-economic well-being and adaptability. It focusses on gender equality, workforce diversity, worker rights and youth engagement in education or employment. These are particularly significant for tourism, which employs more women, minorities and young people. Investments in social protection services – such as child and maternity benefits, unemployment and disability support – enhance labour market resilience, thereby strengthening economic stability. These elements influence tourism investment by creating a stable and productive workforce.
3. *Demand for Travel and Tourism and Its Effects (Seven Indicators):* This pillar measures the risks associated with overcrowding and demand fluctuations in tourism. Uncontrolled tourism growth can lead to overburdened infrastructure, environmental degradation, higher living costs and reduced quality of life for residents. Such problems can negatively impact visitor and resident satisfaction, ultimately decreasing a destination's attractiveness. Key indicators include the length of visitors' stay, seasonality, tourism distribution, and how economic benefits are shared with local communities. Addressing these issues through better management can help reduce overcrowding, promote local businesses, expand travel opportunities and enhance the overall travel experience.

In a regional comparison, the sustainability of tourism in Eastern European and Balkan regions is the least competitive and capable of development compared to other European countries (Table 7.1). These countries need to catch up regarding socio-economic resilience and the conditions that most influence

Table 7.1. Development Index of the Sustainability of Travel and Tourism in Selected European Countries.

Country	Placement in the Global Ranking	Environmental Sustainability	Socioeconomic Resilience and Circumstances	The Demand for Travel and Tourism and Its Effects
Spain	3	4.3	5.3	3.8
Italy	10	4.3	5.7	3.7
Portugal	16	4.2	5.5	3.8
Greece	28	4.4	4.8	3.4
Croatia	46	4.5	5.1	2.8
Malta	35	4.3	5.3	4.2
Turkey	45	3.6	3.7	3.5
Cyprus	31	4.3	5.3	4.1
South Europe		**4.2**	**5.1**	**3.7**
France	4	4.7	5.7	3.4
Germany	5	4.7	5.9	3.9
United Kingdom	8	4.9	5.3	4.4
Switzerland	6	5.2	5.6	4.0
Austria	11	5.1	6.0	3.8
Netherlands	14	4.8	6.1	3.9
Luxembourg	21	4.9	5.6	3.7
Belgium	22	4.4	5.6	4.1
Ireland	24	4.5	5.7	4.6
Czech Republic	26	4.5	5.8	3.7
West Europe		**4.8**	**5.7**	**4.0**
Slovenia	39	4.8	6.0	3.1
Poland	30	4.1	5.2	3.8
Bulgaria	41	4.6	4.8	3.8
Hungary	37	4.5	4.7	3.9
Romania	53	4.3	4.4	4.0
Slovakia	56	4.6	5.4	3.5
Montenegro	67	4.0	4.5	4.0
Serbia	70	3.8	4.4	3.7
Albania	72	4.4	4.7	3.4
North Macedonia	87	3.7	4.2	3.3

Table 7.1. (*Continued*)

Country	Placement in the Global Ranking	Environmental Sustainability	Socioeconomic Resilience and Circumstances	The Demand for Travel and Tourism and Its Effects
Moldova	77	4.1	4.9	3.8
Bosnia-Herzegovina	95	3.5	4.4	3.3
Balkan and Eastern Europe		**4.2**	**4.8**	**3.6**

Note: The results for larger regions are presented in bold.

Source: WEF (2022).

them, so they should pay much more attention to their development in the future than at present. Another aspect of sustainable tourism is the circular economy approach, where Cafuli and Vangjel (2022) identify the problems associated with the implementation of a circular economy in travel and tourism across the macro-environmental level (legal, technological, economic, social), micro-environmental level (infrastructural, value chain) and organisational level (culture, cost structure, income inflows, strategy, etc.).

The infrastructure sub-index measures the availability and quality of each economy's physical infrastructure and comprises three components:

4. *Air Transport Infrastructure (Four Indicators):* Air connectivity is essential for easy travel to and from countries and for moving between many countries. This pillar measures air transport volume by indicators such as available seat kilometres, number of departures, airport density, number of operating airlines and air transport infrastructure quality for domestic and international flights.
5. *Land and Port Infrastructure (Seven Indicators):* The tourism and travel sector needs effective and accessible transit to essential business hubs and tourist destinations. This necessitates a sufficiently wide network of roads and railways, along with appropriate density and infrastructure for roads, railways and ports that adhere to world standards of comfort, safety and modal efficiency. The pillar also takes into account dirt roads that facilitate local connectivity and have the potential to attract tourists.
6. *Tourism Service Infrastructure (Five Indicators):* The presence of appropriate, high-calibre lodging, resorts and recreational amenities in a country can serve as a considerable competitive advantage. The quality of tourism service infrastructure is assessed by the quantity of hotel accommodations and the availability of services like car rentals and ATMs. Competition among tourism services must be taken into account, as it affects price and service quality.

In an international comparison, the aviation infrastructure in the Eastern European and Balkan regions is the least competitive compared to other European countries (Table 7.2). Therefore, in the case of the countries in this region,

Table 7.2. Development Index of Infrastructural Elements in Selected European Countries.

Országok	**Placement in the Global Ranking**	**Air Transport Infrastructure**	**Land and Port Infrastructure**	**Tourist Service Infrastructure**
Spain	3	5.3	5.1	6.1
Italy	10	4.8	4.8	5.8
Portugal	16	4.4	4.5	6.3
Greece	28	4.5	4.0	5.6
Croatia	46	3.2	4.1	6.4
Malta	35	3.9	3.9	5.3
Turkey	45	5.0	4.0	4.2
Cyprus	31	4.1	3.3	5.6
South Europe		**4.4**	**4.2**	**5.7**
France	4	5.1	5.6	5.4
Germany	5	5.1	5.4	4.9
United Kingdom	8	5.3	5.3	5.0
Switzerland	6	4.9	6.5	5.3
Austria	11	4.2	5.7	5.9
Netherlands	14	5.1	6.0	5.4
Luxembourg	21	3.3	6.3	4.6
Belgium	22	4.0	5.4	4.0
Ireland	24	4.1	4.4	4.7
Czech Republic	26	3.6	5.7	4.3
West Europe		**4.5**	**5.7**	**4.8**
Slovenia	39	2.1	4.9	4.9
Poland	30	3.6	4.8	3.8
Bulgaria	41	3.3	3.8	4.8
Hungary	37	3.4	5.5	3.8
Romania	53	3.2	3.6	4.0
Slovakia	56	2.2	4.4	3.8
Montenegro	67	2.6	3.5	5.7
Serbia	70	3.2	3.7	3.6
Albania	72	2.7	3.3	3.8
North Macedonia	87	2.4	3.0	3.4

Table 7.2. (*Continued*)

Országok	Placement in the Global Ranking	Air Transport Infrastructure	Land and Port Infrastructure	Tourist Service Infrastructure
Moldova	77	2.5	3.4	3.0
Bosnia-Herzegovina	95	2.2	3.8	3.5
Balkan and Eastern Europe		**2.8**	**3.9**	**4.0**

Note: The results for larger regions are presented in bold.

Source: WEF (2022).

it would be crucial to develop the aviation infrastructure to increase the competitiveness and development of tourism. In the Balkans and Eastern Europe subregions, the share of tourism in the GDP is lower than in the case of most other European subregions. Consequently, their competitiveness should be improved to continuously increase the number of arrivals and maximise their potential from tourism. However, the region is still below the European average in terms of competitiveness, except for price competitiveness, which indicates the need for further development, especially in the case of infrastructural elements (WEF, 2022).

5. The Airport Carbon Dioxide Emission Reduction Accreditation Programme

The ACA programme is the only officially recognised certification standard for managing airport carbon dioxide emissions. This chapter explains the programme's origins and how it has reshaped the approach to carbon management in the aviation sector. The initiative, launched by ACI EUROPE (Airports Council International Europe) during its 2009 annual congress, has since become a global framework, extending beyond major hubs to include regional, general aviation and cargo airports.

The programme sets airport-specific carbon management standards based on internationally accepted methodologies. It independently evaluates and certifies airports' efforts to monitor, manage and reduce carbon emissions through a multi-level accreditation system. These certification levels reflect an airport's current progress in carbon management and environmental impact. As of 2024, the programme offers seven levels of accreditation (Fig. 7.2):

Level 1: Mapping – This initial level involves measuring and documenting the airport's carbon footprint. To achieve this, airports must define their 'organisational boundaries' and identify all GHG emissions. Data collection and calculation of annual carbon emissions are required, along with regular preparation of carbon footprint reports.

Level 2: Reduction – This level focusses on implementing effective carbon management strategies to reduce emissions. Airports must meet all the requirements of Level 1 and demonstrate progress through emissions reduction targets and reports, using a 3-year rolling average to track results.

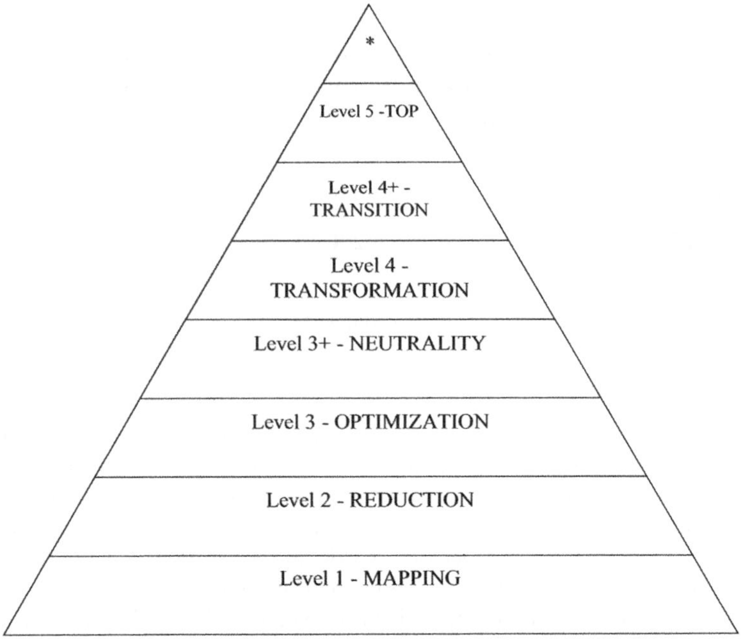

Fig. 7.2. The Seven Levels of ACA (https://www.airportcarbonaccreditation.org/about/7-levels-of-accreditation/). *Source*: Author's edition on the ACA (2023, p. 10).

Level 3: Optimisation (Optimisation) – This level requires the involvement of third parties, such as airlines and service providers, to reduce the airport's carbon footprint. It also includes establishing collaborative channels with authorities and users. To achieve this level, the airport must meet the requirements of both mapping and reduction. Additionally, it must expand its carbon footprint to account for third-party emissions and provide evidence of ongoing cooperation with these stakeholders to implement emission reduction measures.

Level 3+: Neutrality – This stage focusses on neutralising remaining carbon emissions through verified offset programmes. The airport must fulfil all requirements for mapping, reduction and optimisation. It must also offset residual emissions using internationally recognised carbon offsets and provide a detailed carbon footprint report.

Level 4: Transformation – This level signifies a shift in airport operations and collaboration with business partners to achieve maximum emissions reduction. The airport must produce an expanded carbon footprint report and adopt a long-term absolute emissions reduction target in alignment with the 1.5°C or 2°C climate pathway set by the Intergovernmental Panel on Climate Change. The airport must outline necessary steps, establish milestones and present evidence of leadership efforts to engage third parties in emission reduction initiatives.

Level 4+: Transition – This level includes all transformation requirements and requires the airport to offset any remaining emissions using internationally recognised carbon offsets.

Level 5: Net-Zero Emissions – The highest level in the programme, Level 5, represents full achievement of net-zero emissions.

Global Certification Overview (ACA, 2024):

Europe:

- 147 certified airports.
- 48 mapped their carbon footprints.
- 33 actively reduced emissions.
- 16 optimised operations by involving third parties.
- 50 achieved carbon neutrality.
- North America: 47 certified airports.
- Latin America & Caribbean: 24 certified airports.
- Africa: 14 certified airports.
- Asia-Pacific: 55 certified airports.

Global Performance as of June 2024:

- 140 airports mapped their carbon footprints.
- 202 airports actively reduced CO_2 emissions.
- 105 airports involved third parties in CO_2 reduction.
- 34 airports achieved carbon neutrality.
- 28 airports aligned CO_2 management with global climate goals.
- 48 airports implemented conversions and compensated for remaining emissions.
- 62 airports reached Level 4+ Transition or Level 5 accreditation.

Case Study: Budapest Ferenc Liszt International Airport:

Budapest Airport is the only airport in Hungary that participates in the ACA programme. It has achieved Level 4+ Transition, making it the first in Central Europe to reach this status under the ACI's accreditation framework. The next objective is to attain Level 5, achieving net-zero emissions (International Airport Review, 2024).

The map shows that Eastern European and Balkan regions lag other European countries in terms of airport accreditation for carbon dioxide (Fig. 7.3).

6. International Initiatives to Make Airports More Sustainable

6.1. Global Sustainability Standards

The concept of sustainability was solidified by the United Nations' adoption of the 17 Sustainable Development Goals (SDGs) in 2015 (UN Global Compact Guide, 2015). Airports often align their sustainability efforts with these goals, applying frameworks like the Global Reporting Initiative (GRI) Sustainability Reporting Guidelines and the Airport Operators Sector Supplement (AOSS, 2011). While each airport may prioritise actions based on local needs, SDG 13 – Climate Action remains a universally critical objective.

In December 2019, the European Commission (EC) introduced the European Green Deal, aiming to make Europe the world's first climate-neutral continent by 2050. This initiative seeks to combat rising emissions from sectors such as

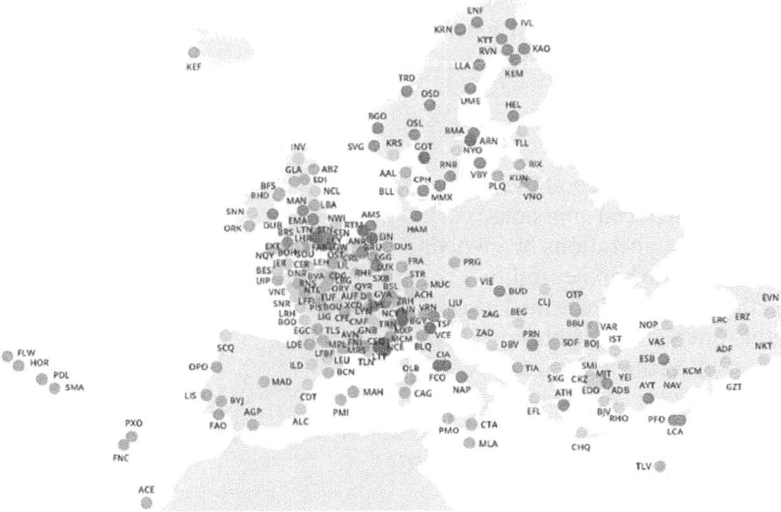

Fig. 7.3. Location of Accredited Airports in Europe, 2023. *Source*: ACA (2024).

aviation and shipping, which have increased by over 50% since 1990. The Sustainable and Smart Mobility Strategy, published in December 2020, set forth several key objectives to advance sustainability in air transport (EC, 2020):

- Making all modes of transport more sustainable by promoting environmentally friendly practices across the sector.
- Accelerating the adoption of low- and zero-emission vehicles and encouraging the use of renewable and low-carbon fuels across road, rail, water and air transport.
- Establishing ambitious energy efficiency standards for aircraft and ships to reduce emissions.
- Transforming airports and ports into zero-emission hubs, enhancing their role in international connectivity and regional economies by integrating sustainable operations and infrastructure.
- Increasing public and private investment in local renewable energy production, sustainable multimodal access and fleet modernisation to improve transport efficiency.

These measures aim to develop an environmentally sustainable and economically resilient transport network. However, many airports face challenges related to the economic downturn and limited access to resources, which complicates their efforts to achieve sustainability. Despite these challenges, the current crisis presents an opportunity to reassess and reform existing systems and practices, strengthening the aviation industry and making it more sustainable.

6.2. Other Global Initiatives Promoting Airport Sustainability

The International Civil Aviation Organization (ICAO) reviews and updates its relevant guidelines and practices for environmental protection every 3 years. In 2015, the ICAO Council also adopted its environmental protection strategic objectives, which aim to minimise the harmful environmental effects of civil aviation activities (ICAO, 2015).

EUROCONTROL has contributed significantly to the aviation sustainability debate with two major reports. The first, *Aviation Outlook 2050 (EAO 2050)*, projects 16 million flights by 2050 and estimates net CO_2 emissions for the first time, analysing pathways to achieve net-zero emissions by 2050 (EUROCONTROL, 2022a). The second, *Objective Sky Green*, builds on these scenarios, thoroughly examining emission reduction strategies and the financial investments needed for decarbonisation (EUROCONTROL, 2022b).

The European Union Aviation Safety Agency (EASA) has focussed on sustainability by addressing noise reduction, air quality improvement and climate change mitigation. EASA's *European Aviation Environmental Report* serves as a comprehensive resource on the environmental performance of the European aviation sector (EASA, 2023).

The Federal Aviation Administration (FAA) has also prioritised sustainability in the United States. In 2011, the FAA launched a pilot initiative to integrate sustainability into airport design. This was followed by the 2012 *Aviation Environmental and Energy Policy Statement*, which affirmed the FAA's commitment to fostering environmentally sustainable growth in aviation (FAA, 2012). The FAA continues to update its environmental policy and operates programmes such as the *Noise Compliance Program* and the *Voluntary Airport Low Emissions (VALE) Program* to help airports meet sustainability targets (FAA, 2020).

BREEAM (Building Research Establishment Environmental Assessment Method) provides a globally recognised sustainability certification process adaptable to various building types, including airport infrastructure. Its primary aim is to guide architectural projects towards improved sustainability outcomes (BREEAM, 2021).

CEEQUAL (Civil Engineering Environmental Quality Evaluation and Award System) is another critical tool for assessing the sustainability of civil infrastructure projects. Widely used in both civilian and military aviation sectors, it evaluates sustainability performance across various airport facilities, including runways, taxiways and operational areas (CEEQUAL, 2007).

7. The Future Strategy of Sustainable Airports Should Be Based on a Balanced Business Model

Today, a sole focus on environmental impacts is no longer sufficient, and the airport industry must comprehensively address the three most important dimensions of sustainability – environmental, social and economic factors (Fig. 7.4). Therefore, ACI EUROPE created its Airport Sustainability Strategy, which provides an industry-wide framework and guidelines around a shared vision of a sustainable future airport (ACI-ACA, 2023). The primary objective of this strategy is to provide general guidance and detailed guidelines for the sustainability efforts of European airport operators (Airports Council International, 2020).

It identifies recommended actions to help airports become more sustainable and provides indicative metrics to measure progress and identify areas for further improvement.

Environmental effects	Social influences	Economic effects
Climate changes Local air quality Material resources Water Biological diversity	Human rights, values and ethics Noise and the quality of life of local communities Experience and commitment of employees Quality of services and passenger experiences	Economic development Sustainable supply chain Sustainable destinations Intermodality *

Fig. 7.4. The Main Pillars of the New Sustainable, Balanced Business Model. *Source*: Airports Council International (2020, p. 16). *Note*: *The meaning of 'intermodal' refers to the connection of different modes of transport, which creates an opportunity for passengers to travel more efficiently and sustainably. Intermodal transport systems allow people to use a combination of other modes of transport (e.g., train, bus, subway) during a trip – the definition based on ScienceDirect (https://www.sciencedirect.com/topics/social-sciences/intermodality).

8. Good and Not-So-Good Examples of How to Make Regional Airports More Sustainable

8.1. The Main Characteristics and Sustainability Activities of Budapest Airport

On June 6, 2007, the consortium led by HOCHTIEF Airport purchased the shares of Budapest Airport Zrt., the operator of Liszt Ferenc International Airport, the owner's loan and interest granted to Budapest Airport Zrt., and the parent company of Budapest Airport Zrt., BUD Holding Zrt. t. To carry out the transaction, the consortium established two holding companies in Hungary, Airport Holding Tanácsadó Kft and its 100% subsidiary Airport Hungary Tanácsadó Kft. The purchase price (GBP 1,309 million) was paid in two steps: In the first step, Airport Hungary Kft. bought 75% of Budapest Airport Zrt.'s ordinary shares minus one vote by paying GBP 1,020 million at the time of the transaction and Budapest Airport Zrt. all preferred shares. The second purchase price instalment (289 million British pounds, 444,234,027 euros plus accrued interest) was due in 2011 to the Royal Bank of Scotland and BAA International Holdings Limited from Airport Hungary Kft. The purchase price payment was arranged by the members of the Company's owner partly with an owner's loan and partly with a capital increase. On July 18, 2011, the minority owner of Budapest Airport Zrt. (MNV Zrt.) exercised its right to sell shares and sold its 25% plus one voting share in Budapest Airport Zrt. to Airport Hungary Kft. for EUR 136,178,979 (HUF 36.6 billion), thus AHUK Kft. Became the sole shareholder in Budapest Airport

Zrt. In September 2013, the Canadian pension fund, the Public Sector Pension Investment Board (PSP Investments), purchased 100% of the HOCHTIEF Group's stake in HOCHTIEF AirPort GmbH. Soon after, HOCHTIEF AirPort GmbH was renamed AviAlliance GmbH. Currently, the consortium that manages the parent company (Airport Holding Kft.) has three members: AviAlliance GmbH, Caisse de dépot et placement du Québec, Malton Investment Pte Ltd. (Airport Hungary Tanácsadó Kft, 2023, p. 12).

8.1.1. AviAlliance Is Currently Positioned in the World's Airport Operations Sector

AviAlliance, a prominent global independent airport operator and investor, manages five major international airports: Athens, Budapest, Düsseldorf, Hamburg and San Juan. It operates as a wholly owned subsidiary of PSP Investments, one of Canada's largest pension fund managers. Headquartered in Germany, AviAlliance has played a pioneering role in airport privatisation, with its origins dating back to the 1930s when its predecessor, the construction firm HOCHTIEF, entered the airport industry. In the 1980s, HOCHTIEF expanded into airport financing and established HOCHTIEF AirPort in 1997 to oversee its airport management operations. Over the years, the company developed a strong portfolio with significant operational control of its holdings. In 2013, HOCHTIEF AirPort GmbH was acquired by the PSP Investments and rebranded as AviAlliance.

PSP Investments, a leading global institutional investor, reported C$243.7 billion in net assets under management as of March 31, 2023. Established in 1999, this AAA-rated Canadian Crown Corporation manages pension funds for public sector plans, including those for the Canadian Armed Forces, Royal Canadian Mounted Police, and Reserves. Its diversified global portfolio spans public markets, real estate, private equity, infrastructure, private debt and natural resources. AviAlliance, as a fully owned subsidiary, benefits from PSP Investments' strong financial resources, enhancing its stability and capacity to form long-term strategic partnerships in the global airport industry (Novoszath, 2015) (Table 7.3).

8.1.2. The Environmental Protection Policy of Budapest Airport – The Green Airport Program

Budapest Airport joined the ACA Program in 2011. Over the next decade, it reduced its direct carbon dioxide emissions by 50% and cut emissions per passenger by one-third. In December 2021, the airport received certification from ACI, recognising its fulfilment of sustainability commitments despite the challenges posed by the pandemic on the aviation sector. With this achievement, Budapest Airport became one of 362 airport operators globally to operate responsibly and achieve full carbon offset (ACA, 2023; Budapest Airport, 2021).

In 2015, Budapest Airport launched the Green Airport Program, a collaborative initiative to reduce the environmental impact of Hungary's primary international airport (Budapest Airport, 2020). This programme encourages cooperation among the various organisations operating at the airport to minimise its carbon

Table 7.3. AviAlliance's Airport Portfolio.

	Athens Airport	**Budapest Airport**	**Düsseldorf Airport**	**Hamburg Airport**	**San Juan Airport**
Development of the number of passengers in 2022 (million people)	22.7	12.2	16.1	11.1	10.3
Development of the number of passengers in 2019 (million people)	25.6	16.2	25.5	17.3	9.4
Share of AviAlliance	40%	55%	30%	49%	40%
Duration of concession	Until 2046	Until 2080	–	–	Until 2053
EBITDA indicator in 2022 (million €)	329.5	59.9[a]	90.8	32.9	215.6
EBITDA indicator in 2019 (million €)	348.4	244.1	187.8	94.9	79.8
Level of carbon accreditation in 2024	4+	3+	3	3+	1[b]

Source: Own editing based on data from the beginning of January 2024 in the database of accredited airports of AviAlliance (2023, pp. 4–19) and the ACA website (2024).

[a]2021 data.

[b]The San Juan Daily Star (2023).

footprint. The initiative focusses on reducing carbon dioxide emissions through a series of targeted measures, including:

- reduction of airport energy consumption,
- creating the opportunity to use renewable energy sources,
- the development of electric mobility,
- further development of selective waste collection at the airport.

8.1.3. Improvements to Budapest Airport for More Sustainable Operation

Budapest Airport has implemented several significant developments to make the airport more sustainable. In recent years, the airport's heating centres and boiler house have been modernised, and the development of a geothermal heating system has begun, thanks to which the airport will be able to completely switch to environmentally friendly heating soon, replacing the previously typical natural gas consumption and significantly reducing carbon dioxide emissions. To reduce the airport's electricity consumption, indoor and outdoor lighting is constantly being replaced with LED light sources. The lighting of the passenger compartments, public parking lots, fuel stations, vehicle repair bases and internal service roads was made more sustainable. Significant progress has also been made in the field of e-mobility; at the end of 2022, approximately 10% of Budapest Airport's vehicle fleet consisted of electric or hybrid vehicles, and the number of more sustainably operated cars and equipment in the vehicle fleet of the airport's ground servers has also increased. By the end of 2022, more than 65% of Budapest Airport's electricity needs will be covered by green energy. From January 2023, 100% of the airport's electricity supply will come from renewable sources (Budapest Airport, 2023a).

8.1.4. ESG (Environmental, Social and Governance) Rating of Budapest Airport

Budapest Airport continuously monitors and measures its sustainability activities. According to the ESG assessment, the airport operator achieved a low-risk rating, confirming that the company pays special attention to ESG aspects during its investment decisions. In the Sustainalytics ESG risk management rating process 2023, Budapest Airport received a score of 13.2. It was ranked 49th among the 187 transportation companies evaluated worldwide and 995th in the 15,718 globally rated companies list. During the risk analysis, Sustainalytics primarily evaluated the companies based on the market situation and the leading global and regional indicators in the context of a full-scale ESG risk analysis, which included more than 70 management indicators. In the process, the Budapest Airport, for example, became the European leader in the traffic of environmentally friendly planes. Budapest Airport also continuously consults with its airline partners regarding introducing sustainable solutions. One of the most significant results is that from April to August 2023, nearly a third of the aircraft movements were carried out with new-generation aircraft that are significantly more environmentally friendly than older types. This was one of Europe's highest rates during this period (Budapest Airport, 2023b).

8.2. The Main Characteristics and Sustainability Strategy of TIA

TIA has changed its shareholders over time. Initially, when TIA was privatised in 2005, the principal shareholders were a consortium led by the German construction company HOCHTIEF, along with the Albanian-American Enterprise Fund and DEG (Deutsche Investitions- und Entwicklungsgesellschaft). As of the most recent updates, TIA was operated by the China Everbright Limited and Friedmann Pacific Asset Management consortium, which acquired the airport in October 2016. This consortium managed TIA through a concession agreement with the Albanian government. As of December 18, 2020, Kastrati Group SHA, a leading independent company based in Albania, established in 1990, owns 100% of the share capital of TIA. Kastrati Group SHA is well positioned globally in Albania through its broad domestic and international activities and network.

8.2.1. ESG Rating of TIA

Since 2006, TIA has operated an Environmental and Quality Management System aligned with ISO standards 14001:2004 and 9001:2000. This system ensures compliance with air quality, wastewater, potable water and noise standards established by Albania, the European Union (EU) and the World Health Organization.

TIA became the first private company in Albania to build its wastewater treatment plant. After the new passenger terminal opened in 2007, TIA introduced modern waste management practices, providing separate bins for recyclable and non-recyclable waste to facilitate proper disposal by passengers and users.

Social responsibility initiatives complement TIA's environmental efforts. By collaborating with local authorities and communities, the airport has supported projects such as developing a tourism plan for Preza Castle and organising environmental awareness activities such as guided tours of the concession area.

Since 2011, TIA has implemented an energy and carbon management system, calculating and reporting CO_2 emissions based on the Greenhouse Gas Protocol. External auditor TUV Hellas (TUV Nord) S.A. verified the airport's carbon management processes. In January 2013, TIA achieved Level 1 'Mapping' accreditation under the ACA programme. By February 2018, TIA advanced to Level 2 'Reduction', underscoring its commitment to reducing CO_2 emissions while managing increased air traffic. These efforts aim to lower electricity and fuel consumption, control CO_2 emissions and promote sustainable development.

By 2015, TIA had significantly improved environmental performance compared to the 2011 baseline. Traffic units increased by over 8%, while the total carbon footprint decreased by 6%. Carbon emissions per traffic unit dropped by 13% to 0.49 kg CO_2, and fuel consumption per unit decreased by 16% to 0.1 L per unit. The total CO_2 footprint in 2015 was 976,000 kg, 96% of which were scope one emissions from airport activities, with the remaining 4% from scope two indirect emissions due to electricity purchases (Tirana International Airport, n.d.).

In 2021, the total CO_2 emissions under TIA's direct control (scope one and scope two) reached 1,363 tonnes, increasing to 1,449 tonnes when including process emissions. These figures represent only 4% of the airport's combined scope 1, 2 and 3 emissions, which amounted to 36,998 tonnes of CO_2. Aircraft movements and landside ground access accounted for 94% of these emissions (Tirana International Airport, n.d.).

Over the past 3 years, TIA's carbon footprint has fluctuated between 1,100 and 1,300 tonnes, with emissions per traffic unit remaining between 0.4 and 0.5 kg CO_2. A comparison of 2011, 2019 and 2021 data shows a 37% and 18% improvement in CO_2 emissions per passenger, reflecting an average emission rate of 0.49 kg per traffic unit. This progress demonstrates TIA's effective and commendable environmental management.

8.2.2. Traffic Units

TIA reported handling over 7.2 million passengers in 2023, a 40% increase from the previous year. This significant growth underscores the airport's role in enhancing regional connectivity and providing excellent service to passengers. The airport has continuously invested in infrastructure development, substantially increasing seat capacity and air traffic movements.

In 2024, TIA is projected to handle a significant volume of passenger traffic, reflecting its role as the primary international gateway to Albania. The total number of passengers is around 3 million, including global and domestic travellers. TIA is also expected to manage substantial cargo traffic, with an estimated total cargo volume of 20,000 metric tonnes. This includes import and export goods, highlighting the airport's importance in facilitating trade and commerce. The number of flight movements (takeoffs and landings) is projected to be approximately 35,000 for the year. This includes commercial airlines, cargo flights and private jets.

8.2.3. Carbon Footprint for 2024

TIA's total carbon footprint for 2024 is projected to be around 900,000 kg of CO_2. This includes emissions from various sources within the airport's operations, such as ground support equipment, airport vehicles and energy consumption. The carbon emissions per traffic unit are expected to be around 0.45 kg of CO_2 per traffic unit. This represents a continued effort to reduce emissions relative to the volume of airport activity, demonstrating TIA's commitment to sustainability.

- Scope 1 Emissions: Direct emissions from TIA's operations, including airport vehicles and ground support equipment, account for approximately 92% of the total emissions.
- Scope 2 Emissions: Indirect emissions from purchased electricity and heating account for 8% of the total emissions.

The largest source of CO_2 emissions for TIA is scope one, primarily due to diesel consumption by fleet vehicles and ground service equipment. The second most significant contributor is diesel consumption for heating in the terminal building. Mitigation efforts to reduce emissions should focus on these areas. Scope 2 emissions come from purchased electricity, mainly carbon-neutral in Albania due to the country's reliance on hydropower plants. However, efforts should still be made to improve resource availability and efficiency.

8.3. The Main Characteristics and Sustainability Strategy of the Vinci S.A. Group

Under the European Merger Regulation, the EC (2023) approved a joint acquisition agreement on December 13, 2023 (File No. M.11339), granting Hungarian-based Corvinus International Investments Zrt. and French-based VINCI Airports shared control of Airport Holding Tanácsadó Kft. (Budapest Airport Holding). This decision has sparked interest in understanding how VINCI Airports addresses airport sustainability and the practices it employs across its extensive operations, which will be relevant for the future of Budapest International Airport.

After over a year of negotiations, the purchase contract for Budapest Airport Zrt. was finalised on June 6, 2024. This transaction marked the airport's return to majority national ownership, with the Hungarian state acquiring an 80% stake and VINCI Airports obtaining 20%. The purchase price was set at €3.1 billion, with an extended loan agreement of €1.44 billion for the creditor consortium. Through this agreement, Hungary partners with a globally recognised operator with expertise in managing world-class airports across multiple continents.

As a leading global operator, VINCI Airports managed 65 airports across 12 countries in Europe, Asia and the Americas by 2022. It leverages its capabilities to finance, develop and modernise airport infrastructure, ensuring operational optimisation and environmental sustainability. In Europe, VINCI operates key airports in Portugal (serving 55.7 million passengers), France (16 million passengers), the United Kingdom (including London Gatwick with 32.8 million passengers) and Serbia (Belgrade Airport with 5.6 million passengers). In Asia, it manages airports in Cambodia and Japan, handling over 22 million passengers. In Latin America, VINCI Airports holds concessions for multiple airports in Brazil, Costa Rica, the Dominican Republic and Chile. Additionally, VINCI became the largest shareholder in Mexico's OMA Group, which operates 13 airports.

VINCI Airports reported revenues of €1.78 billion in the first half of 2023, an 8% increase from pre-pandemic levels in 2019. This growth was fuelled by rising passenger demand, expanded airline seat capacity and new route openings. Passenger traffic reached 123 million in the first half of 2023, a 36% increase over the same period in 2022, with record numbers achieved at airports in Portugal, Mexico, the Dominican Republic and Serbia.

The company's profitability also improved significantly. In the first half of 2023, VINCI Airports' EBIT rose to €780 million, a 105% increase from the previous year, driven by higher revenues, controlled costs, and the integration of the OMA Group. Similarly, EBITDA reached €1.08 billion, marking a 71% increase, with the margin improving to 60.8%.

In July 2023, VINCI Airports, alongside its Portuguese subsidiary ANA, secured a 40-year concession for managing seven airports in Cape Verde, which served 2.8 million passengers in 2019. This expansion underscores VINCI's ongoing strategy to enhance its global airport portfolio and sustainable operations. The group remains committed to reducing its environmental impact, optimising infrastructure and fostering sustainable development across its airports worldwide.

8.3.1. Environmental Protection Policy of the Vinci S.A. Group

VINCI Airports is committed to achieving net-zero emissions across all its airports by 2050. To support this goal, the company continues implementing various decarbonisation initiatives. In 2022, VINCI Airports inaugurated three new solar power plants at Faro, Belgrade and Lyon-Saint Exupéry (parking lot P3), generating carbon-free energy to meet its operational needs. Additionally, the company has reduced its carbon footprint by upgrading infrastructure and equipment. These measures include replacing traditional light bulbs with energy-efficient LEDs, installing more efficient heating and air conditioning systems, and transitioning to electric service vehicles and machinery. One notable achievement is the deployment of the first fully electric aircraft de-icer at Clermont-Ferrand Auvergne Airport.

In response to the energy crisis, VINCI Airports launched an energy efficiency plan during the 2022–2023 winter season, which includes maintaining temperature control at 17°C, particularly in high-capacity areas. By the end of 2022, these combined efforts resulted in a 44% reduction in the direct carbon footprint of the company's activities.

VINCI Airports has initiated a reforestation programme to offset residual emissions from its airport operations, with projects already underway in France and Portugal. In France, these initiatives adhere to the Ministry of Ecological Transition's Label Bas Carbone standards, ensuring compliance with nationally recognised low-carbon benchmarks. In addition to addressing direct emissions, VINCI Airports focusses on reducing indirect emissions by collaborating with partners and encouraging airlines to decarbonise their activities. These efforts aim to foster a comprehensive, industry-wide approach to sustainability and environmental responsibility (Vinci, 2023a, p. 40).

8.3.2. Participation of the Airports of the Vinci S.A. Group in the ACA Program

The VINCI Group operates Toulon Hyères Airport in France, Beja, Madeira and Ponta Delgada airports in Portugal. These airports are among the first 10 worldwide to achieve Level 5 certification under the ACA Program. This certification represents a holistic approach to carbon management, emphasising significant reductions in direct emissions, achieving a net-zero carbon balance and fostering partnerships to minimise third-party emissions (International Airport Review, 2024).

Achieving Level 5 highlights advanced carbon management practices based on the following criteria:

- *Significant CO_2 reduction*: Airports have decreased CO_2 emissions by at least 90% under their direct control:

  o Toulon reduced emissions by 90% in 2022 compared to 2018.
  o Ponta Delgada achieved a 96.16% reduction between 2022 and 2014.
  o Madeira lowered emissions by 96.74% in the same period.
  o Beja Airport recorded a 98.1% reduction between 2022 and 2014.

- *Investment in carbon removal*: Airports have funded nature-based projects, such as afforestation and reforestation, to offset residual emissions, providing additional environmental benefits.
- *Carbon management plan*: Airports have implemented tailored investment strategies and measures to achieve long-term emission targets.
- *Comprehensive carbon footprint mapping*: Airports have mapped all key upstream and downstream Scope 3 emissions in line with the GHG Protocol's Scope 3 Guidance.
- *Stakeholder engagement*: Airports have developed partnership plans to actively involve third-party stakeholders in reducing emissions across the airport ecosystem.

VINCI Airports has demonstrated its leadership in sustainability by becoming the largest international contributor to the ACI ACA programme, with 52 accredited airports (Vinci, 2023b). Of these, the VINCI Group operates 3 airports at

Level 1 (Mapping), 5 airports at Level 2 (Reduction), 14 airports at Level 3 (Optimisation), 9 airports at Level 4+ (Transition) and 4 airports at Level 5 (Net-Zero) (Table 7.4).

These accomplishments reflect VINCI Airports' long-term commitment to reducing its global carbon footprint.

8.4. Main Characteristics and Sustainability Activities of TIA

TIA, or Mother Teresa Airport, is near Tirana, Albania's capital. As the country's primary international gateway, TIA has modern facilities that have undergone substantial upgrades and expansions to meet the growing demand for passenger and cargo services. The airport offers a full range of amenities, including advanced baggage handling systems, efficient customs and immigration services, and state-of-the-art facilities for cargo operations, making it a key hub for passenger and freight transport.

TIA is designed to handle a high volume of flights and passengers annually. It is supported by multiple runways and taxiways that optimise aircraft movements, reduce delays and enhance operational efficiency. The airport also employs advanced air traffic control systems, automated check-in kiosks, and robust security measures, which improve safety, efficiency and the overall travel experience.

TIA is well connected to Tirana and other regions through various transportation options, such as buses, taxis and private vehicles, ensuring seamless connectivity for domestic and international travellers (TIA, 2024).

8.4.1. Participation of Albanian Regional Airports in the ACA Program

Since 2006, TIA has maintained an Environmental and Quality Management System in accordance with ISO 14001:2004 and ISO 9001:2000 standards. This system includes rigorous monitoring of air quality, wastewater, potable water and noise levels, ensuring full compliance with environmental and safety regulations established by Albania, the EU and the World Health Organization.

TIA has achieved Level 2 'Reduction' accreditation under the ACA programme. This level signifies that TIA has successfully implemented measures to manage and reduce its carbon emissions, reflecting its commitment to minimising its environmental impact. TIA became the first private company in Albania to develop and operate its own wastewater treatment plant, setting a benchmark for environmental responsibility and sustainability in the country's private sector.

The airport has adopted modern waste management practices, providing separate bins for recyclable and non-recyclable waste and promoting sustainable waste disposal methods. TIA has significantly improved energy efficiency. The airport employs various energy-saving technologies and practices to reduce electricity and fuel consumption while maintaining high operational standards.

TIA actively engages in local development projects and environmental awareness initiatives. In collaboration with local authorities and residents, the airport contributes to tourism development plans, such as those for Preza Castle, and organises activities to raise environmental consciousness. TIA is actively investing

Table 7.4. Level of Carbon Accreditation of Airports Operated by the Vinci Group at the Beginning of 2024.

	Code	Region	Country	Level
Annecy Haute Savoie Mont-Blanc Airport	NCY	Europe	France	Level 1
Belfast International Airport	BFS	Europe	United Kingdom	Level 2
Belgrade Airport	BEG	Europe	Serbia	Level 2
Chambéry Airport	CMF	Europe	France	Level 3
Clermont-Ferrand Auvergne Airport	CFE	Europe	France	Level 3
Dinard Bretagne Airport	DNR	Europe	France	Level 1
Grenoble Alpes Isère Airport	GNB	Europe	France	Level 3
Nantes Atlantique Airport	NTE	Europe	France	Level 3
Pays d'Ancenis Airport	LFFI	Europe	France	Level 2
Phnom Penh International Airport	PNH	Asia	Cambodia	Level 3
Rennes Bretagne Airport	RNS	Europe	France	Level 3
Saint-Nazaire Montoir Airport	SNR	Europe	France	Level 3
Siem Reap International Airport	REP	Asia	Cambodia	Level 2
Sihanoukville International Airport	KOS	Asia	Cambodia	Level 2
Stockholm Skavsta Airport	NYO	Europe	Sweden	Level 1
Toulon Hyères Airport	TLN	Europe	France	Level 5
Arroyo Barril Airport	EPS	Latin America	Dominica	Level 3
Gregorio Luperón International Airport	POP	Latin America	Dominica	Level 3
La Isabela International Airport	JBQ	Latin America	Dominica	Level 3
Las Américas International Airport	SDQ	Latin America	Dominica	Level 3
María Montez International Airport	BRX	Latin America	Dominica	Level 3
Samaná El Catey International Airport	AZS	Latin America	Dominica	Level 3

(*Continued*)

Table 7.4. (*Continued*)

	Code	Region	Country	Level
Lyon-Bron Airport	LYN	Europe	France	Level 4+
Lyon-Saint Exupéry Airport	LYS	Europe	France	Level 4+
Beja Airport	BYJ	Europe	Portugal	Level 5
Faro Airport	FAO	Europe	Portugal	Level 4+
Flores Airport	FLW	Europe	Portugal	Level 4+
Horta Airport	HOR	Europe	Portugal	Level 4+
Lisbon Airport	LIS	Europe	Portugal	Level 4+
Madeira Airport	FNC	Europe	Portugal	Level 5
Ponta Delgada	PDL	Europe	Portugal	Level 5
Porto Airport	OPO	Europe	Portugal	Level 4+
Porto Santo Airport	PXO	Europe	Portugal	Level 4+
Santa Maria Airport	SMA	Europe	Portugal	Level 4+
Salvador Bahia International Airport	SSA	Latin America	Brazil	Level 3

Source: Own editing, based on data from the beginning of January 2024 in the database of accredited airports on the ACA website.

in renewable energy initiatives, such as installing solar panels, to decrease its reliance on non-renewable energy sources and reduce its environmental footprint. These efforts are integral to the airport's comprehensive strategy for promoting sustainable development and long-term environmental stewardship.

9. Conclusions and Suggestions

The sustainability of tourism and regional airports in Central-Eastern Europe and the Balkans is a multifaceted issue that requires a comprehensive and integrated approach. This study has highlighted the significant efforts and initiatives undertaken by regional airports such as Budapest Airport and TIA and the operations under AviAlliance Holding and the Vinci S.A. group. These case studies have demonstrated that while notable successes exist, challenges must be addressed to achieve broader and more effective sustainability outcomes.

Budapest Airport's 'Green Airport Program' exemplifies proactive measures to reduce energy consumption, promote renewable energy, and enhance electric mobility. TIA's achievement of Level 2 'Reduction' accreditation under the ACA programme and its implementation of modern waste management and energy efficiency practices illustrate significant progress towards sustainability. In 2023, TIA further advanced its sustainability efforts, achieving a 10% reduction in its total carbon footprint compared to 2015, resulting in a total CO_2 emissions footprint of 880,000 kg, with a carbon emission rate of 0.47 kg per traffic unit. These improvements were attributed to advanced energy-saving technologies and practices, enhancing energy efficiency by 20% since 2015. Additionally, fleet fuel consumption per traffic unit was reduced to 0.08 L per traffic unit. TIA also reported handling over 7.2 million passengers in 2023, marking a 40% increase from the previous year, underscoring the airport's role in enhancing regional connectivity and providing excellent service.

In 2021, TIA's total carbon footprint, accounting for scope 1 and scope 2 CO_2 emissions under direct airport control, amounted to 1,363 tCO_2, and including process emissions, it increased to 1,449 tCO_2. These emissions represented about 4% of the airport's total scope 1, 2 and 3, which amounted to 36,998 tCO_2. The most significant contributors to these emissions were aircraft traffic movements and landside ground access, which accounted for 94% of the total. Over the last 3 years, TIA's carbon footprint ranged between 1,100 and 1,300 tonnes, with carbon emissions per traffic unit in the 0.4–0.5 kg range. There was an approximately 37% and 18% improvement in CO_2 emissions per passenger when comparing 2019 and 2021 with 2011 data, resulting in an average relative carbon emission of 0.49 kg per traffic unit.

However, the study also reveals that financial constraints, lack of awareness and infrastructural limitations often impede the broader implementation of sustainable practices. To overcome these barriers, increased investment in sustainability initiatives, enhanced policy support and greater stakeholder collaboration are needed. Governments, private sector entities and international organisations must work together to create an enabling environment that fosters adopting sustainable practices in the tourism and aviation sectors.

The findings underscore the importance of holistic and integrated approaches to sustainability that encompass environmental, social and economic dimensions. Regional airports must not only focus on reducing carbon emissions but also consider the socio-economic impacts of their operations. This includes engaging with local communities, promoting social inclusion and ensuring equitable economic benefits.

In conclusion, achieving sustainability in tourism and regional airports in Central-Eastern Europe and the Balkan regions requires a concerted and collaborative effort. By learning from successful practices and addressing existing challenges, regional airports can significantly contribute to SDGs. This study provides practical recommendations and highlights the critical role of international cooperation in driving the sustainability agenda forward. All stakeholders must remain committed to continuous improvement and innovation in sustainable practices to ensure the long-term viability and competitiveness of the tourism and aviation sectors in these regions.

9.1. Suggestions

- Governments and private sector entities should prioritise funding sustainable technologies such as electric vehicles, renewable energy sources and energy-efficient infrastructure. Financial incentives and subsidies can encourage airports to adopt these technologies.

- Policymakers should develop and enforce regulations promoting sustainability in aviation and tourism. This includes setting targets for carbon emissions reductions and implementing standards for sustainable practices.
- Stakeholders, including governments, private sector companies and international organisations, must collaborate to share best practices, knowledge and resources. Regional and international partnerships can help airports implement effective sustainability initiatives.
- Airports should actively engage with local communities to address socio-economic impacts and promote social inclusion. This involves transparent communication, involving community members in decision-making processes, and ensuring that economic benefits are equitably distributed.
- It is crucial to increase awareness among airport staff, passengers and the local community about the importance of sustainability. Education programmes and campaigns can highlight the benefits of sustainable practices and encourage participation.
- Airports should establish robust systems for monitoring and reporting their sustainability performance. Regular assessments can help identify areas for improvement and ensure accountability.
- As TIA's largest source of CO_2 emissions, mitigation efforts should focus on reducing diesel consumption by fleet vehicles and ground service equipment. Implementing alternative fuels and upgrading to more efficient equipment can significantly reduce emissions.
- Despite Albania's reliance on hydropower, there should still be efforts to improve energy use efficiency at airports. This includes investing in energy-efficient technologies and infrastructure to reduce overall consumption.

References

Airport Carbon Accreditation (ACA). (2023). *Airports responding to climate change. Issue 7 December 2023*. https://www.airportcarbonaccreditation.org/wp-content/uploads/2023/08/ACI-ACA-brochure-2023-v6.pdf

Airport Carbon Accreditation (ACA). (2024). *Reducing carbon and increasing airport sustainability*. https://www.airportcarbonaccreditation.org/

Airport Hungary Tanácsadó Kft. (2023, April 28). *Additional appendix to the December 31, 2022 annual report* (pp. 1–15).

Airports Council International. (2020). *Sustainability strategy for airports* (2nd ed.). https://www.acieurope.org/downloads/publications/ACI%20EUROPE%20SUSTAINABILITY%20, STRATEGY%20-%20SECOND%20EDITION.pdf

Altuntas, O. (2014). Calculation of domestic flight-caused global warming potential from aircraft emissions in Turkish airports. *International Journal of Global Warming*, *6*, 367–379.

AOSS. (2011). *Sustainability reporting guidelines and airport operators sector supplement. Version 3.1./AOSS final version*. https://www.yumpu.com/en/document/read/21480009/airport-operators-sector-supplement-global-reporting-initiative

Atasoy, V. E., Suzer, A. E., & Ekici, S. (2021). Environmental impact of pollutants from commercial aircraft at Hasan Polatkan airport. *Aircraft Engineering and Aerospace Technology*, *93*(3), 417–428.

AviAlliance. (2023). *The airport management company. Identifying potential – Creating value* (p. 12). AviAlliance GmbH. https://www.avialliance.com/avia_en/data/pub/AviAlliance_Corporate_brochure_2023.pdf

Bajrami, H., Fejza, E., & Ismajli, A. (2015). The role of public institutions toward the sustainable tourism development study case: Albanian Alps touristic region. *European Scientific Journal, 11*(1), Article w/5453.

Boussauw, K., & Vanoutrive, T. (2019). Flying green from a carbon neutral airport: The case of Brussels. *Sustainability, 11*(7), 1–19.

BREEAM. (2021, December 1). *BREEAM international new construction Version 6.0, Technical manual, SD 250.* https://files.bregroup.com/breeam/technicalmanuals/sd/international-new-construction-version6/?utm_campaign=2241538_BREEAM%20NEW%20NC%20manual%20downloads&utm_medium=email&utm_source=BRE&dm_i=47CQ,1C1KY,8LDHYQ,667EQ,1

Brokaj, R., & Murati, M. (2014). Sustainable tourism development in Albania through stakeholders involvement. *Academic Journal of Interdisciplinary Studies, 3*(2), Article 313.

Budapest Airport. (2020, June 16). *BUD Green Partner Program Tájékoztató kiadvány* (Information Publication, p. 2). https://www.bud.hu/file/documents/0/0069/bud_tajekoztato_la4_hun_press.pdf

Budapest Airport. (2021, December 1). *Karbonsemlegesség: a világ élmezőnyében a Budapest Airport (Carbon neutrality: Budapest Airport is at the forefront of the world).* https://www.bud.hu/budapest_airport/media/hirek/aktualis_sajtokozlemenyek/karbonsemlegesseg_a_vilag_elmezonyeben_a_budapest_airport.html

Budapest Airport. (2023a, November 12). *Fenntarthatósági jelentés* (Sustainability Report, p. 77). https://www.bud.hu/file/documents/7/7115/bud_fenntarthatosagi_jelentes_2022_1.pdf

Budapest Airport. (2023b, December 14). *Repülőtéri értesítő – fenntarthatósági különszám 2023 (Airport bulletin – Sustainability special issue).* https://www.bud.hu/budapest_airport/media/hirek/aktualis_sajtokozlemenyek/20231214_repuloteri_ertesito_fenntarthatosagi_kulonszam.html

Budd, T., Budd, L., & Ison, S. (2015). Environmentally sustainable practices at UK airports. *Proceedings of the Institution of Civil Engineers, 168*(2), 116–123.

Cafuli, A., & Vangjel, R. (2022). Travel and tourism sector in a circular economy. In *International conference on circular economy: Opportunities and challenges* (pp. 69–76). Central European Initiative (CEI), Editura Universitară Danubius, 2023, ISBN 978-606-533-587-5.

Carlucci, F. V., Cirà, A., & Coccorese, P. (2018). Measuring and explaining airport efficiency and sustainability: Evidence from Italy. *Sustainability, 10,* Article 400. https://solar.italy-albania-montenegro.eu/sites/solar.italy-albania-montenegro.eu/files/2023-05/D.T1.2.1._PP4_Low_Carbon_Plan_ACAA.pdf

CEEQUAL. (2007). *The civil engineering environmental quality assessment and award scheme manual for projects. Version 3.1.* https://www.sustainabilityexchange.ac.uk/ceequal-the-civil-engineeringenvironmental-quality

Ciro, A., & Toska, M. (2021). Entrepreneurial eco-systems for sustainable community-based tourism development in Albania. In J. R. R. Soares (Ed.), *Innovation and entrepreneurial opportunities in community tourism* (pp. 109–137). IGI Global.

Dincer, M. Z., & Dincer, F. I. (2013). *Economic significance of the tourism sector in Balkan countries and an analysis of the tourism relations between Turkey and Balkan countries.* http://dspace.epoka.edu.al/handle/1/319

EUROCONTROL. (2022a). *Aviation Outlook 2050 main report, April 2022.* https://www.eurocontrol.int/publication/eurocontrol-aviation-outlook-2050

EUROCONTROL. (2022b). *Objective Sky Green 2022–2030: The economics of aviation decarbonisation towards the 2030 Green Deal milestone.* https://www.eurocontrol.int/

sites/default/files/2022-05/eurocontrol-objective-skygreen-2022-2030-report-20220523.pdf

European Commission (EC). (2020). *Sustainable and smart mobility strategy – Putting European transport on track for the future* (Brussels, 9.12.2020 COM (2020) 789 final). https://eur-lex.europa.eu/resource.html?uri=cellar:5e601657-3b06-11eb-b27b-01aa75ed71a1.0001.02/DOC_1&format=PDF

European Commission (EC). (2023). *Hungarian Representation – A Bizottság engedélyezte, hogy a Corvinus Zrt. és a VINCI Airports felvásárolják a Budapest Airport Holdingot* (The commission authorized the acquisition of Budapest Airport Holding by Corvinus Zrt. and VINCI Airports). https://hungary.representation.ec.europa.eu/bizottsag-engedelyezte-hogy-corvinus-zrt-es-vinci-airports-felvasaroljak-budapest-airport-holdingot-2023-12-13_hu

European Union Aviation Safety Agency (EASA). (2023). *European aviation environmental report 2022*. https://www.easa.europa.eu/eco/sites/default/files/2023-02/230217_EASA%20EAER%202022.pdf

Federal Aviation Administration (FAA). (2012, July). *Aviation environmental and energy policy statement*. Department of Transportation Federal Aviation Administration. https://www.faa.gov/sites/faa.gov/files/about/office_org/headquarters_offices/apl/FAA_EE_Policy_Statement.pdf

Federal Aviation Administration (FAA). (2020). *Voluntary airport low emissions (VALE) program*. https://www.faa.gov/sites/faa.gov/files/airports/news_information/2020/VALE brochure-2020.pdf

Gaspari, A. (2015). Albanian hotels and sustainable tourism practices. *European Scientific Journal*, *11*(10), Article w/6158.

Giurea, R., Precazzini, I., Ragazzi, M., Achim, M. I., Cioca, L., Conti, F., Torretta, V., & Rada, E. C. (2018). Good practices and actions for sustainable municipal solid waste management in the tourist sector. *Resources*, *7*(3), Article 51.

Hellmeister, A., & Richins, H. (2019). Green to gold: Beneficial impacts of sustainability certification and practice on tour enterprise performance. *Sustainability*, *11*(3), Article 709. https://doi.org/10.3390/su11030709

ICAO. (2015). *Annual report of the ICAO Council: 2015 strategic objectives: Environmental protection*. https://www.icao.int/annual-report-2015/Pages/progress-on-icaos-strategic-objectives-safety-environmental-protection-home-page.aspx

International Airport Review. (2024, May 2). *Budapest Airport becomes the first in central Europe to achieve global carbon management certification*. https://www.internationalairportreview.com/news/221005/budapest-airport-becomes-first-in-central-europe-to-achieve-global-carbon-management-certification/#:~:text=What%20is%20the%20airport%20carbon%20accreditation%3F%20Airport%20carbon,scheme%2C%20on%20a%20scale%20of%20one%20to%20five

Jordão, T. C. (2009). A sustainability overview of the best practices in the airport sector. *Scientific Papers of the of Pardubice, Series D. Faculty of Economics and Administration*, *15*, 21–35.

Karagkouni, A., & Dimitriou, D. J. (2022). Sustainability performance appraisal for airports serving tourist islands. *Sustainability*, *14*(20), Article 13363. https://doi.org/10.3390/su142013363

Lushaj, A., Lushaj, A., Seenappa, S. N., Butina-Watson, G., Lushaj, B. M., Malsia, V., Doçi, D., Hunt, M., & Buçpapaj, E. (2012). Challenges and opportunities for biodiversity conservation and sustainable development of ecotourism in Lalzi Bay, Durres County, Albania – Today's science for tomorrow's management. A methodology guide with a concrete example by Lalzi Bay, Durres County, Albania. *International Journal of Humanities and Social Sciences*, *6*, 3201–3218.

Novoszath, P. (2015). A PSP Investments, a kanadai állami nyugdíjalap legfőbb erényei. PRO PUBLICO BONO: MAGYAR KÖZIGAZGATÁS; A NEMZETI KÖZSZOLGÁ

LATI EGYETEM KÖZIGAZGATÁS-TUDOMÁNYI SZAKMAI FOLYÓIRATA (2), pp. 83–93. ISSN 2063-9058. http://real.mtak.hu/id/eprint/92612

Prather, C. D. (2016). *Sustainable approach and practice on environmental management and carbon emission reduction in the tourism industry*. Airport Cooperative Research Program. https://doi.org/10.4028/www.scientific.net/AMR.573-574.885

Radnić, R. A., Milojica, V., & Roblek, V. (2015). *The importance of sustainable tourism in the context of regional development: Case of Western Balkans region*. https://www.croris.hr/crosbi/publikacija/prilog-skup/639344

Radovanov, B., Dudić, B., Greguš, M., Marcikić Horvat, A., & Karovič, V. (2020). Using a two-stage DEA model to measure tourism potentials of EU countries and Western Balkan countries: An approach to sustainable development. *Sustainability*, *12*, Article 4903.

Sarbassov, Y., Venetis, C. A., Aiymbetov, B., Abylkhani, B., Yagofarova, A., Tokmurzin, D. Z., Anthony, E. J., & Inglezakis, V. J. (2020). Municipal solid waste management and greenhouse gas emissions at international airports: A Astana International Airport case study. *Journal of Air Transport Management*, *85*, Article 101789.

Serio, R. G., Dickson, M. M., Giuliani, D., & Espa, G. (2022). *Toward environmental sustainability: An empirical study on airports efficiency*. https://doi.org/10.48550/arXiv.2210.02736

Setiawan, M. I., Dhaniarti, I., Utomo, W. M., Sukoco, A. B., Mudjanarko, S., Hasyim, C., Prasetijo, J., Kurniasih, N., Wajdi, M. B., Purworusmiardi, T., Suyono, J., Sudapet, I. N., Nasihien, R. D., Wulandari, D., Ade, R. T., Atmaja, W., Sugeng, & Wulandari, A. (2018). The correlations between airport sustainability and Indonesian economic growth. *IOP Conference Series: Earth and Environmental Science*, *140*(1), Article 012089.

Song, S.-K., & Shon, Z.-H. (2012, April 30). Emissions of air pollutants and greenhouse gases from aircraft activities at the Gimhae International Airport. *Journal of Korean Society for Atmospheric Environment*, *28*, 190–202. https://doi.org/10.5572/kosae.2012.28.2.190

Sreenath, S., Sudhakar, K., & Yusop, A. F. (2021). Sustainability at airports: Technologies and best practices from ASEAN countries. *Journal of Environmental Management*, *299*, Article 113639.

The San Juan Daily Star. (2023, April 27). *LMM airport completes the first phase of green accreditation*. https://www.sanjuandailystar.com/post/lmm-airport-completes-first-phase-of-green-accreditation

Tirana International Airport. (n.d.). Corporate responsibility. Retrieved June 22, 2025, from https://www.tirana-airport.com/en/article/61/Corporate-Responsibility

UN global compact guide to the SDGs. (2015). https://d306pr3pise04h.cloudfront.net/docs/issues_doc%2Fdevelopment%2FGCforSDbrochure.pdf

Vinci. (2023a). *Forging a sustainable world. 2022 universal registration document*. https://www.vinci.com/publi/vinci/vinci-2022-universal-registration-document.pdf

Vinci. (2023b). *Half-year financial report at 30 June 2023* (p. 78). https://www.vinci.com/publi/vinci/vinci-half-year-financial-report-at-30-june-2023.pdf

World Economic Forum (WEF). (2022, May 24). *Travel and tourism development index 2021 rebuilding for a sustainable and resilient future insight report* (p. 91). https://www.weforum.org/reports/travel-and-tourism-development-index-2021/explore-the-data

Yilmaz, I. (2017). Emissions from passenger aircraft at Kayseri Airport, Turkey. *Journal of Air Transport Management*, *58*, 176–182.

Yordanov, D. (2019). Low-cost air carriers as a factor for developing sustainable regional tourism. *Trakia Journal of Sciences*, *17*(Suppl. 1), Article 541.

Chapter 8

Policy Strategies for Sustainable Development and Green Innovation

Kirti Prashar, Shubh Arora and Madhu Verma

Centre of Distance and Online Education, Sharda University, Greater Noida, UP, India

Abstract

Purpose: The paper compares policy strategies to support green innovation and achieve sustainable development in developing and developed nations. It aims to learn ways of Integrating Sustainability into Economic growth through practical policies.

Need for the study: The work addresses the importance of Sustainable Development and Green Innovation and challenges in achieving environmental sustainability and economic development to balance the short-term results and future-oriented goals in various developed and developing countries.

Methodology: In the current sociological study, the author uses qualitative data to examine and analyse policy interventions, green innovation and sustainable development for different nations.

Findings: The paper compares the policies for sustainable development in developed and developing countries and finds that many have mechanisms similar to those used for green investment projects along with carbon prices and other emissions, but that depending on the socio-economic context of the situation, different policy measures required in some specific areas; industrialised countries are more concerned with infrastructure, trade, poverty, etc., while others focus on technology, innovation, etc.

Practical implications: The research will assist in developing better policies and frameworks to enhance green innovation in sustainable development. Businesses that seize legislation opportunities to introduce sustainable policies have more competitive advantages while managing risks.

Sustainable Development and Green Innovation: Managing Risk through Interdisciplinary Approaches and Policy Strategies, 179–198

Published under exclusive licence by Emerald Publishing Limited
doi:10.1108/978-1-83608-462-420251008

Keywords: Policy interventions; green innovation; sustainable development; economic growth; sustainable development goals; developed nations; developing nations

JEL codes: Q1; Q44; Q55; H23; R58; F64; O33

Introduction

According to the United Nations Environment Programme (2020), sustainability refers to an ecosystem's ability to maintain long-term ecological balance by preserving natural resources and gradually reducing environmental degradation. It emphasises activities like preserving biodiversity, reducing pollution and utilising renewable energy (RE) sources to sustain the ecosystem's viability over time (Rockstrom et al., 2009). Conversely, economic growth involves the enhancement of a nation's wealth and quality of life through the equitable distribution of capital to produce goods and services (Mankiw, 2014). Key contributors to economic growth include technological advancements, infrastructure development and the creation of employment opportunities, all of which play a significant role in poverty reduction and improving material living standards.

Sustainable development has been established as the foundation for the present and future generations, thanks to the collective efforts of global organisations. Liberal development is 'The development that maximises the potential or current capacity for utilising resources to fulfil human needs and ambitions through strategic resource use, investment trends, innovation direction and institutional improvements'. European countries have introduced several eco-innovation tools to support regional efforts, including the Competitiveness and Innovation Framework Programme, the Environmental Technology Action Plan and Accelerating Eco-Innovation Policies. Subsequently, non-European countries have adopted regulations established by the European Commission and European governments to formulate national policies and create territorial frameworks for promoting eco-innovation (OECD, 2011). Most earlier academic studies on eco-innovation focussed on industrialised nations, particularly in Europe and analysed eco-innovation practices within these countries. However, eco-innovation in emerging economies, especially in Asian nations, warrants greater attention. Asia accounts for 55.0% of the global population and contributes 32.7% of the worldwide gross domestic product (GDP; Eurostat, Asia-Europe Meeting [ASEM], 2014). The rapid economic growth facilitated by global firms' production has significantly increased the environmental burden on Asian nations. The region is responsible for 67.8% of global CO_2 emissions from fuel combustion (International Energy Agency [IEA], 2013). Adopting eco-innovation practices in Asia could contribute significantly to achieving green growth and fostering sustainable global development (http://www.un-documents.net/wced-ocf.htm) Government involvement is crucial for implementing and promoting eco-innovation. Governments can establish social frameworks to support the production of eco-friendly goods and services (Lee, 2002). Legislative regulations are often necessary in the early stages of eco-innovation. Governments possess the authority to design and execute policy tools for eco-innovation, such as financial plans, R&D support programmes, environmental legislation and eco-markets (https://mnre.gov.in/renewable-energy-targets-and-incentives). Policy tools can encourage businesses and industries to adopt eco-innovation as a policy objective (Bleischwitz et al., 2009).

Despite the growing global focus on sustainable development, there are limited comprehensive and systematic evaluations of emerging economies' strategies to balance growth and sustainability effectively (Shayan et al., 2022). Existing studies often concentrate on specific aspects of environmental preservation or economic growth but fail to adopt a holistic approach to examining how these goals can complement each other in the context of developing countries.

Background

Although sustainable development is a worldwide phenomenon, there aren't many thorough and organised evaluations of the tactics used by emerging economies to meet the goals of sustainability and growth (Shayan et al., 2022). Typically, available research tends to focus on individual goals, such as environmental conservation or economic growth, with minimal exploration of their compatibility – especially in the context of developing countries. Some global political policies have driven the adoption of clean technologies. For instance, Germany has set ambitious yet unclear targets for RE, supported by effective regulatory instruments like feed-in tariffs. Additionally, the European Union's (EU) ambitious Green Deal, which aims to make the EU carbon-neutral by 2050, outlines investment programmes, regulations and support for green businesses, projects and products (Khan et al., 2022). These initiatives demonstrate that the strategies implemented in developed countries leverage advanced technical and financial structures to harmonise environmental and economic goals. However, achieving such a balance remains challenging, particularly when attempting to reconcile future objectives with the demands of economic transformation and global competitiveness.

Despite these advancements, developed countries struggle to balance environmental conservation with employment creation and investment promotion, often facing resistance from traditional industrial sectors. Similarly, attempts to create and apply green technologies for sustainable development in developing countries encounter unique challenges. The immense socio-economic needs of these nations compel them to prioritise poverty eradication and economic growth over environmental concerns (https://morth.nic.in/green-transport-initiatives). For example, liberalisation and globalisation have fuelled urbanisation and industrialisation in countries like China and India, causing environmental pollution. Addressing these issues requires robust legislation to promote responsible behaviours. Governments have introduced measures such as pollution taxes, emission caps and subsidies for RE to combat these challenges.

Efforts like China's Belt and Road Initiative highlight the potential for incorporating green innovation into development programmes. However, sustainable policies in underdeveloped countries are often constrained by limited resources, weak institutions and competing development priorities, causing social injustices and ecological threats (Menyelim et al., 2011). Despite these obstacles, industrialised and developing countries can collaborate to exchange experiences and best practices that contribute to green innovation and sustainable development globally. Frameworks like the United Nations Sustainable Development Goals (SDGs) offer strategic avenues for addressing global environmental concerns and advancing the 2030 Agenda. Developed nations can expedite the adoption of green technologies in developing countries by providing enhanced financial, human and technical resources. However, dismantling structural barriers – such as unequal power dynamics, inadequate resource distribution and policy disparities – is essential to fostering meaningful partnerships between the Global North and the Global South.

In conclusion, achieving green innovation and sustainable development requires addressing the unique challenges and opportunities faced by developed and developing nations. While the developed world must demonstrate leadership in environmental sustainability and technological advancement, emerging economies must balance inclusive growth and poverty alleviation. International cooperation, knowledge sharing and a balance between these divergent interests are necessary for creating effective policy solutions. The international community can create a sustainable and just future for future generations by combining the resources and knowledge of both rich and developing countries.

Methodology

The methodology used is analysing the available literature and conducting a qualitative analysis of selected data. By examining the results of prior research, the study provides systematic, comprehensive and compelling insights into how various policy measures impact green innovation and sustainable development across different countries. The paper aims to evaluate a paradigmatic case and derive best practices and practical recommendations for policymakers interested in fostering balanced and sustainable development in the future.

Literature Review and Gap Analysis

The need for economic growth, social well-being and environmental preservation has brought about a significant shift in the public discourse surrounding the development of sustainable and green innovation (Sachs, 2015). According to the World Commission on Environment and Development's definition (WCED, 1987), sustainable development is an advancement that meets present-day requirements without sacrificing the resources required by future generations. Since then, it has encompassed many policy instruments, including regulatory, economically induced and voluntary policies (Jänicke, 2008; Meadowcroft, 2007; OECD, 2011). Additional tools that play a significant role in enforcing sustainability measures include regulatory instruments such as emission standards and environmental impact assessments. Subsidies and tax incentives address inherent market inefficiencies and promote deploying technological and environmental products and systems (OECD, 2011). The industry also supports governmental organisations by implementing voluntary initiatives that allow firms and non-commercial organisations to share experiences and achieve sustainability goals (Delmas & Terlaak, 2001).

Technological analysis is a factor in sustainability solutions as it seeks to provide measures that minimise negative impacts on the natural environment (green innovation). Technological innovation includes RE technologies, as defined by Carrillo-Hermosilla et al. (2010), while non-technological innovation encompasses sustainable business models. However, the movement towards green innovation faces several challenges. For instance, high costs often create market barriers, necessitating substantial investment in research and development (Horbach, 2008). Additionally, regulatory barriers exacerbate these challenges, impeding the expansion of green technologies due to regulatory unpredictability and a lack of supportive policies.

There remains a lack of research on the comprehensive dynamics and productivity of various policy measures relating to sustainable development and green innovation. For instance, as Kivimaa and Kern (2016) noted, while numerous studies focus on individual policy measures such as international carbon pricing or RE subsidies, relatively little research examines the combination and interaction of multiple policy instruments. For example, how do regulatory actions interact with economic incentives to foster or impede green innovation? Additionally, socio-political factors, such as public acceptance and political stability, help implement sustainable development policies. Another significant deficiency is the limited assessment of the long-term environmental consequences of green innovations. Much of the existing research highlights the positive externalities of green technologies without adequately considering their life cycles or potential side effects. For example, while electric cars reduce CO_2 emissions, their production and disposal processes may not be environmentally friendly (Hawkins et al., 2013). Furthermore, economic and social components of sustainable development are frequently addressed in isolation, ignoring the interconnection of these dimensions. This approach risks implementing policies prioritising one aspect of sustainability at the expense of others (Adams, 2006).

Finally, the intersection of digital innovation and sustainability remains an emerging topic with insufficient research. Technologies such as Internet of Things (IoT), artificial intelligence (AI) and blockchain have the potential to advance green concepts and practices due to their efficiency, transparency and data-processing capabilities (Kouhizadeh et al., 2020). However, their negative impacts – such as increased energy and resource consumption – must be carefully analysed to ensure their overall ecological benefits.

Future research should explore the multidimensionality of policy combinations, the socio-political acceptance of policy requirements, the long-term sustainability of systems, regional and cross-country policy changes and the potential role of digital technology in sustainability strategies. Addressing these gaps is critical for developing strategic frameworks facilitating green innovation and global, harmonious and balanced development. This study aims to bridge these gaps by examining the relationships between various policy tools, socio-political factors and technology in advancing sustainable development and green innovation.

The Importance of Sustainable Development and Green Innovation

Sustainable development and green innovation are two complex concepts to understand in the contemporary world of globalisation and growing interest in environmentalism. These concepts highlight the importance of balancing social equality and justice, protecting the natural environment and managing economic resources for the benefit of all. This study explores the relevance of these ideas and how they interrelate. Sustainable development and green innovation contribute to environmental sustainability and advance the United Nations SDGs. Green technology, which refers to sustainable and eco-friendly products and processes, is essential for reducing the carbon footprint and achieving the SDGs. This invention can be explored using eco-innovation, green funding, creativity and other methods. Each technique is critical for lowering costs and waste, enhancing environmental performance and generating economic growth.

(1) *Understanding sustainable development*: According to the UN, the concept of sustainable development is a development that adequately meets current requirements in such a way as to compromise the opportunities for future generations to meet their requirements. It is based on three pillars. The first is economic sustainability, which refers to the management and enhancement of long-term economic growth for the benefit of the community. The second is environmental conservation, and the third is collaborative efforts to preserve the ecosystem and other natural resources sustainably. Social sustainability preserves phenomena that are traditions of culture, equity and human rights.

(2) *Green innovation*: It is the development of new products, processes and/or services that cause little environmental harm. It is the driving force behind progress, allowing individuals to reduce resource consumption by using sustainable products, enhancing the circular economy and incorporating recycled materials into products. Learn how to fight climate change by designing cars with technologies to capture carbon and clean energy, improving ecosystem production and implementing organic farming practices.

(3) *Economic benefits*: Green innovation may stimulate economic prosperity, dispelling the myth that sustainability impedes progress. Green technology gives rise to new sectors and employment prospects. It also contributes to cost savings through resource optimisation and energy efficiency reducing running expenses. Environmentally conscious businesses are currently given top priority by many investors.

(4) *Social impact*: Green innovation and sustainable development benefits society by reducing pollution, improving air and water quality and encouraging public health. Access to clean water and energy can help reduce global inequality. Furthermore, sustainable urban planning strengthens a community's ability to adapt to climate-related dangers.

(5) *Green finance and sustainable development*: Green financing, such as green credit, is critical for increasing financial flows to green initiatives and promoting sustainable development.
(6) Reducing carbon emissions is essential to reaching sustainable development objectives. The study highlights the necessity to investigate eco-innovation, green finance and creativity.
(7) *Global initiatives*: Some of the global initiatives in this regard include; The Paris Agreement is a worldwide agreement that focusses on mitigating the effects of global warming. The 17 (SDGs) of the United Nations address environmental degradation, poverty, inequality and justice. The EU Circular Economy Action Plan provides a framework for resource usage that is sustainable.
(8) Governments play a vital role in promoting research and development, enforcing emission limitations and carbon prices and offering tax breaks to environmentally conscientious firms and consumers.
(9) *Single action*: Everyone can help by making conscious product choices (e.g., buying eco-friendly goods), recycling and trash reduction and endorsing eco-friendly companies and regulations.

Integrating Sustainability in Economic Growth

Economic growth and ecological sustainability refer to the interaction between an economy and a healthy ecosystem. It understands that rather than perceiving economic growth and environmental protection as competing factors, merging the two can provide long-term success. This synergy respects SDGs and ecological constraints while fostering economic growth. It involves reducing negative environmental impacts, promoting resource efficiency and implementing sustainable practices. By incorporating ecological considerations into economic decision-making, the aim is to promote sustainable economic growth that preserves and maintains the environmental systems on which it relies. A healthy environment provides essential resources such as clean air, water, fertile soil and diverse ecosystems that are vital for economic production and human well-being. Ecological sustainability ensures the availability of natural resources and the stability of ecosystems, while environmental degradation introduces risks and vulnerabilities (https://www.gov.br/mme/pt-br/assuntos/energias-renovaveis).

From a traditional economic growth perspective, GDP growth is the primary indicator of wealth and development. While economic advancement has improved living standards, it has also significantly harmed the environment. It is essential to emphasise that the traditional understanding of economic growth is evolving, with environmental challenges becoming increasingly urgent. Sustainability goals, circular economy principles and green technologies are now incorporated into economic policies and practices (Fernandes et al., 2021).

Numerous examples demonstrate how ecological and economic sustainability are correlated. These examples highlight that economic growth and environmental conservation are not mutually exclusive. Here are a few notable instances:

(1) *Costa Rica's Green Economy*: In addition to growth, the country has placed a great emphasis on ecological sustainment as well (Granoff et al., 2015; Green Fiscal Policy Network, 2019). It has achieved an equilibrium through careful and deliberate investments and policies. Costa Rica's forest cover has steadily increased, and more than half of its territory has been protected, enabling sustainable expansion. It is a key global RE producer, relying on it for essential electricity. This study discusses the role and influence of ecotourism on the country's economic income and the conservation of various wildlife.
(2) *Denmark's Circular Economy*: Denmark has also started paying more attention to the circular economy, focussed on enhancing resource utilisation and reducing waste (Thorin, 2020). The country has been incorporating modern provisions and measures like recycling, energy recovery from waste and eco-design. Denmark, as we can see, is a very wealthy country and despite this, it has been able to decouple economic growth from both resource use and waste generation.
(3) *Germany's Energiewende*: It is also referred to as the energy transformation where Germany aims at developing a long-term energy mix that will have the least dependence on fossil fuels, and instead will become more reliant on energy efficiency and RE sources (World Nuclear Association, 2020) and has boosted employment standards, new technologies and most importantly, the production of RE. Moreover, Germany could be a model for sustainable environmental protection and innovative economic development due to the country's recent success in decreasing greenhouse gas emissions while maintaining a robust industrial sector.

Challenges in Achieving Environmental Sustainability and Economic Development

Among the complex and contextual challenges of implementing public policies for sustainable development is the interrelation between governmental institutions and agencies. The difficulty arises from the central and regional focus that involves numerous bodies and organisations in policymaking and actions. The specifics of sustainable development objectives necessitate cooperation among various government agencies. However, fragmented and poorly coordinated policy frameworks often result in redundancy and inefficiency due to compartmentalisation. For example, agency initiatives on sustainable development can be compromised when economic and environmental policies from different agencies are misaligned.

In addition to limitations on information and resources, variability in agencies' goals, missions and priorities significantly hinders effective coordination. Another critical issue is the inability to adapt policies to regional conditions. Federal policies often originate from broad mandates and are not always suitable for local contexts. For instance, Indonesia, an archipelagic nation with a unique geographical structure and population distribution, requires tailored policies to address its needs. Various studies have shown that policies that work well in one setting can be damaging in another. It underscores the need for a more participatory and flexible system for developing and implementing policies considering local dynamics. To address the unique situations and demands, periodic reviews of existing strategies are essential.

A major challenge in sustainable development is the availability of capital. Even when the need and rationale for specific policies are evident, their implementation often requires significant funding, which is frequently insufficient and can lead to reduced programme scope and quality and delays in implementation. Financial constraints may arise from reduced government funding, limited private sector support, or a lack of international assistance. Governments must explore innovative solutions to address these challenges. Conventional approaches take years to implement. Alternatively, unconventional and more radical solutions could yield results within months.

Finally, raising public awareness is another critical issue. Sustainable development requires the active support and participation of all societal institutions. A significant gap often exists between public understanding and engagement and the successful implementation of policies. For instance, in a survey I conducted with 100 respondents, 80% were unaware of the importance of sustainable development or how they could contribute to it. Adequate outreach and communication strategies are essential to raise awareness. Moreover, involving communities in policymaking and implementation fosters a stronger sense of responsibility towards sustainability goals.

Innovations Driving Sustainable Economic Development

Innovations driven by digital technology are key determinants of sustainable economic development. They enable efficiency improvements, reduce resource usage and support a growing population. In industries such as IoT, AI and blockchain, the deployment of innovative technologies leads to cost reductions, optimised organisational resource usage and waste minimisation. RE management, precision agriculture and smart cities exemplify how digital advancements contribute to sustainability. Additionally, digital channels can extend financial services and market access to unbanked populations and small businesses, fostering opportunities for equitable development. These innovations enhance productivity while delivering long-term positive impacts on the economy and people's welfare through sustainable economic growth.

Industrial activities are increasing to generate economic growth causing environmental challenges such as greenhouse gas emissions, use of non-RE sources and associated ecological issues (Mehmood, 2021; Shahbaz et al., 2021). These issues have prompted both industrialised and developing countries to focus on RE sources (Li et al., 2022).

According to the Kyoto Protocol signed in 1997, adopting RE is a critical strategy for reducing CO_2 emission intensity. The international community recognises that RE provides a cost-effective approach to ensuring sustainable development compared to other energy resources (Liu et al., 2017). While sustainable development and RE are distinct concepts, they are intrinsically linked. Sustainable development is incomplete without addressing environmental, economic, social and cultural dimensions (Apergis et al., 2018; Dogan & Seker, 2016). Under the triple-bottom-line paradigm, sustainable development represents a collaborative, comprehensive approach to formulating policies that integrate environmental, economic and societal goals (Elkington, 1994).

Joshi et al. (2010) suggest that RE is vital for economic development, as it reduces CO_2 emissions and mitigates environmental degradation. A stronger emphasis on eco-innovations and clean energy sources is necessary to demonstrate the robust relationship between sustainable energy and economic growth (Debrah et al., 2020; Ministry of Energy, 2019). Investments in environmentally friendly electrical systems are critical to alternative energy sources and achieving ecological benefits (Meng et al., 2022). Sustainable growth depends on eco-innovation (Anwar et al., 2021b; Dogaru, 2020), classified into three categories: eco-organisational innovation, eco-product innovation and eco-process innovation (Anwar et al., 2021a; Cheng et al., 2014; Dogan et al., 2022).

Effective management is the key to accelerating economic growth in developing nations. Sensible policies, efficient resource allocation and a favourable business environment can improve the standard of living. Sustainable economic success relies on inclusive management practices that engage stakeholders and focus on long-term strategies. Good management involves making informed decisions, effective planning, meticulous organisation and vigilant monitoring. Implementing these practices can create a stable corporate environment, increase productivity, minimise resource waste and attract investment incentives (Yasa & Alfarisi, 2024).

Policy Strategies for Sustainable Development and Green Innovation by Developing Nations

India

Policy strategies for sustainable development and green innovation in India involve a multi-faceted approach, considering the country's vast population, diverse economy and significant environmental challenges. Here are some key strategies:

(1) National Action Plan on Climate Change (NAPCC): India's NAPCC lists the following plans for climate change mitigation: Promotion of RE production, improvement of energy efficiency and sustainable agriculture (Government of India, 2008).
(2) *RE targets and incentives*: India has set ambitious targets for renewable energy (RE) deployment and offers a range of incentives to support these goals, including tax credit schemes, subsidies, and feed-in tariffs for RE projects (Ministry of New and Renewable Energy, 2020).
(3) *Green transport initiatives*: Improving facilities of green carriages and increasing use of electric vehicles (EVs), better public transport and eco-friendly city planning of new India to curtail pollution and oil imports (PDMA Sec 70, Ministry of Road Transport and Highways, 2020).

(4) *Waste management and circular economy*: India is working towards effective waste management and promoting the circular economy through waste segregation, recycling and resource recovery (Ministry of Environment, Forest and Climate Change, 2021).

China

Low-carbon transition tactics in four areas of focus: China is focussing its efforts on four main sectors: transportation, industry, energy and building in both urban and rural regions.

(1) Energy: China's energy demand has increased over the past three decades, but growth has slowed since 2013. China has three primary strategies for its energy transformation. The nation is working towards electrification and energy saving from the demand side. It has established a goal to increase RE sources and decrease its reliance on fossil fuels from a supply standpoint. Lastly, China is working towards energy security by developing a robust smart grid and diversifying its supplies.
(2) Transportation: China aims to create a low-carbon, ecologically friendly transportation system centred on the energy transition. China focusses on electrification, and construction of efficient and integrated transportation systems, and the greater use of RE in the transportation industry.
(3) In the industrial sector, the Green Development Plan, presented by China's Ministry of Industry and Information Technology (MIIT) during the 14th Five-Year Plan, highlights three additional themes. These include restructuring the industrial sector's structure and layout, improving energy efficiency, establishing a circular economy and improving green manufacturing systems. These plans are in addition to the Opinion and Action Plan. The Plan specifies that China will create a plan for peak emission for the four industries with the highest emissions intensity: nonferrous metals, steel, petrochemicals and building materials.
(4) Urban and rural construction: In China's cities, industrial operations are the primary source of emissions, in contrast to Western countries where households contribute the highest amount of emissions in metropolitan areas. As a result, China may witness a decrease in emissions from the industrial sector as a result of restructuring its industrial structure and delaying the development of its infrastructure, but an increase in emissions from the household sector as a result of things like city transportation, residential space heating and other facilities. Three more aspects are highlighted in the Green Development Plan, which was released by China's MIIT during the 14th Five-Year Plan. These include restructuring the industrial sector's structure and layout, improving energy efficiency, establishing a circular economy and improving green manufacturing systems.

Brazil

Brazil has actively been after projects on sustainable development and green innovation, especially regarding environmental challenges that have appeared in the Amazon rainforest and other parts of the nation. Key national efforts are described here, with references listed:

(1) National Policy on Climate Change: It includes general guidelines for mitigation, such as reducing 'greenhouse gas emissions, promoting the use of RE' and regulating 'deforestation' (Brazilian Ministry of the Environment, 2008).
(2) *RE expansion*: Hydropower, wind and solar energy sources indicate that the country has invested in harnessing RE to reduce its reliance on fossil fuels and enhance energy quality.
(3) *Forest code*: Brazil has amended the forest code by making land use and inherent forest conservation as well as restoration policies and standards more stringent to minimise deforestation and increase proper usage of lands (Brazilian Ministry of the Environment, 2008).
(4) *Sustainable Agriculture Programmes*: Therefore, Brazil has launched several programmes to promote recap Ultimate Brazilian government resources and incentives for sustainable agriculture at the country level according to the Brazilian Ministry of Agriculture, Livestock and Food Supply, the programmes available are agroforestry system, conservation agriculture and biological farming.

Policy Strategies for Sustainable Development and Green Innovation by Developed Nations

Denmark

With a significant emphasis on RE and environmental protection, Denmark has been a leader in sustainable development and green innovation. Here are a few of Denmark's initiatives:

(1) *Energy policy and RE targets*: Denmark hopes to have a 100% RE system by 2050. The country has set high goals for RE. The nation's 2020 goal of obtaining 30% of its energy from renewable sources has been attained.
(2) *Wind power development*: Denmark is a pioneer in wind energy, having invented and applied wind turbine technology early. In 2020, wind power accounted for around 48% of Denmark's total electricity consumption (Lehmann, 2006).
(3) *Offshore wind farms*: Denmark invested in offshore wind farms; crucial to the nation's shift to RE sources.
(4) *Energy efficiency and green building standards*: Denmark has enacted stringent energy efficiency laws for buildings, and new construction must meet energy performance requirements. Denmark also promotes green construction concepts through groups such as the Green Construction Council.
(5) *District heating and cogeneration*: Denmark has a large-scale district heating system that uses an insulated pipe network to deliver heat to homes and businesses. A significant amount of the system's power comes from cogeneration facilities, which generate heat and electricity to increase overall energy efficiency (Sarkar, 2013).

(6) *Circular economy and waste management*: Denmark has put in place a thorough waste management system that places a major focus on waste-to-energy and recycling technology. The nation wants to move towards a circular economy, in which waste is minimised through the recycling and reuse of resources.

Australia

Australia has launched several programmes to support green innovation and sustainable development. These are a few of the major initiatives:

(1) *RE target*: Australia's electricity must come from renewable sources by 2020, with a minimum of 33,000 GWh required. It has resulted in significant investment in RE projects, particularly those that use wind and solar power (Falk & Ryan, 2007).
(2) The Emissions Reduction Fund incentivises companies and institutions to implement procedures and technological advancements that lower greenhouse gas emissions. The government buys carbon credits from projects having the go-ahead through a crediting and purchasing system (Galindo-Martín et al., 2020).
(3) *Clean Energy Finance Corporation (CEFC)*: The government-owned green banks invest in low-emission, energy-efficient and RE technologies. Since its inception in 2012, the CEFC has committed to investing around $7.8 billion in sustainable energy projects (Courvisanos, 2009).
(4) *Australian Renewable Energy Agency (ARENA)*: The ARENA is a government organisation that finances and supports the development, testing and resale of RE technologies. It has invested in ventures, including large-scale solar, energy storage and hydrogen generation.
(5) *National Energy Productivity Plan (NEPP)*: From 2015 to 2030, the NEPP seeks to increase Australia's energy productivity by 40%. It focusses on strategies to improve energy efficiency and reduce waste in industries, including manufacturing, transportation and buildings.
(6) *Climate solutions fund*: This fund contributes to carbon reduction by funding activities such as garbage management, savanna fire control and revegetation.

Hong Kong

Being a heavily populated and urbanised city, Hong Kong has launched several programmes to support green innovation and sustainable development. Here are a few significant initiatives:

(1) Hong Kong's decarbonisation policy is outlined in the Climate Action Plan 2030+, which aims to reach carbon neutrality by 2050 and reduce carbon emissions by 25–35% by 2030 compared to 2005 levels (Fu & Ng, 2020).
(2) *RE feed-in tariff scheme*: Started in 2018, this programme provides dollar incentives to businesses and every person who invests in the acquisition of renewable electricity from wind or solar resources (Humbatova et al., 2024; Inder et al., 2022).

(3) *Initiatives for waste reduction and recycling*: The government of Hong Kong has presented and adopted several measures that aim at reducing waste and enhancing recycling for instance the Producer Responsibility Schemes for the waste electrical and electronic equipment, the plastic and glass beverage containers and municipal solid waste charging schemes (Tsang & Lee, 2014).
(4) *Green building initiatives*: To ensure that sustainable building design and construction are achieved in the area, the following green building certification programmes are provided in Hong Kong; the Leadership in Energy and Environmental Design certification and the Building Environmental Assessment Method Plus.
(5) *District cooling system*: In a bid to promote energy conservation as well as the reduction of greenhouse gas emissions, Hong Kong entails district cooling that involves and aggregates air condition services for buildings within certain areas.
(6) *Green transport initiatives*: The government of Hong Kong has offered tax relief to those who use EVs and hybrid vehicles, and has over the years shown its commitment to encouraging a clean environment through the provision of transport through the development of the metro and the introduction of environmentally friendly buses (Awamleh et al., 2024; Li et al., 2024).

Comparing Strategies of Developed and Developing Nations

Industrialised and developing nations are expected to pursue distinct paths to green growth due to differences in economic development and environmental deterioration (De Angelis et al., 2019; Shahbaz et al., 2019). For instance, while wealthy nations are the largest producers of CO_2 emissions, their emission rates are declining. In contrast, developing nations experience higher pollution rates (De Angelis et al., 2019). According to Shahbaz et al. (2019), industrialised nations like the United States have implemented 'scale effect' initiatives to reduce carbon emissions. These efforts include funding technical innovations, optimising capital use and disseminating accurate information about how trade liberalisation has contributed to reduced CO_2 emissions. Similarly, policies that simultaneously promote economic growth and environmental preservation have led to better CO_2 emission management in Western Europe (Paramati et al., 2017). However, this success is not mirrored in Eastern Europe, where developing nations prioritise employment generation, wealth creation and economic growth over environmental considerations, resulting in rising CO_2 emissions (Paramati et al., 2017).

This trend is common in many developing nations due to a lack of institutional frameworks for enforcing environmental legislation. Reports from developing economies often emphasise human rights, education, equity, inclusion and diversity efforts, whereas reports from developed economies focus more on sustainable production, distribution chains, carbon dioxide emissions and value leadership. Aye and Edoja's (2017) analysis indicates that growing economies negatively impact carbon emissions. Conversely, Iwata et al. (2012) found no significant link between atmospheric carbon dioxide levels and the economic development of wealthy nations.

Furthermore, industrialised and developing nations differ significantly in their approaches to green building education and research. While industrialised nations have established extensive educational and research programmes on green building, developing nations have yet to fully implement such policies in their educational systems. For example, the United States and the Netherlands have published more studies and training programmes for green building stakeholders than Nigeria (Onuoha, 2017). Nigerian literature primarily focusses on raising awareness about the latest developments in green construction expertise. However, due to the limited prioritisation of research and education by the Nigerian government and building industry professionals, there remains a lack of understanding (Nduka & Ogunsamni, 2015; Onuoha, 2017). Nigeria could benefit significantly from adopting the research and teaching experiences of countries like the United States and the Netherlands (Onuoha & Okeahialam, 2018).

The development of green construction policies in countries like the United States and the Netherlands, as well as in developing nations such as South Africa and Nigeria, is rooted in historical policies and initiatives. Although both rely on previous policy developments, the United States and the Netherlands have more established frameworks compared to South Africa and Nigeria. Only decades after green building promotion began in the United States and the Netherlands did Nigeria and other African countries follow suit. Moreover, while federal governments in the Netherlands and the United States influence green building regulations, state governments play a more significant role in advancing these initiatives (Onuoha & Okeahialam, 2018).

Interest in green building has only recently grown in South Africa and Nigeria. These nations lack the robust and long-standing policies found in the Netherlands and the United States. As a result, green buildings remain relatively new in South Africa and especially in Nigeria, leading to fewer constructions compared to the United States and the Netherlands (Alabi, 2012). Many developing nations have adopted international grading systems or similar frameworks tailored to their environments. However, these systems often reflect the sustainability challenges of their countries of origin, limiting their applicability to developing nations. This limitation underscores the need for developing nations to create rating systems based on their specific sustainability indicators (Iwaro et al., 2014). Consequently, there is a shortage of practical discourse and references on applying sustainability principles to building construction in many developing countries. Nonetheless, like their industrialised counterparts, these nations are beginning to establish frameworks to assess housing durability and integrate sustainability concerns into government policies and decisions.

Conclusion

The research underscores the importance of incentives for social justice, environmentally sustainable development and sustainable economic growth in accelerating progress towards substantiated and environmentally sound development. Especially for developing countries, the analysis raises questions about integrated policies that should address the requirements of sustainable development across social, environmental and economic dimensions. While developed countries have made significant strides in supporting eco-innovation and sustainable development, they face unique challenges in balancing ecological considerations, economic progress and poverty eradication. The findings emphasise the importance of international collaboration and knowledge sharing to address these concerns, particularly in alignment with the United Nations' SDGs

The study also highlights how governments can adopt and promote eco-innovation policies through funding, research and development, legislation and the implementation of environmental regulations. Civil society and individual participation are crucial in advocating for legislative support for environmental protection. Additionally, the study notes that industries and firms can be encouraged to adopt eco-innovation practices through the use of effective policy instruments. Consequently, the contingent nature of effective policy solutions necessitates avoiding overly polarised approaches while fostering global cooperation and information sharing. This research suggests that the international community is building a more inclusive and sustainable trajectory, focussing on shared resources and knowledge to benefit future generations in both developing and developed countries.

The study has significant implications, emphasising the need for a comprehensive roadmap for the practical application of sustainability, particularly concerning its social, environmental and economic impacts. It highlights the importance of policies that address the unique challenges faced by developing countries while safeguarding the potential of transitional periods. Additionally, it fosters international collaboration among researchers and institutions.

From a practical standpoint, the project offers policymakers valuable guidance for implementing effective sustainable development and green innovation frameworks. Organisations leveraging legal incentives may reduce their vulnerability to sustainability-related legal risks while gaining a competitive advantage. The study further emphasises the role of collective participation and civil society in driving legislative changes towards a sustainable future.

In a broader context, the research provides actionable insights into the legislative measures required to address green innovation and sustainable development, with particular attention to developing countries. It equips authorities with strategies to enhance green innovation and sustainable practices. Legislative incentives encourage companies to adopt sound policies, reducing their environmental risks and operational costs. The findings are valuable for business leaders, executives, investors, workers, suppliers, governments and policymakers committed to the sustainable development of the world.

References

Adams, W. M. (2006). *The future of sustainability: Re-thinking environment and development in the twenty-first century*. Report of the IUCN Renowned Thinkers Meeting. https://portals.iucn.org/library/sites/library/files/documents/Rep-2006-001.pdf

Alabi, A. A. (2012). Comparative study of environmental sustainability in building construction in Nigeria and Malaysia. *Journal of Emerging Trends in Economics and Management Sciences*, *3*(6), 951–961.

Anwar, A., Sharif, A., Fatima, S., Ahmad, P., Sinha, A., Khan, S. A. R., & Jermsittiparsert, K. (2021a). The asymmetric effect of public–private partnership investment on transport CO_2 emission in China: Evidence from quantile ARDL approach. *Journal of Cleaner Production, 5*(2), 288–297.

Anwar, A., Sinha, A., Sharif, A., Siddique, M., Irshad, S., Anwar, W., & Malik, S. (2021b). The nexus between urbanization, renewable energy consumption, financial development, and CO_2 emissions: Evidence from selected Asian countries. *Environment, Development and Sustainability, 6*(2), 1–21.

Awamleh, F. T., Alarabiat, Y. A., & Bustami, A. N. (2024). Enhancing sustainable development through international performance indicators: The role of business intelligence techniques. *Challenges in Sustainability, 12*(3), 203–218.

Apergis, N., Jebli, M. B., & Youssef, S. B. (2018). Do renewable energy consumption and health expenditures decrease carbon dioxide emissions? Evidence for sub-Saharan African countries. *Renewable Energy, 127*(1), 1011–1016.

Aye, G. C., & Edoja, P. E. (2017) Effect of economic growth on CO_2 emission in developing countries: Evidence from a dynamic panel threshold model. *Cogent Economics & Finance, 5*(1), 1379–1382.

Bleischwitz, R., Bahn-Walkowiak, B., Irrek, W., Schepelmann, P., Schmidt-Bleek, F., Giljum, S., ... & Pratt, N. (2009). *Eco-innovation-putting the EU on the path to a resource and energy efficient economy* (No. 38). Wuppertal Spezial.

Brazilian Ministry of the Environment. (2008). *Fourth national communication of Brazil to the United Nations framework convention on climate change*. Government of Brazil. https://unfccc.int/resource/docs/natc/bra_nc4_eng.pdf

Carrillo-Hermosilla, J., del Río, P., & Könnölä, T. (2010). Diversity of eco-innovations: Reflections from selected case studies. *Journal of Cleaner Production, 18*(10–11), 1073–1083.

Cheng, C. C. J., Yang, C. L., & Sheu, C. (2014). The link between eco-innovation and business performance: A Taiwanese industry context. *Journal of Cleaner Production, 64*, 81–90.

Courvisanos, J. (2009). Regional innovation for sustainable development: An Australian perspective. *Journal of Innovation Economics, 1*(1), 119–143.

De Angelis, E. M., Di Giacomo, M., & Vannoni, D. (2019) Climate change and economic growth: The role of environmental policy stringency. *Sustainability, 11*(1), 2273–2285.

Debrah, S. K., Nyasapoh, M. A., Ameyaw, F., Yamoah, S., Allotey, N. K., & Agyeman, F. (2020). Drivers for nuclear energy inclusion in Ghana's energy mix. *Journal of Energy, 17*(2), 36–82.

Delmas, M., & Terlaak, A. (2001). A framework for analyzing environmental voluntary agreements. *California Management Review, 43*(3), 44–63.

Dogan, B., Ghosh, S., Hoang, D. P., & Chu, L. K. (2022). Are economic complexity and eco-innovation mutually exclusive to control energy demand and environmental quality in E7 and G7 countries? *Technology in Society, 68*(2), 43–57.

Dogan, E., & Seker, F. (2016). Determinants of CO_2 emissions in the European Union: The role of renewable and non-renewable energy. *Renewable Energy, 94*(4), 429–439.

Dogaru, L. (2020). Eco-innovation and the contribution of companies to sustainable development. *Procedia Manufacturing, 46*(1), 294–298.

Elkington, J. (1994). Towards the sustainable corporation: Win–win–win business strategies for sustainable development. *California Management Review, 36*(2), 90–100.

Eurostat, Asia-Europe Meeting (ASEM). (2014). *A statistical portrait*. Eurostat.

Falk, J., & Ryan, C. (2007). Inventing a sustainable future: Australia and the challenge of eco-innovation. *Futures, 39*(2–3), 215–229.

Fernandes, C. I., Veiga, P. M., Ferreira, J. J. M., & Hughes, M. (2021). Green growth versus economic growth: Do sustainable technology transfer and innovations lead to an imperfect choice? *Business Strategy and the Environment*, *30*(4), 2021–2037.

Fu, J., & Ng, A. W. (2020). Green finance reform and innovation for sustainable development of the Greater Bay Area: Towards an ecosystem for sustainability. *Sustainable Energy and Green Finance for a Low-carbon Economy: Perspectives from the Greater Bay Area of China*, *1*(1), 3–23.

Galindo-Martín, M. A., Castano-Martinez, M. S., & Méndez-Picazo, M. T. (2020). The relationship between green innovation, social entrepreneurship, and sustainable development. *Sustainability*, *12*(11), 44–67.

Government of India. (2008). *National action plan on climate change*. http://www.moef.gov.in/wp-content/uploads/2016/09/national-action-plan-on-climate-change.pdf

Granoff, I., Araya, M., Ulbrich, P., Pickard, S., & Haywood, C. (2015). Bridging Costa Rica's green growth gap: How to support further transformation toward a green economy in Costa Rica. *Deutsche Gesellschaft für Internationale Zusammenarbeit (GIZ) GmbH*, *1*(1), 236–248.

Hawkins, T. R., Singh, B., Majeau-Bettez, G., & Strømman, A. H. (2013). Comparative environmental life cycle assessment of conventional and electric vehicles. *Journal of Industrial Ecology*, *17*(1), 53–64.

Horbach, J. (2008). Determinants of environmental innovation—New evidence from German panel data sources. *Research Policy*, *37*(1), 163–173.

Humbatova, S. I., Hajiyeva, N., Fodor, M. G., Sood, K., & Grima, S. (2024). The impact of economic growth on the ecological environment and renewable energy production: Evidence from Azerbaijan and Hungary. *Journal of Risk and Financial Management*, *17*(7), 275.

Inder, S., Sood, K., & Grima, S. (2022). Antecedents of behavioural intention to adopt internet banking using structural equation modelling. *Journal of Risk and Financial Management*, *15*(4), 157.

International Energy Agency (IEA). (2013). *World energy outlook 2013*. OECD Publishing.

Iwata, H., Okada, K., & Samreth, S. (2012) Empirical study on the determinants of CO_2 emissions: evidence from OECD countries. *Applied Economics*, *44*(27), 3513–3519.

Iwaro, J., & Mwasha, A. (2014). Achieving building sustainability using a sustainable building envelope. *Construction Materials and Structures*, *18*(2), 1345–1351.

Jänicke, M. (2008). Ecological modernization: New perspectives. *Journal of Cleaner Production*, *16*(5), 557–565.

Joshi, A. S., Dincer, I., & Reddy, B. V. (2010). Role of renewable energy in sustainable development. In A. S. Joshi, I. Dincer, & B. V. Reddy (Eds.), *Global warming* (Vol. 1, pp. 71–87). Springer.

Khan, S., Yahong, W., & Zeeshan, A. (2022). Impact of poverty and income inequality on the ecological footprint in Asian developing economies: Assessment of Sustainable Development Goals. *Energy Reports*, *8*(1), 670–679.

Kivimaa, P., & Kern, F. (2016). Creative destruction or mere niche support? Innovation policy mixes for sustainability transitions. *Research Policy*, *45*(1), 205–217.

Kouhizadeh, M., Saberi, S., & Sarkis, J. (2020). Blockchain technology and the sustainable supply chain: Theoretically exploring adoption barriers. *International Journal of Production Economics*, *231*, 107831.

Lee, M. (2002), A study on the relationship between corporate's environmental innovation and environmental policy. *Korean Journal of Public Administration*, *40*(1), 159–188.

Lehmann, M. (2006). Government–business relationships through partnerships for sustainable development: The green network in Denmark. *Journal of Environmental Policy and Planning*, *8*(3), 235–257.

Li, Q., Wu, H., Zhang, B. Q., Dong, Z. H., & Ling, T. (2024). Safety system study of gas stations based on preliminary hazard analysis and fault tree analysis. *Journal of Information Systems Engineering & Management*, *3*(3), 149–163.

Liu, X., Zhang, S., & Bae, J. (2017). The impact of renewable energy and agriculture on carbon dioxide emissions: Investigating the environmental Kuznets curve in four selected ASEAN countries. *Journal of Clean Production*, *164*(4), 1239–1247.

Mankiw, N. G. (2014). *Principles of economics* (7th ed.). Cengage Learning.

Meadowcroft, J. (2007). National sustainable development strategies: Features, challenges, and reflexivity. *European Environment*, *17*(3), 152–163.

Mehmood, U. (2021). Renewable-non-renewable energy: Institutional quality and environment nexus in South Asian countries. *Sustainability*, *10*(1), 235–257.

Menyelim, C. M., Babajide, A. A., Omankhanlen, A. E., & Ehikioya, B. I. (2011). Financial inclusion, income inequality, and sustainable economic growth. *Sustainability*, *13*(1), 1780–1792.

Ministry of Energy. (2019). Ghana Energy Policy, 2019: Energy sector as engine for economic growth and sustainable development. *Sustainability*, *13*(1), 1659–1685.

Ministry of Environment, Forest and Climate Change. (2021). Waste management and circular economy. *Environmental Science and Pollution Research International*, *28*(21), 16278–16466.

Ministry of New and Renewable Energy. (2020). *Annual report 2019–20*. Government of India. https://mnre.gov.in/img/documents/uploads/file_f-1585729816925.pdf

Ministry of Road Transport and Highways. (2020). *Road accidents in India – 2019*. Government of India. https://morth.nic.in/sites/default/files/Road_Accidents_in_India_2019.pdf

OECD. (2011). *Better policies to support eco-innovation: OECD studies on environmental innovation*. OECD Publishing.

Onuoha, I. J., & Okeahialam, S. A. (2018). Comparison study on green and sustainable building policies in developed and developing countries. *Journal of Construction Project Management and Innovation*, *8*(1), 1797–1813.

Paramati, S. R., Shahbaz, M., & Alam, M. S. (2017) Does tourism degrade environmental quality? A comparative study of Eastern and Western European Union. *Transportation Research Part D: Transport and Environment*, *50*(1), 1–13.

Rockstrom, J., Steffen, W., Noone, K., Persson, Å., Chapin, F. S., Lambin, E. F. & Foley, J. A. (2009). Planetary boundaries: Exploring the safe operating space for humanity. *Ecology and Society*, *14*(2), 32–45.

Sachs, J. D. (2015). *The age of sustainable development*. Columbia University Press.

Sarkar, A. N. (2013). Promoting eco-innovations to leverage sustainable development of eco-industry and green growth. *European Journal of Sustainable Development*, *2*(1), 171–171.

Shahbaz, M., Gozgor, G., Adom, P. K., & Hammoudeh, S. (2019) The technical decomposition of carbon emissions and the concerns about FDI and trade openness effects in the United States. *International Economics*, *15*(1), 56–73.

Shahbaz, M., Trabelsi, N., Tiwari, A. K., Abakah, E. J. A., & Jiao, Z. (2021). Relationship between green investments, energy markets, and stock markets in the aftermath of the global financial crisis. *Energy Economics*, *104*(5), 105655–105672.

Thorin, T. (2020). Circular opportunities in the Danish waste system. *Energy Economics*, *37*(2), 2879–2928.

Tsang, E. P. K., & Lee, J. C. K. (2014). ESD projects, initiatives, and research in Hong Kong and Mainland China. *Schooling for Sustainable Development across the Pacific*, *1*(1), 203–221.

World Commission on Environment and Development (WCED). (1987). *Our common future*. Oxford University Press.

Yasa, I. P. B., & Alfarisi, M. S. (2024). The importance of effective management in driving economic growth in developing countries. *JIHAD: Jurnal Ilmu Hukum dan Administrasi*, *6*(1), 245–276.

Zarghami, E., & Fatourehchi, D. (2020). Comparative analysis of rating systems in developing and developed countries: A systematic review and a future agenda towards a region-based sustainability assessment. *Journal of Cleaner Production*, *254*(27), 1201–1224.

Chapter 9

Policy Instruments for Promoting Green Innovation in Economic Development: The Case of Georgia

Tinatin Nozadze[a], *Nino Chanadiri*[a] *and Zarina Burkadze*[a,b]

[a]*Ilia State University, Georgia*
[b]*Women Researchers Council (WRC), Azerbaijan State University of Economics (UNEC)*

Abstract

Introduction: Economic growth plays a crucial role in fostering good governance and democratic stability by redistributing public goods, creating jobs and promoting the middle class. It also helps reduce corrupt practices and supports the enforcement of universal norms, which are essential for building more inclusive institutions. However, there are limits to growth and global economic development that may have detrimental effects on the environment if world economies do not design policy instruments to mitigate these harmful effects (Meadows et al., 1972). Developing a combination of policy instruments can encourage eco-friendly economic behaviours and practices.

Purpose: This study aims to examine various policy instruments that contribute to sustainable development and green innovation. Our goal is to provide a comprehensive analysis of policy strategies, environmental regulations and subsidising funding mechanisms that support green innovations. Additionally, we seek to raise awareness and transfer knowledge about the importance of environmental protection, while fostering cooperative networks among key stakeholders to develop innovative solutions and implement carbon pricing.

Methodology: The study employs qualitative methodology to offer a comprehensive analysis of green policy strategies and to explain how they foster green innovation, while supporting economic development in the case study of Georgia.

Sustainable Development and Green Innovation: Managing Risk through Interdisciplinary Approaches and Policy Strategies, 199–218

Published under exclusive licence by Emerald Publishing Limited
doi:10.1108/978-1-83608-462-420251009

Findings: The results of this analysis indicate that Georgia still lacks effective policies and strategies related to eco-innovation and that the existing green subsidies are inadequate. Key stakeholders within the policy framework do not have clearly defined roles, and additional measures are necessary to raise awareness about the importance of collaboration in sharing expertise and engaging societal actors.

Keywords: Economic development; sustainable development; green policy instruments; green innovations; cooperation; knowledge transfer; and funding mechanisms

JEL codes: O44; Q01; Q56; Q58

Introduction

Georgia began promoting green policies during the late Soviet era, when the grassroots environmental movement established the Georgian Green Party in 1989. The Georgian Green Party is a centre-left political party that advocates for environmental issues (Green Party of Georgia, 2024). Georgia's turbulent political history has been marked by separatist conflicts, the Tbilisi Civil War, and chaotic post-Soviet political developments, which have hindered the prioritisation of green policies at the state level. Environmental concerns have often been overshadowed by existential threats and by power struggles among political elites. Since the Rose Revolution and the first-ever peaceful transfer of political power in 2012, Georgia has proactively engaged with the European Union (EU) by concluding the Association Agreement (2014–2016) and implementing the Visa Liberalization Policy (2017) (EU Relations with Georgia). The EU integration process enabled the Georgian government to place greater emphasis on environmental issues. In 2021, the Georgian Parliament, in collaboration with CENN, prepared the Green Budget Guideline. The purpose of this document was to analyse the 2019 budget from an environmental perspective and to provide recommendations for integrating environmental considerations into future policies and budgets (Gaphrindashvili, 2023). One of the primary recommendations for the Parliament of Georgia is to focus on the following areas:

> i. Elaboration of a policy document on the development of green business; ii. Improvement of the legislative framework relevant for conducting green business and ensuring its enforcement; iii. Activation of information campaigns on the practice of green business and on its auxiliary (financial-technical) instruments; iv. Minimization of risks related to transformation into a green business using various insurance mechanisms; v. Development of mechanisms stimulating the formation of a business culture with high environmental responsibility. (Environmental Protection and Natural Resources Committee of the Parliament of Georgia, 2021)

In 2019, the EU4Environment Programme began supporting Georgia in implementing smart environmental regulations and minimising environmental impacts. EU4Environment introduced a free course in Georgian to disseminate knowledge about the 'Green Economy' and released e-cards to illustrate the benefits of green investments to the entrepreneurs in Georgia (EU4Environment, 2021–2022). The aim of the EU4Environment is to achieve the following results: '1. Greener Decision-Making; 2. Circular Economy and New Growth Opportunities; 3. An Environmental Level Playing Field; 4. Ecosystem Services and Livelihoods; 5. Knowledge Sharing and Coordination' (EU4Environment, 2021–2022).

In 2015, a small Georgian company called 'Qartuli Ferma' joined the Resource Efficient and Cleaner Production (RECP) assistance programme and was monitored by EU4Environment (2024). 'Qartuli Ferma' produces dairy products such as milk, cottage cheese, sour cream and matsoni (yoghurt), using energy sources, electricity and water. After implementing resource efficiency strategies, the company successfully reduced its waste.

Table 9.1 highlights how savings are achieved through three actions: (1) insulating the surface of the steam boiler; (2) installing an additional tank for the cooling water circulation; and (3) replacing the electric water heater with a heat exchanger. As a result, the company successfully reduced its consumption of water, energy and natural gas.[1]

From the current perspective, it is essential to review key policy instruments for sustainable development and green innovation. Several policy instruments, including environmental regulations, subsidised funding mechanisms, awareness raising and knowledge transfer campaigns and the establishment of cooperative networks among governments, industries, academia and civil society, are crucial for developing innovative solutions. Additionally, carbon pricing mechanisms play a significant role in managing risks through interdisciplinary approaches and policy strategies. Reviewing the policy instruments in the context of Georgia presents several potential benefits. Firstly, we examine the literature that addresses the challenges arising from the lack of regulatory frameworks and necessary funding mechanisms to promote green innovations in economic development. Secondly, the chapter highlights the importance of establishing cooperative networks among key stakeholders to sustain economic growth in alignment with green innovations. It also investigates existing carbon pricing mechanisms in Georgia. Thirdly, we analyse the effectiveness of knowledge transfer and awareness-raising campaigns related to the aforementioned instruments. This study aims to provide a comprehensive descriptive analysis of the Georgian case, which will be valuable for scholars, policymakers and stakeholders seeking to identify potential areas for improvements in policy strategies. Finally, it will open new research avenues for scholars interested in green politics and sustainable development. Our guiding research question is: What are the main policy instruments employed in Georgia to promote green innovations in economic development?

[1]EU4Environment (2024, p. 3).

Table 9.1. Saving Achievements.

	Investment (euros)	**Saving (euros/year)**	**PBP (years)**
Option 1	85	219	0.4
Option 2	490	1,371	0.4
Option 3	200	1,151	0.2
Total	775	2,741	–
	Water (M^3/year)	Energy (kWh/year)	Fuel (natural gas) (M^3/year)
Option 1	–	7,200	735
Option 2	810	–	–
Option 3	–	21,513[a]	1,109
Total	810	28,713	1,844
	CO_2-eq (t/year)	Wastewater (M^3/year)	
Total	4,756	810	

Source: Adapted from EU4Environment (2021–2022, p. 3).

[a]The resource savings from electricity (10,646 kWh) and natural gas (10,867 kWh).

To address this research question, this chapter is organised into three main sections. The first section presents a comprehensive literature review on green policy instruments. The second section provides methodological insights. In the third section, a detailed empirical analysis of the Georgian case is conducted. Furthermore, the concluding section discusses the implications of the study (Humbatova et al., 2024; Inder et al., 2022).

Literature Review on Green Policy Instruments

The increasing ecological degradation we face today necessitates adequate government intervention. Studies show that government environmental regulations play a crucial role in guiding companies towards green transformation. By implementing these regulations, governments encourage the companies to develop environmentally friendly strategies that comply with established standards (Fang et al., 2021, pp. 294–295).

> Firms may take the initiative to carry out green technology innovation to achieve the goal of reducing pollution emissions and optimizing the production process. Therefore, the pressure of environmental regulations may generate an innovation impetus that is beneficial to environmental protection.

Scholarly research indicates that government subsidies positively influence green innovations. When combined with appropriate environmental regulations, these subsidies enhance performance efficiency, which varies across non-state-owned, high-tech and low-pollution industries. Furthermore, government subsidies improve technological capabilities, address funding limitations and foster innovative capacities (Duan et al., 2024). In this context, the literature emphasises the importance of green finance (GF). This instrument enables the mobilisation of financial resources to support environmentally sustainable projects and initiatives. GF plays a crucial role in facilitating the transition to a low-carbon economy, whereas traditional funding mechanisms often fall short in promoting such shifts (Agrawal et al., 2024). Scholarly research indicates that effective government policies should be complemented by awareness raising and knowledge transfer campaigns. Communicating the significance of green initiatives and policy instruments to the public makes them more informed and willing to allocate resources for environmental purposes. This approach also encourages taxpayer engagement in green policymaking and planning (Khatibi et al., 2021).

In today's global environment, the development in any sector of society is closely linked to the interaction and collaboration among various stakeholders, including academia, civil society organisations, and both the private and public sectors. This cooperation fosters the sharing of knowledge and experiences, ultimately enhancing capacities. Furthermore, collaboration across different sectors increases economic opportunities by transferring knowledge and skills that were previously confined to a limited number of sectors. It is widely acknowledged that partnerships among industry, academia and government enhance knowledge transfer to the local community (Awamleh et al., 2024; Li et al., 2024). This collaboration generates research and consultancy, supports domestic and regional development and facilitates the dissemination of innovation to society (Nawaz & Koç, 2020). The most efficient model of interaction among government, industry and academia is perceived as one, in which the actors operate independently and are interrelated, yet remain beyond the full control of the government. Other models include instances where the key role lies with the industry, which based on its interests, mentors the other two stakeholders. In these cases, the government and academia assume more supportive roles to the industry rather than equal partners (Nawaz & Koç, 2020). The term 'interrelated' can be referred to the cooperation models in which the efforts of various actors support one another, enhancing collaboration and exchange. Other notable examples include collaborative research, partnership for innovation, and jointly supported start-ups focused on innovative ideas, all of which contribute to enhancing the country's innovation capacity (Nawaz & Koç, 2020). The cooperation model can be schematically depicted as follows:

As illustrated in Fig. 9.1, the interdependence of the three actors is crucial in the relational model, in contrast to models where governments or industries play a dominant role. This cooperative model is founded on the balanced roles of each actor and involves reinforcing one another's efforts. The cooperation model benefits the public in three areas: generating economic opportunities, fostering innovations and promoting general progress in sustainable development. On the one hand, it enhances economic opportunities and yields positive outcomes by making knowledge and research from academic institutions accessible to industries. The availability of such science-based findings enables industries to effectively

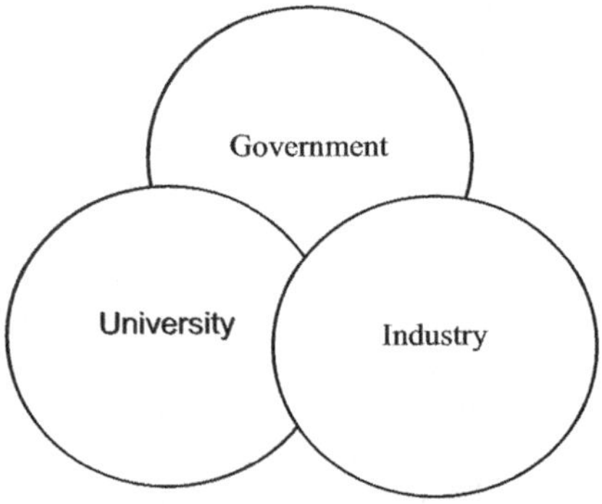

Fig. 9.1. The Cooperation Model of Key Stakeholders in Green Politics. *Source*: Adapted from Nawaz and Koç (2020, p. 3).

absorb and implement the innovations developed by academia (Nawaz & Koç, 2020). On the other hand, the demand for innovations in the industry may serve as a driving force for advancements in research and academia. Consequently, this process is cyclical, as illustrated in Fig. 9.1.

It is also important to emphasise the crucial role of the government in creating supportive political environments that foster innovation and economic opportunities. Such supportive political environments are essential for ensuring the sustainability of the process itself. They may include relevant institutional and legislative frameworks, as well as the presence of supportive programmes. The government should be willing to collaborate with other stakeholders (Nawaz & Koç, 2020).

Collaboration for innovation and economic opportunities should incorporate sustainable development principles. The ideological consensus surrounding the Sustainable Development Goals among different actors is not surprising, as sustainable development is widely regarded as beneficial (O'Riordan & Voisey, 2007), making association with it desirable. Many countries endorse sustainability initiatives and foster both domestic and international cooperation with diverse actors, including the private sector, on various initiatives. This collaboration can focus on different objectives, whether they are the United Nations (UN)-defined Sustainable Development Goals themselves or the components that facilitate the achievement of these goals.

However, as noted above, the characteristics of political settings and the mechanisms of cooperation are significant. Similarly, it is important to consider who the initiators are, as the type and degree of the support may vary under different circumstances. The case study of Georgia presented below illustrates the context of policy and cooperation practices that have evolved around carbon emissions and the process of 'greening the economy'.

We aim to examine these multifaceted theoretical assumptions through a case study of Georgia and assess the extent to which it has developed these instruments for effective green policy planning and implementation.

Methodology

We consider qualitative methodology to be a valuable tool for studying green policy instruments in the context of Georgia. There are several reasons for this belief. First and foremost, green policy is a relatively novel topic in Georgia, and this uncharted field requires careful examination in terms of its policy instruments. Second, Georgia presents an intriguing case, as the selected instruments have varied since its independence and continue to evolve. Third, in the context of its Europeanisation, Georgia has embarked on transitional green policies, and understanding the external impacts on the evolution of green policy instruments provides important insights. Conceptually, we define green policy instruments along five key dimensions – *environmental regulations*, *subsidised funding mechanisms*, *awareness raising and knowledge transfer policies*, *cooperative networks among key stakeholders*, and *carbon pricing mechanisms*. These dimensions are crucial for explaining how an interdisciplinary approach can facilitate the reconciliation of green innovations with economic growth.

In order to identify the guiding principles for the regulations that Georgia employs to support the environmental resilience, as well as subsidising mechanisms, the primary source of data was the Georgian national legislation, specifically the Law on Environmental Protection, which is discussed below. This law outlines the principles that all entities engaged in relevant activities must consider. Based on these principles, taxes and fines are also imposed in cases of violations. Additionally, the law specifies some supportive and subsidisation mechanisms for environmental actions.

To determine the direction of green transformation in Georgia, two crucial documents have been analysed: Georgia's SME Development Strategy 2021–2025 and the Green Budget Guideline prepared by CENN. Additionally, an interview with Nino Chkhobadze, the Chair of the Greens Movement of Georgia/Friends of the Earth – Georgia, has been taken into account. The first document aims to promote the development of a green economy for small- and medium-sized enterprises (SMEs), while the second provides recommendations for Georgian officials on integrating environmental considerations into future budgets and policies. The interview, published on the official website of the Green Movement, was highly informative and facilitated the identification of various projects and activities related to environmental protection and awareness in Georgia. Furthermore, we examined research on to gauge the current state of environmental awareness in the country. We also highlighted the success story of a small Georgian company that received assistance from EU4Environment.

To analyse carbon pricing mechanisms in Georgia and the cooperative strategies employed by various stakeholders – such as the government, industries and academia – that are believed to be effective in achieving desirable policy outcomes, two primary policy documents have been examined. The findings are presented below. The first document, *Georgia's Long-Term Low Emission Development Strategy*, was developed and adopted by the Georgian government in 2023. This document outlines a roadmap for Georgia to achieve carbon neutrality by 2050. Studying this document is important for two main reasons. First, it outlines the country's objectives for reducing emissions across various economic sectors and describes both positive and negative scenarios regarding the results that needed to achieve the desired outcomes by 2050. Consequently, the document provides a roadmap for different economic sectors. Second, it includes an implementation strategy that identifies the responsible entities for overseeing the execution of this strategy. It also highlights strategically important collaborations that enhance the potential for achieving the desired results. Our interest lies in identifying the multi-actor cooperation mechanisms that are either established or lacking in Georgia, particularly concerning environmental action and, specifically, carbon emission reduction. This document serves as a valuable resource for understanding the government's perspective and readiness to involve stakeholders such as the private sector and academic institutions in the strategy implementation process, as well as clarifying the roles of these stakeholders. However, it is important to note that the aforementioned document is a broad strategy with long-term goals extending to 2050. To effectively identify the role of cooperation in the implementation process, it is essential to examine the short-term plans that outline specific goals and measurable outcomes, as well as the responsible entities and their partners in achieving these results. To this end, we also analysed the Action Plan for 2024–2025, which addresses Climate Change in Georgia (2024) with the objective of reducing carbon emissions by 15% across various economic sectors. This detailed plan includes targets, challenges, necessary actions, and the responsible actors involved, along with their partners. Therefore, it was beneficial to study the plan to determine the presence or absence of a credible link to the broader strategic orientations outlined in *Georgia's Long-Term Low Emission Development Strategy*.

Environmental Regulations and Subsidising Mechanisms

The Ministry of Environmental Protection and Agriculture (MEPA) of Georgia is the institution responsible for implementing environmental protection policies and promoting a green economy in the country. To enhance the environmental situation in Georgia, the Government of Georgia developed a national budget-planning document known as the Basic Data and Directions (BDD) (Gaphrindashvili, 2023).

> BDD 2023–2026 indicates that the state aims to develop a Georgian taxonomy of sustainable financing, the purpose of which will be to clearly define which business activity, program of project can be considered to be resource-efficient, energy-efficient, green, sustainable and inclusive.

One of the policy documents for Georgia that outlines the requirements of the strategy of 'green growth' is the SME Development Strategy of Georgia.[2] A primary focus of Georgia's SME Development Strategy 2021–2025 is to promote 'the development of a green economy for SMEs'. In the case of Georgia, eco-

[2]SMEs – small and medium enterprises.

tourism and eco-friendly agricultural production hold significant potential. By engaging local communities in the development of ecotourism, it is possible to enhance environmental awareness and reduce pollution. Unfortunately, funding in Georgia primarily benefits large companies. As a result, the loans available are often too large for small and medium enterprises, leaving them excluded and with limited opportunities to contribute to the growth of the green economy (Ministry of Economy and Sustainable Development, 2021a, 2021b, 2021c).

> Green investment cannot occur while Georgian SMEs experience wider challenges in accessing finance. The venture capital environment in Georgia could be further strengthened to foster improved access to capital for small and dynamic growing businesses. A fund could be established to act as a catalyst for private capital and to match early investment in SMEs with high-growth potential. (Organisation for Economic Cooperation and Development [OECD], 2019)

At the legislative level, Georgia considers several environmental principles that obligate 'Government bodies, physical and legal entities (regardless of ownership and organizational-legal form) to be guided by the basic principles of environmental protection' (Law of Georgia on Environmental Protection, adopted in 1996).[3] Based on these fundamental principles, the law addresses taxes and fines

---

[3]According to the Law of Georgia on Environmental Protection, the guiding principles include: (i) 'Principle of the risk reduction' – that obliges a body undertaking an activity to consider necessary actions to reduce the risks of damage to the environment and people's health. (ii) 'Principle of sustainability' – use of the environment and natural resources when there is no danger to the development of society and the protection of the environment and natural resources from irreversible quantitative and qualitative changes. (iii) 'Principle of prioritising' – an action that can have a negative impact on the environment and human health can be replaced by another, less risky, even more expensive action. A more expensive action is given priority if its cost does not exceed the cost of compensation for damage caused by a less expensive action. (iv) 'Principle of use of nature for a fee' – the use of land, water, forest, flora and fauna, minerals and mineral natural resources is for a fee for the body that undertakes activity. (v) 'Principle polluter pays' – the body that undertakes activity is obliged to pay for the damage caused by the action to the environment. (vi) 'Principle of maintaining biodiversity' – the activity should not cause irreversible degradation of biodiversity. (vii) 'Principle of minimising the waist' – the priority is given to the technology that supports minimising the waist while undertaking the activity. (viii) 'Principle of recycling' – when carrying out activities, preference is given to reusable or recyclable, biologically degradable or environmentally friendly substances, materials, and chemical compounds. (ix) 'Principle of restitution' – the environment degraded as a result of the activity should be restored to its original state as close as possible. (x) 'Principle of environmental impact assessment' – the body that is undertaking the activity is obliged to take into account and evaluate the possible impact of this activity

related to environmental protection, such as fees for utilising natural resources and penalties for pollution caused by certain types of agencies. A clear example of how these principles are applied in Georgia on a daily basis, and how citizens perceive the impact of regulations in their lives, is in the area of air pollution dimension. Citizens can be fined by the police if their vehicles are visibly contributing to air pollution. In 2023, fines started at 100 Georgian Lari (GEL) for individuals and 500 GEL for legal entities (IPN, 2023).

However, it is also important to support the environmentally significant projects that signal state's commitment to creating an environmentally friendly society. The same law regarding environmental protection also takes into account economic mechanisms in the field, such as 'economic stimulation' for promoting environmental protection.

> The purpose of economic stimulation of environmental protection is to facilitate the development and implementation of efficient, environmentally acceptable, ecologically clean, low-waste best technology and techniques, the use of secondary raw materials, and the implementation of effective environmental projects that can be implemented. (Law of Georgia on Environmental Protection, adopted in 1996)

The law identifies three mechanisms for promoting environmental issues: advertising, tax benefits and preferential state credit. According to the Tax Code of Georgia, which provides a more detailed definition of tax benefits, profits derived from the production and sale of renewable energy sources – such as solar, wind, geothermal, biomass energy and hydropower – as well as energy-saving devices, including energy-saving lamps, are exempted from profit tax (Tax Code of Georgia adopted in 1997). However, it is challenging to find statistics on the number of such activities that have received benefits over the years. Thus, Georgian legislation is not environmentally blind; it acknowledges both the fundamental principles of environmental protection and various mechanisms for economic stimulation, including fines for violations of these principles. However, more data are needed to demonstrate the trends in the implementation of these principles and to understand how this process is perceived by industries and the public.

Georgia, like other democratic countries, recognises the importance of property rights and has established effective mechanisms to protect and regulate these rights. Property rights are enshrined in the Constitution of Georgia. The first legislation addressing property rights was the *Law of Georgia on Agricultural Land*

---

on the environment in accordance with the law while projecting or planning of its activity. (xi) 'Principle of public participation in decision-making process' – the public participation is ensured while making important decisions related to the activity. (xii) 'Principle of information accessibility' – the information about the conditions of the environment is open and accessible for the public. Available at https://matsne.gov.ge/en/document/view/33340?publication=21.

Ownership, which focused on land ownership. As the country has developed, its legal framework has evolved. Economic growth and the attraction of foreign investment are vital for developing countries like Georgia. Protecting property rights is essential for attracting foreign investors and indirectly supporting sustainable growth (Kartozia, 2022; Muradov & Hajiyeva, 2022).

> Property rights or tenure to natural resources are a key policy apparatus for promoting sustainable resource use and protection. ... Clear and enforced property rights are crucially necessary for keeping ecosystems healthy and safe. So that the proper regulation and effective application of property rights prevent the destruction of the ecosystem, can encourage the provision of ecosystem services and help invest in the protection and efficient use of natural resources. (Muradov & Hajiyeva, 2022, p. 27)

It is important to note that the 'European Neighbourhood Program for Rural and Agricultural Development' (ENPARD) has been both helpful and beneficial for Georgia. With the support of the EU and the United Nations Development Program (UNDP), in cooperation with the Rural Development Agency (RDA), the Green Grant Program was developed.

> As of July 31, 2022, 106 agreements were signed with 106 unique beneficiaries within the framework of the Green Grant Program. ... The Green Grant Program was implemented to facilitate access to energy-efficient/renewable energy technologies for rural area and the existing business sector, save energy costs, mitigate the impact of climate change, and reduce pressure on natural resources (especially forest resources).[4]

In 2016, Georgia signed the 'Accession of Georgia to the Treaty Establishing the Energy Community', under which the country committed to incorporating all the regulations of the EU energy sector into its national legislation. As a result, Georgia developed the National Renewable Energy Action Plan (NREAP, 2019).

The primary objectives of this document are to:

a. outline the current state of affairs as relates to the legislative and institutional framework for renewable energy as per the requirements of the Renewable Energy Directive.
b. propose a number of policy and investment measures to be undertaken to meet the target of 30% of energy consumed coming from renewable energy for 2020 and implement the Renewable Energy Directive – including likely costs associated with their implementation.[5]

---

[4]Rural Development Agency.

[5]Ministry of Economy and Sustainable Development of Georgia (2021a, 2021b, 2021c).

The Georgian Ecotourism Association operates in Georgia and is one of the oldest organisations dedicated to establishing ecotourism as a significant branch of tourism in the country. The Association aims to promote ecotourism and contribute to environmental protection.[6] Green tourism in Georgia extends beyond ecotourism activities; it also encourages environmentally friendly practices by training staff in sustainable behaviours and enhancing environmental awareness among visitors during tours. For instance, Georgia Insight, one of the successful tour operators, states that they avoid tours that would have a significant impact on the environment, such as off-road jeep tours. They also strive to walk as much as possible and refrain from visiting locations that cannot be accessed by bus.[7]

Awareness Raising and Knowledge Transfer

The Constitution of Georgia includes a separate chapter that focuses on environmental protection. Within the Law of Georgia on Environmental Protection, one can read:

> The main objectives of this Law are to: a) protect and maintain a safe environment for human health; b) provide a legal framework for the protection of the environment from adverse impacts; c) ensure the maintenance or the improvement of environmental quality; d) ensure an optimum balance between (or a harmonious combination of) the environmental, economic and social interests of society; e) provide a legal framework for managing the use of natural resources, taking into consideration the principles of potentials and the sustainable development of the environment; f) ensure the efficient functioning of the unified system of regulation of genetically modified living organisms. (Gaphrindashvili, 2023)

The Greens Movement of Georgia/Friends of the Earth – Georgia is one of the oldest Georgian environmental protection organisations, which was established in 1989. Its mission is to protect the environment, promote sustainable development and establish eco-technologies. Since 1989, its inception, the organisation has had numerous projects, including forestation, environmental remediation, etc., and has played a crucial role in raising public awareness about the significance of environmental protection. One of the prosperous initiatives of the Greens Movement of Georgia is called Clean Region, launched in 2015, and it engages the public from all over the country every year (Global Compact Network Georgia, 2019).

The Greens Movement of Georgia, also known as Friends of Earth – Georgia, is a partner of the Government of Sweden. 'Facilitating reduction of global climate-change-induced greenhouse gas emissions and environmental protection, and the implementation of tenets of circular economy are the main goals

[6]The Georgian Ecotourism Association.

[7]Steffen Schulein (n.d.).

of this cooperation' (Global Compact Network Georgia, 2019). The most pivotal projects financed by the Government of Sweden were Clean Up Georgia (2010–2018) and Keep Georgia Tidy (2018) with the aim to raise public awareness about waste management. 'With project components, complete monitoring is carried out for the implementation of 5-year plans for municipal waste. Four campaigns are ongoing: Clean Up Georgia, Clean Up the World, Keep Georgia Tidy, Blue Stream, Clean Region Competitions' (Global Compact Network Georgia, 2019). As a result of these projects and competitions, public interest in environmental protection has increased, and the regions of Georgia have begun competing to reduce waste. The Greens Movement of Georgia/Friends of the Earth – Georgia also assisted municipalities in developing 5-year plans for waste management and acquiring essential equipment (Global Compact Network Georgia, 2019).

In 2015, the Government of Georgia signed the Paris Agreement.

> By signing this agreement Georgia also assumed an obligation and set a goal to promote the introduction of modern climate-smart technology in energy, manufacturing, agriculture and waste management sectors, implementation of coast protection measures in the river channels and the shoreline of the Black Sea, reduction of the risks of flash floods and mud flows in high mountain areas, fighting against desertification in the regions of east Georgia and protection of the population at high risk. (Global Compact Network Georgia, 2019)

One of the significant steps that Georgia took was to limit emissions from transportation. To reduce air pollution in the country, the Government of Georgia adopted regulations that made technical inspections of vehicles mandatory starting in January 2019. Additionally, the importation of cars manufactured before 2013 was prohibited on January 1, 2024 (MEPA of Georgia, 2023).

The Institute of Social Studies and Analysis, in collaboration with the Environmental Information and Education Centre, UNDP, and Sweden, conducted research on *assessing the level of environmental education and awareness in Georgia*. According to the findings, 62% of the population believes that the effects of climate change are already evident in Georgia, and 53% believe that reducing climate change is achievable through societal efforts. Additionally, 52% of respondents think that regulations or laws should be enacted to manage waste. The research indicates that 59.7% of respondents received environmental education at the school education level, while only 34.7% received it at the university level, 22.8% at the technical education level, and just 22.5% through informal education. Furthermore, 59% of the population expressed a desire to enhance their knowledge about environmental protection. The majority of respondents recognise that exhaust emissions from transportation pose a significant threat to public health (Institute of Social Studies and Analysis, 2022).

In 2023, CENN launched the Green Agenda project in Georgia. This initiative resulted from the collaboration between the Stockholm Environment Institute and the government of Georgia, and it was financed by the Swedish International Development Cooperation Agency.

> [...] the project encompasses areas such as climate change, energy efficiency, sustainable construction, smart mobility, circular economy, pollution reduction, food systems and ecosystem conservation. ... In addition, the project will deliver awareness-raising activities to foster understanding and support for the roadmap.[8]

The Green Agenda Project will be active from September 2023 to March 2026 (CENN, 2023).

Cooperative Networks and Carbon Pricing Mechanisms

Georgia is a small Eastern European country with a hybrid political regime (Freedom House, 2024). Its political institutions are still developing and are often overwhelmed by political struggles. In this context, international organisations and their local representatives initiate and maintain cooperative projects among various stakeholders to foster innovative ideas and create a supportive ecosystem for diverse developmental activities. For instance, regarding climate action, initiatives by international organisations focused on environmental issues include the establishment of local multi-actor platforms composed of representatives from both the private and public sectors. These platforms aim to identify the needs for climate services in targeted areas and address them through innovative practices (CENN, 2022).

Georgia has been striving to align its climate policy with the Sustainable Development Goals, receiving significant support from the international community, particularly the EU and the UN. Georgia's aim to bring more 'green action' in economy is closely linked to its international obligations, and most importantly, the EU Association Agreement, which has driven policy changes in various areas. The EU has set an ambitious goal to achieve climate neutrality by 2050 (The European Union and Georgia, 2023). Georgia's aims also encompass improvements in green economy and reductions in carbon emissions. Furthermore, international involvement is crucial for the country in this endeavour. The importance of external support in 'greening' the economy and fostering more climate-resilient society was emphasised by representatives of the UNDP during a high-level conference in Tbilisi in 2022, which focused on Georgia's prospects in the carbon market (UNDP, 2022).

> Swapping carbon credits is a win-win idea that limits carbon emissions and brings much-needed financing to countries like Georgia to help in their green transition – UNDP representative said.[9]

Even though Georgia's economy is not emission-intensive, ranking among the lowest in terms of emissions among the Eastern Partners of the EU, the OECD

---

[8] A Roadmap for Climate Neutrality 2050.

[9] UNDP (2022).

reported in 2021 that, as of 2019, Georgia was emitting more than three times the amount of greenhouse gases per unit of GDP compared to the OECD average (0.35 $kgCO_{2e}$ per USD in 2012) (OECD, 2021).

In 2023, the Georgian government prepared and adopted the Long-Term Low Emission Development Strategy. The strategy was developed with the support of the EU and the UNDP. Subsequently, the strategy was presented at a conference hosted by the MEPA. The conference received support from the German International Climate Initiative project, which also contributed to the update of the Climate Action Plan for 2024–2025, as discussed below (International Climate Initiative, 2023).

The *Long-Term Low Emission Development Strategy*, to 2050, outlines the goals to be achieved. Both positive and negative scenarios are examined regarding the elimination of emissions across various sectors of the economy. The conclusion drawn is that by 2050, regardless of whether the scenario is optimistic or pessimistic, Georgia should aim to become carbon neutral (*Georgia's Long-Term Low Emission Development Strategy*, 2023).

The strategy is reflected in the 2024–2025 Climate Action Plan. This plan includes seven goals aimed at reducing greenhouse gas emissions, with specific targets for various sectors, including energy, transportation and agriculture.[10] It outlines the necessary activities for each goal, identifies the responsible parties for each activity, and addresses potential challenges. According to the plan, carbon emissions should be reduced by 15% in certain areas, such as energy. In exchange, innovative practices should be established to ensure the continued effective production of energy.

As noted above, for the sustainability of the process and to enhance its positive effects on society, it is crucial that the strategy implementation and coordination process include various stakeholders, such as businesses, non-governmental organisations (NGOs) and academic institutions. Mainstreaming these coordination initiatives into the implementation plans of state strategies is essential for these stakeholders, as it demonstrates the government's willingness to involve them in the process. This inclusion can influence businesses, for example, by creating incentives for their participation and fostering potentially positive collaborative experiences.

While studying *Georgia's Long-Term Low Emission Development Strategy*, it becomes evident that the primary entity responsible for overseeing and coordinating the implementation of this strategy is the inter-agency Climate Change Council. This council is led by the MEPA and comprises various ministries and agencies within the Georgian executive branch.[11] The strategy document outlines the competencies of each governmental entity and its role in the process. The

[10]Source: Climate Change in Georgia, 2024–2025 Action Plan.

[11]'*Georgia's Long-Term Low Emission Development Strategy*', 2023. https://unfccc.int/sites/default/files/resource/Georgia%27s%20LT-LEDS%202023-eng.pdf (accessed June 23, 2024).

Climate Change Council has two advisory bodies: the Coordination Team of the municipalities and the Working Group.[12]

According to the document:

> The Coordination Team is a mechanism for coordination between the government and self-governing bodies in the field of climate change, consisting of the mayors of CoM signatory municipalities, the deputy mayor of the Tbilisi Municipality and the governors (state representatives). The working group is a mechanism to address specific climate change policy issues in the economic and social sectors, consisting of public officials, experts, NGOs, and academic representatives.[13]

Thus, the strategy emphasises the importance of including various stakeholders beyond the government, such as social and economic sectors, experts, NGOs and academic institutions. Another aspect highlighting the role of external actors, particularly the private sector, is in funding mechanisms. The strategy identifies public–private partnerships as essential, describing them as 'a fundamental element of the funding and investment mechanism', which fosters trust.[14]

It is interesting to examine whether and how the broad initiative of cooperation has been reflected in the aforementioned Climate Action Plan. The plan itself places less emphasis on collaboration with actors outside the government. These external partners are not included among the partner institutions listed for the responsible agencies, which consist of ministries, city halls, public agencies and other state institutions. This trend is also evident among the partner institutions, despite the presence of activities that require innovative research, such as establishing practices for utilising renewable energy. This endeavour appears challenging without the involvement of research institutions. Other examples include activities with a specific focus, such as on the arrangement of the passenger railway system between Tbilisi and surrounding municipalities.[15] In this activity, the responsible agency is the Tbilisi City Municipality, while the supporting agencies include the Transport and Urban Development Agency of Tbilisi Municipality and JSC 'Georgian Railway'. The plan does not identify any academic or nongovernmental institutions as partners capable of conducting relevant research

---

[12] '*Georgia's Long-Term Low Emission Development Strategy*', 2023. https://unfccc.int/sites/default/files/resource/Georgia%27s%20LT-LEDS%202023-eng.pdf (accessed June 23, 2024).

[13] '*Georgia's Long-Term Low Emission Development Strategy*', 2023. https://unfccc.int/sites/default/files/resource/Georgia%27s%20LT-LEDS%202023-eng.pdf (accessed June 23, 2024).

[14] '*Georgia's Long-Term Low Emission Development Strategy*', 2023. https://unfccc.int/sites/default/files/resource/Georgia%27s%20LT-LEDS%202023-eng.pdf (accessed June 23, 2024).

[15] Source: Climate Change in Georgia, 2024–2025 Action Plan.

directly. However, it is possible that these institutions may become involved later in the process and provide services to the partners mentioned in the plan.

Based on the reviews of key documents, it can be concluded that carbon emission reduction is a crucial objective for Georgia, with the government playing a pivotal role in both implementing the strategy and securing necessary funding. The government recognises the importance of establishing cooperative networks with entities outside of the public sector, such as the private sector, NGOs and academia, by involving them in advisory roles. However, there is still a need to enhance their participation in short-term action plans as well. Given Georgia's strong dependence on international support, organisations and partners such as the EU and the UN play a significant role in promoting the concept of the economy and encouraging collaboration among various sectors within society based on their own successful practices. As mentioned earlier, some international organisations do facilitate such collaborations within the framework of their projects. Therefore, the contribution of international experience and support is essential for advancing a green economy.

Conclusion

Georgia still lacks effective policies and strategies related to eco-innovation, and the existing green subsidies are insufficient. The MEPA of Georgia should take necessary measures to increase awareness about waste management, monitor air quality, control water pollution, develop green economy initiatives and encourage companies to implement environmentally friendly innovations. These steps can be taken in close cooperation with international partners, particularly in alignment with EU policy frameworks to facilitate Georgia's integration processes. Additionally, following a review of key strategy documents and the action plan, the Georgian model of cooperation regarding carbon emission mechanisms involves the following steps: With the support of international partners and in accordance with internationally assumed obligations, the Georgian government initiates mechanisms for various sectors of the economy to reduce carbon emissions, sets targets for 2050, and develops action plans for shorter timeframes leading up to 2050. The government plays a crucial role as an initiator by involving other societal sectors in the implementation of its strategy. Nevertheless, it still lacks clearly defined roles concerning specific activities and detailed short-term action plans. Consequently, there is room for further improvement by raising awareness about the importance of cooperation, which can lead to effective results by reaching a broader segment of society and by sharing the expertise of various stakeholders.

It is evident that Georgia still has a long way to go in achieving significant progress in establishing multi-sector cooperation practices. Further research and analysis are required, particularly regarding stakeholder engagement, to understand the deeper nature of interactions and the constraints that different actors, such as the public sector and academia, may experience in relation to government bodies. This research should be accompanied by a study of political culture and behaviour, as the existence or non-existence of cooperation practices and their characteristics can be closely linked to established political and societal behaviours, as well as the expectations regarding the roles of different actors that the current political and cultural reality may be reluctant to challenge. For future research, it would be interesting to investigate whether Georgian politicians incorporate environmental issues into their election campaigns and discuss them in their public speeches. Another area of research could explore whether a focus on environmental protection and 'green growth' could have an effect on voting choices.

What is more, as Georgia has occupied territories – Abkhazia and the Tskhinvali region/South Ossetia – that remain beyond Georgia's effective control, it is important to conduct further research on how environmental practices, whether regulatory or subsidising mechanisms, as well as established or planned cooperation practices, can be applied to these occupied territories, even after their reintegration into Georgia.

References

Agrawal, R., Agrawal, S., Samadhiya, A., Kumar, A., Luthr, S., & Jain, V. (2024). Adoption of green finance and green innovation for achieving circularity: An exploratory review and future directions. *Geoscience Frontiers, 15*(4), Article 101669.

Awamleh, F. T., Alarabiat, Y. A., & Bustami, A. N. (2024). Enhancing sustainable development through international performance indicators: The role of business intelligence techniques. *Challenges in Sustainability, 12*(3), 203–218.

CENN. (2022). *Annual report 2022: Contributing to 17 SDGs*. Retrieved June 23, 2024, from https://www.cenn.org/app/uploads/2024/02/CENN-Annual-Report-2022-1.pdf

CENN. (2023). *Launch of the Green Agenda project: Georgia's step towards sustainability and EU integration*. Retrieved June 26, 2024, from https://www.cenn.org/launch-of-the-green-agenda-project-georgias-step-towards-sustainability-and-eu-integration/

Climate Change in Georgia. (2024, November 27). *2024–2025 Action plan*. 2030%20Strategy%20of%20Climate%20Change%20of%20Georgia%202024-2025%20action%20plan%20(2).pdf

Duan, Y., Xi, B., Xu, X., & Xuan, S. (2024). The impact of government subsidies on green innovation performance in new energy enterprises: A digital transformation perspective. *International Review of Economics & Finance, 94*, Article 103414.

Environmental Protection and Natural Resources Committee of the Parliament of Georgia. (2021). *Green Budget Project*. https://environment.cenn.org/app/uploads/2021/02/EN_Green_Budget_A4_Print.pdf

EU4Environment. (2021–2022). *Green economy in Eastern Partner countries. Towards a green economy with EU4Environment in Georgia*. https://www.eu4environment.org/app/uploads/2021/10/Towards-a-green-economy-in-the-Eastern-Partner-countries-web.pdf

EU4Environment. (2024, June 25). *Green economy in Eastern Partner countries. Resource efficient and cleaner production project in Georgia*. https://eecgeo.org/recp/index.htm

EU Relations with Georgia. (2024, November 27). *Georgia*. https://www.consilium.europa.eu/en/policies/eastern-partnership/georgia/

Fang, Z., Kong, X., Sensoy, A., Cui, X., & Cheng, F. (2021, March 11). Government's awareness of environmental protection and corporate green innovation: A natural experiment from the new environmental protection law in China. *Economic Analysis and Policy, 70*(C), 294–312.

Freedom House. (2024). *Georgia's country profile*. https://freedomhouse.org/country/georgia

Gaphrindashvili, N. (2023). Environmental policies and practice in Georgia: Some indications to consider on the way to sustainability. *Public Policy and Administration, 22*, 594–608.

Georgia's Long-Term Low Emission Development Strategy. (2023). Retrieved June 23, 2024, from https://unfccc.int/sites/default/files/resource/Georgia%27s%20LT-LEDS%20 2023-eng.pdf

Global Compact Network Georgia. (2019). *Green projects of greens movement*. Retrieved June 24, 2024, from https://unglobalcompact.ge/sustainability-spotlight/en/mwvaneta-modzraobis-mwvane-proeqtebi/

Green Party of Georgia. (2024). *National Parliamentary Library of Georgia*. http://www.nplg.gov.ge/gwdict/index.php?a=term&d=35&t=127

Humbatova, S. I., Hajiyeva, N., Fodor, M. G., Sood, K., & Grima, S. (2024). The impact of economic growth on the ecological environment and renewable energy production: Evidence from Azerbaijan and Hungary. *Journal of Risk and Financial Management, 17*(7), Article 275.

Inder, S., Sood, K., & Grima, S. (2022). Antecedents of behavioural intention to adopt internet banking using structural equation modelling. *Journal of Risk and Financial Management, 15*(4), Article 157.

Institute of Social Studies and Analysis. (2022). *Assessing the level of environmental education and awareness in Georgia*. UNDP. Retrieved June 26, 2024, from https://georgia.un.org/en/254717-assessing-level-environmental-education-and-awareness-georgia

International Climate Initiative. (2023). *Georgia's path to a carbon-neutral future*. Retrieved June 23, 2024, from https://www.international-climate-initiative.com/en/iki-media/news/georgias-path-to-a-carbon-neutral-future/

IPN. (2023). *The representative of environmental protection explains what the driver has the right to in case of a car fine for emissions*. Retrieved June 29, 2024, from https://www.interpressnews.ge/ka/article/768412-garemos-dacvis-carmomadgeneli-ganmartavsrisi-upleba-akvs-mzgols-gamonabolkvze-mankanis-dajarimebis-shemtxvevashi/

Kartozia, M. (2022, November 27) Actual issues of property rights reform in Georgia. *The Caucasus and the World*, No. 26. https://journals.4science.ge/index.php/journal/article/view/1522

Khatibi, F. S., Dedekorkut-Howes, A., Howes, M., & Torabi, E. (2021) Can public awareness, knowledge and engagement improve climate change adaptation policies? *Discover Sustainability, 2*, Article 18.

Law of Georgia on Environmental Protection, adopted in 1996. Retrieved June 29, 2024, from https://matsne.gov.ge/ka/document/view/33340?publication=33

Li, Q., Wu, H., Zhang, B. Q., Dong, Z. H., & Ling, T. (2024). Safety system study of gas stations based on preliminary hazard analysis and fault tree analysis. *Journal of Engineering Management and Systems Engineering, 3*(3), 149–163.

Meadows, D. H., Meadows, D. L., Randers, J., & Behrens, W. W., III. (1972). *The limits to growth: A report for the Club of Rome's project on the predicament of mankind*. Universe Books.

Ministry of Economy and Sustainable Development of Georgia. (2021a). *National renewable energy action plan*. Retrieved June 29, 2024, from https://www.economy.ge/index.php?page=home

Ministry of Economy and Sustainable Development of Georgia. (2021b). *Periodic technical inspection of vehicles*. Retrieved June 25, 2024, from https://www.economy.ge/?page=economy&s=126&lang=en

Ministry of Economy and Sustainable Development of Georgia. (2021c). *SME development strategy of Georgia, 2021–2025*. Retrieved June 29, 2024, from https://www.economy.ge/?page=ecopolitic&s=45&lang=en

Ministry of Environmental Protection and Agriculture (MEPA) of Georgia. (2023, June 12). *The Government of Georgia decided to implement the Euro 5 car emission standards to reduce air pollution across the country*. Retrieved June 25, 2024, from https://mepa.gov.ge/En/News/Details/21297

Muradov, A., & Hajiyeva, N. (2020). Economic and legal assessment of illicit activities during the occupation of Karabakh and its adjacent districts. *Society and Politics, 14*(1), 22–44.

National Renewable Energy Action Plan (NREAP). (2019). *NREAP, Georgia*. https://www.economy.ge/uploads/files/2017/energy/samoqmedo_gegma/nreap_v_3_eng_21022020.pdf

Nawaz, W., & Koç, M. (2020). *Industry, university and government partnerships for the sustainable development of knowledge-based society drivers, models and examples in US, Norway, Singapore and Qatar*. Springer, pp. 2–5.

Organisation for Economic Cooperation and Development (OECD). (2021). *"Sustainable infrastructure investment in Georgia" in "Sustainable infrastructure for low-carbon development in the EU Eastern partners: Hotspot analysis and needs assessment"*. Retrieved June 23, 2024, from https://read.oecd-ilibrary.org/environment/sustainable-infrastructure-for-low-carbon-development-in-the-eu-eastern-partnership_0d3170fa-en#page1

O'Riordan, T., & Voisey, H. (2007). The political economy of sustainable development. *Environmental Politics, 6*(1), 1–23.

Rural Development Agency. *Green grants program*. Retrieved June 29, 2024, from https://www.rda.gov.ge/en

Schulein, S. (n.d.). *Green tourism in Georgia. 12 portraits of practitioners*. Georgian National Tourism Administration. https://gnta.ge/wp-content/uploads/2018/12/Green-Tourism-in-Georgia.pdf

Tax Code of Georgia adopted in 1997. Retrieved June 29, 2024, from https://matsne.gov.ge/en/document/view/31690?publication=86

The European Union and Georgia. (2023). *Delegation of European Union in Georgia*. Retrieved June 23, 2024, from https://www.eeas.europa.eu/georgia/european-union-and-georgia_en?s=221

The Georgian Ecotourism Association. Retrieved June 29, 2024, from https://ecotourism.ge/

UNDP. (2022). *Carbon trade to promote green economy in Georgia*. Retrieved June 23, 2024, from https://www.undp.org/georgia/press-releases/georgia-carbon-market

Chapter 10

Corruption Perception in the Light of Green Transition Indicators

Szilárd Malatyinszki[a], Botond Géza Kálmán[a], Szonja Jenei[b], Kobla Sewornu Afadzinu[c] and Zsuzsanna Zugor[d]

[a]*Economic Research Institute and Department of Economics and Management, Faculty of Economics, Kodolányi János University, Székesfehérvár, Hungary*
[b]*Department of Management and Marketing, Kautz Gyula Faculty of Economics, Széchenyi István University (SZE), Győr, Hungary*
[c]*Doctoral School in Economics, University of Szeged, Szeged, Hungary*
[d]*Chancellor's Office, Kodolányi János University, Székesfehérvár, Hungary*

Abstract

Purpose: This study explores the relationship between green transition areas that promote sustainability and the perceived level of corruption across 41 countries.

Need for the study: Corruption undermines sustainability efforts and environmental governance, creating a need to understand its interaction with green transition indicators.

Methodology: The study uses data from the Bertelsmann Stiftung (BS) Sustainable Governance Indicators (SGI) 2022 report and Transparency International's Corruption Perceptions Index (CPI), deploying statistical methods to examine how environmental policy and participation in international treaties affect corruption.

Findings: State performance in environmental policy significantly influences corruption perception, with effects enhanced by international cooperation. Gross greenhouse gas emissions emerge as the most influential indicator, negatively affecting corruption perception by increasing its presence.

Sustainable Development and Green Innovation: Managing Risk through Interdisciplinary Approaches and Policy Strategies, 219–236

doi:10.1108/978-1-83608-462-420251010

Practical implications: These findings call for integrating anti-corruption measures into environmental policy frameworks, fostering international collaboration, and enhancing transparency to advance sustainable development and reduce corruption risks.

Keywords: Corruption; sustainability; environmental policy; green transition indicators

JEL codes: D73; P28; P18; N50

Literature review

The United Nations (2018) has estimated that corruption imposes an economic burden of at least 5% of the global gross domestic product (GDP) annually, with more than $1 billion exchanged in bribes around the world each year. This widespread issue disrupts social, economic, and institutional stability in virtually every country. While the economic and political consequences of corruption are widely acknowledged, its effects in specific sectors such as environmental and resource management are not as thoroughly understood. Within industries like agriculture, forestry, fisheries and the management of protected areas and wildlife, corruption has deeply entrenched itself. These illicit practices compromise both ecological and economic systems, ultimately creating negative repercussions for social well-being. Combatting systemic corruption in these sectors requires targeted policy strategies based on collective action theory, emphasising collaborative solutions to reduce its pervasive impacts (Tacconi & Williams, 2020). Governments bear the primary responsibility for achieving a balance between environmental sustainability and economic growth. Sustainable development is inherently linked to a nation's financial systems, regulatory policies, and institutional frameworks. The interplay of these factors illustrates the importance of stringent environmental policies, greater adoption of renewable energy technologies, and robust anti-corruption measures. By implementing comprehensive regulatory frameworks, governments can mitigate environmental harm while fostering sustainable growth. A well-functioning institutional structure is crucial in this context, as it provides the foundation for effective policy enforcement and sustainable development practices (Balsalobre-Lorente et al., 2023).

The complex connections among corruption, renewable energy use, economic development and carbon emissions highlight the long-term challenges of sustainability. Evidence points to a strong correlation between corruption and carbon dioxide emissions, as well as between economic growth and environmental degradation. While international trade and renewable energy adoption contribute to mitigating climate challenges, the negative influence of corruption often offsets these benefits. Effective governance, therefore, is essential to manage the interplay of these variables and ensure positive environmental outcomes (Leitão, 2021). An important study by Iglesias Troche and Martí Trull (2020) analysed the relationship between the Corruption Perception Index and greenhouse gas emissions, finding that corruption significantly impacts environmental performance. Their findings reveal a particularly strong correlation when measuring emissions against GDP per $1,000, as opposed to considering temporal changes. Between 1990 and 2008, countries with lower corruption levels achieved greater reductions in greenhouse gas emissions compared to highly corrupt nations. This finding emphasises the role of good governance in addressing climate challenges. Further research demonstrates that countries with moderate corruption levels are better equipped to utilise climate finance for emission reduction efforts than those with severe corruption problems. For instance, a one-point improvement in the Corruption Perception Index increases the likelihood of reducing emissions by 2.46%. However, underdeveloped nations often fail to exploit climate finance opportunities fully, limiting the effectiveness of such initiatives in mitigating climate change (Lyeonov et al., 2023). Interestingly, while corruption generally correlates negatively with CO_2 emissions across different income groups, high-income nations show a positive association, suggesting unique dynamics in these contexts.

Institutional quality, which encompasses the degree of corruption, plays a critical role in determining per capita emissions. Corruption exacerbates production inefficiencies and leads to emissions 'leakage', where production relocates from wealthier to lower-income countries to circumvent stringent regulations. This form of moral corruption undermines global emission reduction efforts by shifting the burden to nations with weaker regulatory frameworks (Devlina & Sahu, 2022). Transparent governance, characterised by reduced corruption, has been shown to significantly lower air pollution levels, both directly by enforcing regulations and indirectly through economic growth stimulation (Liu & Dong, 2021). Additionally, corruption has been identified as a key driver of environmental crimes such as illegal deforestation and hazardous waste dumping, further illustrating its profound impact on environmental health (Ngamkaiwan, 2023). The intersection of corruption and public policies, particularly those related to environmental regulation, has received increasing attention over the past few decades. Corruption weakens societal well-being by reducing the effectiveness of environmental policies and restricting access to public resources. Research highlights the critical role of institutional trust in mediating the influence of corruption. Trustworthy institutions foster a balance between industrial and environmental interests, thereby mitigating corruption's impact on regulatory frameworks. A robust institutional system not only facilitates the implementation of effective environmental policies but also strengthens international cooperation. This collaboration is essential for developing governance frameworks capable of reducing corruption on a global scale (Dincer & Fredriksson, 2018; Pellegrini & Vujic, 2003).

Morse (2006) undertook a comprehensive exploration of the relationship between corruption and environmental sustainability, focussing on how perceptions of corruption influence the progress of environmental protection measures. His research concluded that perceived corruption explains up to 20% of the variability in environmental indicators. Specifically, countries with higher levels of perceived corruption tend to exhibit weaker climate policies. This connection is particularly evident in nations with loose, market-oriented climate strategies, where corruption is closely linked to industries benefiting from substantial environmental tax exemptions and other financial advantages. Interestingly, this relationship holds even in countries with traditionally strong governance structures characterised by high levels of trust and low corruption (Rafaty, 2018). Despite numerous political economy theories and documented examples of corruption in resource management, efforts to combat such practices remain largely ineffective. This ineffectiveness continues to pose significant threats to both environmental sustainability and the economic systems integral to achieving it (Leitão, 2016).

The concept of green consumption emphasises the environmentally conscious use of goods and services, aiming to minimise harm to ecosystems. However, corruption can disrupt this process by inflating production costs or undermining public accountability for sustainable practices. For instance, corrupt practices may lead to weaker implementation of policies designed to promote green consumption (Lu & Li, 2023). Energy productivity and efficiency, often used as benchmarks for sustainability, are also heavily influenced by corruption control. Research by Akorli and Adom (2023) highlights that in African nations with lower energy efficiency, reducing corruption significantly enhances energy performance, showcasing how effective governance is key to fostering sustainable energy transitions.

The green transition – a shift towards renewable energy and sustainable practices – depends on well-implemented regulatory frameworks. Corruption and bureaucratic inefficiencies often undermine these efforts, hindering progress in achieving ecological balance. A longitudinal study spanning 30 years (Xu et al., 2024) revealed that while green transitions improve biocapacity, addressing corruption and improving bureaucratic quality are essential to achieving ecological sustainability.

Corruption's impact on the carbon footprint is complex and multifaceted. While it may lead to a temporary reduction in emissions, its long-term effects often result in higher overall emissions. Additionally, corruption consistently exacerbates the ecological footprint, a phenomenon closely tied to political instability. Key factors accelerating environmental degradation include rapid urbanisation, increased foreign direct investment (FDI), and rising energy consumption. To combat these challenges, strengthening political stability and implementing robust anti-corruption measures are imperative (Asif et al., 2023). Research by Dada et al. (2023) examining 25 years of data further emphasises this point. They found that corruption-driven shadow economies, alongside financial development, economic growth, and urbanisation, significantly increase the ecological footprint. Conversely, they found that trade openness mitigates environmental harm. Their findings also revealed that while urbanisation and economic growth diminish biocapacity, a strong financial system can mitigate the shadow economy's negative effects on environmental degradation. Waste management presents another critical issue where corruption is a significant factor. In developed economies, wealthier nations often transfer waste disposal to lower-income countries, where regulatory compliance is less expensive. Corruption facilitates this process, as low-income officials in these nations may accept bribes to overlook environmental violations. A game theory analysis by Cesi et al. (2019) demonstrated that corruption enables illegal waste disposal and encourages higher waste production, echoing the Jevons (1865) paradox. This paradox, established over 150 years ago, illustrates how increased efficiency in resource use often leads to higher overall consumption.

Urban solid waste management, a vital public service, has also been scrutinised for its connection to corruption. Italy, which ranks high in corruption among European nations, has faced persistent challenges in managing waste, especially during crises. Studies have shown that regions with higher levels of corruption generate more waste per capita, requiring additional financial and logistical resources for treatment. Such behaviour creates opportunities for criminal activity, undermining public administration and harming citizens. However, no significant differences were observed in selective waste collection rates or landfill utilisation across these regions (Romano et al., 2021). Electronic waste recycling is another area heavily impacted by corruption. Due to the hazardous nature of electronic waste for both human health and the environment, strict regulations govern this sector. Nonetheless, illegal recycling practices persist, particularly in developing nations where informal processing dominates. Policymakers aim to integrate informal recycling into formal systems, often through financial incentives. However, these subsidies can inadvertently foster corruption. To address this, government authorities are increasingly establishing interface organisations that redirect illegally recycled components into legitimate reuse channels, reducing the environmental and health risks associated with informal recycling (Williams et al., 2013).

After analysing the existing body of literature, the researchers developed the following key questions for their study:

Q1. How can the sample analysed in this study be described in terms of the environmental sustainability indicators identified in the literature?

Q2. What impact do the chosen environmental sustainability indicators have on shaping perceptions of corruption?

Methods

The authors utilised statistical analysis to address the research questions, drawing data from the BS SGI 2022 database. This dataset, publicly accessible at https://www.sgi-network.org/2022/, provides extensive information on governance and sustainability metrics for 41 EU and Organisation for Economic Co-operation and Development (OECD) countries. It serves as a valuable resource for understanding governance effectiveness and environmental performance across nations. The database includes an index evaluating the effectiveness of anti-corruption efforts, as well as several sustainability-related indicators. Among these are measures of environmental policy performance, material footprint, and participation in multilateral environmental agreements (MEAs). The authors specifically selected indicators that directly relate to corruption, such as those addressing the trade of emission quotas and decision-making processes in environmental policies.

Using the BS methodology, these indices are constructed from statistical data and scored on a scale from 1 to 10, where higher values indicate stronger performance. A score of five serves as the theoretical midpoint, offering a benchmark for evaluating relative performance. This standardised scoring system ensures consistency and comparability across countries, allowing for meaningful cross-national analysis. For their study, the authors focussed on a subset of SGI indices most relevant to the research objectives. These indicators, detailed in Table 10.1, form the analytical basis for examining the relationship between corruption perception and environmental sustainability. By leveraging this rich dataset, the authors aimed to uncover critical insights into how governance and sustainability interact, shedding light on the dynamics that influence corruption and environmental outcomes.

To analyse corruption levels, the authors relied on time-series data from Transparency International's CPI, a well-established measure that reflects the perceived levels of corruption in various countries. This index served as the dependent variable in their statistical modelling framework. The research process began with the generation of descriptive statistics, which provided a comprehensive summary of the dataset's key features. As part of the preliminary analysis, the authors assessed

Table 10.1. Indicators Used by Authors.

Index Name	**Definition**
Corruption Prevention	This indicator examines the measures implemented by governments and societies to ensure that public officials and politicians refrain from engaging in bribery. It focusses on the mechanisms established to uphold the ethical conduct and integrity of officeholders
Environmental Policy	This indicator evaluates governmental efforts to conserve natural resources and reduce pollution. It addresses three core aspects: the level of ambition reflected in the government's environmental policies, the tangible outcomes of these initiatives, and the extent to which environmental considerations are integrated into broader policy frameworks
MEAs	This metric assesses the percentage of a country's participation in global and regional MEAs, reflecting its commitment to collaborative international environmental efforts
Material Footprint	This indicator measures the total volume of raw materials extracted to meet the consumption needs of a population. Measured as material footprint per capita, it is typically higher in wealthier nations, which often rely on resources from other countries to sustain their elevated living standards

Source: Authors' own.

the normality of the sample distribution using the Shapiro–Wilk test (Shapiro & Wilk, 1965) and evaluated homoscedasticity – the assumption of equal variance across the dataset – using Levene's test (Levene et al., 1960). These diagnostic tests were essential for determining whether parametric statistical techniques could be applied or whether nonparametric methods would be more appropriate for further analyses.

Building on these foundational steps, the authors sought to understand the relationship between environmental sustainability metrics and corruption prevention efforts. To address this, they constructed a regression model in which the CPI served as the dependent variable, representing corruption levels. The independent variables included various environmental indices, chosen for their potential influence on corruption dynamics. The regression analysis aimed to uncover both the magnitude and direction of these relationships, exploring how environmental factors impact efforts to reduce corruption. By structuring the model in this way, the researchers could assess whether robust environmental policies and practices correlate with improved governance and reduced corruption, providing valuable insights into the interconnectedness of sustainability and governance.

Results

Table 10.2 shows the results of the descriptive statistics. The analysis included data from 41 countries, with no missing values, ensuring a comprehensive dataset. The Shapiro–Wilk (1965) test was employed to evaluate the normality of the indices.

Table 10.2. Descriptive Statistics for the Sample.

	2014	**2015**	**2016**	**2017**	**2018**	**2019**	**2020**	**2021**	**2022**	**Shapiro–Wilk's *p***
Corruption_Prevention – mean	6.41	6.39	6.51	6.56	6.54	6.44	6.32	6.24	6.34	0.958
Multilateral_Environmental_Agreements – mean	7.33	7.33	6.66	6.46	6.88	6.71	6.79	6.81	6.93	<0.001
Material_Footprint – mean	5.82	5.88	5.93	5.91	5.98	5.91	5.88	5.91	5.95	0.028
Environmental_Policy – mean	5.98	6.07	6.07	6.15	6.05	6.12	6.17	6.17	6.22	0.051
N	41	41	41	41	41	41	41	41	41	–
Missing	0	0	0	0	0	0	0	0	0	–

Source: Authors' own.

Most indices met the normality assumption; however, the 'MEAs' indicator was an exception, failing the normality test with a significance level of $p<0.001$. Due to this, the study adopted non-parametric statistical methods, which are more suitable for datasets that do not meet normality requirements. An examination of the Corruption Prevention indicator shows that all countries achieved results above the theoretical midpoint, indicating generally positive trend. While this suggests progress in efforts to prevent corruption, it also indicates the need for further advancements to strengthen governance and integrity across the board. Both the Environmental Policy indicator and the MEAs indicator exceeded the theoretical average, reflecting strong international engagement and commitment to environmental protection initiatives. These results suggest that the examined countries actively participate in and fulfil their roles within global environmental agreements, demonstrating their alignment with international sustainability goals.

The Material Footprint indicator also scored above the theoretical average. However, this higher value is a cause for concern, unlike the previous indicators. It indicates an excessive use of natural resources, resulting in an unsustainably large ecological footprint. This finding underscores the need for improved resource management practices and more sustainable consumption patterns, particularly in wealthier nations that contribute disproportionately to global resource extraction and consumption. The findings, illustrated in Fig. 10.1, reveal a mixed picture of sustainability performance among the analysed countries. While progress is evident in areas like corruption prevention and environmental policy, challenges remain in reducing material consumption and promoting long-term environmental sustainability. These results emphasise the importance

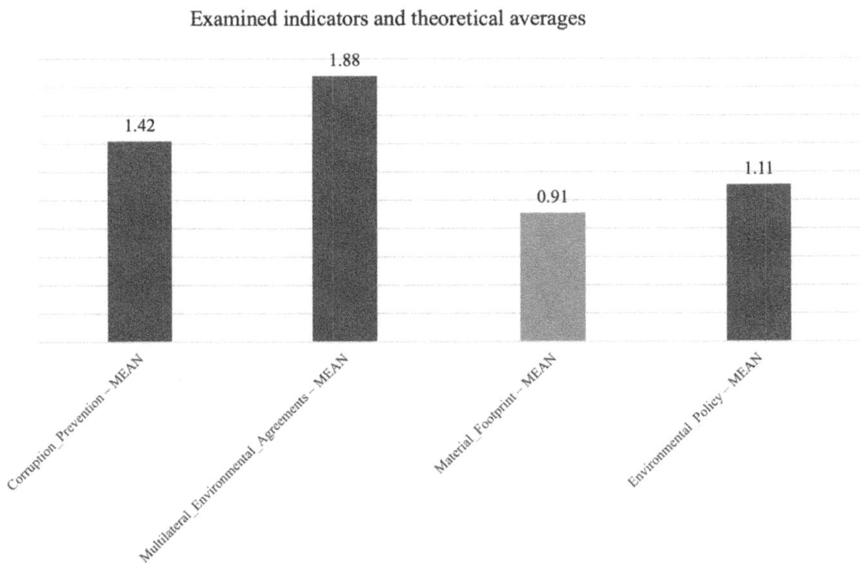

Fig. 10.1. Favourable (Dark Teal) and Unfavourable (Red) Indicator Averages. *Source*: Authors' own.

of addressing resource overuse and aligning national policies with global efforts to combat environmental degradation and ensure sustainable development.

Tables 10.3 and 10.4 present the details of the regression model. The model explains 49.4% of the variation in corruption prevention as influenced by environmental indicators (R^2=0.494). The results indicate a good fit, with statistical significance confirming that the observed effects are not due to chance (p<0.001). Additionally, the variance inflation factor values for the variables range from 1.12 to 5.33, well within the acceptable limit of 10, ensuring no issues with multicollinearity.

Table 10.4 highlights that environmental policy and material footprint have a significant impact on corruption prevention. Effective compliance with environmental policy plays a critical role in enhancing corruption control, primarily by reducing the risk of exploitation through legal loopholes. Additionally, the influence of environmental policy is likely strengthened by the involvement of MEAs, which promote international cooperation and provide a framework for enforcing stricter environmental standards. This interconnectedness illustrates the value of aligning environmental governance with anti-corruption measures to achieve better outcomes.

Discussion

The interplay between corruption and environmental sustainability emerges as a critical area of inquiry, particularly in the context of achieving green transition goals. The present study advances our understanding by demonstrating the nuanced relationships between environmental policy, MEAs, material footprints,

Table 10.3. Overall Test Results of Regression Model.

	Overall Model Test					
Model	***R***	***R*²**	***F***	***df1***	***df2***	***p***
1	0.703	0.494	90.6	3	359	<0.001

Source: Authors' own.

Table 10.4. Regression Model Coefficients.

Predictor	**Estimate**	**SE**	***t***	***p***
Model Coefficients – Corruption_Prevention				
Intercept	2.7554	0.6307	4.369	<0.001
Environmental_Policy	0.4928	0.0536	9.199	<0.001
Material_Footprint	0.1767	0.0247	7.162	<0.001
Multilateral_Environmental_Agreements	0.0504	0.0546	0.923	0.356

Source: Authors' own.

and corruption perception. This discussion synthesises the findings of the study with extant literature to contextualise the implications and provide a foundation for future research directions.

Influence of Environmental Policy on Corruption Perception

The study underscores the paramount role of environmental policy in shaping perceptions of corruption. The regression model reveals that robust environmental policies significantly enhance the effectiveness of corruption prevention mechanisms. These findings align with Balsalobre-Lorente et al. (2023), who highlighted that stringent environmental policies, coupled with economic and institutional advancements, can mitigate ecological footprints. The ability of environmental policies to close legal loopholes appears to be a critical factor, as it diminishes opportunities for corrupt practices to exploit ambiguities in regulatory frameworks.

Moreover, the integration of environmental aspects into broader policy agendas fosters transparency and accountability, thereby reducing the scope for corruption. This is consistent with Liu and Dong (2021), who found that the integrity of institutional frameworks directly correlates with reductions in pollution and corruption. The present findings reinforce the argument that comprehensive environmental policies are not only pivotal for ecological outcomes but also integral to governance quality. Additional evidence from Rafaty (2018) highlights that nations with stringent environmental regulations exhibit higher public trust in governance and lower perceived corruption, emphasising the dual benefits of proactive policy frameworks.

A growing body of literature emphasises the role of stringent environmental standards in curbing opportunities for rent-seeking and collusion. For example, Dincer and Fredriksson (2018) observed that countries with robust environmental regulatory frameworks tend to have lower levels of corruption due to reduced discretionary power among public officials in environmental permitting processes. This finding shows the potential for environmental policies to establish systematic checks that preclude corrupt practices.

Furthermore, effective environmental policy aligns with sustainable development goals (SDGs), particularly those that emphasise institutional strength and transparency. This linkage is evident in studies by Xu et al. (2024), which demonstrated that green electricity transitions and environmental regulatory quality are significantly impeded in contexts of high corruption. By fostering an environment of accountability, environmental policies protect natural resources and contribute to institutional credibility.

Environmental policies' intersection with digital governance innovations offers another promising dimension. The integration of digital tools in monitoring emissions and enforcing compliance has proven effective in reducing opportunities for corruption. According to Shang et al. (2025), digital transparency mechanisms in environmental governance have increased accountability and curbed bribery in high-risk sectors. This technological approach provides a template for enhancing policy effectiveness while minimising corrupt interference.

The interplay between public participation and environmental governance is also crucial. Public participation in policy formulation and implementation fosters transparency and accountability, reducing the scope for malpractice. Lyeonov et al. (2023) demonstrated that countries with higher levels of civic engagement in environmental decision-making report lower corruption indices and improved environmental outcomes. Thus, policies that encourage public oversight and participation are essential in the fight against corruption.

Lastly, policies must address the role of the private sector in environmental governance. Corporate compliance with environmental standards is often influenced by the stringency of regulations and the likelihood of enforcement. According to Lu and Li (2023), businesses operating under robust regulatory environments are more likely to adopt ethical practices, thereby reducing corrupt transactions associated with environmental non-compliance.

MEAs and Corruption

The study's findings underline the importance of MEAs as instruments for fostering international accountability and combating corruption. These agreements establish normative frameworks that promote transparency, thereby reducing opportunities for corruption in environmental governance. However, the study indicates that their direct impact is less significant than that of robust national environmental policies. Bäckstrand et al. (2017) similarly highlight that MEAs often require integration into domestic governance systems to achieve meaningful outcomes. Nations with weak institutional capacities may struggle to enforce MEA provisions, thereby allowing corruption to persist, particularly in sectors like resource management and emissions regulation.

Beyond fostering regulatory frameworks, MEAs play a critical role in knowledge dissemination and institutional learning. Countries participating in MEAs can adopt global best practices and leverage innovative solutions for environmental challenges. As emphasised by Chayes and Chayes (1995), compliance with MEAs often hinges on the ability of international institutions to provide technical support and capacity-building for member states. By embedding global standards into local governance contexts, MEAs help create an environment less conducive to corruption, particularly in resource-intensive sectors.

However, translating MEAs into actionable outcomes remains challenging, as disparities in their implementation often reflect governance issues at the national level. Purdon (2015) suggests that such disparities may stem from insufficient regulatory capacity, lack of political will, or conflicting economic interests. Moreover, Böhringer and Löschel (2006) caution that the economic incentives tied to MEA participation might sometimes create opportunities for rent-seeking behaviour, thereby inadvertently fostering corruption.

In addition, MEAs' impact on corruption may also depend on the transparency of international institutions themselves. Gupta and Mason (2016) argue that ensuring accountability within MEAs requires robust mechanisms for monitoring and reporting compliance. Without such mechanisms, MEAs risk being undermined by non-compliance and corrupt practices within participating states.

Broader Implications for Environmental Governance

The implications of MEAs extend beyond corruption control to addressing the complexities of transboundary environmental challenges. These agreements foster collaboration among nations, enabling collective action to tackle issues like climate change, biodiversity loss, and pollution. Biermann, Betsill, et al. (2010) and Biermann, Zelli, et al. (2010) emphasise that MEAs function as essential instruments for building global partnerships and promoting shared environmental goals. Their success, however, hinges on the synergy between international frameworks and domestic governance. Weak institutional capacities at the national level often undermine the implementation of MEA objectives, as highlighted by Gupta et al. (2016), who note that disparities in governance structures across nations present significant barriers to uniform enforcement.

Strengthening the interface between international and domestic governance systems is critical. For MEAs to achieve their full potential in reducing corruption and promoting sustainable development, they must be tailored to the specific needs of participating countries. Adaptive governance, as explained by Hovi et al. (2009), provides flexibility in how MEAs are put into action, allowing them to fit different institutions and levels of ability. This approach minimises corruption risks by aligning MEA commitments with the realities of local governance contexts.

A recurring theme in this discussion is the role of institutional capacity in mediating the effectiveness of MEAs. Countries with robust institutions are better equipped to translate MEA commitments into actionable policies, reducing corruption risks and enhancing environmental outcomes. Conversely, nations with weak institutions often struggle with enforcement, creating opportunities for corruption to thrive. As noted by Ostrom (2010), institutional diversity and polycentric governance systems can offer resilience by distributing authority and creating multiple layers of accountability.

The study underscores the importance of integrating anti-corruption strategies into broader environmental governance frameworks. This aligns with findings by Persson et al. (2019), who argue that addressing corruption in environmental governance requires targeted reforms, such as enhancing transparency, fostering civic engagement, and strengthening judicial systems. For instance, participatory governance models, which involve multiple stakeholders in decision-making processes, have been shown to improve accountability and reduce corruption. The OECD (2018) highlights that such models are particularly effective in ensuring that MEA implementation aligns with national priorities and public interests.

Financial mechanisms, including international funding and climate finance, are pivotal in supporting MEA implementation. However, they also introduce risks of mismanagement and corruption. Climate finance, in particular, is vulnerable to diversion and inefficiencies in countries with limited regulatory oversight. Transparency International (2020) identifies several best practices for mitigating these risks, such as establishing independent audit mechanisms and implementing stringent reporting requirements.

Integrating financial governance reforms into MEA frameworks can further enhance their impact. For example, mechanisms like performance-based funding, which ties financial disbursements to measurable outcomes, can incentivise transparency and reduce corruption. As Cavanagh et al. (2020) note, such approaches ensure that resources are allocated effectively, aligning financial incentives with environmental and governance objectives.

Emerging technologies, including blockchain and digital monitoring systems, present new opportunities for enhancing MEA implementation. Blockchain, with its capacity for secure and transparent record-keeping, has been proposed as a tool for improving the traceability of financial flows and environmental data. As suggested by Kaza et al. (2018), blockchain could be used to track carbon credits, ensuring that they are not subject to fraudulent practices.

Similarly, remote sensing technologies and AI-driven analytics can provide real-time monitoring of environmental indicators, facilitating compliance with MEA commitments. These technologies enable early detection of non-compliance and corruption, allowing for timely interventions. For example, Li et al. (2019) demonstrate the effectiveness of satellite-based monitoring in tracking deforestation, a critical metric in biodiversity-related MEAs.

Addressing Equity and Justice within MEA Frameworks

Equity and justice considerations are integral to the success of MEAs. The disproportionate impact of environmental degradation on low-income nations underscores the need for equitable resource-sharing mechanisms. MEAs must address these disparities to ensure their legitimacy and efficacy. As noted by Newell et al. (2017), equity-focussed approaches, such as differentiated responsibilities and capacity-building initiatives, can enhance the inclusivity and fairness of MEA frameworks.

The inclusion of indigenous knowledge systems and local expertise in MEA implementation is another critical aspect of equity. Indigenous communities often possess unique insights into sustainable resource management, which can complement scientific approaches. Integrating these perspectives, as highlighted by Folke et al. (2021), can strengthen MEA frameworks by making them more contextually relevant and culturally sensitive.

Future Research and Policy Directions

The findings call for a more comprehensive understanding of the interplay between MEAs, corruption, and environmental governance. Future research should explore the long-term impacts of MEA implementation on governance quality and corruption control, particularly in resource-dependent economies. Comparative studies examining MEA efficacy across different institutional and cultural contexts could provide valuable insights into best practices and areas for improvement.

Additionally, policymakers should prioritise capacity-building initiatives that enhance the ability of low-income nations to implement MEAs effectively. This includes providing technical assistance, fostering knowledge exchange, and ensuring equitable access to financial resources. Collaborative approaches that involve governments, civil society, and the private sector are essential for addressing the systemic challenges identified in this study.

Material Footprint and Governance Challenges

The material footprint indicator provides valuable insights into the intersection of resource consumption and corruption. High material footprints, as observed in affluent nations, signal disproportionate resource extraction, often from lower-income countries. This dynamic creates fertile ground for corruption, as highlighted by Devlina and Sahu (2022), who discussed emissions leakage and its moral implications. The current study reinforces the necessity for equitable resource management practices and stringent oversight mechanisms to address these disparities.

The relationship between material footprints and corruption underscores the systemic challenges in balancing economic growth with sustainability. For instance, Akorli and Adom (2023) demonstrated that energy efficiency transitions are heavily influenced by regulatory quality and corruption control. These findings collectively underscore the critical need for policies that promote resource efficiency while ensuring transparency in governance structures.

Broader Implications for Green Transition

The broader implications of this study are profound, especially in light of global green transition efforts. The findings highlight that the effectiveness of environmental sustainability initiatives is inextricably linked to the governance environment. Corruption not only undermines environmental objectives but also erodes public trust and institutional credibility, creating a vicious cycle that impedes progress.

Several studies corroborate this perspective. Asif et al. (2023) and Rafaty (2018) emphasise the dual role of political stability and anti-corruption measures in fostering effective climate policies. The current findings suggest that addressing corruption is not merely a governance issue but a prerequisite for achieving SDGs.

The study also draws attention to the role of financial incentives in shaping green transitions. While such incentives aim to encourage compliance and innovation, they can inadvertently become sources of corruption if not carefully managed. The literature, including Xu et al. (2024) and Williams et al. (2013), highlights the risks associated with subsidies and other financial mechanisms in sectors like renewable energy and recycling. Establishing robust oversight frameworks is therefore imperative to mitigate these risks and ensure that financial resources are directed towards genuine sustainability objectives.

Future Research Directions

While the study provides critical insights, it also opens avenues for further research. The limited explanatory power of the regression model (49.4%) suggests that additional factors influence the relationship between environmental indicators and corruption perception. Future research could explore the role of variables such as political culture, public awareness, and technological advancements in shaping these dynamics.

Another promising direction is the examination of sector-specific corruption within the green transition. As noted by Romano et al. (2021) and Cesi et al. (2019), sectors like waste management and electronic recycling are particularly susceptible to corrupt practices. Understanding the unique challenges and vulnerabilities of these sectors could inform targeted anti-corruption strategies.

Lastly, longitudinal studies that track changes in corruption perception over time in response to environmental policy interventions would provide valuable insights into causality and long-term impacts. Such studies could also incorporate comparative analyses across regions and income groups to identify best practices and contextual factors.

Conclusion

State institutions play a crucial role in advancing environmental sustainability, relying on effective legislation and law enforcement to implement policies successfully. Significant financial resources are often allocated to support the green transition, funding initiatives such as renewable energy, conservation, and waste management. However, these resources can also become targets for corruption, undermining their intended purpose and outcomes. This study demonstrates a strong connection between environmental sustainability indicators and perceived levels of corruption. The proposed model explains nearly 50% of this relationship, highlighting the critical role of effective environmental policy in shaping corruption perceptions. Participation in international environmental agreements further reinforces this effect, as global cooperation and coordinated actions strengthen governance and contribute to reducing corruption and improving its perception. Stronger anti-corruption measures impose stricter regulatory environments, increasing the risks and costs associated with legal violations and profiteering. As these measures take hold, privileges tied to political connections and corrupt practices are eroded. In response, companies often shift their focus to socially responsible initiatives to rebuild their reputation or distance themselves from past misconduct. The fight against corruption also enhances external oversight and increases stakeholder scrutiny, driving companies to improve their corporate social responsibility performance. Furthermore, anti-corruption efforts liberate resources previously misused through corrupt practices, enabling firms to reinvest in socially and environmentally beneficial activities. By dismantling corrupt systems and fostering transparency, anti-corruption measures pave the way for improved governance, stronger societal trust, and enhanced sustainability outcomes.

References

Akorli, C. D., & Adom, P. K. (2023). The role of corruption control and regulatory quality in energy efficiency transition tendencies in Africa. *iScience*, *26*(3), 106262. https://doi.org/10.1016/j.isci.2023.106262

Asif, K., Sabir, S., & Qayyum, U. (2023). Corruption, political instability, and environmental degradation in South Asia: A comparative analysis of carbon footprint and ecological footprint. *Journal of the Knowledge Economy*, *15*, 4072–4096. https://doi.org/10.1007/s13132-023-01133-y

Bäckstrand, K., Kuyper, J. W., Linnér, B. O., & Lövbrand, E. (2017). Non-state actors in global climate governance: From Copenhagen to Paris and beyond. *Environmental Politics*, *26*(4), 561–579. https://doi.org/10.1080/09644016.2017.1327485

Balsalobre-Lorente, D., Topaloglu, E. E., Nur, T., & Evcimen, C. (2023). Exploring the linkage between financial development and ecological footprint in APEC countries: A novel view under corruption perception and environmental policy stringency. *Journal of Cleaner Production*, *414*, 137686. https://doi.org/10.1016/j.jclepro.2023.137686

Biermann, F., Betsill, M. M., Gupta, J., Kanie, N., Lebel, L., Liverman, D., Schroeder, H., & Siebenhüner, B. (2010). Earth system governance: A research framework. *International Environmental Agreements: Politics, Law and Economics*, *10*(4), 277–298. https://doi.org/10.1007/s10784-010-9137-

Biermann, F., Zelli, F., Pattberg, P., & Van Asselt, H. (2010). The architecture of global climate governance: Setting the stage. In F. Biermann, P. Pattberg, & F. Zelli (Eds.), *Global climate governance beyond 2012. Architecture, agency and adaptation* (pp. 15–24). Cambridge University Press. https://portal.research.lu.se/en/publications/the-architecture-of-global-climate-governance-setting-the-stage

Böhringer, C., & Löschel, A. (2006). Promoting renewable energy in Europe: A hybrid CGE approach. *Energy Journal*, *27*(3), 135–150. https://doi.org/10.5547/ISSN0195-6574-EJ-VolSI2006-NoSI2-7

Cavanagh, C., Benjaminsen, T. A., & Vedeld, P. (2020). Climate finance and carbon colonialism: The political economy of forest carbon in sub-Saharan Africa. *Geoforum*, *117*, 132–141. https://doi.org/10.1016/j.geoforum.2020.08.010

Cesi, B., D'Amato, A., & Zoli, M. (2019). Corruption in environmental policy: The case of waste. *Economia Politica*, *36*(1), 65–78. https://doi.org/10.1007/s40888-017-0087-x

Chayes, A., & Chayes, A. H. (1995). *The new sovereignty: Compliance with international regulatory agreements*. Harvard University Press. https://doi.org/10.4159/9780674262638

Dada, J. T., Ajide, F. M., Arnaut, M., & Adeiza, A. (2023). On the shadow economy-environmental sustainability nexus in Africa: The (ir)relevance of financial development. *International Journal of Sustainable Development & World Ecology*, *30*(1), 6–20. https://doi.org/10.1080/13504509.2022.2115576

Devlina, R. R. R., & Sahu, S. K. (2022). Corruption and carbon emission: An empirical investigation. *International Journal of Green Economics*, *16*(4), 355–388. https://doi.org/10.1504/IJGE.2022.129000

Dincer, O. C., & Fredriksson, P. G. (2018). Corruption and environmental regulatory policy in the United States: Does trust matter? *Resource and Energy Economics*, *54*, 212–225. https://doi.org/10.1016/j.reseneeco.2018.10.001

Folke, C., Polasky, S., Rockström, J., Galaz, V., Westley, F., Lamont, M., Österblom, H., & Steffen, W. (2021). Our future in the anthropocene biosphere. *Ambio*, *50*(4), 834–869. https://doi.org/10.1007/s13280-021-01544-8

Gupta, A., & Mason, M. (2016). *Transparency in global environmental governance: Critical perspectives*. MIT Press. https://muse.jhu.edu/pub/6/edited_volume/book/33383

Gupta, J., van Asselt, H., & Biermann, F. (2016). *Cross-cutting issues: International environmental law and governance in the anthropocene*. Edward Elgar Publishing.

Hovi, J., Sprinz, D. F., & Underdal, A. (2009). Implementing long-term climate policy: Time inconsistency, domestic politics, international anarchy. *Global Environmental Politics*, *9*(3), 20–39. https://doi.org/10.1162/glep.2009.9.3.20

Iglesias Troche, I., & Martí Trull, N. (2020). *Are greenhouse gas emissions correlated with corruption?: A study on the relation between pollution and corruption through the Kyoto Protocol participants* [Universitat Pompeu Fabra]. http://repositori.upf.edu/handle/10230/46464

Jevons, W. S. (1865). *The coal question; An inquiry concerning the progress of the nation, and the probable exhaustion of our coal-mines* (1st ed.). MacMillan and Co. http://archive.org/details/coalquestionani00jevogoog

Kaza, S., Yao, L. C., Bhada-Tata, P., & Woerden, F. V. (2018). *What a waste 2.0: A global snapshot of solid waste management to 2050*. World Bank Publications. https://doi.org/10.1596/978-1-4648-1329-2

Leitão, A. (2016). Corruption and the environment. *Journal of Socioeconomics*, *5*(3), 1–5. https://doi.org/10.4172/2167-0358.1000173

Leitão, N. C. (2021). The effects of corruption, renewable energy, trade and CO_2 emissions. *Economies*, *9*(2), Article 2. https://doi.org/10.3390/economies9020062

Levene, H. (1960). Robust tests for equality of variances. In I. Olkin et al. (Eds.), *Contributions to probability and statistics: Essays in Honor of Harold Hotelling* (pp. 278–292). Stanford University Press. https://www.semanticscholar.org/paper/Robust-tests-for-equality-of-variances-Levene/3eb99d37fef7c5b23ea3ecb4e1a7de65b0af59ed

Li, T., Wang, D., Zhang, L., & Chen, X. (2019). Satellite monitoring of forest loss and recovery to support sustainable development goals. *Remote Sensing*, *11*(19), 2219. https://doi.org/10.3390/rs11192219

Liu, Y., & Dong, F. (2021). Haze pollution and corruption: A perspective of mediating and moderating roles. *Journal of Cleaner Production*, *279*, 123550. https://doi.org/10.1016/j.jclepro.2020.123550

Lu, J., & Li, H. (2023). The impact of environmental corruption on green consumption: A quantitative analysis based on China's Judicial Document Network and Baidu Index. *Socio-Economic Planning Sciences*, *86*, 101451. https://doi.org/10.1016/j.seps.2022.101451

Lyeonov, S., Toušek, Z., Bozhenko, V., & Erdeiné, K.-G. S. (2023). The impact of corruption in climate finance on achieving net zero emissions. *Journal of International Studies*, *16*(1), 142–159. https://www.ceeol.com/search/article-detail?id=1172309

Morse, S. (2006). Is corruption bad for environmental sustainability? A cross-national analysis. *Ecology and Society*, *11*(1), 1–22. https://www.jstor.org/stable/26267783

Newell, P., & Mulvaney, D. (2017). The political economy of the "just transition": The politics of fossil fuel phase-out. *Energy Research & Social Science*, *38*, 36–44. https://doi.org/10.1016/j.erss.2017.10.008

Ngamkaiwan, C. (2023). Secondary green crime: Bangkok's PM2.5 pollution and policy corruption. *International Journal for Crime, Justice and Social Democracy*, *12*(4), 65. https://doi.org/10.5204/ijcjsd.2857

Ostrom, E. (2010). Polycentric systems for coping with collective action and global environmental change. *Global Environmental Change*, *20*(4), 550–557. https://doi.org/10.1016/j.gloenvcha.2010.07.004

Pellegrini, L., & Vujic, S. (2003). *Corruption, economic development and environmental policy*. Institute for Environmental Studies. https://www.feem-web.it/ess/ess03/students/pellegr.pdf

Persson, A., Weitz, N., & Nilsson, M. (2019). Follow-up and review of the sustainable development goals: Alignment vs. internalization. *Review of European, Comparative & International Environmental Law*, *28*(1), 59–68. https://doi.org/10.1111/reel.12219

Purdon, M. (2015). Advancing comparative climate change politics: Theory and method. *Global Environmental Politics*, *15*(3), 1–26. https://doi.org/10.1162/GLEP_a_00301

Rafaty, R. (2018). Perceptions of corruption, political distrust, and the weakening of climate policy. *Global Environmental Politics*, *18*(3), 106–129. https://doi.org/10.1162/glep_a_00471

Romano, G., Masserini, L., & Lombardi, G. V. (2021). Environmental performance of waste management: Impacts of corruption and public maladministration in Italy. *Journal of Cleaner Production*, *288*, 125521. https://doi.org/10.1016/j.jclepro.2020.125521

Shang, W., Li, H., Ni, X., Chen, T., & Liu, T. (2025). BlockGuard: Advancing digital copyright integrity with blockchain technique. *Computers and Electrical Engineering*, *122*, 109897. https://doi.org/10.1016/j.compeleceng.2024.109897

Shapiro, S. S., & Wilk, M. B. (1965). An analysis of variance test for normality (complete samples). *Biometrika*, *52*(3–4), 591–611. http://links.jstor.org/sici?sici=0006-3444%28196512%2952%3A3%2F4%3C591%3AAAOVTF%3E2.0.CO%3B2-B

Tacconi, L., & Williams, D. A. (2020). Corruption and anti-corruption in environmental and resource management. *Annual Review of Environment and Resources*, *45*, 305–329. https://doi.org/10.1146/annurev-environ-012320-083949

Transparency International. (2020). *Corruption risks in climate finance: Challenges and solutions*. https://www.transparency.org

United Nations. (2018, September 10). Global cost of corruption at least 5 per cent of world gross domestic product, secretary-general tells security council, citing world economic forum data. *Meetings Coverage and Press Releases*. https://press.un.org/en/2018/sc13493.doc.htm

Williams, E., Kahhat, R., Bengtsson, M., Hayashi, S., Hotta, Y., & Totoki, Y. (2013). Linking informal and formal electronics recycling via an interface organization. *Challenges*, *4*(2), Article 2. https://doi.org/10.3390/challe4020136

Xu, R., Pata, U. K., & Dai, J. (2024). Sustainable growth through green electricity transition and environmental regulations: Do risks associated with corruption and bureaucracy matter? *Politická Ekonomie*, *10*(10), 1–23. https://doi.org/10.18267/j.polek.1420

Chapter 11

Financial Market Contribution to Sustainable Development: Two Approaches to Green Bonds ETF's Analysis

Andriy Popovych

Agricultural and Food Economics State Research Institute, Warsaw, Poland

Abstract

Purpose: The objective of this study is to empirically confirm the existence of a premium to the price of bonds with the 'green' status in accordance with climate standards. It differs from previous ones in that it is based on the analysis of green bond exchange-traded funds.

Need for the study: Currently, there is an accelerated development of the green bond market and an increase in their importance in solving the problem of financing environmental projects. At the same time, in the academic literature, the existence of a 'green' premium is not such an unambiguous issue, and the scope of relevant research should be expanded.

Methodology: The chapter analyses the efficiency of investing in green Exchange Traded Funds (ETFs) compared to conventional ETFs using two approaches. The first approach uses various indicators of green bond funds' returns based on the Capital Asset Pricing Model (CAPM) model: Sharpe ratio, risk-adjusted Modigliani–Modigliani ratio, coefficient beta, coefficient Jensen's alpha and value at risk. The second approach is compares the ratio of the current price to the fund's net asset value (NAV).

Findings: The study found evidence of a special premium in green bond funds.

Practical implications: The continued growth of the green bond market confirms the considerable potential of this financial instrument. Understanding the fundamental factors driving the growth of green bond market

Sustainable Development and Green Innovation: Managing Risk through Interdisciplinary Approaches and Policy Strategies, 237–256

doi:10.1108/978-1-83608-462-420251011

is critical to the global sustainability investment agenda as well as the feasibility study of issuing such securities, undergoing additional certification stages, and the costs required to obtain the appropriate label.

Keywords: Green bonds; ESG principles; ETF; NAV; 'green' premium

JEL code: G12; Q01; Q51

Introduction

Globalization of the world economy, increasing negative climate change, growing frequency of natural and manmade disasters, formation of new social consciousness and thinking as well as the rapid development of new information and telecommunication technologies and new market segments are giving rise to revolutionary changes in the capital market. These trends have a direct impact on the behaviour of both small firms and big corporations, private and institutional investors forcing them to pay more attention to their own reputation as contributors to the creation of a fairer and greener world.

One of the drivers of such changes is the concept of sustainable development for preserving peace and achieving a successful future through the connection of three aspects of development: environmental, social and economic. This idea has prompted financial markets to adjust the impact of environmental risks on long-term profitability (Leite & Cortez, 2015).

Due to increased awareness of climate change socially responsible investing is gaining acceptance in the financial sector. This phenomenon is becoming a mainstream idea in understanding the impact of ecological menaces can have on long-term profitability in financial markets. A 'socially responsible' investor is an investor who, when making investment decisions, takes into account the extent to which the project meets the criteria of social and environmental sustainability.

The environmental risks along with poor corporate governance and negative social practices damage a company's long-term value. The sustainable development of the corporation is achieved by combining actions and practices to promote responsibilities to society at the institutional, organisational and individual levels, creating social, environmental and economic value (Khan, 2019).

Companies follow a long-term socially responsible approach in running business because of market conditions or shareholder pressure. Integrating environmental, social and governance (ESG) factors into senior management decisions can deliver higher and more sustainable returns for shareholders in the future. Investors are becoming interested in integrating ESG factors into their investment strategy, with the ability to influence the potential long-term performance of their portfolio management (Nizam et al., 2019). Moreover, they encourage interaction with shareholders (Capelle-Blancard & Monjon, 2014).

Currently, one of the criteria for a company's attractiveness among investors is the presence in its development strategy of the focus on projects and technologies to alleviate global problems and find a way to solve them. Investors are becoming interested in integrating ESG factors into investment strategy because of the ability of potential companies to benefit significantly from eco-efficiency not only through lower costs, but also through the competitive advantage of being first movers and reducing overall risks (Delis et al., 2018).

The ESG projects are growing at a rapid pace around the world because regulators and policymakers have made environmental issues a top policy priority while the increased public awareness of ESG risks has been accelerated by recent coronavirus pandemic. The emergence of a generation of investors who prioritise non-financial factors alongside financial factors has fuelled growth of ESG funds.

In recent years the performance of ESG funds has attracted investor attention. During the COVID-19 sell-off ESG portfolios outperformed their traditional peers. This drives the biggest shift in the European asset and wealth management industry has ever experienced, empowering managers to drive change by playing a key role in mitigating climate risk (El Ghoul et al., 2018).

In the context of the financial crisis and severe volatility in financial markets, investors increasingly began to turn to new socially responsible forms of saving and increasing capital, a special case of which are climate or green bonds. A climate or green bond is a general name for bonds that are issued to finance projects aimed at solving environmental problems. In addition to the assessment of standard financial indicators, such as maturity, coupon, price and credit quality of the issuer, investors are able to assess the environmental goals of a specific project. It should be noted that bonds are one of the most common and convenient debt instruments and companies, non-profit organisations, municipal and federal authorities issue bonds when it is necessary to raise borrowed funds to complete certain tasks or projects.

Due to widespread adoption and support from investors and regulators, green bonds have managed to become one of the most sought-after sources of financing for green investments. The debut issue of green bonds took place in 2007 when the European Investment Bank introduced its Climate Awareness Bonds. With the adoption of the principles and standards, a new, certified stage in the development of green bonds began and continues up to this day. Total issuance of green, social and sustainability (GSS) bonds reached in 2022 around €2.2trn, based on data from Bloomberg New Energy Finance, while European Investment Bank's (EIB) issuance of climate awareness bond (CAB) and sustainability awareness bond (SAB) is approaching €60 billion, making it the largest GSS issuer in its peer group (EIB, 2022).

However, despite the relatively rapid growth, the volume of green bond trading remains significantly smaller than that of traditional bonds. This problem has not yet been sufficiently studied from a scientific point of view, and the academic literature on this issue is very heterogeneous. The overall volume of research lacks a common coordinated approach, and different authors often come to directly opposite conclusions. In this regard, conducting additional research on the prerequisites for the growth of the green bond market and the specifics of pricing on them is appropriate and necessary.

The Concepts of 'Green' Bonds and 'Green' Premium

The solution to environmental problems depends on the development of new technologies, often the implementation of quite costly projects that require significant funds. Therefore, the main problem in achieving global sustainable development goals is the financial gap between the necessary and actually implemented investments. To address this problem, national authorities around the world are taking active measures to mobilise private green capital. The growing demand for sustainable investments, as well as a number of initiatives at the national and supranational levels, has contributed to the emergence of new financial instruments that allow funds to be channelled into sustainable development projects (Leins, 2020; McKinsey, 2022).

As realising these ambitions requires unprecedented investment, one of the priorities for the global community is to find additional opportunities to mobilise green finance. Thus, according to Organisation for Economic Co-operation and Development (OECD) estimates, developing countries are short of about $4.2 trillion in annual investment required to achieve the 17 UN Sustainable Development Goals by 2030. The European Commission reports that just to achieve the goals of the Paris Agreement, the EU will require between 175 billion and 290 billion euros of annual investment over the next decades. It is estimated that nearly $9 trillion in annual sustainable and green investments will be needed to achieve carbon neutrality for the global economy by 2050.

One of these measures is the issue of green bonds, the funds raised from which are used to finance green projects. In the process of issuing of such bond an assessment of the environmental goals of a specific project is added to the standard indicators, such as price, coupon, maturity, and credit rating of the issuer. Experts from the International Capital Markets Association define 'green' bonds as any type of bond, the proceeds of which will be used exclusively to finance or refinance, partially or fully, new and existing green projects (Gianfrate & Peri, 2019). However, a relatively large share of green bonds comes from sectors exposed to environmental credit risks (Ehlers & Packer, 2017).

A climate bond is a general name for bonds that are issued to finance projects aimed at solving environmental problems. Projects that meet relevant national or international standards or certifications in the following areas are called 'green': (1) renewable energy; (2) energy efficiency; (3) prevention of pollution; (4) management of natural resources; (5) land use; (6) protecting biodiversity; (7) 'green' transport; (8) management of water resources; (9) climate change adaptation; (10) circular economy; and (11) environmentally friendly buildings (Tolliver et al., 2020).

This growth is explained by a number of reasons. Firstly, the advantages of green bonds, such as flexible coupon payment schedules, the possibility of long-term financing of green projects and other benefits from lower costs of debt securities. They allow municipalities to cover budget shortfalls in capital-intensive infrastructure financing schemes. Corporate issuers benefit from improved financial performance and lower coupon interest rates. Secondly, government measures stimulating 'green' investments, such as tax incentives and guarantees, as well as risk hedging because 'green' bonds are less sensitive to market volatility, protection from inflation, etc., have an impact. In addition, to obtain 'green' status. For their bonds, issuers must undergo special procedures to confirm compliance with established standards, and after their issue, regularly submit reports with information about their sustainability for interested parties. All this increases the transparency and attractiveness of this financial instrument. Finally, the positive environmental effects that 'green' bonds are actually aimed at achieving attract a wide range of 'socially responsible' investors (Tolliver et al., 2020).

Companies that adhere to socially and environmentally responsible practices receive economic benefits in the form of a lower cost of capital due to higher investor demand and lower risks (El Ghoul et al., 2016). An additional factor of investment attractiveness in green investments is the business reputation of a socially and environmentally responsible company (Boutin-Dufresne & Savaria, 2004). Thus, even taking into account the additional costs associated with the requirements of global exchanges, green bonds are relatively more convenient for issuers as they can reduce the cost of debt financing (Gianfrate & Peri, 2019).

The main advantage of green bonds over conventional ones is their relatively low cost. In some cases, even small differences in bond prices can have a significant impact on long-term sustainability (e.g., in the energy sector and large industrial facilities). Therefore, assessing the 'convenience' of green bonds in terms of the return to be paid to investors is of paramount importance (Gianfrate & Peri, 2019).

Moreover, in the modern world, the shift in emphasis from finance in the broad sense of the concept to narrower categories – green finance and sustainable development finance, gives corporations a new way to hedge future risks associated with environmental and social scandals. Thus, corporations that produce large amounts of environmental pollution, as well as those producing products and services related to weapons, nuclear technology, tobacco products, alcohol, gambling, medical cannabis products, etc., face higher risks of prosecution, systematic risks and risks of being blacklisted by institutional investors (Hong & Kacperczyk, 2009).

This raises questions about whether green bonds improve an issuer's credit rating, how issuing green bonds affects other debt instruments such as conventional bonds, and how authorities can encourage investors to invest in green bonds. The analysis showed that higher coupons paid on ordinary bonds more often lead to bankruptcy of issuers. Accordingly, lower-cost green investments contribute to greater financial strength of their issuers, which in turn improves their credit ratings and helps reduce the risk premium on bond yields. In addition, the attractiveness of 'green' bonds increases the quality and timely development of new technologies (Agliardi & Agliardi, 2019).

The high demand for these financial products reflects the interest of investors willing to finance green projects. The driving forces behind this demand are related to the image of investment funds as socially responsible institutions. In addition, a growing number of institutional investors are decarbonising their portfolios and redirecting funds to green investments as they view climate change as a growing threat to long-term economic growth (Gianfrate & Peri, 2019).

Although most green bonds are virtually identical to their so-called 'conventional' equivalents, it would be reasonable to expect the price and yield to be roughly the same. Nevertheless, there is a popular opinion in the financial community about the existence of 'green' premium, that is, the premium that the issuer of a bond receives for this very 'greenness' of a given security.

There is a bulk of the literature on the topic of green bonds particularly on 'green' premium, but there is no general approach for estimating the cost of capital for green investments. The most common technique is when the standard model is modified by adding a specific green premium to the investor's expected return. Although the majority of authors do not specify what this premium should be, the narrative most often implies that it should be positive, providing the investor with a higher return on investment in projects with additional 'green value' (Noh, 2019).

Research into the price differential between green and traditional bonds in global capital markets typically asks whether investors are willing to pay a premium for green bonds over conventional bonds, that is, whether the green label gives issuers an incentive to raise funds by issuing 'green' securities, and investors have the opportunity to diversify the return on their investments. Generally, the conclusion is that green securities can meet global green investment needs, so it is necessary to support the growth of the green investment market to mitigate climate change (Nanayakkara & Colombage, 2019).

The monetary value of certifying a green bond as compliant is beyond doubt, as is the generally more expensive issuance and servicing of green bonds. The question is which party, issuer, investor or third party will bear these costs. Arguably, if the cost of certification is borne by the issuer, then there is no green premium and green bond prices are equal to the prices of corresponding conventional bonds, as shown in a study of municipal bond initial offerings in the United States (Larcker & Watts, 2020). If the cost of certification is borne by the investor, in whole or in part, a green premium is observed and the price of green bonds is higher than the price of corresponding conventional bonds, as has been shown in studies of initial offerings (Ehlers & Packer, 2017; Zerbib, 2018).

It can also be assumed that investors value third-party certification and accept lower yields in this case (Baker et al., 2022). However, over time, in the secondary market, the yield of green bonds equals the yield of conventional bonds, as this may be due to at least two reasons in secondary market research. First, the cost of certification, if assumed by the investor as a premium to the bond's offering price, is spread out over time. Secondly, those investors who are not willing to overpay for the special status of the bond can buy a bond on the secondary market, while investors purposefully participate in the primary placement willing to pay a higher price for a green bond (Hachenberg & Schiereck, 2018).

Another finding is that the green bonds were on average priced at a premium to regular bonds when issued, but performed similarly in the secondary market over time. The main determinants of lower green bond yields are ratings and issuer type. This feature of the green bond market is explained by the fact that institutional investors have an accumulated positive reputation and a kind of positive green credit history. In contrast, the other companies with investments in green bonds may sometime violate covenants and may be regarded as more risky and less responsive to the specific requirements and preferences of green investors (Bachelet et al., 2019).

One of the obstacles is that the green investment sector has insufficient investment attractiveness. This problem is associated with the novelty of technology, the corresponding high risks and problems with the credit risks of borrowers and issuers (Kaminker & Stewart, 2012). In this regard, the role of the state in the processes of development of the green economy is to promote legislation on green and hybrid financing instruments, which reduce financial risks and the cost of financing for this sector (Braun & Hazelroth, 2015).

In many countries, there are major problems in the development of the green economy: a lack of expertise in the implementation of green investment projects, the volume of national capital markets is not large enough to finance the required volume of green investments, the sectors of green financial instruments in the capital market are experiencing liquidity problems, the cost of capital in the country is comparatively high; there are administrative barriers and high transaction costs for large institutional investors, etc. (Taghizadeh-Hesary & Yoshino, 2017).

It is argued that lower yield spreads for green bonds could compensate the issuer for the higher cost of issuing payment-related verification and third-party certification (Hachenberg & Schiereck, 2018). However, the existence of too large a negative yield premium for green bonds has the danger of disincentivizing green investors from sticking to their financial strategies (Zerbib, 2018).

The results of a number of empirical studies on the issue of determining the premium of green bonds compared to traditional ones have shown great contradictions and a lack of unity of opinions. Some studies find a green premium (Baker et al., 2022; Karpf & Mandel, 2018), some find a green discount (Hachenberg & Schiereck, 2018) and some simply claim that there is no premium (Larcker & Watts, 2020; Tang et al., 2020). At the same time, premiums vary greatly, ranging from a negative premium of 18 basis points (Ehlers & Packer, 2016) to a positive premium of 12 basis points (Bachelet et al., 2019).

Analysis of Index Strategies of Green Bond Exchange-traded Funds

Much of the academic research on green bonds focusses on the issue of pricing green bonds compared to conventional bonds. This study, unlike the above-mentioned, focusses on studying green bond ETFs and the study question is whether such funds have a 'green' premium or a 'green' discount.

One of the latest trends in private investing in the stock market is the index investing which can be characterised as investing financial resources in instruments that partially or completely duplicate various stock indices. This method of investment is passive in nature and does not require the active participation of the investor in managing his own investments. ETF is a financial instrument whose versatility lies in the fact that these funds can be used by a private investor, large asset managers, and an enterprise planning to place temporarily available funds (Lamothe & Seetohul, 2019).

The index investing is carried out mainly with the help of exchange-traded investment funds, ETFs, this is due primarily to the fact that exchange-traded funds provide a high level of diversification due to collective investment in assets combined in any index, as well as due to a wide coverage, the fund provides returns corresponding to a specific financial index (Lamothe & Seetohul, 2019).

The index ETP exactly repeats the structure of the stock index that underlies the fund. The main task of such an exchange-traded fund is to follow the index values as accurately as possible. This gives a great advantage to the investor in clearly diversifying investor's investments, allowing to know exactly where and in what proportion the funds are invested. However, this same factor can also work at a loss: in situations where the market falls, the ETP will completely replicate the market, and in the case of managed funds, the fall, as a rule, is limited by the actions of managers. Bond ETFs, just like equity funds, follow the structure and movement of country or global bond indices.

ESG mutual funds are becoming increasingly popular among investors as they take into account a wide range of ESG factors that are consistent with their objectives and strategies when selecting investments. The performance of ESG funds in different economic scenarios is determined by comparing their returns with those of traditional funds over the business cycle, both in periods of growth and decline, and assessing the correlation with the business cycle.

Different researchers may understand the term 'premium' to be opposite entities: either a premium as a premium to the price and a lower profitability, or a premium as a premium to the profitability and a lower price. In this study, the term 'green premium' refers to the higher returns of a green bond fund compared to corresponding conventional bond funds. The lower yield of a green bond fund is what the term 'green discount' refers. In addition, the difference when the price of a green bond fund is higher than the NAV is also called the green premium and when the price of a green bond fund is lower than the NAV is also called the green discount.

Approaches and Methodology to Measuring the 'Green' Premium

The purpose of this study is to empirically confirm or refute the existence of a green premium by determining the performance of a green fund by comparing their returns with returns of conventional bond funds. This study tries to prove the existence or absence of a green premium by utilising two approaches. The first method uses various green bond fund returns characteristics from the CAPM. The second approach uses analysis of the ratios of the price of green ETF to its NAV and compares it with the dynamics of market benchmark indices.

For the first approach such ETF return characteristics as annualised return and volatility, beta and Jensen's alpha, as well as measures of risk-adjusted performance, such as Sharpe ratio, M2 ratio, and value at risk which are widely used in the literature for evaluation of the performance of actively managed portfolios (Ambler et al., 2001) are calculated and analysed.

The most commonly used investment performance indicator in the professional investment analyst community is the Sharpe ratio, which evaluates the risk-adjusted return on a financial instrument, that is, it evaluates the adequacy of obtaining additional return with an increase in risk by one unit. Since differences in risk perception can lead to an incorrect assessment of the return and the chosen investment strategy, the Sharpe ratio, using excess return and standard deviation, ensures the comparability of assets with different risks. The Sharpe ratio also makes it possible to compare the performance of funds and their benchmark indices. Mathematically, the Sharpe ratio is calculated as follows:

$$\mathrm{SR} = (R_I - R_F)/\sigma_I,$$

where R_I is the return of the asset, R_F is the risk-free return and σ_I is the standard deviation, that is, the risk, of the asset.

As a basic measure of risk-adjusted return, the Sharpe ratio has its drawbacks. If the return is associated with negative asymmetry, it underestimates the risk. To overcome the lack of actual numerical comparability of the Sharpe ratio the Modigliani–Modigliani ratio, or M2, is often used, which evaluates the risk-adjusted annual performance of a portfolio relative to a market benchmark, thus showing how effective the fund was in relation to the market. Mathematically, the M2 coefficient is calculated as follows:

$$\mathrm{M2} = (R_I - R_F)\,\sigma_M/\sigma_I + R_F,$$

where σ_I is the standard deviation of the return of the asset, that is, the risk of the asset, and σ_M is the standard deviation the of the return of the market, that is, the risk of the market.

The risk-adjusted ratios are generally not enough to determine how efficient the financial instruments are relative to each other. Hence, the alpha and beta values calculated using the univariate capitalization-weighted (CAP-based) index model should also be determined. However, these indicators are sensitive to the chosen benchmarks and determine the portfolio manager's ability to select funds and manage the movement of funds in the market.

Beta from the CAPM model estimates systematic or non-diversifiable market risk, that is, the expected premium for an investor taking market risk. Mathematically, beta is calculated as follows:

$$\beta_I = \mathrm{cov}(R_I, R_M)/\mathrm{var}(R_M).$$

Jensen's alpha is another CAPM indicator, which is used to determine the excess return of a portfolio expressed as the difference between the fund's average return and the market return, that is, it estimates how much extra return the portfolio has earned over and above the expected return (Dayaratne et al., 2010). Mathematically, Jensen's alpha is calculated as follows:

$$\alpha Ji = E(R_I) - [R_F + \beta_I (E(R_M) - R_F)],$$

where αJi is the excess return, $E(R_I)$ is the theoretical expected return obtained using CAPM. β_I is beta from the CAPM model.

A positive Jensen's alpha indicates that an actively managed fund outperforms the index.

Value at risk calculates the potential loss of an investment within a given timeframe and confidence level. It takes into account only negative fluctuations and the shape of the distribution, but depends on the choice of significance level for the individual investor (Hendricks, 1996). Although there are several different methods for calculating VaR, the historical method is the simplest. Mathematically, historical VaR is calculated as follows:

$$\text{VaR} = V_M (V_I / V_{(I-1)}),$$

where M is the number of days from which historical data is taken, V_I is the number of variables on the day I.

The second approach to the analysis of return of ETFs is based on the fact that funds are traded on an exchange and they have a current market price, which may be more or less than its actual value, which is measured by the NAV at the end of each day and the intraday NAV (iNAV) at midday. In relatively calm markets, ETF prices and NAV tend to remain close. However, when financial markets become more volatile, ETF prices reflect changes in market sentiment more quickly, while NAV may take longer to adjust, resulting in premiums and discounts. If the ETF's price is above its NAV, the ETF is said to be trading at a 'premium', and conversely, if the ETF's price is below its NAV, the ETF is said to be trading at a 'discount'. This can happen throughout the entire trading day because the ETF and its underlying securities are actually two separate pools of liquidity that are loosely coupled. Sometimes charts showing premiums and discounts can give the impression of a significant price change when a transaction occurs. However, as a rule, premiums and discounts are short-lived (Kreis & Licht, 2018).

An ETF typically underperforms its benchmark index due to a variety of factors, including the fund's total expense ratio (TER), trade execution costs, management fees, cash drag, exchange rate volatility and rebalancing costs, but can end up in positive territory, if it outperforms its index, for example, as a result of gains from stock lending. If optimistic investors begin to aggressively bid up the price of an ETF to more than their underlying securities, the ETF's price may rise faster than the price of its underlying securities and therefore it may trade at a premium. Likewise, if pessimistic investors aggressively sell an ETF largely than its underlying securities, the ETF may trade at a discount (Lamothe & Seetohul, 2019).

Since most exchange-traded funds are passive instruments that seek to track the performance of their chosen benchmark, which could be the S&P 500 or similar, as well as a specially created index of securities of companies related to green investments, there are fund performance metrics such as tracking error and tracking differential. Tracking errors and tracking differences provide insight into a passive mutual fund's ability to replicate its benchmark index. Investors should consider both metrics when assessing the performance of a passive fund and its ability to deliver desired investment results.

Tracking error measures the level of consistency or discrepancy between the performance of a passive mutual fund (index fund or ETF) and its target index and provides insight into return volatility by measuring the persistence of a portfolio's tracking differential over time. Tracking error is mathematically calculated as the annual standard deviation of the difference in return between a passive fund and its underlying index:

$$\mathrm{TE} = \sqrt{(\Sigma(r_i - r_b)^2/(n-1))},$$

where r_i is daily return of the fund portfolio and r_b is daily return of the reference index.

Tracking error is usually expressed as a percentage, which indicates the variability of a fund's performance relative to the index over a specified period. A higher tracking error suggests that a passive fund deviates more from its benchmark, resulting in a larger difference in performance. This indicates that the fund's returns are less predictable and may differ significantly from the performance of the benchmark it 'tracks'. This may arise due to factors such as the fund's additional expenses as well as how closely the fund manager can replicate the weighting of stocks in an index. Thus, a fund with less tracking error is more desirable but tracking error alone does not determine the overall quality of a passive fund.

In order to determine whether there are statistically significant differences in the central tendency of multiple independent samples another nonparametric statistical test should be applied. The Kruskal–Wallis test is used in the context of time series data, for comparing groups representing different time intervals within the series as an indicator of differences in medians especially when distributions are similar because differences in mean ranks imply differences in medians.

The rationale of using the Kruskal–Wallis test is that if the distributions are similar, ordinal variables are sufficient, since non-parametric tests do not use differences in values, but ranks of the data within these intervals. Therefore, the Kruskal–Wallis test is also often called the one-way analysis of variance on ranks test.

The test statistic is given by

$$H = (N-1)\, g\Sigma_{\,i=1}(r_{\,i-r})^2/g\Sigma_{i=1\ ni}\,\Sigma_{j=1}\,(r_{ij}-r)^2,$$

where N is the total number of observations across all groups, g is the number of groups, n_i is the number of observations in group i, r_{ij} is the rank (among all observations) of observation j from group i, r_i is the average rank of all observations in group i is the average of all the r_{ij}.

This question position then leads to the null and alternative hypotheses between three or more groups in a data set. The null hypothesis is that all independent samples have the same central tendency and therefore come from the same population. The alternative hypothesis is that at least one of the independent samples does not have the same central tendency as the other samples and therefore comes from a different population. A low *p* value suggests that there are significant differences between groups, warranting the presence.

Data Characteristics

The history of green bonds covers more than 15 years and during this period, a sufficient amount of material for research has been accumulated. At the same time, the complexity of assessment lies in the significant diversity of these tools, as well as methods and practices for presenting results.

Data for analysis in this study were collected from several public databases: Euronext, J.P. Morgan Asset Management, Amundi Asset Management, Yahoo Finance, S&P. The databases consist of time series based on the returns of exchange trading of primary investment funds. An exceptional focus for this asset class is bond funds, both climate or green and conventional.

The maximum period of consideration for bond funds is 5 years and the minimum is a year. But for the purpose of this study to assess the profitability, the activities of the funds for the last two years, from April 2022 to April 2024, are considered, and to assess the difference in the price of the asset and its NAV, the periods from issue date to April 2024.

The Euronext database was used to check the presence of a green premium based on the yield estimation method. The Euronext database lists 26 green bond funds identified as green by Environmental Finance, meaning that green bonds made up at least half of their weighting, met time requirements and had historical data available.

The study set includes a total of nine green bond funds and 11 conventional bond funds of the same issuer for comparison. The launch date, assets value and TER of the green bond funds included in the analysis are shown in Table 11.1.

Determination of the green premium based on a comparison of price and NAV of the fund used data from J.P. Morgan Asset Management. Here are four green funds available, and four more conventional bond funds selected for comparison. Fund launch, ongoing charge and the value of fund assets of the green bond funds included in the analysis are shown in Table 11.2.

All of the funds listed are denominated in euros because, although US dollar bonds have the largest weight in the funds, they are traded on European exchanges. In Euro funds, US dollar bonds are not classified separately in the analysis because each portfolio is geographically diversified and includes both corporate and government bonds.

The study used a matching index matching method, in which a target fund or target group of green bond funds is compared with a reference fund or conventional bond funds issued by the same issuer. The matching index shows the quality of investment in green bond funds and how green bond funds compare favourably with conventional funds.

The most accurate results would be obtained if it were possible to track the performance of each bond fund first as a conventional fund and then as a green

Table 11.1. Green Bond Funds.

	Launch Date	Assets Value	TER (%)
Lyxor Green Bond (DR) UCITS ETF	2 March 2017	33.3	0.25
BNP Paribas Easy FTSE EPRA Nareit Developed Europe EX UK Green	6 November 2019	Approximately 70.0	0.4
Lyxor Euro Government Green Bond (DR) UCITS ETF	6 July 2021	25.5	0.2
Lyxor Corporate Green Bond (DR) UCITS ETF	24 August 2021	52.3	0.2
Franklin Euro Green Bond UCITS ETF	15 September 2021	36.5	0.18
BNP Paribas Easy FTSE EPRA Nareit Global Developed Green CTB UCITS ETF	17 March 2022	Approximately 100.0	0.4
BNP Paribas Easy JPM ESG Green Social and Sustainability IG EUR Bond UCITS ETF	7 April 2022	Approximately 100.0	0.25
Ishares € Green Bond UCITS ETF	17 October 2020	40.0	0.2
JPM Green Soc Sust Bond UCITS ETF	16 February 2022	65.3	0.25

Source: Euronext, Yahoo Finance, S&P, Amundi.

fund. Since this is impossible, control groups of issuers were selected in such a way that the conventional bond funds they issued met the requirements for green bonds in most respects. To evaluate different selection methods, the trade-off between the number of matching characteristics and their quality was taken into account.

In determining the return on an investment portfolio, standard portfolios of the relevant financial instruments are used as a benchmark. The choice of index is an important task since it can significantly affect the assessment of the return on the portfolio. For the purposes of this study, two indices were selected, namely the Global Securities Market Index (S&P500) and the S&P Green Bond Market Index (S&PGBI).

Measuring the Performance of Green Bond Funds

Within the framework of the first approach the first group of green bonds ETFs with ordinary bonds ETFs, the average annual return and average annual volatility adjusted to the average number of trading days (252) were obtained. On that basis, the main coefficients of the investment performance characteristics of nine

Table 11.2. Green Bond Funds NAV.

	Fund Launch	Fund Assets	Ongoing Charge (%)
Green Social Sustainable Bond **ETF**	12 October 2018	36.5	0.32
Corporate Bond 1–5-Year Research Enhanced Index (ESG) **UCITS ETF**	6 December 2018	270.3	0.04
Corporate Bond Research Enhanced Index ESG ETF	23 February 2023	122.5	0.04
Corporate Bond Research Enhanced Index (ESG) UCITS ETF	22 January 2021	53.2	0.19

Source: J.P. Morgan Asset Management, Yahoo Finance, S&P.

green bond funds and 11 ordinary bond funds included in the study were calculated. The results of a comparative analysis are presented in Table 11.3.

All green bond funds analysed in this study show positive returns, while two of the seven selected conventional bond funds show negative returns. At the same time, the maximum returns of green bond funds were lower than those of the conventional bond funds analysed. At the same time, the underlying indices were either negative or quite low, and therefore all of them outperformed the market relative to any benchmark index. The average return of green bond funds was 8.2%, exceeding not only the risk-free return of 3%, but also exceeding the benchmark index return of about 5%.

As follows from the analysis, the higher returns of green bond funds are associated with greater risk, and the green bond fund with the highest return bears the first largest risk. Thus, the results of the study show that although green bond funds are better investments, they are riskier than conventional bond funds, but

Table 11.3. Comparative Analysis of Investment Performance of Bond ETFs.

	Green Bonds ETFs				Ordinary Bonds ETFs			
	Min	**Max**	**Median**	**Mean**	**Min**	**Max**	**Median**	**Mean**
Annualized return	0.009	0.216	0.040	0.082	–0.020	0.060	0.018	0.019
Annualised volatility	0.054	0.290	0.080	0.127	0.039	0.061	0.052	0.051
Sharpe ratio	–0.384	0.623	0.134	0.202	–1.222	–0.182	–0.751	–0.727
M2	–0.043	0.148	0.055	0.068	–0.040	0.057	0.020	0.014
Beta	0.000	0.012	0.002	0.005	0.002	1.929	0.082	0.524
Jensen alpha	–0.021	0.186	0.010	0.052	–0.050	0.016	–0.013	–0.015
Value at risk	0.006	0.030	0.008	0.013	0.039	0.061	0.052	0.002

Source: Euronext, Yahoo Finance, S&P.

less risky than the benchmark index. The S&P500 World Index has a higher standard deviation than the selected green bond funds, which is explained by the fact that stocks are a riskier asset than bonds. The risk and return indicators of the studied green bond funds are much closer to those of the S&PGBI.

This study examines the characteristics obtained from the Sharpe ratio and M2 ratio. Five out of seven green bond funds have positive Sharpe ratios. This means that most green bond funds exceed the risk-free return. The Sharpe ratio of green bond funds is 0.20 and the M2 ratio is 0.07, which is ahead of conventional bond funds. In addition, the Beta and Alpha coefficients show that the green bond fund has virtually no market risk, and also significantly improves the active management indicators. They also outperform green bond funds in terms of value at risk.

The second group of green bonds ETFs and their ordinary bonds analogues are analysed comparing the price to NAV ratio. To graphically compare each pair of the ETFs correctly the lesser period of the two is chosen so that number of trading days are the same. The results are presented in Fig. 11.1, green bonds ETFs are on the left side, ordinary bonds ETFs are on the right side.

A graphical comparative analysis of various funds gives an idea of the trajectory of the price to NAV ratio, from which we can draw a conclusion about the differences both between different categories of funds, and between funds of the same category. However, it does not allow making an unambiguous conclusion about the presence of a green premium or discount due to the different lengths of the time series.

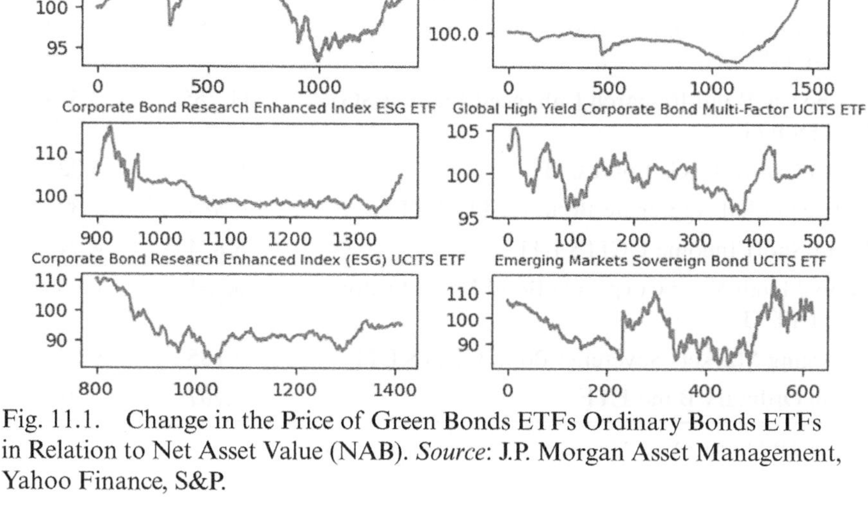

Fig. 11.1. Change in the Price of Green Bonds ETFs Ordinary Bonds ETFs in Relation to Net Asset Value (NAB). *Source*: J.P. Morgan Asset Management, Yahoo Finance, S&P.

To test the divergence between the price behaviour of green bonds ETFs and the price behaviour of a benchmark Tracking Error (TE) indicator is calculated. Tracking error for second group of green bonds ETFs and their ordinary counterparts is reported as a standard deviation percentage difference for both S&P500 and S&PGBI benchmarks, which reports the difference between the return an investor receives and that of the benchmark. In general, the closer both indicators are to zero, the better a passive ETF replicates its underlying index. The results of tracking error test are presented in Table 11.4.

As follows from the test results, green bond funds perform worse than regular funds in tracking general index but comparatively better in relation to the specialised benchmark. There are many risk factors that can lead to higher tracking error, including fees that can affect returns, rebalancing costs, and un-invested cash remaining in the fund at the end of the day's trading.

Going further the Kruskal–Wallis test was conducted to test whether there is similar pattern in ETFs price to NAV performance between each green bond fund and its ordinary counterpart. The results of the Kruskal–Wallis test are presented in Table 11.5.

The results of Kruskal–Wallis test show that there was a significant difference between different categories of funds. The test results indicate that the samples do not come from the same distribution and p value associated with the test statistic is below the selected significance level, therefore, given the available data, the null hypothesis of the pairwise similarity of funds is rejected.

Table 11.4. Tracking Error Test Results.

	TE S & P500	**TE S & PGBI**
Green Social Sustainable Bond ETF	1.675	0.578
Corporate Bond 1–5-Year Research Enhanced Index (ESG) **UCITS ETF**	8.336	2.524
Corporate Bond Research Enhanced Index ESG ETF	4.497	1.912
Corporate Bond Research Enhanced Index (ESG) UCITS ETF	11.755	3.529
Mean Green (ESG) Bond ETF	6.566	3.221
Active Global Aggregate Bond UCITS ETF	5.883	7.321
Ultra-Short Income UCITS ETF	3.824	4.041
Global High Yield Corporate Bond Multi-Factor UCITS ETF	3.735	6.963
Emerging Markets Sovereign Bond UCITS ETF	6.185	9.875
Mean Ordinary Bond ETF	4.907	8.915

Source: J.P. Morgan Asset Management, Yahoo Finance, S&P.

Table 11.5. Kruskal–Wallis Test Results.

Green Bonds ETF	Ordinary Bonds ETF	Statistic	p-value
Green Social Sustainable Bond ETF	Active Global Aggregate Bond UCITS ETF	5.713	0.017
Corporate Bond 1–5-Year Research Enhanced Index (ESG) UCITS ETF	Ultra-Short Income UCITS ETF	8.175	0.004
Corporate Bond Research Enhanced Index ESG ETF	Global High Yield Corporate Bond Multi-Factor UCITS ETF	149.617	0.000
Corporate Bond Research Enhanced Index (ESG) UCITS ETF	Emerging Markets Sovereign Bond UCITS ETF	9.740	0.002

Source: J.P. Morgan Asset Management, Yahoo Finance, S&P.

To determine the total premium and discount based on the ratio of a fund's price to its NAV, it is necessary to analyse the number of periods in which the fund trades above the NAV and the number of periods in which the fund trades below the NAV. In addition, the size of the deviation must be taken into account. The summary statistics of ETFs trading are presented in Table 11.6.

Table 11.6. Summary Statistics of ETFs Trading, Price/NAV.

	Number of Positive	Number of Negative	Percentage of Positive	Percentage of Negative	Mean Positive	Mean Negative
GSSB	39	87	31	69	0.449	–1.185
C15REESG	115	263	30	70	0.388	–0.352
CBREESG	225	405	36	64	1.544	–0.365
CBREESGUCITS	334	548	38	62	3.742	–5.015
Mean Green ESG Bond	178	326	34	66	1.531	–1.729
AGAB	40	212	16	84	0.204	–2.082
USI	123	381	24	76	0.129	–1.148
GHYCBMFI	272	484	36	64	2.238	–2.736
EMSB	353	655	35	65	1.044	–3.158
Mean ordinary bond	197	433	28	72	0.903	–2.281

Source: J.P. Morgan Asset Management, Yahoo Finance, S&P.

All the studied funds, both green and conventional, trade at a discount most of the time, with green bond funds having the best ratio of premium to discount periods. They also have less variability within their category. In addition, the average premium and discount for green bond funds are approximately the same, while for conventional bond funds, the discount is on average three times larger than the premium.

Conclusion

The consequences of climate change indicate that a significant part of the resources of the global financial system must be directed to preventing climate catastrophe. Limited fiscal and banking capacity has led to the emergence of new ways to attract private funds to gradually decarbonise the global economy. The emergence of 'green' or climate bonds, on the one hand, is determined by the same factors as the issue of conventional bonds. On the other hand, the focus of funds raised with their help on the implementation of 'green' projects indicates the importance of environmental factors and initiatives within the framework of the Paris Agreement. Climate bonds are a tool through which economically developed countries and many developing countries attract significant amounts of investment to implement projects aimed at preserving the environment.

Currently, the green bond market is a young but dynamically developing structure of the financial sector. In recent years, there has been a trend in the world towards an increase in the importance of climate bond markets; the creation of a financial instrument significantly contributes to solving the problem of financing environmental projects with a developed repayment mechanism. The constant increase in the size of the green bond market confirms the enormous potential of this financial instrument. However, understanding the fundamental factors driving the growth of green bond issuance is critical to advancing the global sustainability investment agenda.

Analysis of the use of such a tool for attracting investments in green projects, such as green bonds and green bond ETFs, carried out on the basis of an available database, using an assessment of risk-adjusted returns, and the ratio of the fund price to its net worth, suggest that green bond funds command a premium over conventional bond funds. At the same time, limited data limits both a broader formulation of the existence of the 'green' premium and the possibility of more accurately determining its size.

References

Agliardi, E., & Agliardi, R. (2019). Financing environmentally-sustainable projects with green bonds. *Environment and Development Economics*, *24*(6), 608–623.

Ambler, T., Kokkinaki, F., Puntoni, S., & Riley, D. (2001). *Assessing market performance: The current state of metrics* [Working Paper No. 01-903]. Center for Marketing.

Bachelet, M. J., Becchetti, L., & Manfredonia, S. (2019). The green bonds premium puzzle: The role of issuer characteristics and third-party verification. *Sustainability*, *11*(4), 1098.

Baker, M., Bergstresser, D., Serafeim, G., & Wurgler, J. (2022). The pricing and ownership of US green bonds. *Annual Review of Financial Economics*, *14*, 415–437.

Boutin-Dufresne, F., & Savaria, P. (2004). Corporate social responsibility and financial risk. *The Journal of Investing, 13*(1), 57–66.

Braun, G., & Hazelroth, S. (2015). Energy infrastructure finance: Local dollars for local energy. *The Electricity Journal, 28*(5), 6–21.

Capelle-Blancard, G., & Monjon, S. (2014). The performance of socially responsible funds: Does the screening process matter? *European Financial Management, 20*(3), 494–520.

Dayaratne, D. A. I., Dharmaratne, D. G., & Harris, S. A. (2010). Measuring the risk and performance in plantation sector using CAPM based Jensen's alpha. *Sabaragamuwa University Journal, 6*(1), 68–81.

Delis, M., De Greiff, K., & Ongena, S. (2018). *Being stranded on the carbon bubble? Climate policy risk and the pricing of bank loans* [Research Paper No. 8-10]. SFI.

Gianfrate, G., & Peri, M. (2019). The green advantage: Exploring the convenience of issuing green bonds. *Journal of Cleaner Production, 219*, 127–135.

Ehlers, T., & Packer, F. (2016). *Green bonds–certification, shades of green and environmental risks*. Bank for International Settlements.

Ehlers, T., & Packer, F. (2017, September). *Green bond finance and certification. BIS Quarterly Review*. https://ssrn.com/abstract=3042378

El Ghoul, S., Guedhami, O., Kim, H., & Park, K. (2018). Corporate environmental responsibility and the cost of capital: International evidence. *Journal of Business Ethics, 149*, 335–361.

European Investment Bank (EIB). (2022). *15 years of EIB green bonds: leading sustainable investment from niche to mainstream*. https://www.eib.org/en/press/all/2022-308-15-years-of-eib-green-bonds-leading-sustainable-investment-from-niche-to-mainstream#:~:text=On%20July%205th%202007,of%20social%20and%20sustainability%20bonds

Hachenberg, B., & Schiereck, D. (2018). Are green bonds priced differently from conventional bonds? *Journal of Asset Management, 19*, 371–383.

Hendricks, D. (1996). Evaluation of value-at-risk models using historical data. *Economic Policy Review, 2*(1), 32.

Hong, H., & Kacperczyk, M. (2009). The price of sin: The effects of social norms on markets. *Journal of Financial Economics, 93*(1), 15–36.

Kaminker, C., & Stewart, F. (2012). *The role of institutional investors in financing clean energy* [OECD Working Papers on Finance, Insurance and Private Pensions 23]. OECD Publishing.

Karpf, A., & Mandel, A. (2018). The changing value of the 'green' label on the US municipal bond market. *Nature Climate Change, 8*(2), 161–165.

Khan, M. (2019). Corporate governance, ESG, and stock returns around the world. *Financial Analysts Journal, 75*(4), 103–123.

Kreis, Y., & Licht, J. W. (2018). Trading on ETF mispricings. *Managerial Finance, 44*(3), 357–373.

Lamothe, C., & Seetohul, Y. (2019). *Deviations between ETF prices & their net asset value* [Master's thesis, Simon Fraser University].

Larcker, D. F., &, E. M. (2020). Where's the greenium? *Journal of Accounting and Economics, 69*(2–3), 101312.

Leins, S. (2020). 'Responsible investment': ESG and the post-crisis ethical order. *Economy and Society, 49*(1), 71–91. https://doi.org/10.1080/03085147.2020.1702414

Leite, P., & Cortez, M. C. (2015). Performance of European socially responsible funds during market crises: Evidence from France. *International Review of Financial Analysis, 40*, 132–141.

McKinsey. (2022). *Environmental, social, and governance (ESG) report*. https://www.mckinsey.com/spcontent/bespoke/esg-2023-sean/pdfs/esg-report-2022-aw6-v12-final.pdf

Nanayakkara, M., & Colombage, S. (2019). Do investors in green bond market pay a premium? Global evidence. *Applied Economics, 51*(40), 4425–4437.

Nizam, E., Ng, A., Dewandaru, G., Nagayev, R., & Nkoba, M. A. (2019). The impact of social and environmental sustainability on financial performance: A global analysis of the banking sector. *Journal of Multinational Financial Management*, *49*, 35–53

Noh, Y. (2019). The effects of corporate green efforts for sustainability: An event study approach. *Sustainability*, *11*(15), 4073.

Taghizadeh-Hesary, F., & Yoshino, N. (2018). Assessment of the channels of transmission of oil price fluctuations to the economy. *Argumenta Oeconomica*, *41*(2), 5–24.

Tang, D. Y., & Zhang, Y. (2020). Do shareholders benefit from green bonds? *Journal of Corporate Finance*, *61*, 101427.

Tolliver, C., Keeley, A. R., & Managi, S. (2020). Policy targets behind green bonds for renewable energy: Do climate commitments matter? *Technological Forecasting and Social Change*, *157*, 120051.

Zerbib, O. D. (2019). The effect of pro-environmental preferences on bond prices: Evidence from green bonds. *Journal of Banking & Finance*, *98*, 39–60.

Chapter 12

Green Growth Policy in Visegrad: Key Drivers from an Economic and Non-economic Perspective

Nazrin Akhundzada and Vusal Ahmadov

Azerbaijan State University of Economics, Baku, Azerbaijan

Abstract

Purpose: This chapter evaluates the state of the implementation of the green growth policies in the Visegrad countries. The authors examine the main determinants of the transition to a green economy.

Need for the study: Conventional economic growth, based on fossil fuel and the extensive use of other natural resources, has created many environmental problems. The current industry-based economic growth in the Visegrad countries is not exempt from these challenges. Therefore, a transition from the current economic growth system in the Visegrad countries to a green growth system is essential.

Methodology: After qualitative analysis of green growth policies, the study applies panel Fully Modified OLS (FMOLS) to estimate the effects of environmental policy strictness, carbon taxes, green finance on greenhouse gas (GHG) emission, the share of renewable energy in total energy consumption, material productivity and green patents.

Findings: The European Union (EU) requirements are the primary motivation for implementing green growth policies in the Visegrad countries. Carbon taxes do not have a sizable effect on GHG emissions or increasing the share of renewable energy consumption. However, green finance has a small positive effect on the number of green patents and material productivity.

Sustainable Development and Green Innovation: Managing Risk through Interdisciplinary Approaches and Policy Strategies, 257–273

Published under exclusive licence by Emerald Publishing Limited
doi:10.1108/978-1-83608-462-420251012

Practical implications: The results of this study can guide policymakers in better formulating a green transition strategy for the Visegrad countries. Green technology is the ultimate driver of green growth. This study's findings highlight that government financial support is crucial for developing new green technologies and implementation of existing technologies for mass production.

Keywords: Green economy; Visegrad; economic growth; green technology; pollution; fossil fuels; energy demand

JEL codes: Q40; Q50; R11

Introduction

Socio-economic development is accompanied by interdependent relationships not only between economic and social dimensions but also between environmental and political ones. Nowadays, one of the key factors essential for ensuring sustainable development is the transition to a green economy. Many countries around the world are facing environmental challenges that are complex and difficult to address. As a part of the EU, the transition to a green economy has been at the forefront of the agenda for the Visegrad countries. The Visegrad economies are specialised in industrial production, which tends to be more polluting and heavily dependent on fossil fuel imports. Given these considerations, the green transition holds particular importance for the Visegrad countries.

The decarbonisation of economy can be achieved through the implementation of various green policies. The most commonly applied policies focus on issues such as promotion of clean technologies, the regulation of energy consumption and the increased use of renewable energy sources. The green economy is viewed as a new development path that promotes higher standards of living while ensuring efficient use of natural resources (Dziekański et al., 2023).

Rising levels of pollution caused by carbon dioxide emissions and other harmful substances, excessive waste generation, and unsustainable use of natural resources are leading to environmental degradation and exacerbating climate change. Compared to conventional economic models that suggest a trade-off between efficiency and equity in allocation of resources, circular economy leans on adaptation of three principles, namely reduction, reuse and recycling.

The degree of success transitioning to a green economy can vary significantly across nations. Some countries may severely lag behind, while others substantially might go ahead in terms of green performance. Several international agreements have been accepted by many nations to mitigate the consequences of climate change. The Paris Agreement, which came into the force since 2016, aims to limit global warming to 1.5°C and reduce GHG emissions by 43% by 2030. Additionally, developed countries are expected to provide financial aid to more vulnerable countries to support their green transitions. In the context of the green transition, policymakers primarily advocate for shifting from the fossil fuels to renewable energy sources.

This chapter investigates the effectiveness of green growth policies in facilitating the transition to a green economy in Visegrad countries. The study evaluates the impact of green growth policies in three categories: market-based instruments, non-market-based instruments and technology policies. A regression model is used to estimate the effects of green growth policies on GHG emission, the share of renewable energy and material productivity in the Visegrad countries.

The Literature Review section introduces the theoretical framework of this study and gives a brief overview of state of green transition in the Visegrad countries. The data and methodology and discussion of finding are stated in the Green Growth Policy in Visegrad Group: Overview section. The Conclusion section concludes and gives policy recommendations.

Literature Review

Most green growth strategies focus on reducing pollution and GHG emissions while coordinating energy demand. The efficient use of energy through new technologies is one of the key requirements for controlling energy consumption. Among other objectives, it is important to highlight the adoption of fuel-efficient and hybrid cars as well as effective waste management. At the same time, a green transition is closely linked to significant changes in social behaviour.

There are several recognised channels through which green policies can contribute to growth (World Bank, 2012). Three of them are the following:

- Green policies foster availability of resources. Better management of physical, human and natural resources can increase productivity.
- Green policies can improve efficiency. For instance, imposition of environmental taxes or congestion taxes can help to finance other environmental projects.
- Green policies promote innovation. This process refers to stimulation of innovative solutions by encouraging patents and increasing spending on R&D.

Furthermore, green growth policies also influence other non-growth dimensions such as job creation, poverty reduction and resilience to environmental shocks. However, despite being both efficient and necessary, the pace of adjustment in the global economy towards green growth is slower than expected. Many countries face serious challenges in achieving climate neutrality. Conflicts of interest often arise due to presence of market failures involving companies and institutions with political side and financial obstacles. A key issue is that the factors such as labour, capital and agglomeration effects tend to weigh more heavily in firms' decision-making processes than environmental policies, which means green growth cannot fully replace them. So-called growth policies that ensure sustainability of financial system and prosperity of business environment may not be fully substitutable by green growth policies. Conversely, economic activity accompanied by environmental degradation results in the depletion of natural resources and threatens the welfare of future generations.

Before moving to a regional analysis of the Visegrad Group, we reconsider the overall framework required for sustainable development by searching for and examining the possible determinants of the transition to a green economy.

Effective material productivity helps to avoid resource waste and reduce detrimental impacts on the environment. The major challenge to successful implementation is the necessity of ensuring that materials are used effectively across all stages, starting from extraction to disposal. As most materials end up as waste, waste management becomes crucial. Overall, there is an upward trend for municipal waste generation in OECD countries.

A low-carbon economy entails the reduction of waste that damages the environment. One approach that can be applied to achieve this goal is zero waste. In this context, waste illustrates the inefficiency and misuse of resources in the region, generated by production and consumption activities. The zero waste approach must follow certain rules, commonly referred to as 5Rs: refuse, reduce, reuse, recycle and compost (rot) (Dziekański et al, 2023). The authors found a significant relationship between households' actions, such as consumption, reuse and recovery actions and environmental protection outcomes, including food management and zero waste concept based on analysis of data from Poland, Slovakia and Ukraine.

OECD (2017) explores a set of indicators illustrating progress towards green growth. One set of indicators captures environmental and resource productivity. These determinants evaluate the level of efficiency achieved in the usage of energy, other natural resources, and environmental services. According to the provided interpretation, resource productivity represents output per unit of CO_2 emitted or total primary energy supplied. In most cases, these indicators are related to the production-based category. Another set of indicators that can be considered for tracking the success of green transition is the stock of renewable and non-renewable natural resources. The next group of factors focusses on economic opportunities and relevant policy responses, particularly in terms of regulation. This group also highlights the importance of technology and innovation in ensuring green growth and achieving investments that align with environmental objectives.

Long-term sustainable growth requires the promotion of innovative solutions that integrate environmental considerations. Weak enforcement of environmental regulations is often associated with low recognition of environmental issues. On the other hand, good institutional quality facilitates the reduction of carbon emissions by implementing effective regulatory policies. Furthermore, various economic tools and policies such as taxation, carbon pricing and transfers can accelerate the transition to a green economy.

Traditional growth theories have not considered the environment as a factor of economic growth (Brock & Taylor, 2010; Nordhaus, 1974; Smulders, 1999). However, Brock and Taylor (2005) introduce the *green Solow model*, which incorporates the environment as a factor in economic growth. This modified version of the classic growth model recognises the environment as a limiting factor for economic growth. The environment acts as a limiting factor due to its finite capacity to provide resources and absorb waste. Environmental assets are public goods and are inherently associated with market failures. Markets for environmental goods cannot achieve social optimality. The depletion of environmental assets by the current generation may deprive future generations of meeting their own needs. Additionally, unregulated pressure on the environment is a major driver of climate change, accompanied by significant threats to human health. The current use of environmental resources reflects underinvestment in natural capital and overinvestment in its destruction. In this context, the environmental cost of using natural inputs is underpriced, while their exploitation is subsidised. Therefore, government intervention is necessary to guide the environmental dimension of economic growth. This involvement, aimed at addressing environmental challenges, is known as *green growth policies* (Rodrik, 2014). The instruments of green growth policies can be separated into two broad categories: *market and non-market instruments* (Serres et al., 2010). Market-based instruments are designed to increase the cost of polluting and incentivising producers to reduce pollution through existing technologies or by adopting cleaner alternatives. These instruments range from environmentally related taxes, fees and charges to subsidies for reduction in pollution. The *non-markets instruments* do not operate by increasing the immediate cost of pollution. They can be divided into two groups. The direct regulations of the use of environment and active technology policies. Also known as command-and-control measures, these entail the enforcement of specific environmental regulations on businesses, such as mandating the use of environmentally friendly technologies or setting performance standards. The creation and implementation of new technologies are complex and resource-incentive processes. They inherently carry two major risks. First, there is uncertainty regarding the success of the project, meaning that if the project fails, the initiator loses the resources invested. Second, even if the project succeeds, other firms may copy the technology and benefit without bearing the initial costs, depriving the creator of significant financial rewards. Given these risks, individual firms are often reluctant to invest in new technologies. Moreover, the development of technologies frequently requires collaboration among various actors. This necessitates government coordination to facilitate these interactions and ensure creation and dissemination of new technologies. Inherent risks of technology creation are present in case of creation of green technologies. Therefore, government should involve in creation and diffusion of green technologies. In order to increase the supply of green technologies, active green technology policies ranges from public investment in environment-related Research and Development (R&D), public funding for private R&D in green projects. At the same time, the financial support to households and small businesses in purchasing the green technologies can be considered as part of green technology policies.

Paramati et al. (2017) employed panel data analysis on 11 developing economies and argued that renewable energy consumption positively influences economic output while also accelerating the reduction of CO_2 emissions. Policymakers should promote incentives for projects that support decarbonisation and emission reductions. The Porter Hypothesis developed by Porter (1991) suggests that firms generating pollution can benefit from strict and well-designed environmental regulation by fostering innovations. As a result, such regulations can lead to increased productivity within firms. Supporting this, Van Leeuwen and

Mohnen (2017) found evidence of a positive role for environmental regulation in generating eco-investments in the Netherlands. Similarly, Zhang and Ullah (2023) argue that internet, environmental policy stringency (EPS) and renewable energy consumption, and R&D promotes green growth. However, an inverse relationship between stringency of environmental regulations and green growth is also possible, overly tight policies could hamper green gross domestic product (GDP) growth (Arjomandi et al., 2022).

Regarding the socio-economic aspects of growth, quality of life is closely linked to exposure to air pollution. As is well known, air pollution poses serious health risk to society.

Green Growth Policy in Visegrad Group: Overview

The implementation of comprehensive environmental policies is essential to reduce reliance on fossil fuel energy. Numerous efforts have been made to develop public policies aimed at transition to a green economy. Notably, the EU launched its European Green Deal which aims to achieve climate neutrality by 2050. This initiative represents a new carbon-free growth pathway that ensures both prosperity and sustainability.

However, due to their various levels of development, geographical factors and other considerations, EU member states exhibit different positions and performances in adopting green policies. Among these, Visegrad countries formed distinct cluster. These four countries are characterised by a heavy reliance on fossil fuels in their industries and energy sectors, coupled with weaker commitment to decarbonising their economies.

In 2019, EU member states, including the Visegrad Group, prepared National Energy and Climate Plans for the period 2021–2030. These plans outline broad goals and prioritise five key dimensions: decarbonisation, energy efficiency, energy security, the internal energy market and research, innovation and competitiveness. While the Visegrad Group adheres to EU regulations, their progress in achieving green transition goals varies significantly.

Despite being a unified block, the Visegrad countries achieved different levels of progress in their green transition. Historically, these nations were former socialist countries that faced significant challenges during the transition period of the 1990s. As a result, these factors promoted regional cooperation (Jonek-Kowalska & Rupacz, 2024). After integrating into the world market, V4 countries experienced substantial economic growth from 1991 to 2019 accompanied by a rising level of energy consumption. Simultaneously, CO_2 emission rates declined steadily from 1999 to 2020. Among Visegrad countries, Poland and Czechia consistently recorded the highest emission rates (see Fig. 12.1). This can largely attributed to the heavy reliance of their economies on coal mining.

A comparative analysis by Riepl and Zavarská (2023) assessed the green transition across three dimensions: the share of renewable energy sources, the level of energy efficiency and resource productivity. According to available data, Slovakia ranked first among Visegrad countries, with renewable energy accounting 17% of

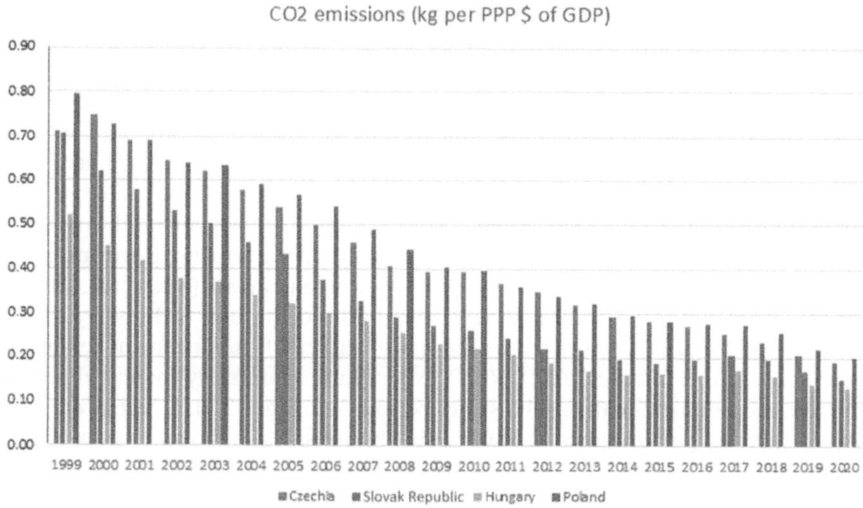

Fig. 12.1. CO_2 Emissions. *Source*: World Bank (https://databank.worldbank.org/source/world-development-indicators).

energy mix. Conversely, Hungary ranked last in this group. Overall, the Visegrad region lagged behind the EU-27 in adopting renewable energy sources. Limited financial capacity and a shortage of adequate technical skills contributed to these slower advances in the green transition.

The transition to renewable energy sources is closely associated with a reduction in emissions of harmful substances, particularly carbon dioxide. At the same time, environmental policy is recognised as one of the key factors contributing to enhancement of renewable energy. Electricity generation constitutes the largest share of renewable energy use across EU member states. For the three countries of Visegrad, except Poland, nuclear power was the leading source of electricity production, contributing more than 30% of their electricity. In contrast, Poland remains heavily reliant on coal, with over 69% of its electricity generated from this fossil fuel. Statistics show that energy consumption from renewable sources has increased significantly since the 1990s. The overall share of renewable energy in the energy mix remains below 20% across all Visegrad countries, there has been substantial progress in shifting the energy mix towards renewable sources (see Fig. 12.2).

Among the notable achievements of the Visegrad Group, it is worth to mention decoupling of economic growth from GHG emission.

Godawska and Wyrobek (2021) examined the role of the EPS in renewable energy production for Visegrad countries from 1993 to 2012. Authors argue that the implementation of stringent environmental policies positively impacts renewable energy production in the long run and facilitates the replacement of fossil fuels. The EPS index is highlighted as one of the commonly used indicators to measure restrictiveness of environmental policies. The article also incorporated several control variables for analysis, including GDP per capita (GDP_PC) growth, per capita carbon dioxide emission and GINI index. Descriptive statistics revealed an upward trend in EPS, indicating an improvement of environmental regulation across region. Policy instruments can be categorised in two broad categories: market instruments (environmental taxes, emission trading systems and feed-in tariffs) and non-market instruments (emission standards and government subsidies for renewable energy technologies). Authors found that stringency of emission standards and subsidies significantly influences renewable energy production in the long run. Conversely, restrictiveness of environmental taxes was deemed insignificant both in the short- and long-term horizons. Environmental taxes, in fact, can discourage the development of green patents (Shen et al., 2022). On the other hand, innovation should be supported through technology subsidies, as R&D can be considered as the major driver of enhancement for green technology (Fu & Zhang, 2022). R&D expenditure marginally increased across all Visegrad countries during the study period (see Fig. 12.3). Czechia demonstrated the best performance in R&D contributions, while Slovakia showed the lowest.

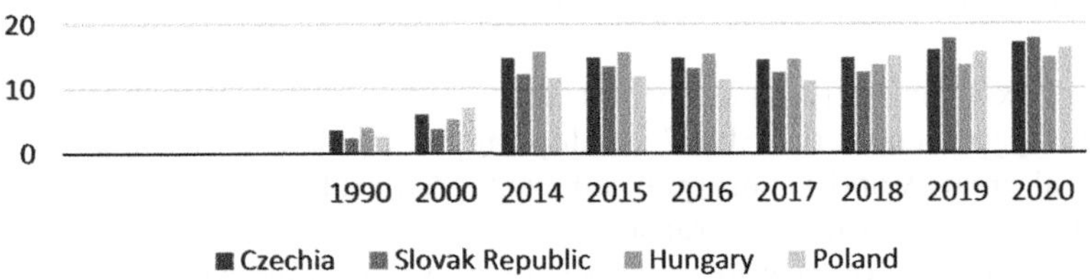

Fig. 12.2. Renewable Energy Consumption in Visegrad Group. *Source*: World Bank Development Indicators (Renewable Energy Consumption; % of Total Energy Consumption) (https://databank.worldbank.org/source/world-development-indicators).

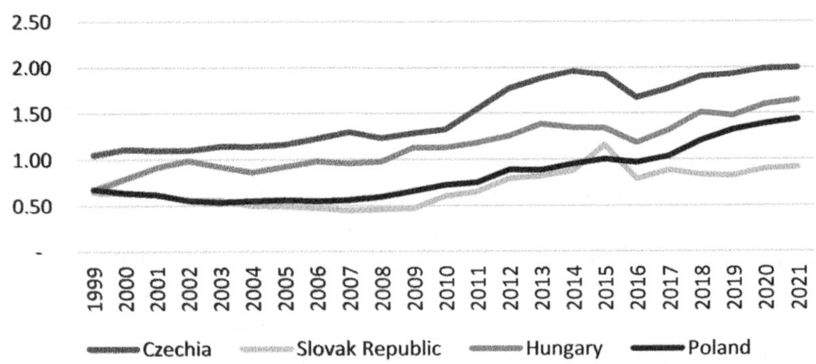

Fig. 12.3. R&D Expenditure as a Percentage of GDP in Visegrad Group. *Source*: World Bank Development Indicators (R&D; % of GD) (https://databank.worldbank.org/source/world-development-indicators).

Empirical Strategy

This section introduces the data and empirical methodology of this study.

Methodology

This study employs Panel FMOLS and Dynamic OLS (DOLS) models. These dynamic regression models are particularly suitable for small panels, especially when the number of time periods is bigger than the number of cross-sections ($T > N$) (Kao & Chiang, 2001). In this study, the number of time periods ($T = 22$) exceeds the number of cross-sections ($N = 4$), making FMOLS and DOLS appropriate for the analysis. An additional advantage of FMOLS and DOLS is their ability to account for cross-sectional heterogeneity (Zu, 2001), resulting in less biased estimates (Kao & Chiang, 2001). Unlike static regression models, FMOLS and DOLS can mitigate endogeneity problems and reduce the estimation bias (Pedroni, 2001).

The following equations present the models:

Model 1:

$$\text{GHG}_{\text{PC}} = \text{Market\_based} + \text{Command\_control} \\ + \text{Tech\_support} + \text{GDP.P.C} + \text{R.D} + \text{Fin\_Dev} + \mu_{i,t}$$

Model 2:

$$\text{MAT.PRD} = \text{Market\_based} + \text{Command\_control} \\ + \text{Tech\_support} + \text{GDP\_PC} + \text{R.D} + \text{Fin\_Dev} + \mu_{i,t}$$

Model 3:

$$\text{RENW.ENRG} = \text{Market\_based} + \text{Command\_control} \\ + \text{Tech\_support} + \text{GDP\_PC} + \text{R.D} + \text{Fin\_Dev} + \mu_{i,t}$$

Model 4:

$$\text{GRN.PTNTS} = \text{Market\_based} + \text{Command\_control} \\ + \text{Tech\_support} + \text{GDP\_PC} + \text{R.D} + \text{Fin\_Dev} + \mu_{i,t}$$

A decline in environmental pollution and reliance on fossil fuels, along with an increase in efficiency of natural resources and green technologies are the main criteria for green growth. Accordingly, data for these criteria are used as indicators of green growth in this study. Greenhouse gas emissions per capita (GHG_PC) serve a proxy for environmental pollution. While environmental pollution encompasses more than just GHG emissions, GHG_PC is a critical determinant of climate change (Mitchell, 1989), making it a primary variable in this analysis. Fossil-based energy contributes significantly to pollution and is *exhaustible*. As oil reserves diminish and the marginal cost of fossil fuel extraction rises, global energy security faces growing threats (Hubbert, 1956). Consequently, transitioning to non-exhaustible energy sources, such as renewable energy, is essential (Rifkin, 2011). The transition to a green economy also depends on technological advancements. Green patents are used proxy for green technology. Efficient use of natural resources, which are finite and exhaustible, is a fundamental component of sustainable development. Material productivity serves as an indicator of production efficiency in this context. From the perspective of green growth policies, study uses the *Market-based, command and control, technology support environmental policies* main explanatory variable to represent green growth policies and Table 12.1 describes them. *Market-based policies* indicate green growth policies with market instruments, *command and control* stands for direct regulations and setting standards and tech-support implies the government supports to shift to green technologies. GDP_PC and R&D and Fin_Dev are the control variables suggested by related studies (Aghion et al., 2009; Tawiah et al., 2021; Yang & Ni, 2022) and represented by GDP_PC (constant 2015 USD), R&D spending (% of GDP) and Financial development index. Data description is provided in Table 12.2.

Unit Root Test

Before performing unit root test, we run cross-sectional dependence. According to the Breusch-Pagan Lagrange Multipliers (LM) test, there is cross-sectional dependence in all series (Table 12.3). Therefore, the second generation unit root test, Pesaran's (2007) Cross-sectionally Augmented Im Pesaran Shin (CIPS) is employed to account for cross-sectional dependence. The result indicates that series are integrated with $I(1)$ except green patents (Table 12.4).

In order to test the long-term relationship between variables, Kao cointegration test (Kao, 1999) is used. All five modifications of Kao test statistics reject the

Table 12.1. The Green Growth Policy Composite Indicators.

Market-based Environmental Policies	**Command-and-Control Environmental Policies**	**Technology Policies**
CO_2 trading scheme	Emissions limit on Nox	Government support low-carbon R&D expenditures
Renewable energy trading scheme	Emissions limit on SO_x	Wind energy support (Auction and FiTs)
Carbon dioxides tax	Emissions limit on PM	Solar energy support (Auction and FiTs)
Nitrogen oxides tax	Sulphur content limit	
Sulphur oxides tax		
Diesel tax		

Source: Authors' own construction.

null hypothesis of no cointegration among series (Table 12.5). Consequently, we conclude that series in all models are cointegrated.

After the Kao test showing the presence of cointegration among variables in all models (Table 12.5), the FMOLS and DOLS demonstrate the long-run relationship between green growth and their determinants. The results show that the market-based environmental policies (MBEP) are effective to reduce the GHGs. The taxes on GHG emission may incentivise enterprises to pollute less in order to pay less taxes (Kotnik et al., 2014). Additionally, trading of pollution permits

Table 12.2. Definitions of Variables.

Type	Variable	Notation	Specification	Source
Dependent	GHG emissions	*GHG_PC*	GHG emissions (metric tons) per capita	World Bank
	Renewable energy	Renewable	The proportion of renewable energy in total final energy consumption	World Bank
	Green patents	*Green_patents*	Patents in environment-related technologies	OECD data
	Material Productivity	*Material_ product*	The amount of economic output generated (in terms of GDP) per unit of materials consumed	OECD data
Independent	Market-based policies	*Market_ Based*	The market-based EPS index	OECD data
	Non-market-based policies	*Non-market_ based*	the non-market based EPS index	OECD data
	Technology support policies	*Tech_support*	Technology support EPS index	OECD data
Control	GDP_PC	*lnGDP.PC*	GDP per capita (constant 2015 US$)	World Bank
	R&D spending	*R&D*	R&D expenditure (% of GDP)	World Bank
	Financial Development index	*Fin_Dev*	Aggregated overall index of financial development	World Bank

Source: Authors' own construction.

Table 12.3. Breusch-Pagan LM Test (Cross-sectional Dependence Test).

Variables	Statistics	*p*-Value
p.c_ghg	59.04	0.000
Renw. energy	18.34	0.000
Greenpatents	13.40	0.037
Material.productivity	83.53	0.000
Market_based	33.85	0.000
Non-market_based	72.06	0.000
tech_support	36.33	0.000
lnGDP.PC	27.41	0.000
R&D	29.22	0.000
Fin_Dev	34.28	0.000

Source: Authors' own construction.

Table 12.4. Stationarity Tests of Variables.

Variables	Level		First Difference		Order of Integration
	CIPS	Truncated CIPS	CIPS	Truncated CIPS	
p.c_ghg	–0.23	–0.23	–3.26***	–3.27***	*I* (1)
Material.productivity	–2.04	–2.04	–4.06***	–4.05***	*I* (1)
Renw. energy	–1.73	–1.73	–4.28***	–4.28***	*I* (1)
Greenpatents	–2.90**	–2.90**	–3.99***	–3.99***	*I* (0)
Market based	–1.43	–1.43	–4.47***	–4.47***	*I* (1)
Non-market based	–0.60	–0.60	–3.17***	–3.17***	*I* (1)
Tech_supports	–1.84	–1.84	–4.67***	–4.67***	*I* (1)
lnGDP.PC	–2.0	–2.01	–2.14***	–2.14***	*I* (1)
R&D	–2.08	–2.08	–3.17***	–3.17***	*I* (1)
Fin_dev	–1.83	–1.83	–4.17***	–4.17***	*I* (1)

Source: Authors' own construction.

Note: * is 10%, ** is 5% and *** is 1% significance levels.

opens opportunities for extra revenue by polluting less. There is a positive association between MBEP and renewable energy. The MBEP may increase the cost of usage of traditional energy and increase the demand for renewable energy (Rastegaret al., 2024). The effect of MBEP on green patents is also positive. It can be

Table 12.5. Kao Cointegration Test.

Kao Test for Cointegration	**Statistic**	***p*-Value**
Modified Dickey Fuller *t*	–3.16	0.001
Dickey Fuller *t*	–2.06	0.019
Augmented Dickey Fuller *t*	6.88	0.000
Unadjusted modified Dickey Fuller *t*	–3.52	0.000
Unadjusted Dickey Fuller *t*	–2.16	0.015

Source: Authors' own construction.

assumed that the market-based tools increase the marginal cost of fossil-based energy, therefore, it may stimulate the enterprise to shift to greener technology, consequently, rise in green patents (Liao, 2018). Lastly, the effect of market-based policies on material productivity is positive as expected. It can be claimed that reduction in GHGs emission makes to use inputs of production efficiently and shift to greener technology brings efficient technologies. As a consequent, it results in rise in efficiency of productivity of material usage.

As expected, command and control (C&C) regulations reduce the GHGs emission. It can be claimed that the obligatory environmental regulation could mitigate the GHGs emissions by both stimulating enterprises to shift to the less energy-intensive and less polluting technologies (Guo et al., 2021). The C&C regulations have a positive effect on renewable energy. By setting limits on emissions, the C&C could motivate the industrial producers to shift to cleaner source of energy, including renewable energy. Additionally, the EU has renewable energy directive with a target of achieving at least 20% of renewable energy of total energy consumption in 2020 and 42.5% in 2030. From the target of this directive, it is also obligatory for companies in certain industries in Visegrad countries to use a certain minimum level of their energy consumption from renewable sources. The results show that there is a positive association between C&C regulations and green patents. The main goal of C&C is to find a long-term solution for environment problems and it can ultimately be achieved by shift to green technology (Lamperti et al., 2020; Rodrik, 2014). In this regard, the C&C regulations can be considered an effective tool to promoting green technologies in Visegrad countries. The effect of the C&C regulations on material productivity is positive. By setting limits on pollution and structure of energy consumption, directive regulations can make producers to improve the efficiency of their technologies and it could result in an increase in productivity.

As expected, the technology support policies have a reducing effect on GHGs emissions and its effects on renewable energy, green patents and material productivity are positive. The shift to green model of growth requires the necessary green technologies and it can be said that the technology support policies are effective to accompany the transition to green technologies in Visegrad countries.

The results show that a rise in GDP_PC result in rise in GHGs emission (Tables 12.6 and 12.7). According to a debated Environmental Kuznets Curve

Table 12.6. Results (FMOLS).

Variables	**(1) GHG P.C**	**(2) Renewable**	**(3) Green_patents**	**(4) Material_productivity**
Market_Based	–0.55***	1.97 ***	0.38***	0.38***
	(0.113)	(0.427)	(0.098)	(0.043)
Non-market	–0.17**	0.80***	0.20**	0.27***
	(0.066)	(0.2081)	(0.095)	(0.024)
Tech_support	–0.07*	0.31**	0.60*	0.13***
	(0.039)	(0.137)	(0.103)	(0.047)
lnGDP.PC	1.23***	0.80***	1.25***	0.20***
	(0.027)	(0.168)	(0.45)	(0.013)
R&D	–2.04***	7.97***	0.11**	0.77***
	(0.224)	(0.861)	(0.048)	(0.11)
Fin_dev	–4.77***	15.87**	9.10***	1.69***
	(1.40)	(2.18)	(0.897)	(0.467)
Observations	84	8	84	84

Source: Authors' own construction.

Note: * is 10%, ** is 5% and *** is 1% significance levels.

Table 12.7. Results (DOLS).

Variables	**(1) GHG P.C**	**(2) Renewable**	**(3) Green_patents**	**(4) Material_productivity**
Market_Based	–0.48***	2.21***	1.83**	0.22*
	(0.152)	(0.580)	(0.91)	(0.088)
Non-market	–0.17**	0.88***	1.57***	0.17***
	(0.080)	(0.288)	(0.37)	(0.043)
Tech_support	–0.07*	0.36*	0.83*	0.12**
	(0.052)	(0.192)	(0.473)	(0.054)
lnGDP.PC	1.22***	–0.66***	0.93***	0.12***
	(0.027)	(0.131)	(0.185)	(0.02)
R&D	–2.04***	9.25***	5.39**	0.78***
	(0.032)	(1.51)	(2.45)	(0.121)
Fin_dev	–4.13**	11.98***	34.99***	1.53
	(2.07)	(3.212)	(6.95)	(0.884)
Observations	84	84	84	84

Source: Authors' own construction.

Note: * is 10%, ** is 5% and *** is 1% significance levels.

hypothesis, after a while of economic growth, pollution should decline (Leal & Marques, 2022). Additionally, the effects of GDP_PC on renewable energy which is counterintuitive. The energy-intensive heavy industries are still dominant in Visegrad countries, and they are still the main locomotive of economic growth. Therefore, it could explain unexpected association of GDP_PC with GHGs emissions and renewable energy. However, the effect of GDP_PC on green patents and material productivity. The positive effect of GDP_PC on green patents can be linked to rise in national income creates available resources to be spent on green technologies. By supporting the improvement of more efficient technology, GDP growth can result in rise in material productivity.

As theory predicts, the R&D spending has a positive effect on reducing GHGs emission, increasing share of renewable energy, green patents and material productivity. All four spheres of green growth ultimately require new green technologies to transit to environmentally sustainable model of economic growth. A higher level of overall innovativeness can facilitate the creation of green technologies (Irandoust, 2016; Mensah et al., 2019).

As expected, the effect of financial development on GHGs emission is negative and it is positive in case of renewable energy, green patents and material productivity. Transition to green growth path requires a considerable amount of investment in capital and technologies and a developed financial system can assist allocation of resources to investment in green transition (De Haas & Popov, 2023). The impact of financial development on green growth indicators in case of Visegrad countries can be explained from this perspective.

Conclusion

This study evaluates the effectiveness of green growth policies in Visegrad countries by employing FMOLS and DOLS models. The results show that market-based, command-and-control, and technology support policies are effective policy tools for reducing GHG emissions, increasing the share of renewable energy, material productivity of inputs, and facilitating green innovation. EU membership played a critical role in design and implementation of green growth policies.

In the long term, the shift to green growth path ultimately depends on green technologies. Due to inherent uncertainly with new technologies, individual entrepreneurs would be reluctant to initiate green innovations. Therefore, governments should share the risk of green innovation with private sector. In its turn, it requires financial resources. However, the Visegrad countries cannot mobilise sufficient resources to create and diffuse green technologies. Finance could be a bottleneck on green innovation in these countries. In this regard, it is necessary to find possible ways of mobilising resources to finance creation and diffusion of green technologies. One way could be to broaden the scope of environmental taxes and use collected resources in transition to green technologies. Additionally, the EU should increase the resources targeted to be used on green technologies in member countries with insufficient financial resources including Visegrad countries. Further research should focus on the investigation of the prospects of creation and implementation of green technology in Visegrad countries. Additionally, the energy-intensive heavy industry with a higher propensity to pollute is the Visegrad economies' cornerstone. Future studies should investigate the dynamics of the evolution of the industrial bases of Visegrad economies in the context of green transition.

References

Aghion, P., Hemous, D., & Veugelers, R. (2009). *No green growth without innovation*. Bruegel.

Arjomandi, A., Gholipour, H., Tajaddini, R., & Harvie, C. (2023). Environmental expenditure, policy stringency and green economic growth: Evidence from OECD countries. *Applied Economics*, *55*(8), 869–884.

Brock, W., & Taylor, S. (2005). Economic growth and the environment: A review of theory and empirics. In P. Aghion & S. Durlauf (Eds.), *Handbook of economic growth* (Vol. 1, part A). Elsevier.

Brock, W., & Taylor, S. (2010). The green solow model. *Journal of Economic Growth*, *15*, 127–153.

De Haas, R., & Popov, A. (2023). Finance and green growth. *The Economic Journal*, *133*(650), 637–668.

Dziekański, P., Popławski, L., Wyszkowski, A., & Wrońska, M. (2023). Assessment of the spatial disparities of the green economy in the voivodeships of Poland in 2010–2020. *Economics and Environment*, *4*, 1–17.

Fu, F., & Zhang, S. (2022). Toward green growth in China: The role of green finance investment, technological capital, and renewable energy consumption. *Environmental Science and Pollution Research*, *30*, 72664–72674.

Godawska, J., & Wyrobek, J. (2022). The impact of environmental policy stringency on renewable energy production in the Visegrad Group Countries. *Energies*, *14*(19), 6225.

Guo, X., Fu, L., & Sun, X. (2021). Can environmental regulations promote greenhouse gas abatement in OECD countries? Command-and-control vs. market-based policies. *Sustainability*, *13*(2), 1–18.

Irandoust, M. (2016). The renewable energy-growth nexus with carbon emissions and technological innovation: Evidence from the Nordic countries. *Ecological Indicators*, *69*, 118–125.

Jonek-Kowalska, I., & Rupacz, S. (2024). Transformation of energy resources in the visegrad group: Strategies, results, and climate effectiveness. *Resources*, *13*(5), 64.

Kao, C. (1999). Spurious regression and residual-based tests for cointegration in panel data. *Journal of Econometrics*, *90*(1), 1–44.

Kao, C., & Chiang, M.-H. (2001). On the estimation and inference of a cointegrated regression in panel data. *Advances in Econometrics*, *15*, 179–222.

Kotnik, Z., Klun, M., & Škulj, D. (2014). The effect of taxation on greenhouse gas emissions. *Transylvanian Review of Administrative Sciences*, *10*(43), 168–185.

Lamperti, F., Napaletano, G., & Roventini, A. (2020). Green transitions and the prevention of environmental disasters: Market-based vs. command-and-control policies. *Macroeconomic Dynamics*, *24*(7), 1861–1880.

Leal, P., & Marques, A. (2022). The evolution of the environmental Kuznets curve hypothesis assessment: A literature review under a critical analysis perspective. *Heliyon*, *8*(11), e11521.

Liao, Z. (2018). Environmental policy instruments, environmental innovation and the reputation of enterprises. *Journal of Cleaner Production*, *171*, 1111–1117.

Mensah, C., Long, X., & Lamina, D. (2019). Technological innovation and green growth in the Organization for Economic Cooperation and Development economies. *Journal of Cleaner Production, 240*(31), 118204.

Mitchell, J. (1989). The "greenhouse" effect and climate change. *Review of Geophysics, 27*(1), 115–139.

Nordhaus, W. (1974). Resources as a constraint on growth. *The American Economic Review, 64*(2), 22–26.

OECD. (2017). *Green growth indicators 2017*. OECD Publishing.

Paramati, S., Mo, D., & Gupta, R. (2017). The effects of stock market growth and renewable energy use on CO_2 emissions: Evidence from G20 countries. *Energy Economics, 66*(3), 360–371.

Pedroni, P. (2001). Fully modified OLS for heterogeneous cointegrated panels. *Advances in Econometrics, 15*, 93–130.

Pesaran, M. H. (2007). A simple panel unit root test in the presence of cross-section dependence. *Journal of Applied Econometrics, 22*(2), 265–312.

Porter, M. (1991). America's green strategy. *Scientific American, 264*(4), 143–168.

Rastegar, H., Eweje, G., & Sajjad, M. (2007). The impact of environmental policy on renewable energy innovation: A systematic literature review and research directions. *Sustainable Development, 32*(5), 2884.

Riepl, T., & Zavarská, Z. (2024). *Towards a greener Visegrád group: Progress and challenges in the context of the European Green Deal* [Vienna, Policy Notes and Reports, No. 64]. The Vienna Institute for International Economic Studies (wiiw).

Rifkin, J. (2011). *The third industrial revolution: How lateral power is transforming energy, the economy, and the world*. Macmillan.

Rodrik, D. (2014). Green industrial policy. *Oxford Review of Economic Policy, 30*(3), 469–491.

Serres, A., Murtin, F., & Nicoletti, G. (2010). *A framework for assessing green growth policies* [Working Paper No. 774]. OECD Economics Department.

Shen, T., Li, D., Jin, Y., & Li, J. (2022). Impact of environmental regulation on efficiency of green innovation in China. *Atmosphere, 13*(5), 767.

Smulders, J. A. (1999). Endogenous growth theory and the environment. In J. C. J. M. Van der Bergh (Ed.), *Handbook of environmental and resource economics* (pp. 610–621). Edward Elgar Publishing.

Tawiah, V., Zakari, A., & Adedoyin, F. (2021). Determinants of green growth in developed and developing countries. *Environmental Science and Pollution Research, 28*, 227–242.

Van Leeuwen, G., & Mohnen, P. (2017). Revisiting the Porter hypothesis: An empirical analysis of Green innovation for the Netherlands. *Economics of Innovation and Technology, 26*(2), 63–77.

World Bank. (2012). *Green growth report*.

Yang, L., & Ni, M. (2022). Is financial development beneficial to improve the efficiency of green development? Evidence from the "belt and road" countries. *Energy Economics, 105*, 105734.

Zu, Y. (2001). *Multivariable system identification for process control*. Elsevier Science & Technology Books.

Chapter 13

A Bibliometric Review on the Literature of Green Banking: Using Scopus Database (1997–2022)

Hem Shweta Rathore[a] *and Dhaval Maheta*[b]

[a]*Amity School of Business, Amity University Uttar Pradesh, Noida, UP, India*
[b]*Department of Business and Industrial Management, Veer Narmad South Gujarat University, Surat, Gujarat, India*

Abstract

Purpose: This study seeks to integrate and visualise research on green banking. The analysis distinguishes central themes, key articles and major gaps to facilitate the understanding of how green banking has been developed and how it contributes to sustainability and environmental protection.

Need for the study: The importance of environment-friendly business practices has raised the interest of scholars in green banking. Even with considerable literature, mapping the body of literature that shows research trends, gaps and future directions will be important in helping scholars and policymakers to bridge the gaps in the less researched aspects of green banking.

Methodology: This study uses a bibliometric analysis of the 114 publications indexed in Scopus using Biblioshiny and Vosviewer software. Measures such as citation trends, keyword frequency, thematic mapping and authors' and institutions' networks were extracted and analysed to understand the discipline comprehensively.

Findings: Research on green banking is concentrated in environmental and management journals, driven by collaborations from Australia, India and Bangladesh, peaking in 2021 with themes like sustainable banking and green credit policies.

Sustainable Development and Green Innovation: Managing Risk through Interdisciplinary Approaches and Policy Strategies, 275–294

doi:10.1108/978-1-83608-462-420251013

Practical implications: The findings provide insights for academicians, policymakers and practitioners, highlighting research trends, guiding global green banking standards and suggesting future exploration of niche topics like green credit and broader database integration.

Keywords: Green banking; bibliometric analysis; sustainable development; climate change; Biblioshiny; VOSviewer; Scopus

JEL Code: Q01; Q56; O16; N20

Introduction

The banking industry is regarded as the largest sector that serves the needs of all social classes, that has an impact on a nation's growth and economic development. Profits and financial expansion serve as a gauge of the banking sector's success. The industry can affect a nation's economic development and progress. An ominous sign that natural resources are being destroyed and may soon disappear from the planet is climate change and global warming. Eco-friendly and green initiatives are required to solve this issue. The banking sector is widely recognised for its relatively low environmental impact in terms of pollution and carbon emissions. Banks are emphasising environmental conservation by implementing green banking practices. It has two aspects: first, the manner banking is conducted, including whether it is paperless or not, and second, where the bank invests its funds in green banking. Banks can leverage their position to finance eco-friendly projects, thus fulfilling their corporate responsibilities while capitalising on new opportunities (Singhal, 2014). The phrase 'green banking', alternatively known as 'moral financial services', is utilised broadly to describe banking practices that are socially and environmentally conscious (Goyal & Joshi, 2011). Green banking emerged as a response to the traditional banking ideology's intended and unintended adverse effects on the environment (Masukujjaman et al., 2016). Green banking is considered sustainable, preventing environmental damage and ensuring lasting economic growth (Islam et al., 2020).

Green banking has emerged as a vital area of focus within the financial sector, driven by increasing concerns over sustainability, environmental preservation and the role of financial institutions in promoting green practices. Research from the past few years reflects a growing interest in how green banking initiatives are implemented globally, highlighting significant trends and challenges. Recent studies show that green banking dynamically aligns financial activities with Sustainable Development Goals. A substantial portion of the literature emphasises green bonds, climate finance and the execution of green banking strategies to reduce carbon emissions and promote renewable energy initiatives. Countries such as China, the United Kingdom and the United States are leading in this research, emphasising green bonds and sustainable finance.

It addresses mitigating climate alteration, preserving the environment and financing purchases of environmental products and services (Lindenberg & Volz, 2016). Banks are promoting corporate social responsibility activities (Scholtens, 2011) because banks and businesses are becoming more aware of the connection between sustainability and environmental and green banking (Kärnä et al., 2003). To present a green image, banks everywhere are investing profoundly in green strategies (Skouloudis & Evangelinos, 2009). Banks, industries and the financial system benefit from greening banking by lowering the carbon footprints of banking activities (Bihari & Pandey, 2015). Costs are minimised, risk is diminished, bank reputations are improved, and environmental sustainability benefits all. These benefits are all achieved through green banking, accomplishing both commercial goals and social responsibility.

Applying quantitative approaches to bibliometric data is encompassed under the bibliometric methodology (Broadus, 1987; Pritchard, 1969). The 1950s saw the beginning of bibliometric discourse (Wallin, 2005). Bibliography studies depict the prevailing state of a study area and outline prospects for researchers to extend their work in that area in the future. Bibliometric analysis is a quantitative technique for evaluating academic literature on a particular topic. This method uses statistical methods to assess research cooperation, publishing patterns and citation trends. The use of bibliometric analysis in business research has grown significantly in the last several years (Donthu et al., 2020, 2021). This growth may be ascribed to advancements in the field and the accessibility of bibliometric tools like Gephi, Leximancer, Vosviewer, Biblioshiny and systematic databases such as Scopus and Web of Science. By analysing publications, bibliometric studies provide an understanding of the development and influence of specific research domains, revealing trends, key contributors and the influence of research outputs. The background of bibliometric analysis can be associated with the early 20th century, with forerunners such as Derek de Solla Price, who introduced the concept of bibliometrics in the 1960s. Price emphasised the importance of citation analysis for evaluating scientific impact. Since then, bibliometric techniques have evolved, incorporating advancements in computational tools and data sources, leading to more sophisticated analyses of scientific literature.

Numerous research is carried out to validate the significance of green banking, its environmental effects and so forth. It is, therefore, imperative to carefully present all previous research to comprehend the body of literature in the field and to direct future scholars towards unexplored areas of study. The study's primary goal is to recognise the key areas of green banking research in the literature. The study's major components include a theme map, keyword analysis, citation analysis, the most fruitful contributions from various universities as well as from countries and geographic distribution of research. The study will give academicians a thorough overview of the history of green banking. Future researchers will benefit from the study's findings as they will learn about the less-explored facets of green banking, and policymakers will have a clear understanding of the standards that must be set to safeguard the environment, achieve sustainability and implement global green banking programmes.

The subsequent segments of the document are organised in the following manner: The Literature Review and Research Gap section offers a comprehensive examination of the existing relevant literature; The Research Design and Frame of Analysis section delineates the methodological approach and theoretical framework employed in the study; The Selection of Database and Data Extraction section articulates the empirical results and provides critical commentary; and the Limitations section concludes the research.

Literature Review and Research Gap

Researcher possibilities for expanding their future work on a particular topic are mapped out in bibliography studies, which map the existing condition of a research area. Bibliometric analysis is a numerical method to assess the academic literature within a specific field. This approach employs statistical tools to evaluate publication patterns, citations and collaboration among researchers. By analysing publications, bibliometric studies provide insights into the development and impact of specific research domains, revealing trends, key contributors and the influence of research outputs. Derek de Solla Price introduced the concept of bibliometrics in the 1960s and emphasised the importance of citation analysis as a tool for evaluating scientific impact. Since then, bibliometric techniques have evolved, incorporating advancements in computational tools and data sources, leading to more sophisticated analyses of scientific literature.

Past literature has focussed on different dimensions of green banking. A steadily increasing body of work addresses green banking from myriad perspectives. Cogent literature delves into its concept (Bukhari et al., 2021; Carnahan, 2001); customer perception (Bukhari et al., 2020a; Burhanudin et al., 2021; Herath & Herath, 2019; Malik & Singh, 2022; Rai et al., 2019); and as a corporate governance prerogative (Bose et al., 2018; Bukhari et al., 2022; Karyani & Obrien, 2020; Okyere-Kwakye & Md Nor, 2021; Sun et al., 2020); as a regulatory imperative (Bose et al., 2021; Khan et al., 2021); and across multiple countries (Ahuja, 2015; Awamleh et al., 2024; Bukhari et al., 2020b; Humbatova et al., 2024; Inder et al., 2022; Khairunnessa et al., 2021; Khatun et al., 2021; Li et al., n.d., 2024; Nguyen et al., Xing et al., 2021). The latest research on green banking highlights its vital function in advancing environmentally conscious growth and tackling environmental issues. Various studies emphasise the need for banks to integrate ecological considerations into their operations, thereby influencing industries to adopt greener practices. The burgeoning literature on green banking has also incorporated review articles that try to analyse the extant literature (Ahuja, 2015; Aracil et al., 2021; Khairunnessa et al., 2021; Sarma & Roy, 2021).

Given the extensive scholarly literature on green banking, there stems a need to document the major areas studied in green banking; summarise the thrust of the studies and chart out a research agenda for future discourses. Contextualising an all-inclusive portrait of research developments on green banking and highlighting the area that have been receiving scant attention should also be addressed.

While acknowledging the research done so far in this interesting area of scholarly interest, the current study tries to address some key research queries:

1. What is the extent of publication on an annual basis for green banking in Scopus Indexed journals from 1997 to 2022?
2. Which articles are the most influential regarding the volume and number of citations?
3. Which are the authors, their countries, institutions and their collaborative status that are producing the most scholarly works on green banking?
4. What is the intellectual structure of the knowledge base viz. keywords, key concepts, emerging themes and conceptual frame of analysis on green banking?
5. What are the vital evolution trends in research on green banking?

Finding suitable answers to these research queries delimits the flow and the structure of our scholarly work.

Research Design and Frame of Analysis

The foundation of the study is an extensive, in-depth study of the scholarly footprint of researchers on green banking across the world. It is a bygone conclusion that such an analysis must be scientifically designed, methodologically sound and do justice to the previous works that painstakingly highlight the aspects of the study area. To capitalise on these prerequisites, the researchers have chosen bibliometric analysis. This is a popular quantitative method used to track the authors and citations of publications within a field of study through time, providing the perception of the dynamic forces of the field (Mathankar, 2018). The initial conversation on bibliometric analysis started in 1950 (Wallin, 2005). Bibliometric analysis is performed for different aims such as to explore emergent tendencies in studies and journal performance, patterns of collaboration and research constituents and to investigate the conceptual framework of a certain field in the body of existing literature (Donthu et al., 2020; Verma & Gustafsson, 2020). Studies of bibliographic reviews are crucial since the idea of a bibliography is common and valued in research (Fernández-Batanero et al., 2019). The review articles assist in gathering information by analysing the most-cited publications and their rates of citation in a particular academic topic (Fardi et al., 2011). The significance of assessment procedures, in particular the use of bibliometric indicators derived from the publication behaviours of authors and criteria for journal editing, is becoming increasingly clear to the scientific community, publishers and policy officials (Moed, 2005).

Selection of Database and Data Extraction

Using the purposive sampling method, the Scopus database, which has the most scholarly journals and publications, assisted as the data source for analysing green banking variables. Software packages – R (Bibliometrix R Package), Biblioshine and VOSviewer – have been utilised for this study. The phrase 'green banking' was looked up in the article's title, abstract, keywords and body text in Scopus. The search yielded 114 documents published between the years of 1997 and 2022. Authors found it prudent to not impose a time frame restriction keeping in mind that the thrust of the current work is to analyse the general trajectory of green banking research. A captive table summarising the descriptive thrust of the bibliometric analysis is given in Table 13.1.

Table 13.1. General Description of the Bibliometric Analysis of Green Banking.

Description	Results
Timespan	1997–2022
Sources (journals, books, etc.)	86
Documents	114
Average years from publication	3.19
Average citations per document	5.044
Average citations per year per document	1.443
References	5,574
Document types	
Article	84
Book	2
Book chapter	6
Conference paper	15
Review	7
Document contents	
Keywords plus (ID)	272
Author's keywords (DE)	354
Authors description	
Authors	252
Author appearances	314
Authors of single-authored documents	16
Authors of multi-authored documents	236
Authors collaboration	
Single-authored documents	18
Documents per author	0.452
Authors per document	2.21
Co-authors per documents	2.75
Collaboration index	2.46

Source: Authors' compilation.

This is evident from Table 13.1 that within the duration of 26 years ranging from 1997 to 2022, 114 documents were published in 86 journals and books, on green banking. These documents include articles, book chapters, conference papers, conference reviews, editorial, review papers, etc. The maximum number of scholarly works was published in the form of research papers (84 articles) and the lowest number was published in the form of books (1 book). These documents were contributed by 252 authors from different countries.

Following the selection of the documents to be utilised, two databases – one for each platform separately for comparison and another combined for specific analyses – were created. The coding method involved creating a database utilising several variables to ascertain information about each article and highlight the productivity of the study field. The process was further complemented by focussing on selecting study areas, country-wise distribution publication organisations and journals. Furthermore, to ensure an in-depth analysis, a section was devoted to the contributing authors, and a summary of the trends was included in the analysis. The year wise break up of retrieved work is presented in Table 13.2.

Table 13.2. Year-wise Break Up of Scholarly Works.

Year	Articles	Year	Articles
1997	1	2017	9
2012	2	2018	11
2013	3	2019	12
2014	4	2020	18
2015	2	2021	25
2016	10	2022	17

Source: Authors' compilation using Biblioshiny.

Annual Scientific Production

Fig. 13.1 shows the annual scientific production of the works on green banking. This represents the scholarly works spread over the 26-year study period. The inference from the graph is that four noteworthy publications were published for the first time in 2014; they quickly fell in 2015 but rebounded after that year. The idea of 'green banking' was not well documented till 2017. Hence, only a modest number of research was done. Researchers began publishing rigorously from the year 2018, and the most significant number of research studies, 25, were produced in the year 2021. Concern over climate change, sustainable development and environmental conservation may have been a factor in the study's rise from the year 2015 to the year 2021.

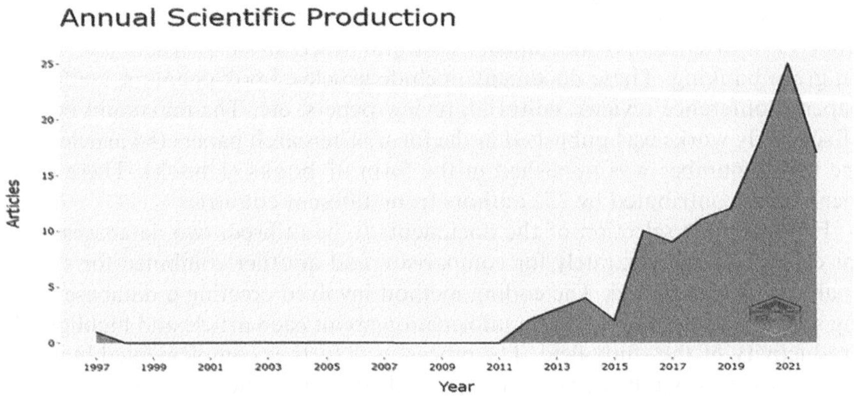

Fig. 13.1. Annual Scientific Production. *Source*: Biblioshiny.

Citation Analysis

In line with the study objectives, the authors also tried to highlight citation analysis specifically by journal, by article, by country and by author. The journals that possess the most referenced publications written in descending order are presented in Table 13.3.

Table 13.3. Most Cited Journal Articles.

Journal Description	Articles
International Journal of Green Economics	8
Environment Development and Sustainability	6
Sustainability (Switzerland)	6
International Journal of Asian Business and Information Management	3
Wit Transactions on Ecology and the Environment	3
Business Strategy and the Environment	2
International Journal of Business Innovation and Research	2
International Journal of Ethics and Systems	2
Journal of Advanced Research in Dynamical and Control Systems	2
Journal of Islamic Marketing	2
Journal of Sustainable Finance and Investment	2
Prabandhan: Indian Journal of Management	2
2014 14th International Conference on Advances in ICT For Emerging Regions ICTER 2014 – Conference Proceedings	1
Academy of Accounting and Financial Studies Journal	1
Academy of Entrepreneurship Journal	1

Table 13.3. (*Continued*)

Journal Description	Articles
Accounting	1
ACM International Conference Proceeding Series	1
Al-Shajarah	1
Arab Law Quarterly	1
Asia Pacific Journal of Environmental Law	1

Source: Authors' compilation using Biblioshiny.

As shown in Table 13.3, it is observed that eight articles received maximum citations and were published in *International Journal of Green Economics*. The journals *Environment Development and Sustainability Journal* and *Sustainability* had six most cited articles each. Out of 20 journals, the majority of journals have one to three articles, which received a good number of citations. An interesting observation that stands out is that most of the journals are environment journals, while journals that cater to the domains of banking and finance journals have not yet published articles on green banking.

In line with our research questions, we have tried to analyse the citations of the research articles in descending order of cited articles (Table 13.4).

Table 13.4. Citation Analysis.

Research Article Details	Total Citations	Total Citations per Year
S. Bose (2018), *Asia Pacific Journal of Management*	59	11.8
H. Sun (2020), *Sustainability*	31	10.3333
C. Zhixia (2018), *Asian Economic Financial Review*	29	5.8
K. Masud Ma (2017), *Sustainability*	26	4.3333
T. Julia (2020), *Journal of Islamic Marketing*	24	8
M. R. B. Rubel (2020), *Employee Relations*	23	7.6667
K. Masud Ma (2018), *Sustainability*	20	4
S. Bose (2021), *Corporate Governance: International Review*	18	9
K. Kumar (2020), *Environment Development Sustainability*	18	6
G. Ibe-Enwo (2019), *Sustainability*	17	4.25
A. Rehman (2021), *Environment Development Sustainability*	15	7.5
T. Julia (2016), *Humanomics*	15	2.1429

(*Continued*)

Table 13.4. (*Continued*)

Research Article Details	Total Citations	Total Citations per Year
K. Sharmeen (2019), *Thunderbird International Business Review*	14	3.5
A. Rifat (2016), *International Journal of Green Economics*	14	2
K. Chatzitheodorou (2021), *Sustainable of Production Consumption*	12	6
Y. Singh (2015), *Journal of Interdisciplinary and Multidisciplinary Research*	11	1.375
Miah Md (2021), *Environment Development Sustainability*	10	5
D. Mckanan (2017), *Eco-Alchemy: Anthroposophy and the History and Future of Environment*	10	1.6667
B. Burhanudin (2021), *International Journal of Consumer Studies*	9	4.5
P. Sarma (2021), *Journal of Sustainable Finance and Investment*	9	4.5

Source: Authors' compilation using Biblioshiny.

An examination of the country-wise distribution of most cited articles (Table 13.5) on green banking, we find that Australia has the maximum cited articles; Brunei and Ghana have non-cited articles.

Table 13.5. Country-wise Break Up of Most Productive Research Studies.

Country	Total Citations	Average Article Citations	Country	Total Citations	Average Article Citations
Australia	81	27.00	United Kingdom	9	3.00
China	77	11.00	Guinea	6	6.00
Bangladesh	66	9.43	Philippines	3	3.00
Malaysia	56	6.22	Poland	2	2.00
India	51	3.40	Kazakhstan	1	1.00
Korea	46	23.00	Romania	1	1.00
Turkey	17	17.00	Saudi Arabia	1	1.00
Indonesia	14	3.50	Brunei	0	0.00

Table 13.5. (*Continued*)

Country	Total Citations	Average Article Citations	Country	Total Citations	Average Article Citations
Greece	12	12.00	Ghana	0	0.00
Pakistan	12	3.00	United Kingdom	9	3.00
Oman	11	5.50	Guinea	6	6.00

Source: Authors' compilation using Biblioshiny.

Table 13.6. Author-wise Article Contribution.

Authors	Articles	Articles Fractionalised	Authors	Articles	Articles Fractionalised
N. Nisha	8	3.75	Md Miah	3	1.00
M. Iqbal	6	1.75	A. Roy	3	1.50
S.A. A. Bukhari	5	1.58	P. Sarma	3	1.50
F. Hashim	5	1.58	S. Singh	3	1.25
A. Rifat	5	1.42	B. Burhanudin	2	0.67
A. Amran	4	1.33	A. Choubey	2	1.00
T. Julia	4	1.83	R. Hasan	2	0.67
S. Kassim	4	1.83	L. Huang	2	0.75
S. Bose	3	0.83	J. D. Kim	2	0.67
Hz. Khan	3	0.83			

Source: Authors compilation using Biblioshiny.

Table 13.6 presents the contribution of authors within the domain of green banking. Out of 20 most contributing authors, the author N. Nisha has published a maximum number of eight articles, other major contributing authors are M. Iqbal, S. A. A. Bukhari, F. Hashim and A. Rifat, they have contributed five or more but less than eight articles on green banking.

Authors Collaboration and Affiliation

Keeping in line with our research questions, the section is devoted to analysing authors from the perspective of collaboration, organisational affiliation and country of origin. Table 13.7 explores the collaborative efforts of the authors. Out of a total of 252 authors, 221 authors have written only a single article to the study, 17 authors have written two articles each and six authors contributed three articles each, in the domain of green banking.

Table 13.7. Author Collaborations.

Documents Written	Number of Authors	Proportion of Authors	Documents Written	Number of Authors	Proportion of Authors
1	221	0.877	5	3	0.012
2	17	0.067	6	1	0.004
3	6	0.024	8	1	0.004
4	3	0.012			

Source: Authors' compilation using Biblioshiny.

Fig. 13.2 presents author affiliations to their respective organisations, universities and/or institutions. Researchers from numerous universities worldwide have published studies on green banking. Sains Malaysia and North South University are the most participating Universities. Authors from these universities have published 13 and 10 studies, respectively. Other universities have published six or less than six studies.

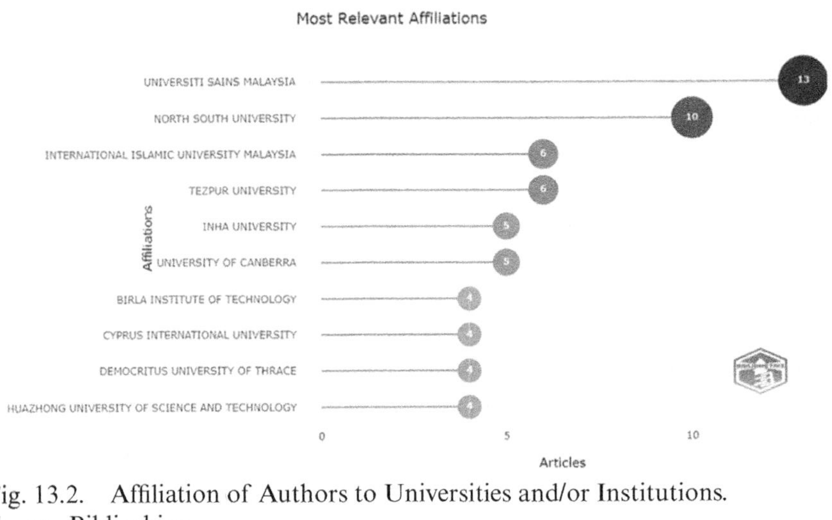

Fig. 13.2. Affiliation of Authors to Universities and/or Institutions.
Source: Biblioshiny.

Analysis of Keywords, Themes and Constructs for Green Banking

The topmost authors' keywords can serve as indicators of the fields' scientists' and researchers' interests and research priorities, according to Zhang et al. (2019). The theme of research publications is reflected in the keywords, which are crucial for indexing those articles. We may gain helpful insight into the primary research areas of interest in a certain field by performing keyword research (Wuni et al., 2019). It was deemed crucial to look at the slant of keywords that authors employed in the carefully chosen articles that made up this bibliometric analysis. The most prominent keyword is green banking. Sustainable development, sustainable banking, sustainability and green finance are among other keywords that were used repetitively in the study. The two main objectives of green banking are environmental preservation and sustainable development. Green banking is a subset of the larger field of green finance. Sustainable banking is promoted by banks implementing green banking practices. Bangladesh is one nation that is actively pursuing green banking (Fig. 13.3).

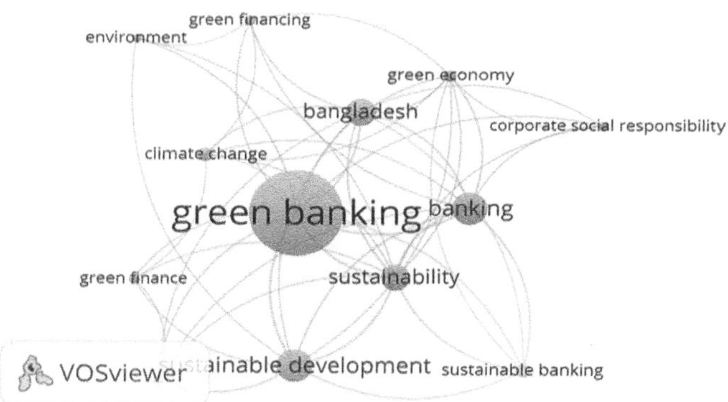

Fig. 13.3. Keyword Analysis. *Source*: VOSviewer.

We now analyse the important themes and niche areas of green banking research using thematic mapping. Figs. 13.4 and 13.5 are thematic maps highlighting the important themes in our analysis. Motor themes (upper-right quadrant) are characterised by both high centrality and density, indicating that such themes have been developed and are important for the research field. The motor themes on 'green banking' are sustainable development, climate change, economics, environmental regulations, investments, energy efficiency, total factor productivity. Themes in the upper-left quadrant are the high developed and isolated themes or niche themes. The niche themes on the topic of 'green banking' are green credit policies and financial institutions. Themes in the lower-left quadrant are the emerging or declining themes representing weakly developed and marginal discussions. The emerging or declining themes on the topic of 'green banking' are carbon footprint and the carbon banking industry. Themes in the lower-right quadrant are known as basic and transversal themes. The basic themes on the topic of 'green banking' are financial system, environmental economics, green economy and environmental policy.

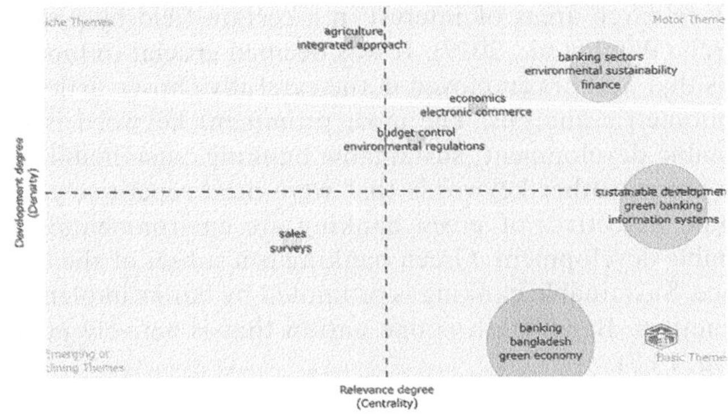

Fig. 13.4. Thematic Analysis I. *Source*: Biblioshiny.

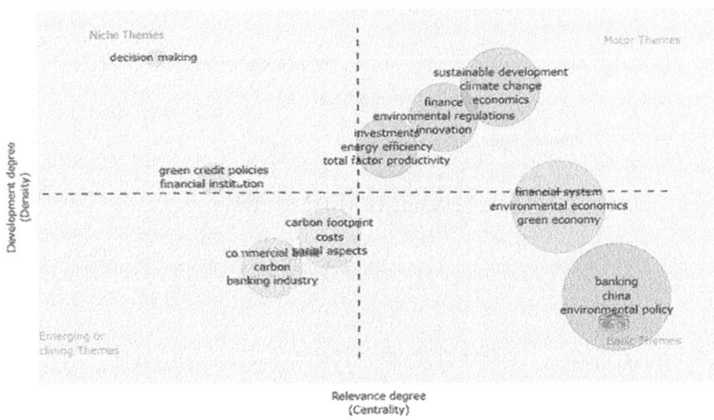

Fig. 13.5. Thematic Analysis II. *Source*: Biblioshiny.

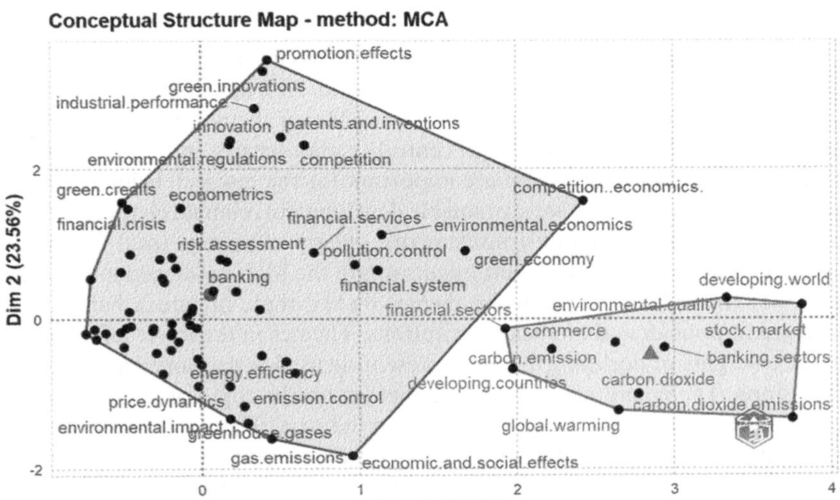

Fig. 13.6. Conceptual Structure of Green Banking. *Source*: Biblioshiny.

Fig. 13.6 presents the concrete construction of the papers published. The conceptual map is a scientific tool that aids co-word analysis to evaluate the co-occurrence of author keywords. Simply put, the map contextualises research focus of the authors. In our analysis, two clusters are seen to be formed. The first structure is more significant, viz., having the most keywords (and hence greater research emphasis), and encompasses themes on green innovations, environmental regulations, environmental economics, econometrics, risk assessment, greenhouse gases, gas emissions and environmental impact. The second cluster has themes on carbon emission, global warming, environmental quality, stock market and banking sectors.

Geographical Spread of the Publications

To analyse the geographical spread of the publications, we analyse the geographic distribution of green banking by country. In terms of publications by a single author, India took the top spot, while Bangladesh took the top spot in terms of international collaboration. Apart from India and Bangladesh, Malaysia, China, Indonesia and Pakistan are a few of the nations that have made more substantial contributions to the literature on green banking than other nations (Table 13.9). Authors have begun to contribute to the expanding body of research on green banking in Australia, the United Kingdom, Korea and Oman (Fig. 13.7). Other nations like Brunei, Ghana, Guinea, Hong Kong and Kazakhstan, have each made a solitary contribution to research in the domain of green banking (Table 13.8 and Fig. 13.7).

Table 13.8. Country-wise Geographical spread of Publications.

Country	Articles	Frequency	SCP	MCP	MCP_Ratio
India	15	0.2174	13	2	0.133
Malaysia	9	0.1304	7	2	0.222
Bangladesh	7	0.1014	1	6	0.857
China	7	0.1014	4	3	0.429
Indonesia	4	0.058	4	0	0
Pakistan	4	0.058	1	3	0.75
Australia	3	0.0435	2	1	0.333
United Kingdom	3	0.0435	3	0	0
Korea	2	0.029	1	1	0.5
Oman	2	0.029	0	2	1
Brunei	1	0.0145	1	0	0
Ghana	1	0.0145	1	0	0
Greece	1	0.0145	1	0	0
Guinea	1	0.0145	0	1	1
Hong Kong	1	0.0145	1	0	0

(*Continued*)

Table 13.8. (*Continued*)

Country	Articles	Frequency	SCP	MCP	MCP_Ratio
Kazakhstan	1	0.0145	1	0	0
Nepal	1	0.0145	1	0	0
Philippines	1	0.0145	1	0	0
Poland	1	0.0145	1	0	0
Romania	1	0.0145	1	0	0

Source: Authors' compilation using Biblioshiny.

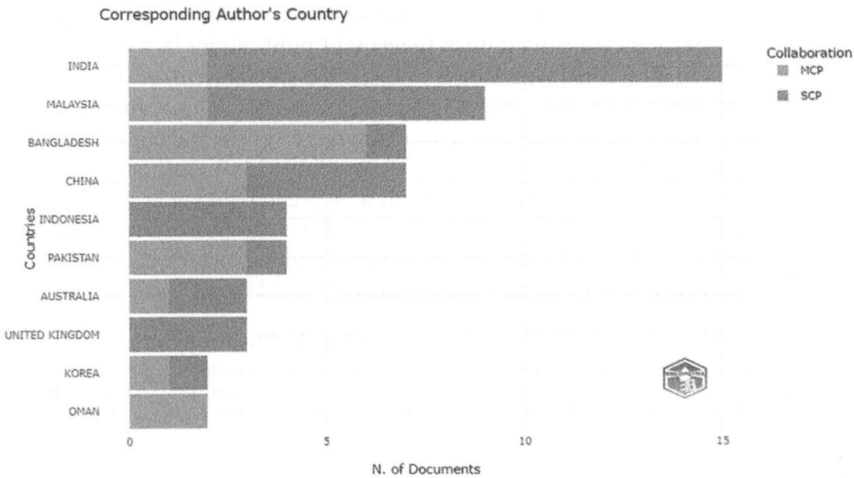

Fig. 13.7. Country-wise Distribution of Publications. *Source*: Biblioshiny.

Table 13.9. Country-wise Frequency of Publication.

Region	Frequency	Region	Frequency
India	51	Greece	5
Malaysia	45	Peru	5
Bangladesh	40	France	4
China	26	Kazakhstan	4
Indonesia	23	Oman	4
Pakistan	17	South Korea	4
United Kingdom	11	Nepal	3
Australia	10	Romania	3
Sri Lanka	6	Belgium	2
Turkey	6	Japan	2

Source: Authors' compilation using Biblioshiny.

Results and Discussion

Green banking as a scholarly domain has received the attention of academic literature as well as practitioner interest. The current study was undertaken to answer some key questions on the thrust and focus of green banking in cogent literature. For this purpose, a bibliometric analysis was undertaken with available Software, viz., VOSviewer and Biblioshiny by scouring articles published in Scopus-indexed journals. A lower cut-off year of 1997 was chosen considering the lean streak of published work on the subject in the Scopus database, while 2022 was the cut-off decided in advance. In keeping with the trends in bibliometric analysis, the five research questions were framed. Accordingly, an exhaustive analysis of the trends and progress of scientific literature on green banking was made. The results showed that 114 documents were published in 86 journals and one book. The maximum number of scholarly works was published in the form of research papers 84 articles and the most significant number of research studies, 25, was produced in the year 2021. Moreover, these articles were published primarily in environment-related or management-centric journals but not a single article was published in banking and finance journals. The highest citation was 59 for an article authored in the *Asia Pacific Journal of Management*. Similarly, the *Journal of Green Economics* has a total of eight cited articles, the highest among all captive journals in our study. Australia as a country has the maximum number of cited articles. The collaboration analysis reveals that most of the works are collaborative in nature. Researchers from numerous universities worldwide have participated in studies on green banking, but Universities Sains Malaysia and North South University record the most published work. Keyword analysis forms an integral analysis of any bibliometric study. The works on green banking reveal that sustainable development, sustainable banking, sustainability and green finance are preferred keywords. A thematic analysis led the authors to believe that the central themes in the published works are sustainable development, climate change, economics, environmental regulations, investments, energy efficiency and total factor productivity. Scholarly attention has been also paid to green innovations, environmental regulations, environmental economics, econometrics, risk assessment, greenhouse gases, gas emissions and environmental impact in published works.

Limitations

While conducting the study, some limitations cropped up invariably. The authors admit that data were extracted only from the Scopus database while other databases like the Web of Sciences and Publons are excluded. Second, the results often contain comparable duplicate data, such as the same keyword used in both the single and plural or using hyphens in the same compound phrase, which somewhat compromises the findings. The authors used VOSviewer, R (Bibliometrix R Package) and Biblioshiny, and hence, the results are delimited to the range of features in the two softwares. Nevertheless, we are impressed with the current themes in Green Banking research and have presented a scientific analysis of the academic works in our study from 1997 onwards.

Future Research Consideration

Future research can expand the database to incorporate other popular databases and conduct co-occurrence and bibliographical coupling with looser threshold values to identify more areas of impactful publications. The authors feel that bibliometric analysis may be constrained by the specific software in use, and extensive analysis can be anticipated by a combination of distinct features of additional software. While a bibliometric analysis is a scientific tool to conduct such research, the analysis can be substantiated by a Systematic Literature review in the field. Finally, the niche areas being marginal and evolving research works contributing to the fields of green credit policies and researchers can take up financial institutions. However, the popularity and sustenance of green banking rests on the publication of works devoted to Green banking. Hence, the publication houses could be open to publishing more research on the themes by inviting author scholars to paper calls, especially by core banking and finance journals. To conclude, green banking is a practice-oriented concept, the evolution of the same can contribute to lasting sustainability for a better world, and research on the theme can be spurred by the practice, theory and publication intent of the stakeholders involved in sustainability discourses.

References

Ahuja, N. (2015). Green banking in India: A review of literature. *International Journal for Research in Management and Pharmacy*, *4*(1), 11–16.

Aracil, E., Najera-Sanchez, J.-J., & Forcadell, F. J. (2021). Sustainable banking: A literature review and integrative framework. *Finance Research Letters*, *42*, 101932. https://doi.org/10.1016/j.frl.2021.101932

Awamleh, F. T., Alarabiat, Y. A., & Bustami, A. N. (2024). Enhancing sustainable development through international performance indicators: The role of business intelligence techniques. *Challenge Sustainability*, *12*(3), 203–218.

Bihari, S. C., & Pandey, B. (2015). Green banking in India. *Journal of Economics and International Finance*, *7*(1), 1–17.

Bose, S., Khan, H. Z., & Monem, R. M. (2021). Does green banking performance pay off? Evidence from a unique regulatory setting in Bangladesh. *Corporate Governance – An International Review*, *29*(2), 162–187. https://doi.org/10.1111/corg.12349

Bose, S., Khan, H. Z., Rashid, A., & Islam, S. (2018). What drives green banking disclosure? An institutional and corporate governance perspective. *Asia Pacific Journal of Management*, *35*(2), 501–527. https://doi.org/10.1007/s10490-017-9528-x

Broadus, R. N. (1987). Toward a definition of "bibliometrics". *Scientometrics*, *12*, 373–379.

Bukhari, S. A. A., Hashim, F., & Amran, A. (2020a). Green banking: A road map for adoption. *International Journal of Ethics and Systems*, *36*(3), 371–385. https://doi.org/10.1108/IJOES-11-2019-0177

Bukhari, S. A. A., Hashim, F., & Amran, A. (2020b). The journey of Pakistan's banking industry towards green banking adoption. *South Asian Journal of Business and Management Cases*, *9*(2), 208–218. https://doi.org/10.1177/2277977920905306

Bukhari, S. A. A., Hashim, F., & Amran, A. (2021). Green banking: A conceptual framework. *International Journal of Green Economics*, *15*(1), 59–74. https://doi.org/10.1504/IJGE.2021.117682

Bukhari, S. A. A., Hashim, F., & Amran, A. (2022). Pathways towards green banking adoption: Moderating role of top management commitment. *International Journal of Ethics and Systems*, *38*(2), 286–315. https://doi.org/10.1108/IJOES-05-2021-0110

Burhanudin, B., Ronny, R., & Sihotang, E. T. (2021). Consumer guilt and green banking services. *International Journal of Consumer Studies*, *45*(1), 38–53. https://doi.org/10.1111/ijcs.12602

Carnahan, I. (2001). Green banking. *Forbes*, *168*(4), 46.

Donthu, N., Kumar, S., Mukherjee, D., Pandey, N., & Lim, W. M. (2021). How to conduct a bibliometric analysis: An overview and guidelines. *Journal of Business Research*, *133*, 285–296.

Donthu, N., Kumar, S., & Pattnaik, D. (2020). Forty-five years of journal of business research: A bibliometric analysis. *Journal of Business Research*, *109*, 1–14.

Fardi, A., Kodonas, K., Gogos, C., & Economides, N. (2011). Top-cited articles in endodontic journals. *Journal of Endodontics*, *37*(9), 1183–1190.

Fernández-Batanero, J. M., Montenegro Rueda, M., Fernández-Cerero, J., & García Martínez, I. (2019). Impact of the information and communication technologies on the education of students with down syndrome: A bibliometric study (2008–2018). *European Journal of Educational Research*, *9*(1), 79–89.

Goyal, K. A., & Joshi, V. (2011). A study of social and ethical issues in banking industry. *International Journal of Economics and Research*, *2*(5), 49–57.

Herath, A., & Herath, S. (2019). Impact of green banking initiatives on customer satisfaction: A conceptual model of customer satisfaction on green banking. *IOSR Journal of Business Management*, *21*, 24–35.

Humbatova, S. I., Hajiyeva, N., Fodor, M. G., Sood, K., & Grima, S. (2024). The impact of economic growth on the ecological environment and renewable energy production: Evidence from Azerbaijan and Hungary. *Journal of Risk and Financial Management*, *17*(7), 275.

Inder, S., Sood, K., & Grima, S. (2022). Antecedents of behavioural intention to adopt internet banking using structural equation modelling. *Journal of Risk and Financial Management*, *15*(4), 157.

Islam, M. J., Roy, S. K., Miah, M., & Das, S. K. (2020). A review on corporate environmental reporting: An emerging issue in the corporate world. *Canadian Journal of Business and Information Studies*, *2*(3), 45–53.

Kärnä, J., Hansen, E., & Juslin, H. (2003). Environmental activity and forest certifcation in marketing of forest products – A case study in Europe. *Silva Fennica*, *37*(2), 848–871.

Karyani, E., & Obrien, V. V. (2020). Green banking and performance: The role of foreign and public ownership. *Jurnal Dinamika Akuntansi Dan Bisnis*, *7*(2), 221–234. https://doi.org/10.24815/jdab.v7i2.17150

Khairunnessa, F., Vazquez-Brust, D. A., & Yakovleva, N. (2021). A review of the recent developments of green banking in Bangladesh. *Sustainability*, *13*(4), 1904. https://doi.org/10.3390/su13041904

Khan, H. Z., Bose, S., Sheehy, B., & Quazi, A. (2021). Green banking disclosure, firm value and the moderating role of a contextual factor: Evidence from a distinctive regulatory setting. *Business Strategy and the Environment*, *30*(8), 3651–3670. https://doi.org/10.1002/bse.2832

Khatun, M. N., Sarker, M. N. I., & Mitra, S. (2021). Green banking and sustainable development in Bangladesh. *Sustainability and Climate Change*, *14* (5), 262–271. https://doi.org/10.1089/scc.2020.0065

Li, Q., Wu, H., Zhang, B. Q., Dong, Z. H., & Ling, T. (2024). Safety system study of gas stations based on preliminary hazard analysis and fault tree analysis. *Journal of Information Systems Engineering & Management*, *3*(3), 149–163.

Li, W., Chen, X., & Yuan, T. (n.d.). Green credit policy and corporate cash holdings: Evidence from China. *Accounting and Finance*, *63*(S2), 2875–2903. https://doi.org/10.1111/acfi.13021

Lindenberg, N., & Volz, U. (2016). *Green banking regulation: setting out a framework* [Report for the Practitioners 'Dialogue on Climate Investments (PDCI)]. Deutsche Gesellschaft für Internationale Zusammenarbeit (GIZ) GmbH.

Malik, G., & Singh, D. (2022). Personality matters: Does an individual's personality affect adoption and continued use of green banking channels? *International Journal of Bank Marketing*, *40*(4), 746–772. https://doi.org/10.1108/IJBM-04-2021-0133

Masukujjaman, M., Siwar, C., Alam, A. S. A., Bashawir, A., & Er, A. (2016). Economy–environment nexus for development: Is Bangladesh on the right track?. *International Journal of Advanced Applied Sciences*, *3*(2), 25–29.

Mathankar, A. R. (2018). Bibliometrics: An overview. *International Journal of Library and Information Science (IJLIS)*, *7*(3), 9–15.

Moed, H. F. (2005). Citation analysis of scientific journals and journal impact measures. *Current Science*, *89*(12), 1990–1996.

Mukherjee, D., Kumar, S., Donthu, N., & Pandey, N. (2021). Research published in management international review from 2006 to 2020: A bibliometric analysis and future directions. *Management International Review*, *61*(5), 599–642.

Nguyen, A. H., Do, M. H. T., Hoang, T. G., & Nguyen, L. Q. T. (n.d.). Green financing for sustainable development: Insights from multiple cases of Vietnamese commercial banks. *Business Strategy and the Environment*, *32*(1), 321–335. https://doi.org/10.1002/bse.3132

Okyere-Kwakye, E., & Md Nor, K. (2021). The intention of banks to adopt green banking in an emerging market: The employees' perspective. *Economic and Political Studies*, *9*(4), 497–504. https://doi.org/10.1080/20954816.2021.1899621

Pritchard, A. (1969). Statistical bibliography or bibliometrics. *Journal of Documentation*, *25*, 348–349.

Rai, R., Kharel, S., Devkota, N., & Paudel, U. R. (2019). Customers perception on green banking practices: A desk review. *The Journal of Economic Concerns*, *10*(1), 82–92.

Sarma, P., & Roy, A. (2021). A Scientometric analysis of literature on Green Banking (1995-March 2019). *Journal of Sustainable Finance and Investment*, *11*(2), 143–162. https://doi.org/10.1080/20430795.2020.1711500

Scholtens, B. (2011). Corporate social responsibility in the international insurance industry. *Sustainable Development*, *19*(2), 143–156.

Singhal, K. (2014). Green banking: An overview. *Asian Journal of Multidisciplinary Studies*, *2*(6), 196–200.

Skouloudis, A., & Evangelinos, K. I. (2009). Sustainability reporting in Greece: Are we there yet? *Environmental Quality Management*, *19*(1), 43–60.

Sun, H., Rabbani, M. R., Ahmad, N., Sial, M. S., Guping, C., Zia-Ud-din, M., and Fu, Q. (2020). CSR, co-creation and green consumer loyalty: Are green banking initiatives important? A moderated mediation approach from an emerging economy. *Sustainability (Switzerland)*, *12*(24), 10688. https://doi.org/10.3390/su122410688

Verma, S., & Gustafsson, A. (2020). Investigating the emerging COVID-19 research trends in the field of business and management: A bibliometric analysis approach. *Journal of Business Research*, *118*, 253–261.

Wallin, J. A. (2005). Bibliometric methods: Pitfalls and possibilities. *Basic & Clinical Pharmacology & Toxicology*, *97*(5), 261–275.

Wuni, I. Y., Shen, G. Q., & Osei-Kyei, R. (2019). Scientometric review of global research trends on green buildings in construction journals from 1992 to 2018. *Energy and Buildings*, *190*, 69–85.

Xing, C., Zhang, Y., & Tripe, D. (2021). Green credit policy and corporate access to bank loans in China: The role of environmental disclosure and green innovation. *International Review of Financial Analysis*, *77*, 101838. https://doi.org/10.1016/j.irfa.2021.101838

Zhang, D., Zhang, Z., & Managi, S. (2019). A bibliometric analysis on green finance: Current status, development, and future directions. *Finance Research Letters*, *29*, 425–430.

Index

Printed and bound by CPI Group (UK) Ltd, Croydon, CR0 4YY

13/09/2026

14961063-0004